Probability and Mathematical
  PURI, VILAPLANA, and ... Applied Statistics
  RANDLES and WOLFE ... Statistics
  RAO • Linear Statistical Inference and Its Applications, *Second Edition*
  RAO • Real and Stochastic Analysis
  RAO and SEDRANSK • W.G. Cochran's Impact on Statistics
  RAO • Asymptotic Theory of Statistical Inference
  ROHATGI • An Introduction to Probability Theory and Mathematical Statistics
  ROHATGI • Statistical Inference
  ROSS • Stochastic Processes
  RUBINSTEIN • Simulation and The Monte Carlo Method
  SCHEFFE • The Analysis of Variance
  SEBER • Linear Regression Analysis
  SEBER • Multivariate Observations
  SEN • Sequential Nonparametrics: Invariance Principles and Statistical Inference
  SERFLING • Approximation Theorems of Mathematical Statistics
  SHORACK and WELLNER • Empirical Processes with Applications to Statistics
  TJUR • Probability Based on Radon Measures

Applied Probability and Statistics
  ABRAHAM and LEDOLTER • Statistical Methods for Forecasting
  AGRESTI • Analysis of Ordinal Categorical Data
  AICKIN • Linear Statistical Analysis of Discrete Data
  ANDERSON, AUQUIER, HAUCK, OAKES, VANDAELE, and WEISBERG • Statistical Methods for Comparative Studies
  ARTHANARI and DODGE • Mathematical Programming in Statistics
  ASMUSSEN • Applied Probability and Queues
  BAILEY • The Elements of Stochastic Processes with Applications to the Natural Sciences
  BAILEY • Mathematics, Statistics and Systems for Health
  BARNETT • Interpreting Multivariate Data
  BARNETT and LEWIS • Outliers in Statistical Data, *Second Edition*
  BARTHOLOMEW • Stochastic Models for Social Processes, *Third Edition*
  BARTHOLOMEW and FORBES • Statistical Techniques for Manpower Planning
  BECK and ARNOLD • Parameter Estimation in Engineering and Science
  BELSLEY, KUH, and WELSCH • Regression Diagnostics: Identifying Influential Data and Sources of Collinearity
  BHAT • Elements of Applied Stochastic Processes, *Second Edition*
  BLOOMFIELD • Fourier Analysis of Time Series: An Introduction
  BOX • R. A. Fisher, The Life of a Scientist
  BOX and DRAPER • Empirical Model-Building and Response Surfaces
  BOX and DRAPER • Evolutionary Operation: A Statistical Method for Process Improvement
  BOX, HUNTER, and HUNTER • Statistics for Experimenters: An Introduction to Design, Data Analysis, and Model Building
  BROWN and HOLLANDER • Statistics: A Biomedical Introduction
  BUNKE and BUNKE • Statistical Inference in Linear Models, Volume I
  CHAMBERS • Computational Methods for Data Analysis
  CHATTERJEE and PRICE • Regression Analysis by Example
  CHOW • Econometric Analysis by Control Methods
  CLARKE and DISNEY • Probability and Random Processes: A First Course with Applications, *Second Edition*
  COCHRAN • Sampling Techniques, *Third Edition*
  COCHRAN and COX • Experimental Designs, *Second Edition*

Applied Probability and Statistics (Continued)

CONOVER • Practical Nonparametric Statistics, *Second Edition*
CONOVER and IMAN • Introduction to Modern Business Statistics
CORNELL • Experiments with Mixtures: Designs, Models and The Analysis of Mixture Data
COX • Planning of Experiments
COX • A Handbook of Introductory Statistical Methods
DANIEL • Biostatistics: A Foundation for Analysis in the Health Sciences, *Fourth Edition*
DANIEL • Applications of Statistics to Industrial Experimentation
DANIEL and WOOD • Fitting Equations to Data: Computer Analysis of Multifactor Data, *Second Edition*
DAVID • Order Statistics, *Second Edition*
DAVISON • Multidimensional Scaling
DEGROOT, FIENBERG and KADANE • Statistics and the Law
DEMING • Sample Design in Business Research
DILLON and GOLDSTEIN • Multivariate Analysis: Methods and Applications
DODGE • Analysis of Experiments with Missing Data
DODGE and ROMIG • Sampling Inspection Tables, *Second Edition*
DOWDY and WEARDEN • Statistics for Research
DRAPER and SMITH • Applied Regression Analysis, *Second Edition*
DUNN • Basic Statistics: A Primer for the Biomedical Sciences, *Second Edition*
DUNN and CLARK • Applied Statistics: Analysis of Variance and Regression, *Second Edition*
ELANDT-JOHNSON and JOHNSON • Survival Models and Data Analysis
FLEISS • Statistical Methods for Rates and Proportions, *Second Edition*
FLEISS • The Design and Analysis of Clinical Experiments
FOX • Linear Statistical Models and Related Methods
FRANKEN, KÖNIG, ARNDT, and SCHMIDT • Queues and Point Processes
GALLANT • Nonlinear Statistical Models
GIBBONS, OLKIN, and SOBEL • Selecting and Ordering Populations: A New Statistical Methodology
GNANADESIKAN • Methods for Statistical Data Analysis of Multivariate Observations
GREENBERG and WEBSTER • Advanced Econometrics: A Bridge to the Literature
GROSS and HARRIS • Fundamentals of Queueing Theory, *Second Edition*
GUPTA and PANCHAPAKESAN • Multiple Decision Procedures: Theory and Methodology of Selecting and Ranking Populations
GUTTMAN, WILKS, and HUNTER • Introductory Engineering Statistics, *Third Edition*
HAHN and SHAPIRO • Statistical Models in Engineering
HALD • Statistical Tables and Formulas
HALD • Statistical Theory with Engineering Applications
HAND • Discrimination and Classification
HOAGLIN, MOSTELLER and TUKEY • Exploring Data Tables, Trends and Shapes
HOAGLIN, MOSTELLER, and TUKEY • Understanding Robust and Exploratory Data Analysis
HOEL • Elementary Statistics, *Fourth Edition*
HOEL and JESSEN • Basic Statistics for Business and Economics, *Third Edition*
HOGG and KLUGMAN • Loss Distributions
HOLLANDER and WOLFE • Nonparametric Statistical Methods
IMAN and CONOVER • Modern Business Statistics
JAGERS • Branching Processes with Biological Applications
JESSEN • Statistical Survey Techniques
JOHNSON • Multivariate Statistical Simulation

(*continued on back*)

Design, Data, and Analysis

by Some Friends of
Cuthbert Daniel

Cuthbert Daniel

Design, Data, and Analysis

by Some Friends of Cuthbert Daniel

Edited by
COLIN L. MALLOWS
AT&T Bell Laboratories

John Wiley & Sons
New York · Chichester · Brisbane · Toronto · Singapore

The text for the book was processed at Bell
Laboratories on a VAX 11/780 computer running
the UNIX* operating system and troff/mm software
driving an APS-5 phototypesetter.

*UNIX is a trademark of Bell Laboratories, Inc.

Copyright © 1987 by John Wiley & Sons, Inc.

All rights reserved. Published simultaneously in Canada.

Reproduction or translation of any part of this work
beyond that permitted by Section 107 or 108 of the
1976 United States Copyright Act without the permission
of the copyright owner is unlawful. Requests for
permission or further information should be addressed to
the Permissions Department, John Wiley & Sons, Inc.

Library of Congress Cataloging-in-Publication Data:

Design, data, and analysis.

  (Wiley series in probability and mathematical
statistics. Applied probability and statistics,
ISSN 0271-6356)
  Bibliography: p.
  Includes index.
  1. Experimental design. 2. Mathematical
statistics. 3. Daniel, Cuthbert. I. Daniel,
Cuthbert. II. Mallows, Colin L. III. Series.
QA279.D464   1987   001.4'34   87-8216
ISBN 0-471-83937-X

Printed in the United States of America

10 9 8 7 6 5 4 3 2 1

Contents

Contributors	ix
Preface	xi
Bibliography of Cuthbert Daniel	xvii

1. Analysis of Unreplicated Factorials Allowing for Possibly Faulty Observations
   George E. P. Box and R. Daniel Meyer   1

2. Variable Selection in Clustering and Other Contexts
   Edward B. Fowlkes, Ramanathan Gnanadesikan, and Jon R. Kettenring   13

3. Weighting Qualitative Data
   Spencer M. Free   35

4. Explaining Experimental Design Fundamentals to Engineers: A Modern Approach
   Gerald J. Hahn, John L. Bemesderfer, and Donald M. Olsson   41

CONTENTS

5. Repeatability and Reproducibility: Some problems in applied statistics
   Hugo C. Hamaker — 71

6. Design, Modelling, and Analysis of Some Biological Data Sets
   Frank R. Hampel — 93

7. Analytical Representation of Dielectric Constants: A Complex Multiresponse Problem
   Stephen Havriliak, Jr. and Donald G. Watts — 129

8. Indirect Measurement of Work
   Mary B. Hovik and Sutton Monro — 159

9. Are Some Latin Squares Better Than Others?
   J. Stuart Hunter — 163

10. Graphical Exploratory Analysis of Variance Illustrated on a Splitting of the Johnson and Tsao Data
    Eugene G. Johnson and John W. Tukey — 171

11. Analysis of a Two-Way Table
    John Mandel — 245

12. Reusing Published Examples: A Case of Caveat Emptor
    Barry H. Margolin and Bruce J. Collings — 261

13. Analysis of Bernoulli Data From a 2^5 Design Done in Blocks of Size Four
    Lincoln E. Moses — 275

14. A 2-Stage Procedure for Guaranteeing Accuracy with Calibration Standards
    Brain R. Schlain — 291

15. Linear Models for Some-Cells-Empty Data:
    The Cell Means Formulation,
    A Consultant's Best Friend
    Shayle R. Searle   305

16. Six-Sequence Carry-Over Design for the
    Determination of the Effect of a Drug
    in Reducing Food Intake
    John C. Thornton, Harry Smith, and Harry R. Kissileff   331

17. Statistics in a Court of Law
    Hans Zeisel   353

    Index   365

Contributors

John L. Bemesderfer
Lebanon, Pennsylvania

George E. P. Box
*Department of Statistics
University of Wisconsin
Madison, Wisconsin*

Bruce J. Collings
*Department of Mathematical
  Sciences
Montana State University
Bozeman, Montana*

Edward B. Fowlkes,
*Statistics Research Group
Bell Communications Research
Morristown, New Jersey*

Spencer M. Free, Jr.
*Statistical Consultant
Newtown Square, Pennsylvania*

Ramanathan Gnanadesikan
*Information Sciences Research
Bell Communications Research
Morristown, New Jersey*

Gerald J. Hahn
*Corporate Research
  and Development
General Electric Company
Schenectady, New York*

Hugo C. Hamaker
Eindhoven, Netherlands

Frank R. Hampel
*ETH
Zürich, Switzerland*

Stephen Havriliak, Jr.
*Research Division
Rohm and Haas Company
Bristol, Pennsylvania*

CONTRIBUTORS

Mary B. Hovik
Zionsville, Pennsylvania

J. Stuart Hunter
Statistical Consultant
Princeton, New Jersey

Eugene G. Johnson
Educational Testing Service
Princeton, New Jersey

Jon R. Kettenring
Statistics Research Group
Bell Communications Research
Morristown, New Jersey

Harry R. Kissileff
St. Luke's-Roosevelt Hospital
  Center
Columbia University
New York, New York

John Mandel
National Measurement Laboratory
National Bureau of Standards
Gaithersburg, Maryland

Barry H. Margolin
Statistics and Biomathematics Branch
National Institute of Environmental
  Health Sciences
Research Triangle Park,
  North Carolina

R. Daniel Meyer
The Lubrizol Corporation
Wickliffe, Ohio

Sutton Monro
Coopersburg, Pennsylvania

Lincoln E. Moses
Department of Statistics
Stanford University
Stanford, California

Donald M. Olsson
Applied Statistics Product Quality
  Systems and Analysis
General Electric Company
Louisville, Kentucky

Brian R. Schlain
Statistical Consultant
New York, New York

Shayle R. Searle
Biometrics Unit
Cornell University
Ithaca, New York

Harry Smith
Durham, North Carolina

John C. Thornton
Department of Biomathematical
  Sciences
Mount Sinai School of Medicine
New York, New York

John W. Tukey
Princeton University
Princeton, New Jersey

Donald G. Watts
Department of Mathematics
  and Statistics
Queens University
Kingston, Ontario, Canada

Hans Zeisel
University of Chicago Law School
Chicago, Illinois

Preface

It was at the annual ASA meetings in Philadelphia in August 1984 that I learned two surprising facts: that Cuthbert Daniel was within a few days of his 80th birthday, and that no suitable public celebration of his achievements had been made. My first reaction was to doubt the accuracy of the report. How could it be that my young friend had managed to accumulate such an impressive number of years? On inquiry it turned out that each part of the data was accurate; being unable to affect the former, I resolved to do something about the latter. The responses to my initial invitations were very enthusiastic, and Bea Shube at Wiley was very encouraging. So here it is; a testimonial to Cuthbert's influence on several generations of designers and analyzers of data. I hope this book will be a worthy commemoration of his influence and tribute to the affection in which he is held by his many friends, admirers, collaborators, proteges, and imitators.

My idea was to invite a collection of chapters containing descriptions of experiments, with analysis, giving the full data, and enough explanation of the context that the reader could embark on independent analysis. Many of the chapters do conform to this model, and give some idea of the range of problems that can confront a practicing statistician. I have also included a few chapters of a more expository nature, containing no data, for the sake of broadening the coverage. The intended audience for the book is students and aspiring statistical consultants. The analyses also provide a timely challenge to designers of statistical computing systems.

Before introducing the papers, I would like to place on record the outline of Cuthbert's unusual career.

After getting a B.S. and M.S. in Chemical Engineering at M.I.T., which was evidently no strain since he also took most of the courses offered in the Math, English, and History departments, as well as some in the Mining department, his first move was to work his way to France on a cattleboat and spend the summer bicycling round Normandy, Brittany, and the Riviera. This was only the first of several career moves that failed to lead to fame and fortune. He spent one year with the Hercules Powder Company, and another at the University of Berlin studying physics while his new wife Janet Goldwater was doing biochemistry at the Kaiser Wilhelm Institute, Dahlem. He decided not to become a physicist. For two years he taught science at Cambridge School, Kendal Green, MA, sharing the oldest house in Cambridge with B.F. Skinner, who is still a close friend. Then for four years he taught physics at Sarah Lawrence College and biology (to teachers) at Bank Street School, in New York City. By this time he was 35 years old and statistics had as yet made no impression on him, nor had he on it.

In 1939-1940 he was a research associate in Evaluation of School Broadcasts at Ohio State. It was here that he discovered statistics, and was soon giving a seminar for the staff. In 1941-42 he was an assistant to Paul Lazarsfeld at the Office of Radio Research, Columbia, and published his first paper. Later he tutored with Alex Mood at Princeton. He went back to Chemical Engineering with Heyden Chemical Corporation, and insisted on applying statistics to their engineering problems. He was fired.

In 1945 he organized and headed the first statistical group at the Oak Ridge Gaseous Diffusion Plant, being responsible for continuous inventory of the U-235.

Finally, in 1947 he decided he was a consultant in engineering statistics, and for nearly forty years has had a vigorous career in that field. Once he found his vocation, his influence grew rapidly. He soon realised that classical statistical methods are often insufficient, and undertook to augment them with new methods of his own. His paper on Half-Normal Plots in the first volume of Technometrics (1959) was a revelation to many; here was a technique that was transparently simple, and obviously useful, but that seemed not to fit into any established theoretical framework. It stimulated many others to develop other novel graphical ideas, and Allan Birnbaum to attempt some relevant theory. His first book, "Fitting Equations to Data" (with Fred S. Wood of Standard Oil) is full of new ways of dealing with problems that had arisen in his practical work, but that had never been properly formulated. It showed that there was much opportunity in applied work for imagination and creativity; and that such work can drive the development of theory in useful directions.

In his second book, "Applications of Statistics to Industrial Experimentation", he showed by example how careful design and imaginative analysis, with much attention paid to the residuals, can lead to important insights. Many of the examples in the book are "classical" data-sets, but Cuthbert found new structure that was missed by the original authors. It was surprising to some, but surely not to anyone who knew him, that in this book he recorded his chagrin that half-normal plots had not been more effective in detecting the peculiarities that he now found interesting. He now realised that signs are often important, and that it is a mistake to cling to old ideas (even one's own) when new and better ones come along.

In 1970 Cuthbert was voted Outstanding Statistician of 1970 by the Chicago Section of the American Statistical Association. In 1971 he gave the Fisher Memorial Lecture at the ASA annual meetings; in 1974 he gave the W. J. Youden Memorial Address at the ASQC meetings. He won the Frank Wilcoxon award for the best practical application paper in Technometrics, 1978. He is a Fellow of ASA, the Institute of Mathematical Statistics, and the American Association for the Advancement of Science, and an Honorary Fellow of the Royal Statistical Society. He has served on a National Academy of Sciences Committee on Pesticide Residues, and on a National Cancer Institute Clinical Investigations Review Committee.

For many years Cuthbert has been in great demand as a speaker at professional meetings, where his insight and wit always assured an appreciative reception. He has had an important influence on many; several of the papers in this volume include sincere testimonials to that effect. In my own case, I remember with great affection many evenings at his house in Manhattan, where I used to go after lecturing at Columbia, and where we struggled together with such problems as the proper interpretation of regression coefficients, and the selection of variables. It was at one of these sessions that the idea for the C_p plot arose; we agreed that the letter C was appropriate, representing our only shared initial.

I turn now to an outline of the contents of this volume.

First, we have two expository chapters. Hahn, Bemesderfer and Olsson describe a course on experimental design that they put together for engineers, scientists, and managers at General Electric.

The material covered includes factorial and fractional factorial experiments, blocking, response surface analysis, Evolutionary Operation, components-of-variance models and nested experiments, and finally an introduction to Taguchi's ideas in process design. This course covers much of what is essential for an industrial statistician. Searle argues vigorously that when dealing with factorial designs where some cells are empty, the usual overparameterized models (with side constraints) are excessively clumsy, and should be replaced by "cell-means models", with explicit careful attention given to elucidating the linear hypotheses that are of interest.

Two chapters are concerned with design issues.

Hunter asks the question "are some latin squares better than others?" His answer is "Yes", at least for the three-factor case, because some can be augmented to Box-Behnken second-order designs using only six extra runs, while others need ten extra runs. Presumably similar results could be obtained for designs in higher dimensions.

Schlain describes how a two-stage procedure can be used to ensure that certain calibration standards conform to desired tolerances.

Twelve chapters are mainly on topics in the analysis of data, though several of these also address design issues.

In his 1959 paper, Cuthbert pointed out that the half-normal plot can help in the identification of (a few) bad values in the data. Here Box and Meyer describe a formal Bayesian approach to this problem. The formality is not so extreme as to disdain the use of graphical methods for summarizing the results.

Fowlkes, Gnanadesikan, and Kettenring discuss and illustrate techniques for selecting a subset of variables, in each of the three problems (i) multiple regression, (ii) discriminant analysis, and (iii) clustering. It is encouraging that, for the data-set that they analyze, using distinct methodologies for these three distinct objectives, they arrive at similar results.

Free contributes the analysis of a small but intriguing experiment of the efficacy of a proposed vaccine for cattle.

Hamaker draws on his experience in the analysis of interlaboratory studies to discuss several issues that arise in that context.

Hampel contributes analyses of eight data sets from biology. As far as I know, Cuthbert has never worked in this field, but it is clear that his methods and philosophy carry over. I draw attention to Hampel's personal preface and dedication.

Havriliak and Watts analyze data from a study of dielectric constants of certain polymers. In this problem, there is a highly-developed theory that suggests a detailed model, but the similarities with Hampel's examples are more striking than the differences.

Hovik and Monro discuss the use of accounting data to measure productivity in an office or shop. The data consists of counts of units produced in various categories, and total time spent (man-hours), for each of a number of workers. It may be of interest to record that a very similar problem was the first that I studied (in 1964) using the C_p plot; my idea was that for some tasks, the time spent per unit might have small variability, while for some other tasks the time spent per unit might expand to fill whatever slack was available (Parkinson's Law). Thus a count of the "small variability" units might be a better predictor of the total time than a count that included the "large variability" units. The analysis was not very successful, though it did suggest that certain tasks could usefully be pooled. Hovik and Monro have a very interesting new approach to the problem.

Johnson and Tukey present a careful analysis of some classical psychometric data, showing (amongst many other things) how (a variant of) Cuthbert's half-normal plot can be used in a complex (not two-level) design, by splitting various sums of squares into one-degree-of-freedom components.

Mandel re-analyses some classical viscosity data, finding a parsimonious "concurrent" model that provides useful insights.

Margolin and Collings follow Cuthbert's lead in being unwilling to take published data and analysis at face value. I have one quibble with their exposition. After spending some time with the Stuart data that they describe, I am unable to find any other strange coincidences. How, then, should the figure of 0.6×10^{-6} be deflated to allow for the fact that it relates to the single most extraordinary coincidence in the data? I suggest a factor of at least 100; but that still leaves 10^{-4} ...

Moses describes the design and analysis of an experiment involving blocking and Bernoulli responses.

Thornton, Smith, and Kissileff present the analysis of a complex experiment involving carry-over effects.

Finally, the collection includes a paper by Hans Zeisel discussing the proper interpretation of "at random" in the context of the selection of juries.

It is a pleasure to acknowledge the meticulous work of Marylyn McGill and Mary Flannelly typesetting this volume at AT&T Bell Laboratories, Murray Hill, and in preparing the figures. Anne Freeny checked some of the analyses (and found a few mistakes!). I apologize to all, but especially to Cuthbert, for not having finished work on this volume sooner.

Colin L. Mallows

Murray Hill, New Jersey
August, 1986

Bibliography of Cuthbert Daniel

BOOKS

Daniel, C. and Gaudet, H. (1941). *Radio Listener Panels.* Washington, D. C.: Federal Radio Education Committee, Federal Security Agency.

Daniel, C. and Wood, F. S. (1971). *Fitting Equations to Data.* New York: Wiley. Second edition 1980.

Daniel, C. (1976). *Applications of Statistics to Industrial Experimentation.* New York: Wiley.

PAPERS

Daniel, C. (1940). "Three Types of 'Like' reactions in judging popular songs," *Journal of Applied Psychology,* **24,** 746-748.

Daniel, C. (1940). "Statistically significant differences in observed per cents," *Journal of Applied Psychology,* **24,** 826-830.

Daniel, C. and Necrema, N. (1950). "Design of experiments for most precise slope estimation or linear extrapolation," *Journal of the American Statistical Association,* **45,** 546-556.

BIBLIOGRAPHY OF CUTHBERT DANIEL

Daniel, C. and Rickett, R. L. (1953). "A comparison of impact testing machines in the 20 to 30 foot pound range," *Proceedings of the American Society for Testing Materials*, **53**, 739-750.

Daniel, C. (1953). Review of *Statistical Mathods for Chemical Experimentation*, by W. L. Gore. *Journal of American Statistical Association*, **48**, 476-485.

Vanderbeck, R. W., Wilde, H. D., Lindsay, R. W., and Daniel, C. (1953). "Statistical analysis of behavior in the transition temperature zone," *The Welding Journal Research Supplement*, **32**, 325-s - 332-s.

Daniel, C. (1954). "Evaluation of several sets of constants and several sources of variability," *Chemical Engineering Progress*, **50**, 81-86.

Daniel, C. (1954). "Finding and measuring the effects of assignable causes." *Transactions of the American Society for Quality Control*, 377-384.

Daniel, C. and Riblett, E. W. (1954). "A multifactor experiment," *Industrial and Engineering Chemistry*, **46**, 1465-1468.

Daniel, C. (1956). "Fractional replication in industrial research." In *Proceedings of the Third Berkeley Symposium on Mathematical Statistics and Probability*, Volume 5. Berkley and Los Angeles: University of California Press, pp. 87-98.

Daniel, C. (1956). "Fractional replication in industrial experimentation," *Transactions of the American Society for Quality Control*, 229-234.

Daniel, C. (1958). "On varying one factor at a time." Note 131, *Biometrics*, **14**, 430-431.

Daniel, C. (1959). "Use of half-normal plots in interpreting factorial two-level experiments," *Technometrics*, **1**, 311-341.

Daniel, C. (1960). "Locating outliers in factorial experiments." *Metropolitan Conference American Society for Quality Control*, 108-116.

Daniel, C. (1960). "Locating outliers in factorial experiments," *Technometrics*, **2**, 149-156.

Daniel, C. (1960). "Parallel fractional replicates," *Technometrics*, **2**, 263-268.

Daniel, C. (1961). "Critique et analyse graphique des resultats de plans d'expérience factoriel 2^n," *Revue de Statistique Appliqueé*, **9** No. 3, 11-26.

Daniel, C. (1962). "Sequences of fractional replicates in the 2^{p-q} series," *Journal of the American Statistical Association*, **57**, 403-429.

Daniel, C. (1963). "Experimental designs for fuel cell research," *Seventeenth Annual Proceedings, Power Research Conference*, May, no page nos.

Daniel, C. (1963). "Use of half-normal plots," *Transactions of the American Society for Quality Control*, 117-123.

Daniel, C. (1963). Discussion on Professor Scheffé's paper, "The simplex-centroid design for experiments with mixtures," *Journal of the Royal Statistical Society, Series B*, **25**, 256-257.

Daniel, C. (1964). Review of *Experimental statistics*, by M. Natrella. Bureau of Standards Handbook No. 91. *Journal of Industrial Quality Control*, 44-45.

Daniel, C. (1966). Review of *Statistics and Experimental Design in Engineering and Physical Sciences*, by N. L. Johnson and F. S. Leone. *SIAM Review*, **8**, 402-404.

Daniel, C. and Wilcoxin, F. (1966). "Factorial 2^{p-q} plans robust against linear and quadratic trends," *Technometrics*, **8**, 259-278.

Daniel, C. (1967). Answer to Query 20, "Analysis of a factorial experiment. (Partially confounded 2^3)," *Technometrics*, **9**, 171-172.

Daniel, C. (1969). "Some general remarks on consulting in statistics," *Technometrics*, **11**, 241-245.

Daniel, C. (1973). "One-at-a-time plans," *Journal of the American Statistical Association*, **68**, 353-368. (The Fisher Memorial Lecture for 1971.)

Daniel, C. (1975). "Calibration designs for machines with carry-over and drift," *Journal of Quality Technology*, **7**, 103-108. (The W. J. Youden Memorial Address for 1974.)

Daniel, C. (1978). "Patterns in residuals in the two-way layout," *Technometrics*, **20**, 385-395.

Daniel, C. and Lehmann, E. L. (1979). "Henry Scheffé, 1907-1977" *Annals of Statistics*, **7**, 1149-1161.

Daniel, C. (1980). Note 1. "A convenient formula for inverting a frequently occuring matrix." Note 2. "Extension of S.S. $(y_1 - y_2) = (y_1 - y_2)^2/2$ to $n = 3$ and 4." *Journal of Statistical Computation and Simulation*, **10**, 160-161.

Daniel, C. (1982). "Weighted 2^k designs," *Utilitas Mathematica*, **21B**, 117-121.

Daniel, C. (1983). "Half-normal plots." In S. Kotz and N. L. Johnson (Eds.), *Encyclopedia of Statistical Sciences*, Volume 3. New York: Wiley, pp. 565-568.

CHAPTER 1

Analysis of Unreplicated Factorials Allowing for Possibly Faulty Observations

George E. P. Box
University of Wisconsin

R. Daniel Meyer
The Lubrizol Corporation

1. INTRODUCTION

Normal probability plotting of orthogonal contrasts (Daniel, 1959) has become a standard technique for interpreting and criticizing unreplicated factorial and fractional factorial experiments. While the primary objective of the normal plot is to determine which effects are distinguishable from noise, Daniel has pointed out that this is not its only function. Various departures from assumptions may be detected by critical inspection of the normal plot. In particular, the presence of one or more faulty observations is marked by a characteristic pattern among the plotted points.

An Example

To illustrate, consider the data in Table 1 for a full 2^4 factorial experiment taken from Box and Draper (1986). With the factors denoted by 1, 2, 3, and 4, this shows the design array, the original observations, and the estimated effects. A normal plot of the effects is shown in Figure 1. From this plot it will be seen that while the main

2   ANALYSIS OF UNREPLICATED FACTORIALS

TABLE 1. The data for the example with the original observations in the right-hand column and the estimated effects along the top.

EST.	−0.80	−4.22	3.71	1.01	0.91	−2.49	−0.58	−0.80	−1.18	1.49	1.20	0.72	0.40	−1.58	1.52	
	1	2	3	4	12	13	14	23	24	34	123	124	134	234	1234	
1	−	−	−	−	+	+	+	+	+	+	−	−	−	−	+	47.46
2	+	−	−	−	−	−	−	+	+	+	+	+	+	−	−	49.62
3	−	+	−	−	−	+	+	−	−	+	+	+	−	+	−	43.13
4	+	+	−	−	+	−	−	−	−	+	−	−	+	+	+	46.31
5	−	−	+	−	+	−	+	−	+	−	+	−	+	+	−	51.47
6	+	−	+	−	−	+	−	−	+	−	−	+	−	+	+	48.49
7	−	+	+	−	−	−	+	+	−	−	−	+	+	−	+	49.34
8	+	+	+	−	+	+	−	+	−	−	+	−	−	−	−	46.10
9	−	−	−	+	+	+	+	+	−	−	+	+	+	+	−	46.76
10	+	−	−	+	−	−	−	+	−	−	−	−	−	+	+	48.56
11	−	+	−	+	−	+	+	−	+	−	−	−	+	−	+	44.83
12	+	+	−	+	+	−	−	−	+	−	+	+	−	−	−	44.45
13	−	−	+	+	+	−	+	−	−	+	−	+	−	−	+	59.15
14	+	−	+	+	−	+	−	−	−	+	+	−	+	−	−	51.33
15	−	+	+	+	−	−	+	+	+	+	+	−	−	+	−	47.02
16	+	+	+	+	+	+	−	+	+	+	−	+	+	+	+	47.90

effects 2 and 3 are largest in absolute magnitude, they do not deviate very much from a line drawn through all the remaining points. One would hesitate therefore to conclude on this basis that they were distinguishable from the noise. There is, however, another feature of the plot which bears further consideration. The points falling near zero appear to follow two different parallel lines rather than one, with negative values on one line and positive values on the other. Daniel points out that such behavior suggests the possibility of a faulty observation. He also suggests (Daniel, 1976) how that observation may be identified, using the fact that if a particular

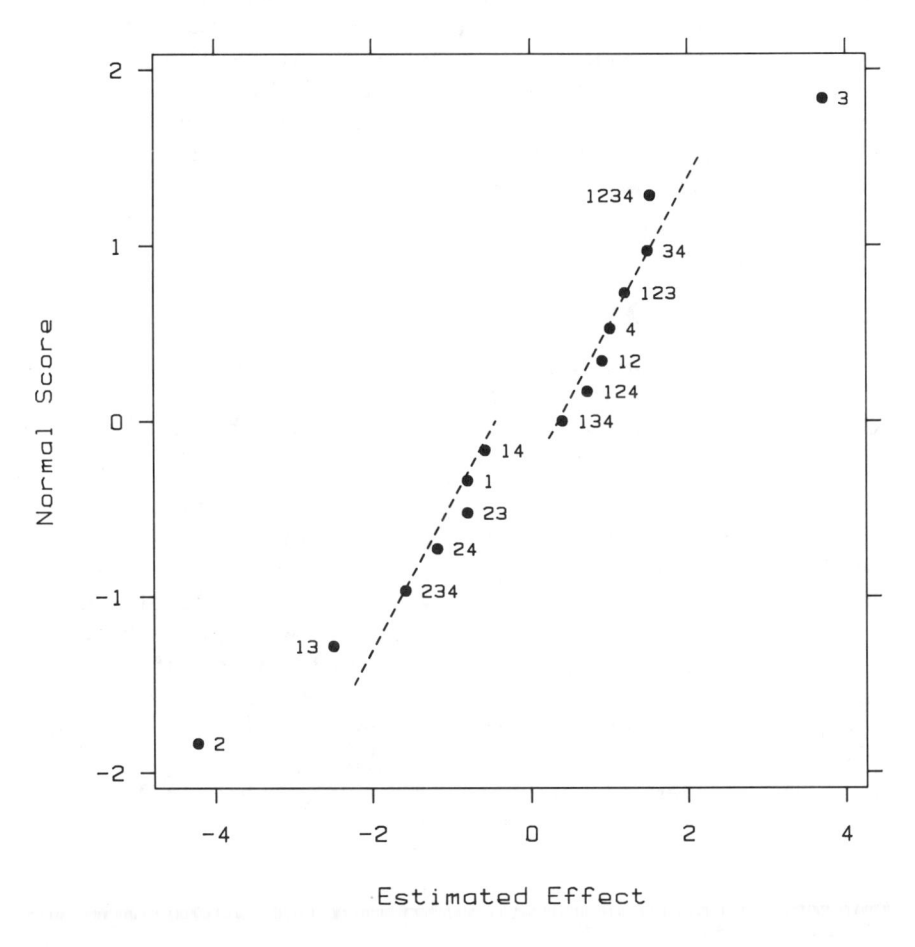

Figure 1. Normal plot of the estimated effects for the data in Table 1. Points near zero appear to follow two different parallel lines, represented by the dashed lines, rather than one.

observation is biased by, say, a positive amount, those contrasts in which the observation enters positively are shifted to the right, and those contrasts in which the observation enters negatively are shifted to the left. This produces a "gap" such as the one seen in Figure 1. Thus the observation, if it exists, which enters positively in the small positive contrasts and negatively in the small negative contrasts will be under suspicion.

Examination of the design array, Table 1, shows that the row of signs corresponding to $y_{13} = 59.15$ matches the signs of all contrasts save one, suggesting that this thirteenth observation is too large. In practice, such a discovery should lead to reconsideration of the data and in particular of what effects might show up if this observation were appropriately adjusted. In an ongoing investigation it should lead the experimenter to consider any special circumstances which might have surrounded the making of this observation and possibly to a repetition of the observation or of some selected part of the design involving this observation.

2. A MORE FORMAL SOLUTION

The remainder of this paper summarizes some recent work on a more formal study which however closely follows the spirit of Daniel's analysis. We emphasize that we regard this work not as replacing this analysis but as perhaps a useful adjunct to it.

The possibility of model inadequacies poses a dilemma for the experimenter rather like that faced by a small country which believes itself in danger of air attack and wonders how it should spend a limited budget on radar apparatus. While some resources should be spent on highly directional radars to monitor with great sensitivity the direction (or directions) regarded as most likely, it might be wise to spend the rest on nondirectional instruments which, while less sensitive, could monitor the whole horizon. Graphical analysis can perform a task like global radar making it possible that the investigator is alerted to contingencies not initially bargained for (see also Box, 1980).

A Model Based on the Effect Sparsity Hypothesis

Clearly implied by Daniel's normal plot analysis is a hypothesis of *effect sparsity* — that most of what is occurring can be accounted for by a few active effects. Suppose **X** is the $n \times n$ design matrix from which the $n-1$ usual estimated effects are calculated, and **y** is the $n \times 1$ vector of observations. If $\mathbf{X}_{(a)}$ denotes the columns of **X** which correspond to active effects $\tau_{(a)}$, then **y** may be described by the relationship

$$\mathbf{y} = \mathbf{X}_{(a)}\tau_{(a)} + \epsilon$$

where ϵ is the $n \times 1$ vector of normally distributed errors with zero mean and variance σ^2. Let α_1 be the prior probability that an effect is active, and let $a_{(r_1)}$ be the event that a particular set of r_1 of the $n-1$ effects is active; $\mathbf{X}_{(r_1)}$ and $\tau_{(r_1)}$ are the columns of **X** and the effects corresponding to $a_{(r_1)}$. The prior distribution of each active effect τ, given σ^2, is an independent normal with mean zero and variance $\gamma^2 \sigma^2$; the prior distributions of the mean τ_0 and log (σ) are locally uniform (see, e.g., Box and Tiao, 1968, 1973). Thus the posterior probability of the event $a_{(r_1)}$ can be written

$$p(a_{(r_1)}|\mathbf{y}) \propto \left(\frac{\alpha_1}{1-\alpha_1}\right)^{r_1} \gamma^{-r_1} \frac{\left|\mathbf{X}'_{(0)}\mathbf{X}_{(0)}\right|^{1/2}}{\left|\Gamma_{r_1}+\mathbf{X}'_{(r_1)}\mathbf{X}_{(r_1)}\right|^{1/2}} \times$$

$$\left[\frac{S(\hat{\tau}_{(r_1)}) + \hat{\tau}'_{(r_1)}\Gamma_{r_1}\hat{\tau}_{(r_1)}}{S(\hat{\tau}_{(0)})}\right]^{-(n-1)/2}$$

where

$$\Gamma_{r_1} = \frac{1}{\gamma^2}\begin{bmatrix} 0 & 0' \\ 0 & I_{r_1} \end{bmatrix}, \quad I_{r_1} = r_1 \times r_1 \text{ identity matrix}$$

$$\hat{\tau}_{(r_1)} = \left[\Gamma_{r_1} + \mathbf{X}'_{(r_1)}\mathbf{X}_{(r_1)}\right]^{-1}\mathbf{X}'_{(r_1)}\mathbf{y}$$

$$S(\hat{\tau}_{(r_1)}) = \left[\mathbf{y} - \mathbf{X}_{(r_1)}\hat{\tau}_{(r_1)}\right]'\left[\mathbf{y} - \mathbf{X}_{(r_1)}\hat{\tau}_{(r_1)}\right].$$

6 ANALYSIS OF UNREPLICATED FACTORIALS

Then, for example, the posterior probability that an effect i is active is

$$p_i = P[\text{effect } i \text{ active } | \mathbf{y}] = \sum_{(r_1): i \text{ active}} p(a_{(r_1)}|\mathbf{y}).$$

In an earlier paper, Box and Meyer (1985) follow such an approach to provide an alternative means of locating active effects and they show that the statistical literature suggests average values for these parameters of $\alpha_1 = 0.2$, $\gamma = 2.5$. They furthermore show that the conclusions about which effects are active are usually insensitive to variations over the ranges of values of (α_1, γ) which appear to be actually encountered.

Faulty Observations

To allow for the possibility of faulty observations (Box and Tiao, 1968; Meyer, 1985), we suppose that the errors associated with such values have an inflated error variance $k^2\sigma^2$ ($k>1$) and occur with some small probability α_2. Thus the error ϵ is supposed to follow the scale-contaminated normal distribution $(1-\alpha_2)N(0,\sigma^2) + \alpha_2 N(0,k^2\sigma^2)$. Let $a_{(r_1,r_2)}$ be the event that a particular set of r_1 effects are active and a particular set of r_2 observations are faulty $\mathbf{X}_{(r_1,r_2)}$ is the matrix of columns and rows of $\mathbf{X}$ corresponding to active effects and faulty observations, and $\mathbf{y}_{(r_2)}$ the elements of $\mathbf{y}$ supposed to be faulty. Then the posterior probability of the event $a_{(r_1,r_2)}$ can be written

$$p(a_{(r_1,r_2)} | \mathbf{y}) \propto \left(\frac{\alpha_1}{1-\alpha_1}\right)^{r_1} \left(\frac{\alpha_2}{1-\alpha_2}\right)^{r_2} \gamma^{-r_1} k^{-r_2} \times$$

$$\frac{|\mathbf{X}'_{(0)}\mathbf{X}_{(0)}|^{\frac{1}{2}}}{|\mathbf{\Gamma}_{r_1}+\mathbf{X}'_{(r_1)}\mathbf{X}_{(r_1)}-\phi\mathbf{X}'_{(r_1,r_2)}\mathbf{X}_{(r_1,r_2)}|^{\frac{1}{2}}} \left[\frac{S\left(\hat{\tau}_{(r_1,r_2)}\right)+\hat{\tau}'_{(r_1,r_2)}\mathbf{\Gamma}_{r_1}\hat{\tau}_{(r_1,r_2)}}{S(\hat{\tau}_{(0)})}\right]^{-(n-1)/2}$$

where

$$\phi = 1 - \frac{1}{k^2},$$

$$\hat{\tau}_{(r_1,r_2)} = \left[\Gamma_{r_1} + X'_{(r_1)}X_{(r_1)} - \phi X'_{(r_1,r_2)}X_{(r_1,r_2)}\right]^{-1}\left[X'_{(r_1)}y - \phi X_{(r_1,r_2)}y_{(r_2)}\right]$$

$$S\left[\hat{\tau}_{(r_1,r_2)}\right] = \left[y - X_{(r_1)}\hat{\tau}_{(r_1,r_2)}\right]'\left[y - X_{(r_1)}\hat{\tau}_{(r_1,r_2)}\right] -$$

$$\phi\left[y_{(r_2)} - X_{(r_1,r_2)}\hat{\tau}_{(r_1,r_2)}\right]'\left[y - X_{(r_1,r_2)}\hat{\tau}_{(r_1,r_2)}\right].$$

Then, for example, the posterior probability that effect i is active is

$$p_i = \sum_{(r_1,r_2):i \text{ active}} p(a_{(r_1,r_2)}|y)$$

and the posterior probability that observation y_j is faulty is

$$q_j = \sum_{(r_1,r_2):y_j \text{ faulty}} p(a_{(r_1,r_2)}|y).$$

Computing the $\{p_i\}$ and $\{q_j\}$ over all combinations $a_{(r_1,r_2)}$ will generally not be feasible. Instead we employ the following iterative approximation. We first compute the probabilities $\{p_i\}$, assuming there are no faulty observations. Then temporarily choose the active effects as those with $p_i > P$. The probabilities $\{q_j\}$ are computed with the active effects held fixed by the above choice. The probabilities $\{p_i\}$ are then recomputed, assuming all observations with $q_j > Q$ to have variance $k^2\sigma^2$, and so on. In most cases convergence is achieved in one or two iterations, with $P = Q = 0.5$. Alternatively, P and Q may be chosen after observing the results of the first iteration as a more exploratory approach. As computing power increases, the simultaneous summation over all combinations of active columns and faulty observations will be the most desirable method of computation.

Analysis of Data Assuming No Possibility of Faulty Observations

Figure 2 shows the posterior probabilities $\{p_i\}$ for the data of Table 1 with $\alpha_1 = 0.2$, $\gamma = 2.5$ when we do *not* allow for faulty observations ($\alpha_2 = 0$). The probabilities suggest, as did the normal plot, that although main effects 2 and 3 are largest in absolute magnitude, the evidence for these effects being active is rather slight.

8 ANALYSIS OF UNREPLICATED FACTORIALS

Analysis of Data Assuming Faulty Observations Possible

Earlier work (Chen and Box, 1979) suggested that this kind of analysis for faulty values is chiefly affected by the parameter $G = \alpha_2 k^{-1}/(1-\alpha_2)$ and that it is fairly insensitive to change. Relying on this work we employ the values $\alpha_2 = 0.05$ and $k = 5$. In practice the analyst may use the computer to experiment somewhat with other values and thus to check on the stability of the conclusions.

In Figure 3, using $\alpha_2 = 0.05$ and $k = 5$, the posterior probabilities $\{p_i\}$ and $\{q_j\}$ are plotted. The value of q_{13} is very close to one, suggesting strongly that observation y_{13} is faulty. The affect on the probabilities $\{p_i\}$ of the automatic downweighting of y_{13} achieved by this analysis is to make the posterior probabilities for main effects 2 and 3 much closer to one, and the probabilities for interactions 13 and 134 also much larger. The conclusions are similar to those suggested by a Daniel plot with data in which y_{13} has been suitably adjusted. Posterior probabilities and revised values of the estimated effects are given in Tables 2 and 3.

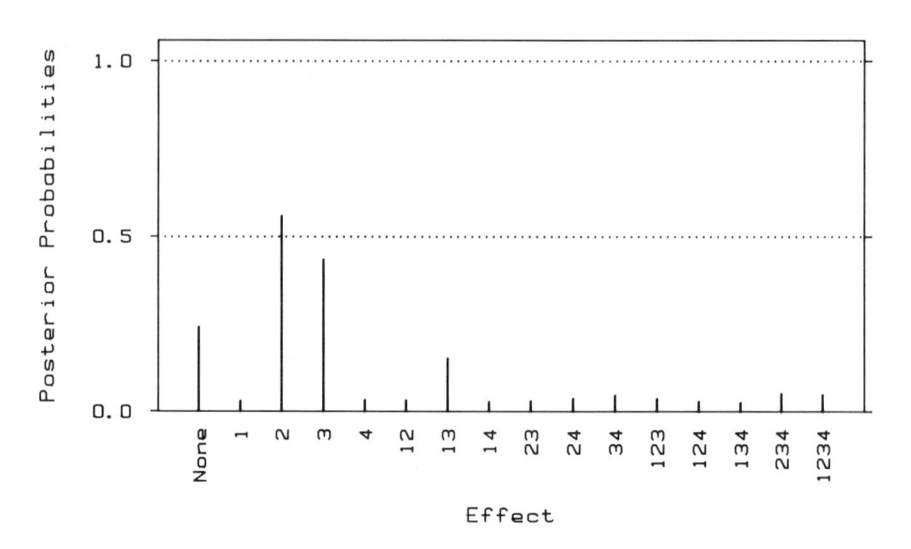

Figure 2. Posterior probabilities $\{p_i\}$ that each effect is active, assuming no faulty observations, with $\alpha_1 = 0.2$, $\gamma = 2.5$.

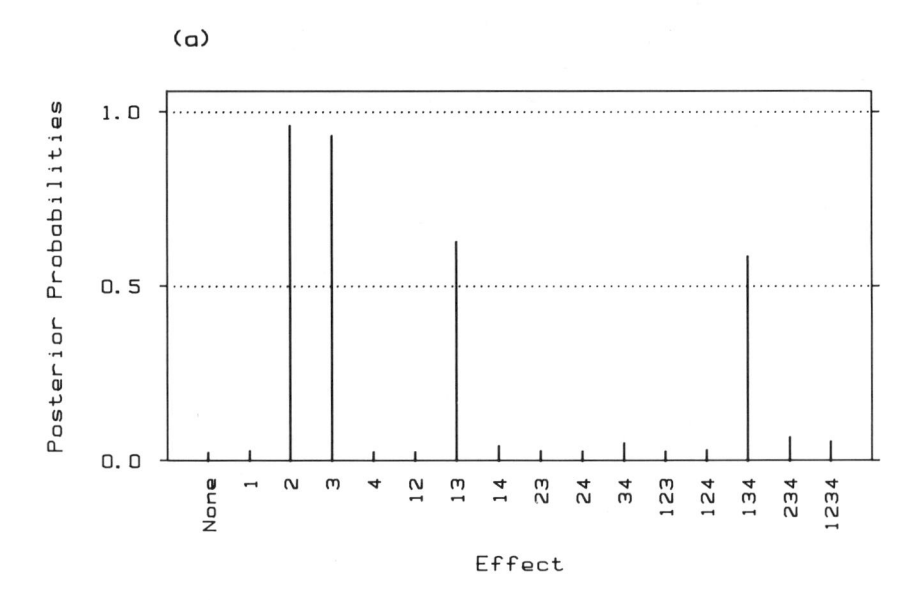

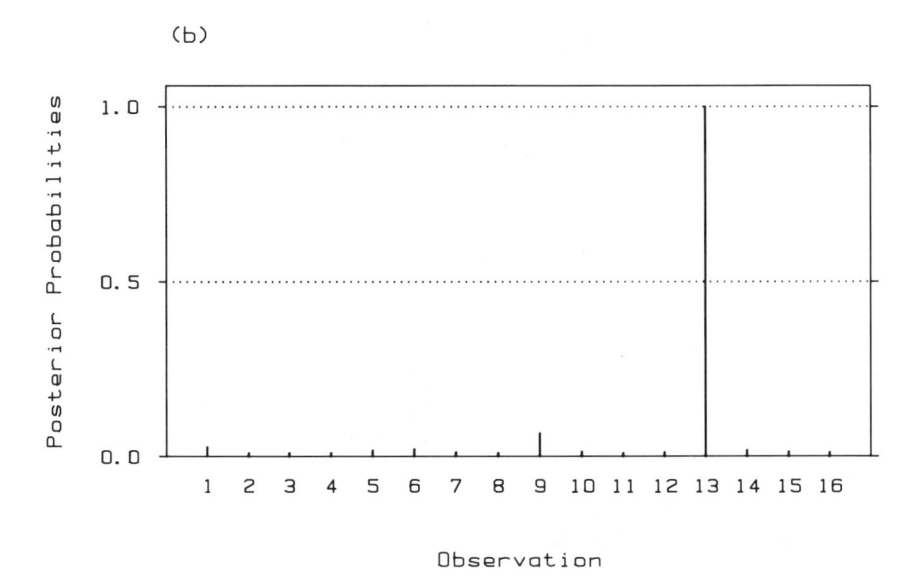

Figure 3. (a) Posterior probabilities $\{p_i\}$ that each effect is active, assuming $y_{13} = 59.15$ has variance $k^2\sigma^2$, with $\alpha_1 = 0.2$, $\gamma = 2.5$, $k = 5$ (b) Posterior probabilities $\{q_j\}$ that each observation is faulty, assuming main effects 2 and 3 and interactions 13 and 134 are active, with $\gamma = 2.5$, $\alpha_2 = 0.05$, $k = 5$.

TABLE 2. Posterior probabilities $\{p_i\}$ and Bayesian estimates of effects with $\alpha_1 = 0.2$, $\gamma = 2.5$, $\alpha_2 = 0.05$, $k = 5$.

Column	Assuming No Outliers Estimated Effect	Assuming No Outliers Posterior Probability	Allowing For Outliers Estimated Effect	Allowing For Outliers Posterior Probability
1	−0.79	.029	0.25	.029
2	−4.18	.557	−3.17	.960
3	3.67	.432	2.68	.931
4	1.00	.032	−0.02	.026
5	0.90	.031	−0.13	.026
6	−2.47	.151	−1.49	.628
7	−0.57	.027	0.48	.043
8	−0.79	.029	0.25	.029
9	−1.17	.036	−0.17	.028
10	1.48	.046	0.52	.051
11	1.19	.036	0.19	.028
12	0.71	.028	−0.33	.032
13	0.40	.025	1.42	.587
14	−1.56	.051	−0.62	.069
15	1.50	.048	0.55	.056

3. CONCLUSION

We feel that with the increase in computational power now becoming available analysis of the kind we suggest here is a practical possibility. Furthermore, experimentation with the parameters α_1, α_2, γ and k can indicate to what extent the conclusions are insensitive to reasonable changes in the probability model. Experience may show that such analysis can usefully augment the highly successful graphical methods of Daniel.

ACKNOWLEDGMENT

Sponsored by the United States Army under Contract No. DAAG29-80-C-0041 and aided by access to the research computer of the University of Wisconsin Department of Statistics.

TABLE 3. Posterior probabilities $\{q_j\}$ that observation are faulty, assuming main effects 2 and 3 and interactions 13 and 134 are active, with $\alpha = 2.5$, $\alpha_2 = 0.05$, and $k = 5$.

Row	Observation	Posterior Probability
1	47.46	.027
2	49.62	.010
3	43.13	.010
4	46.31	.010
5	51.47	.017
6	48.49	.021
7	49.34	.012
8	46.10	.010
9	46.76	.066
10	48.56	.014
11	44.83	.010
12	44.45	.012
13	59.15	1.000
14	51.33	.018
15	47.02	.014
16	47.90	.012

REFERENCES

Box, G. E. P. (1980). "Sampling and Bayes' inference in scientific modelling and robustness." *Journal of the Royal Statistical Society, Series A*, **143**, 383-430.

Box, G. E. P. and Draper, N. R. (1986). *Response Surfaces and Empirical Model Building.* New York: Wiley.

Box, G. E. P. and Meyer, R. D. (1985). "Studies in quality improvement II: an analysis for unreplicated fractional factorials." University of Wisconsin-Madison, Mathematics Research Center Technical Summary Report #2797.

Box, G. E. P. and Tiao, G. C. (1968). "A Bayesian approach to some outlier problems," *Biometrika*, **55**, 119-129.

Box, G. E. P. and Tiao, G. C. (1973). *Bayesian Inference in Statistical Analysis.* Reading, MA: Addison-Wesley.

Chen, G. and Box, G. E. P. (1979). "Further study of robustification via a Bayesian approach." University of Wisconsin-Madison, Mathematics Research Center Technical Summary Report #1998.

Daniel, C. (1959). "Use of half-normal plots in interpreting factorial two-level experiments," *Technometrics*, **1**, 311-341.

Daniel, C. (1976). *Applications of Statistics to Industrial Experimentation.* New York: Wiley.

Meyer, R. D. (1985). "Analysis of factorial experiments." University of Wisconsin-Madison, Mathematics Research Center Technical Summary Report #2865.

CHAPTER 2

Variable Selection in Clustering and Other Contexts

Edward B. Fowlkes
Ramanathan Gnanadesikan
Jon R. Kettenring

Bell Communications Research

ABSTRACT

This paper discusses issues and methods for selecting a subset of initially observed variables in three different statistical data analysis contexts. The first is multiple regression analysis, where the problem is to choose a subset of the independent variables that will do well in predicting the dependent variable in the regression relationship. The second situation is discriminant analysis, where one would like to choose a subset of initially observed variables which would maximally separate prespecified groups from which the observations are known to arise. The third context is that of clustering, wherein the groupings of the observations themselves emerge from the data analysis, and the problem is to select a subset of initially observed dependent variables that would account for cluster structure present in the data. The paper illustrates the uses of the methods for all three contexts in analyzing a real data set.

1 INTRODUCTION

Reduction of dimensionality is an important goal of data analysis. In the analysis of multivariate observations, for instance, it is common practice to look for such reduction via linear combinations of the initial variables. The classical techniques, such as principal components, canonical correlation and discriminant analyses, as well as the more recent work of DeSarbo, Carroll, Clark and Green (1984) on cluster analysis, provide examples of this approach.

From a pragmatic viewpoint, there is another type of reduction which is appealing, viz. selecting a subset of the variables. The main practical advantage here is that there is an actual reduction in the number of variables measured and the avoidance of interpretational difficulties that could arise in looking at linear combinations of very different kinds of variables. It is, of course, common practice to look at the weights of variables in a linear combination and to omit those that have "negligible" weights, but neither is this always easy to do nor are negligible weights always guaranteed.

The main purpose of this paper is to discuss and to illustrate (through the analysis of a specific data set) techniques for selecting a subset from an initial set of variables, given three different contexts of statistical analyses. Specifically, the three contexts of interest for variable selection in this paper are: (1) multiple regression, (2) discriminant analysis, and (3) cluster analysis. Despite a common interest in selecting a subset of the variables, there are clear differences among the three contexts and such differences need to be accommodated by the methods used (see Section 2 below for further discussion of this). The amount of attention paid in the literature to the methods in the three categories tends to be in decreasing order, partly perhaps due to the increasing difficulties inherent in the three settings.

At any rate, variable selection for multiple regression analysis is a problem that Cuthbert Daniel has been very interested in, and he had a key role in stimulating major advances on this front (see, for example, Daniel and Wood, 1980; Gorman and Toman, 1966; Mallows, 1973). The selection of the topic for this paper in the volume honoring him is based on this historic interest of his.

Section 2 discusses the similarities and differences among the three contexts of statistical analyses considered in this paper. It also provides references to discussions of well-known methods of variable selection and brief descriptions of those that are most pertinent. Section 3 illustrates the use of the methods in performing all three types of analyses on a specific data set which is included for possible further analyses by the interested reader. Section 4 consists of summary and conclusions.

2. ALGORITHMS FOR VARIABLE SELECTION

Variable selection in the context of multiple regression analysis is a well-studied problem in the literature. For example, Draper and Smith (1981, Chapter 6) discuss ten types of algorithms, including the popular stepwise and C_p methods. The goal in all of these procedures is to find individual subsets of size p from the complete set of P so-called independent variables which adequately explain or predict a single dependent variable. (For the regression discussion, it is assumed that an intercept term is counted in p and P.)

The large variety of approaches to variable selection for regression includes some that are fairly rigidly specified, based on rules involving significance levels, as in the stepwise procedures, and others that are more informal, based on impressions obtained from graphical displays, as in the C_p method. However, even within the realm of graphical methods, one can distinguish various degrees of formality. In the usual C_p plot, developed by Mallows (1973), one superimposes the line $C_p = p$ to serve as a benchmark. This is an informal guideline which involves limited distributional assumptions. Spjøtvoll (1977) proposes two alternatives. One is to plot $F_p = 1 + (C_p - p)/(P - p)$ against p with the line $F_p = 1$ as the benchmark. (In this expression, it is assumed that all P independent variables are used in obtaining the estimate of σ^2 involved in C_p.) This plot uses a more familiar statistic than C_p but is intended to be equally informal. The other is to plot the significance level of C_p or F_p, based on the usual normality assumptions about the data, versus p. The argument for this approach is that it can help in deciding which deviations from the benchmark line in the C_p or F_p plot are statistically important. Another option, which is applied later in this paper but in another context, is to superimpose an upper percentage point as a second benchmark curve directly on the C_p or F_p plot. The spirit of this suggestion is to maintain the informality of the procedure, but to add a little extra for calibration purposes.

While the state of development of variable selection methods for discriminant analysis is not at the same stage as that for regression, there are nevertheless several formal and informal techniques that are in use. Overviews may be found in Hand (1981, Chapter 6), McKay and Campbell (1982a,b) and Seber (1984, Section 6.10).

The two-group discrimination problem is simpler to treat than the multi-group one. The theory is neater, complications are fewer, and there is a close tie with multiple regression. A standard F-test can be used to check whether a given subset of the variables is adequate in the sense that the complementary subset provides no "additional information" about separation between the groups. McKay (1978) exploits this idea by calculating the significance levels for all possible such tests and then plotting them as in Spjøtvoll's second alternative to the C_p.

The multi-group case is complicated by the need to find subsets of variables which discriminate among all of the groups and not just the most separate ones. McKay (1977) provides a simultaneous test procedure approach based upon an "additional information" test statistic, which fulfills this need. The earlier work of McCabe (1975) may not be as effective for such incremental evaluation but is attractive because of its simplicity and informality. His approach is to compute Wilks' Λ statistic, $U_p = |\mathbf{W}_p|/|\mathbf{T}_p|$, where $\mathbf{W}_p$ and $\mathbf{T}_p$ are the within group and total sums of cross-products matrices, respectively, for each p-subset of variables. These values are ordered separately for each p and then used as a guide for finding important subsets.

As a compromise between the rigorous formal treatment of McKay and the simple ordering idea of McCabe, one can construct a C_p type display based on the "additional information" test idea. Specifically, with n observations and K groups,

$$Q_{P-p} = - \{(n-p-1) - (P-p+K)/2\} \log (U_P/U_p)$$

is an appropriate statistic for testing the significance of the additional (P−p) variables in the presence of a particular p-subset. Its null distribution is approximately $\chi^2_{(P-p)(K-1)}$. This suggests plotting Q_{P-p} versus (P−p)(K−1). The plot can be enhanced with benchmarks as previously discussed for the C_p plot. In contrast to the C_p plot, small abscissa values correspond to cases where the subset included is large. A variation of this plot based upon significance levels has been suggested by McKay and Campbell (1982a).

For cluster analysis problems, explicit variable selection procedures have been considered by Hartigan (1972) and Fowlkes, Gnanadesikan and Kettenring (1985). Clustering methods tend to be used in an exploratory mode without as much information about the background and structure of the data as in regression and discriminant analysis. It may happen that one subset is relevant for one grouping structure but not for others. Indeed, some variables may only constitute "noise" that masks clear cluster structure delineated by other variables. This makes the problem of selecting appropriate subsets crucial for the success of the analysis.

The algorithms proposed by Fowlkes et al. resemble the forward, backward and stepwise ones in regression. While their mechanics depend upon statistics derived from normal theory for discriminant analysis, the associated distribution theory for these statistics is useless because the clusters are determined from the data rather than being prespecified. This makes the analytical determination of benchmarks extremely difficult, and it is necessary to resort to simulation.

The algorithms have been developed explicitly for use with hierarchical clustering, but the general approach could be applied to any partitioning procedure. The forward selection version — the only one used in this paper — begins by forming P hierarchical trees of the data, one for each variable. The tree is derived starting with distances between each pair of data points and merging points or groups of points according to a particular rule such as complete linkage (see Seber, 1984, Section 7.3). A cut is made at various levels of the tree to form $K = 2, 3, \ldots, K_{max}$ groups. For each K, a traditional eigenvalue-based statistic is used to measure group separation. With $p = 1$, this is of course a trivial calculation. The example in Section 3 utilizes a version of Pillai's (1955) trace statistic, namely, $S(K) = tr(T_p^{-1} B_p)/p$, where $B_p = T_p - W_p$, but others such as U_p could be used as well. The statistics minus their estimated null expected values, i.e., $S(K) - E(S(K))$, are plotted against K, separately for each tree, and one of the variables is selected as the first to enter on the basis of these P plots. The next stage proceeds in the same manner, but now all (P−1) combinations of two variables, including the one already selected, are used, leading to (P−1) new plots to be examined. The forward selection procedure continues until the plots no longer indicate strong evidence for bringing in an additional variable.

The expected values are estimated via simulation. The null condition used as background is random sampling from a P-dimensional spherical normal distribution. For more details, see Fowlkes et al. (1985).

A hypothetical example of the use of this method is shown in Figure 1. Two variables, 1 and 2, have already been entered and the addition of a third is being considered. The two panels show the plots of $S(K) - E(S(K))$ corresponding to adding either variable 3 or variable 4. There is strong evidence for preferring variable 3 because the subset {1,2,3} gives rise to uniformly higher values with a sharp peak corresponding to three clusters. (In plots of this type, small negative values may occur; these are rounded to zero.)

18 VARIABLE SELECTION IN CLUSTERING AND OTHER CONTEXTS

Assessment of Cluster Separation

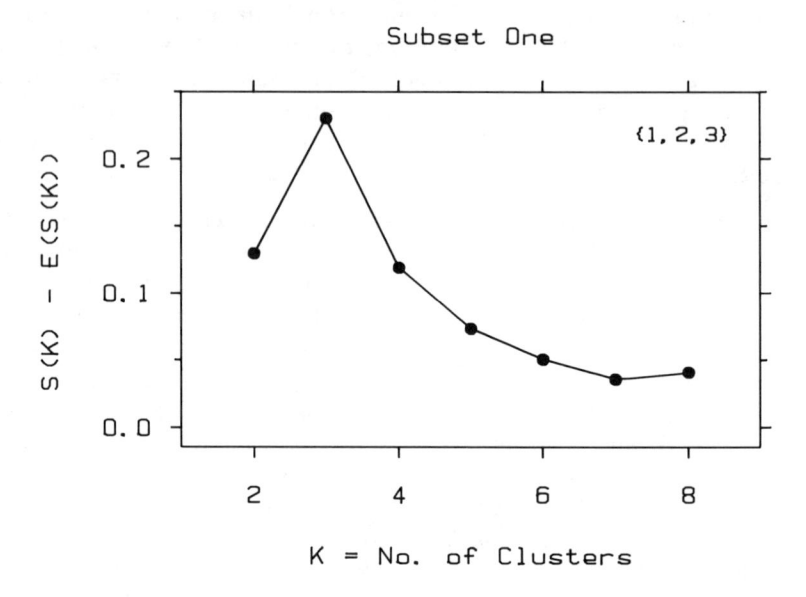

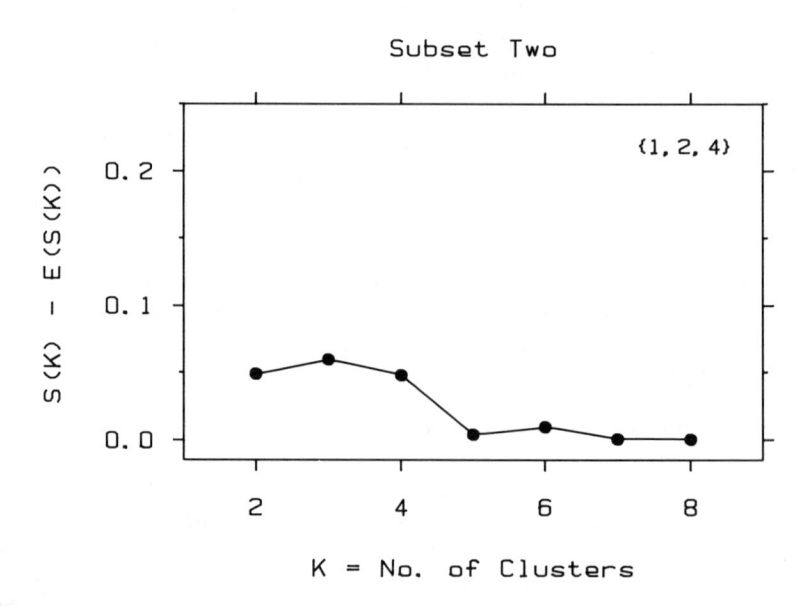

Subset One

Subset Two

Figure 1. Cluster separation plots for two hypothetical subsets of three variables.

3. AN EXAMPLE OF THREE VARIABLE SELECTION CONTEXTS

In this section a real data example is considered. The data comprised nine variables recorded on 56 automobiles, as shown in Table 1. Half of the autos were foreign built, and half were manufactured by American auto makers. The data represents a subset of data used by Chambers, Cleveland, Kleiner, and Tukey (1983). It was found from analysis of the full complement of autos that the most prominent structure in the data corresponded to ones that are large, expensive and domestic versus the rest. The former group was removed in order to look for more subtle structure. Some reasonable questions to ask about this data are: which subset of the other variables, including a dummy variable for foreign versus domestic, best predicts EPA mileage (variable 2); which subset of the variables best discriminates between foreign and domestic autos; and which subset of variables best reveals cluster structure (if such structure is indeed present).

First, the forward selection algorithm for hierarchical clustering, discussed in Section 2, was applied to the auto data, having standardized each of the nine variables to have unit standard deviation, and using $S(K)$ as a measure of cluster separation. Distances between pairs of autos were measured by the Euclidean metric applied to the standardized variables, and the complete linkage method was used in the hierarchical clustering. The maximum number of clusters for consideration was selected as eight. Figure 2 shows plots of $S(K) - E(S(K))$ versus the number of clusters, K, for the second step of the forward selection process, variable 8 (displacement) having been selected in the first step. The figure shows eight separate plots, one for each two-variable subset. The subset which shows the most cluster separation is {8,1} for displacement and price. Not only does {8,1} have the largest single separation value (viz., largest ordinate value), but its separation values tend to be larger than the corresponding values for other subsets. Since the plot for displacement and price reaches a somewhat sharp maximum at $K = 3$, there is an indication that there are three clusters. The decision was made to select variable 1 (price) at the second step, and the apparent clustering for variables 8 and 1 was checked by making a scatter plot, shown in Figure 3, of displacement versus price and identifying the points by cluster number. The clusters are entirely separated, and the contents correspond roughly to luxury, foreign cars; small, low cost, foreign and domestic cars; and large, low cost, domestic cars. There is one striking anomaly with this clustering; the Buick Opel and Chevrolet Chevette, both small, fuel-efficient cars, clustered with the large domestic autos.

20 VARIABLE SELECTION IN CLUSTERING AND OTHER CONTEXTS

TABLE 1. 1979 data on nine variables for fifty-six automobiles.

Make & Model	Price $	EPA Mileage mpg	Rear Seat ins	Trunk Space cu ft	Weight lbs	Length ins	Turn Circle ft	Displacement cu ins	Gear Ratio
AMC Concord	4099	22	27.5	11	2930	186	40	121	3.58
AMC Pacer	4749	17	25.5	11	3350	173	40	258	2.53
AMC Spirit	3799	22	18.5	12	2640	168	35	121	3.08
Audi 5000	9690	17	27.0	15	2830	189	37	131	3.20
Audi Fox	6295	23	28.0	11	2070	174	36	97	3.70
BMW 320i	9735	25	26.0	12	2650	177	34	121	3.64
Buick Century	4816	20	29.0	16	3250	196	40	196	2.93
Buick Le Sabre	5788	18	30.5	21	3670	218	43	231	2.73
Buick Opel	4453	26	24.0	10	2230	170	34	304	2.87
Buick Regal	5189	20	28.5	16	3280	200	42	196	2.93
Buick Skylark	4082	19	27.0	13	3400	200	42	231	3.08
Chev. Chevette	3299	29	26.0	9	2110	163	34	231	2.93
Chev. Malibu	4504	22	28.5	17	3180	193	41	200	2.73
Chev. Monte Carlo	5104	22	28.5	16	3220	200	41	200	2.73
Chev. Monza	3667	24	25.0	7	2750	179	40	151	2.73
Chev. Nova	3955	19	27.0	13	3430	197	43	250	2.56
Datsun 200-SX	6229	23	21.0	6	2370	170	35	119	3.89
Datsun 210	4589	35	23.5	8	2020	165	32	85	3.70

AN EXAMPLE OF THREE VARIABLE SELECTION CONTEXTS 21

Datsun 510	5079	24	22.0	8	2280	170	34	119	3.54
Datsun 810	8129	21	27.0	8	2750	184	38	146	3.55
Dodge Colt	3984	30	24.0	8	2120	163	35	98	3.54
Dodge Diplomat	5010	18	29.0	17	3600	206	46	318	2.47
Fiat Strada	4296	21	26.5	16	2130	161	36	105	3.37
Ford Fiesta	4389	28	26.0	9	1800	147	33	98	3.15
Ford Mustang	4187	21	23.0	10	2650	179	42	140	3.08
Honda Accord	5799	25	25.5	10	2240	172	36	107	3.05
Honda Civic	4499	28	23.5	5	1760	149	34	91	3.30
Mazda GLC	3995	30	25.5	11	1980	154	33	86	3.73
Merc. Bobcat	3829	22	25.5	9	2580	169	39	140	2.73
Merc. Monarch	4516	18	27.0	15	3370	198	41	250	2.43
Merc. Zephyr	3291	20	29.0	17	2830	195	43	140	3.08
Olds. Cutlass	4733	19	28.0	16	3300	198	42	231	2.93
Olds. Cutlass Supreme	5172	19	28.0	16	3310	198	42	231	2.93
Olds. Omega	4181	19	27.0	14	3370	200	43	231	3.08
Olds. Starfire	4195	24	25.5	10	2720	180	40	151	2.73
Peugeot 604 SL	12990	14	30.5	14	3420	192	38	163	3.58
Plym. Arrow	4647	28	21.5	11	2360	170	37	156	3.05
Plym. Champ	4425	34	23.0	11	1800	157	37	86	2.97
Plym. Horizon	4482	25	25.0	17	2200	165	36	105	3.37
Plym. Sapporo	6486	26	22.0	8	2520	182	38	119	3.54
Plym. Volare	4060	18	31.0	16	3330	201	44	225	3.23

TABLE 1. 1979 data on nine variables for fifty-six automobiles, (cont'd).

Make & Model	Price $	EPA Mileage mpg	Rear Seat ins	Trunk Space cu ft	Weight lbs	Length ins	Turn Circle ft	Displacement cu ins	Gear Ratio
Pont. Firebird	4934	18	23.5	7	3470	198	42	231	3.08
Pont. Grand Prix	5222	19	28.5	16	3210	201	45	231	2.93
Pont. Le Mans	4723	19	28.0	17	3200	199	40	231	2.93
Pont. Phoenix	4424	19	27.0	13	3420	203	43	231	3.08
Pont. Sunbird	4172	24	25.0	7	2690	179	41	151	2.73
Renault Le Car	3895	26	23.0	10	1830	142	34	79	3.72
Subaru	3798	35	25.5	11	2050	164	36	97	3.81
Toyota Celica	5899	18	22.0	14	2410	174	36	134	3.06
Toyota Corolla	3748	31	24.5	9	2200	165	35	97	3.21
Toyota Corona	5719	18	23.0	11	2670	175	36	134	3.05
Volvo 260	11995	17	29.5	14	3170	193	37	163	2.98
VW Dasher	7140	23	37.5	12	2160	172	36	97	3.74
VW Rabbit	4697	25	25.5	15	1930	155	35	89	3.78
VW Rabbit Diesel	5397	41	25.5	15	2040	155	35	90	3.78
VW Scirocco	6850	25	23.5	16	1990	156	36	97	3.78

AN EXAMPLE OF THREE VARIABLE SELECTION CONTEXTS 23

Given the reasonableness of this clustering (aside from the anomaly), it was decided to go to a third step in forward selection, where variables 8 and 1 appear in each subset. Figure 4 shows plots of the separation statistic for each of the seven subsets. The choice of which variable to enter next is not so clear-cut. However, the subsets {8,1,3}, {8,1,5}, and {8,1,9} appear to be very good prospects. For subset {8,1,3}, which enters variable 3 (rear seat room) at step three, there is an indication of three clusters since the configuration reaches a sharp maximum for K = 3. When this clustering was inspected, the cluster membership was almost identical to that found for the two-variable subset {8,1}, and the anomaly of the Opel and Chevette was still present. The set {8,1,3} was therefore rejected as a candidate. Of the two remaining subsets, {8,1,5} exhibited the most overall separation, and variable 5, weight, was tentatively selected. The configuration for {8,1,5} attains a maximum at K = 4, indicating four clusters. The clustering for this subset was checked by making scatter plots of the three variables, labeling the points by cluster number, and looking at the cluster memberships. The scatter plots are shown in Figure 5; each of the tentative clusters is separated in at least one of the panels. The cluster memberships are identical to those for the subset {8,1} except that a new cluster containing the Opel and

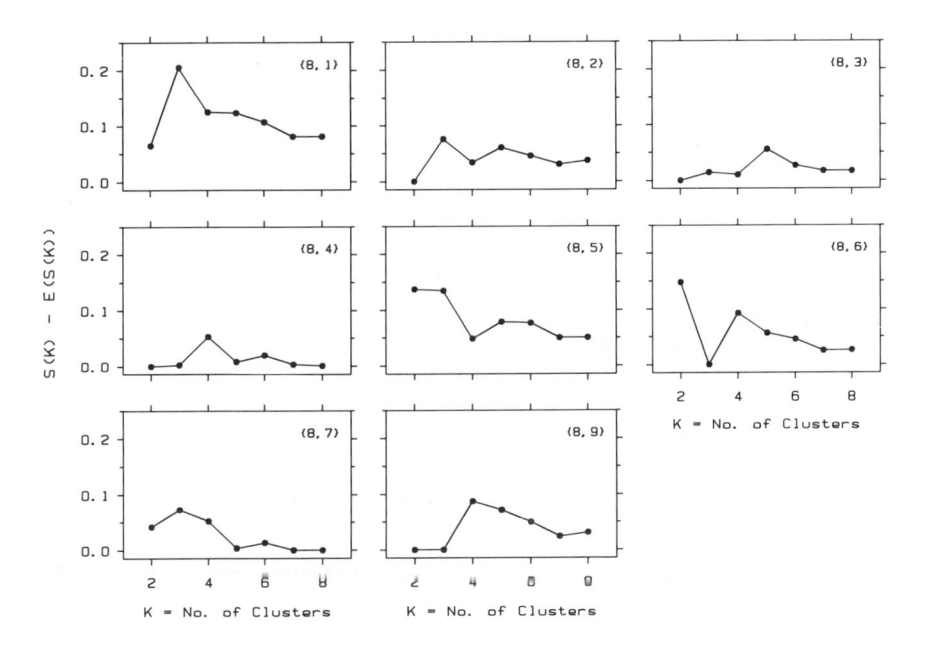

Figure 2. Cluster separation plots for subsets of two variables.

24 VARIABLE SELECTION IN CLUSTERING AND OTHER CONTEXTS

Chevette has formed. This new cluster stands out strikingly in the weight versus displacement scatter plot; this plot indicates that the Opel and Chevette have low weight and very high displacement. Since both of these cars are small, and displacement is a measure of engine size, this result seemed odd. (It has been found that the displacement values for these two autos were erroneously recorded! The displacement values should be 111 inches and 98 inches respectively for the Opel and Chevette rather than 304 inches and 231 inches, as given in Chambers et al.)

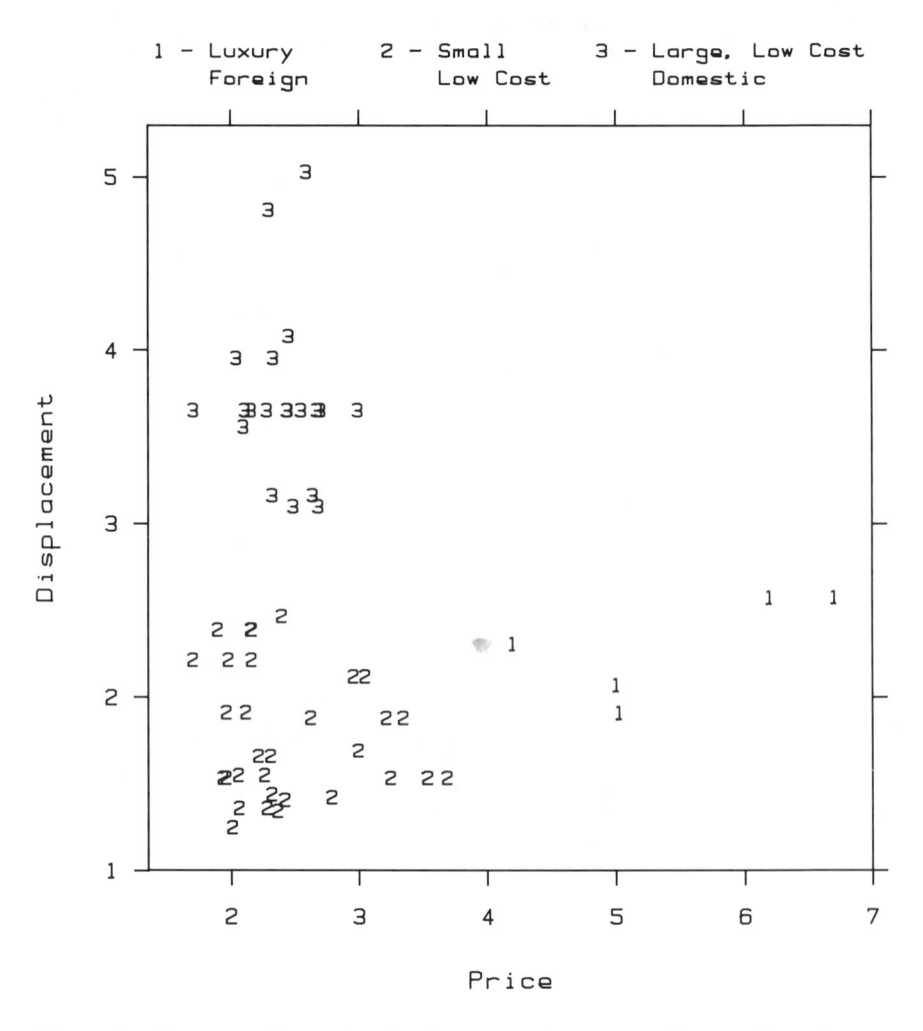

Figure 3. Scatter plot of displacement versus price with cluster identifications.

AN EXAMPLE OF THREE VARIABLE SELECTION CONTEXTS 25

The selection process was continued until five variables had been entered; 9 (gear ratio), and 2 (EPA mileage) were added to {8,1,5}. There was an indication of five clusters in the cluster separation plot for {8,1,5,9,2}. The cluster memberships were the same as those for {8,1,5} except that a new cluster containing highly fuel-efficient foreign cars, like the Volkswagen Rabbit Diesel, was carved away from the cluster containing the small, low cost, foreign and domestic autos. The final clustering is shown in Table 2.

A dendrogram resulting from the hierarchical clustering of the autos according to the five selected variables is given in the top panel of Figure 6. The nodes (corresponding to individual autos) of the dendrogram have been coded by cluster membership. It is interesting to consider what would have happened to the five clusters if all nine variables had been used in calculating the inter-auto distances. A clustering was carried out using these distances, and the result is shown by the dendrogram in the lower panel of Figure 6. The nodes are again coded according to the five clusters identified with the subset of five variables. The result of using all nine variables is striking; the five clusters, that were found to have a reasonable interpretation, have become muddled. This can be seen from common cluster numbers not appearing together in the tree.

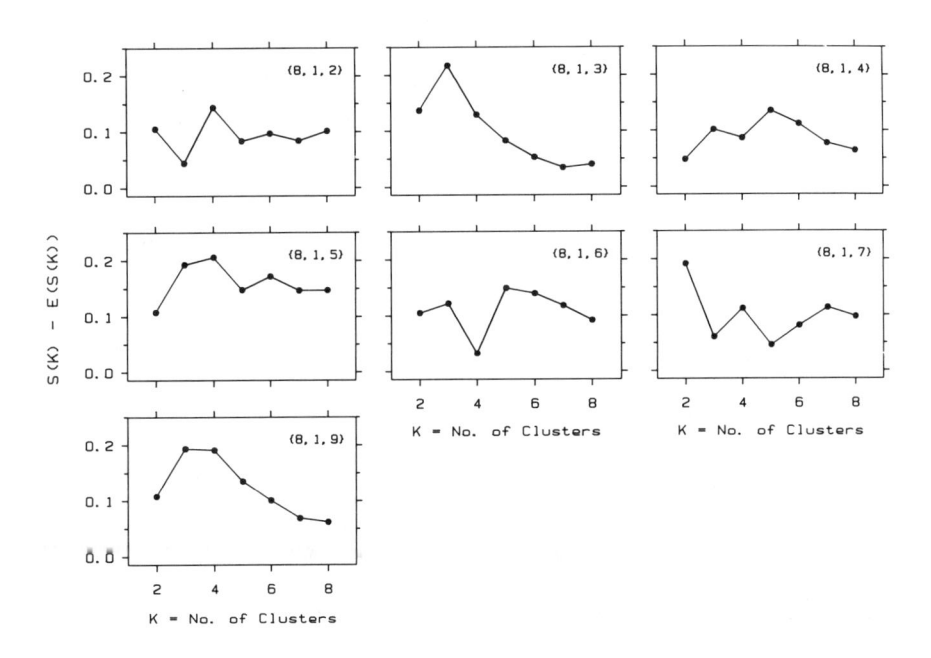

Figure 4. Cluster separation plots for subsets of three variables.

There are two major flaws with the nine variable clustering. The expensive, foreign car group (cluster 1) is split, and small, inexpensive foreign and domestic cars (cluster 2) start combining with large, inexpensive domestic cars (cluster 3) at low levels of the hierarchy. No cut of the second tree produced interpretable clusters.

The results will now be compared with those from regression and discriminant analysis. First, in regression it might be desired to predict EPA mileage from a subset of price, weight, displacement, etc. plus a dummy variable for the comparison of foreign versus domestic.

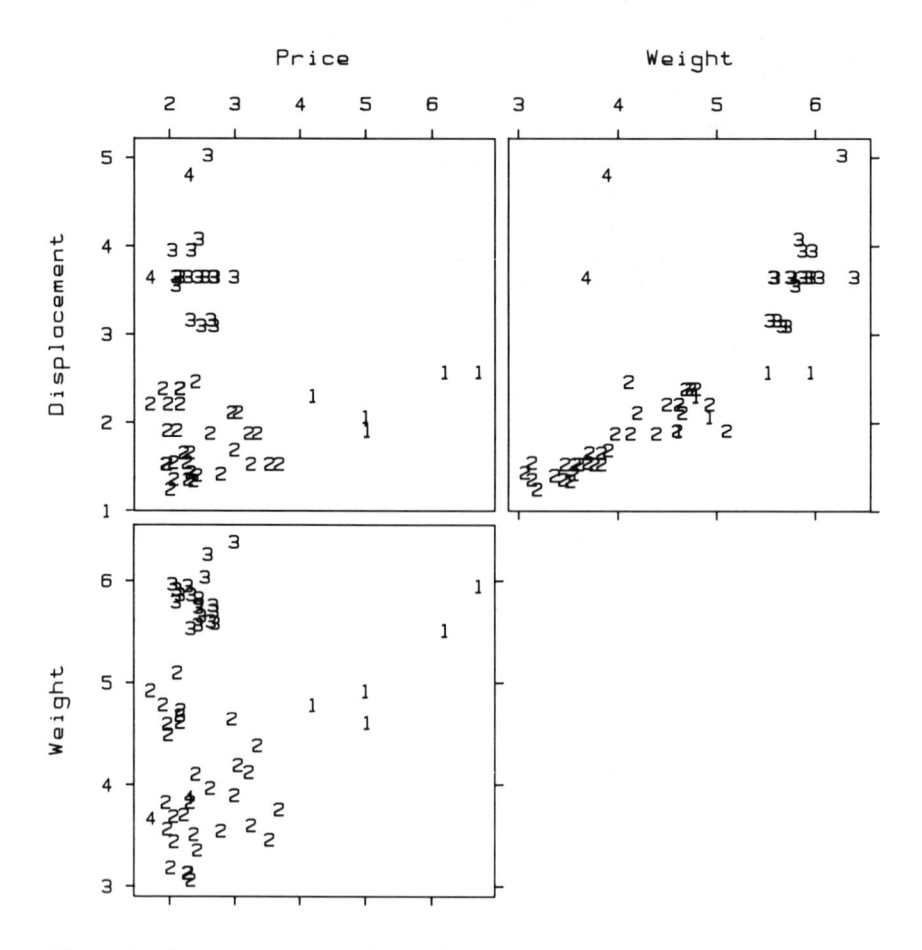

Figure 5. Pairwise scatter plots of price, weight, and displacement with cluster identifications.

AN EXAMPLE OF THREE VARIABLE SELECTION CONTEXTS 27

TABLE 2. Contents of clusters based on displacement, price, weight, gear ratio, mileage.

Cluster One

Honda Civic	Ford Fiesta	Plym. Champ
Renault Le Car	VW Rabbit	VW Scirocco
Audi Fox	Fiat Strada	VW Dasher
Toyota Corolla	Honda Accord	Datsun 510
Plym. Arrow	Datsun 200-SX	Toyota Celica
Plym. Sapporo	Toyota Corona	Plym. Horizon
Merc. Bobcat	AMC Spirit	Ford Mustang
Pont. Sunbird	Olds. Starfire	Chev. Monza
Merc. Zephyr	AMC Concord	

Cluster Two

BMW 320i Datsun 810 Audi 5000 Volvo 260 Peugeot 604 SL

Cluster Three

Chev. Malibu	Pont. Le Mans	Pont. Grand Prix
Chev. Monte Carlo	Buick Century	Buick Regal
Olds. Cutlass	Olds. Cutl. Supr.	Plym. Volare
AMC Pacer	Merc. Monarch	Olds. Omega
Buick Skylark	Pont. Phoenix	Chev. Nova
Pont. Firebird	Dodge Diplomat	Buick Le Sabre

Cluster Four

Mazda GLC Datsun 210 VW Rabbit Diesel Subaru Dodge Colt

Cluster Five

Buick Opel Chev. Chevette

28 VARIABLE SELECTION IN CLUSTERING AND OTHER CONTEXTS

(a) Displacement, Price, Weight, Gear Ratio, Mileage

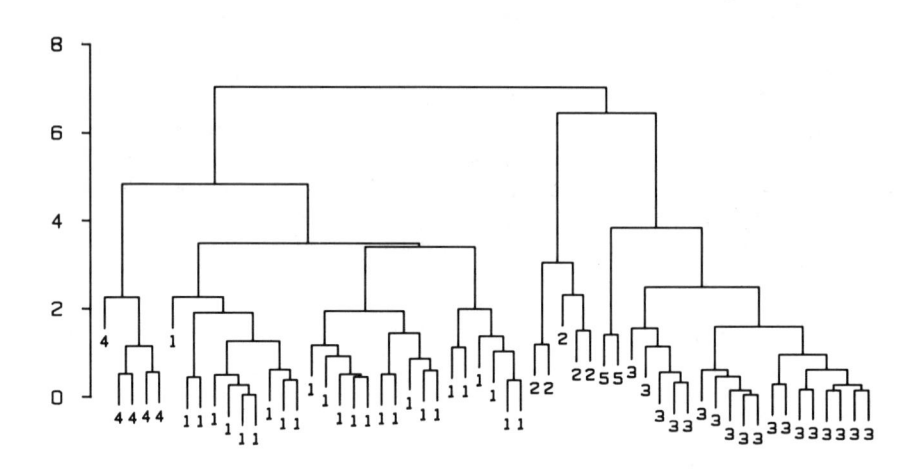

(b) All Variables

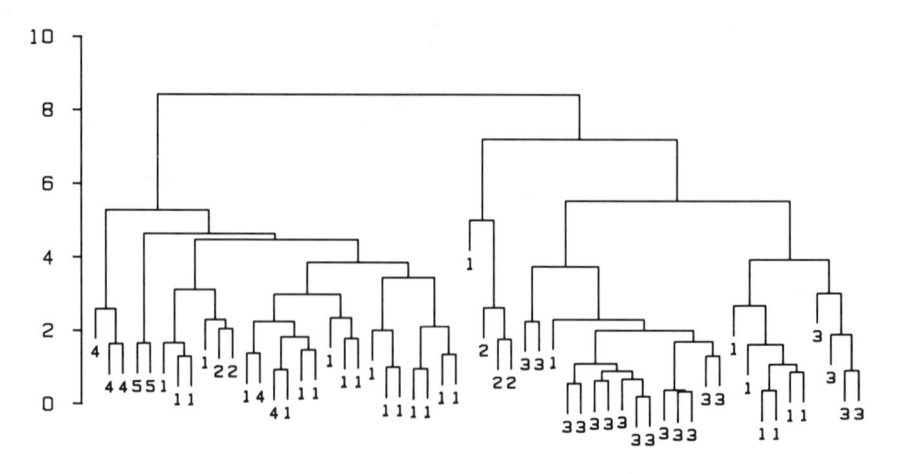

Figure 6. Hierarchical trees for clusterings based on five and nine variables.

AN EXAMPLE OF THREE VARIABLE SELECTION CONTEXTS

Figure 7 shows a C_p plot for all subset regressions (including an intercept) in this context, where the values of the C_p statistic for each subset of predictors are plotted versus the number of variables, p. Some of the subset models involving variables 4 (weight), 1 (price), and 9 (foreign vs. domestic) have been identified on the plot. For example, the label "4" indicates a model where only weight is present, while the label "14" denotes a model with both price and

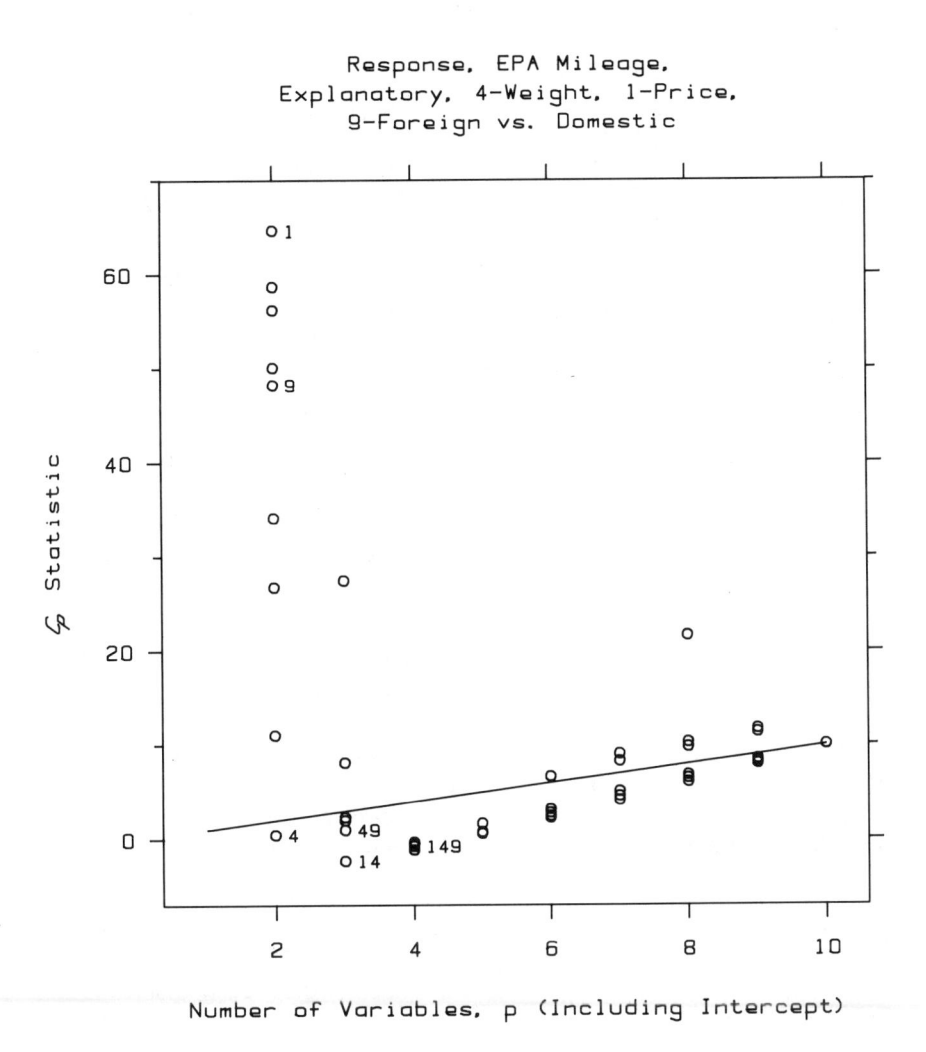

Figure 7. C_p plot for all subset regressions of EPA mileage on remaining eight variables plus indicator variable for foreign versus domestic.

weight. In addition, the straight line, $C_p = p$ is superimposed on the plot. Good models are indicated by points that fall near the straight line whose values of p are small. Such models fit well with few parameters. From this plot we see that weight (4) alone is a good model for the data. However the addition of price (1) produces a significant improvement in the fit, and the pair "14" is the best two-variable model. Model "14" would have also been selected in the second step of a forward selection algorithm in this context. Three autos, Audi 5000, Volvo 260, and Peugeot 604sl, were flagged as having high leverage (Belsley, Kuh, and Welsch, 1980, Chapter 2). Also three autos, Datsun 210, Rabbit Diesel, and Subaru, were identified as being outliers. It is interesting to note that the high leverage points comprise three of five autos in the luxury, foreign car cluster, and the outliers comprise three of five points in the high efficiency, foreign cluster, these clusters having been found in the hierarchical clustering of this data.

Finally, the problem was considered in the context of discriminant analysis, where all possible subset discriminant analyses were carried out to classify the autos as foreign or domestic, based on the nine variables. Since there are only two groups, this may be carried out via all possible subset regressions where the response is a dummy variable indicating whether an auto is foreign or domestic. The results are summarized by the C_p plot shown in Figure 8. The value of the C_p statistic is shown on a natural log scale, and the lines $C_p = p$ and $y = (P-p)(F_{.99, P-p, n-P} - 1) + p$ also superimposed. The first point to lie close to the $C_p = p$ line is for the subset of variables $\{1,5,8,9\}$, and the next is $\{1,2,5,8,9\}$. Variable 2 (EPA mileage) is not a strong discriminator between foreign and domestic autos in this data set. This is reflected in the small difference in C_p values for the two subsets. The subset $\{1,2,5,8,9\}$ is the same one that was selected in the hierarchical clustering. Although the smaller subset may be preferred for discriminating between foreign and domestic autos, the larger one leads to an interesting refinement found in the clustering context, where the foreign/domestic categorization was further split into subcategories which made intuitive sense.

The C_p concept can be extended as shown in Section 2 to accommodate the multiple group case. If the five clusters found in the hierarchical clustering context are considered as fixed groups, this extension can be used to identify subsets that best discriminate between these five groups. Figure 9 shows a plot of the statistic, Q_{P-p}, versus the degrees of freedom, $df = (P-p)(K-1)$. In addition, a solid line is plotted at $y = x$, where the statistic is equal to its degrees of freedom, and a dashed line is plotted at $y = \chi^2_{.99, df}$. On this plot,

AN EXAMPLE OF THREE VARIABLE SELECTION CONTEXTS   31

one is looking ideally for points in the vicinity of the benchmarks which correspond to a small number of variables and are well separated. The subset {1,2,5,8,9} found in the clustering context is identified in the plot and is the "best" subset of five variables. The subset {1,2,5,8} is at least as attractive because of the gap in the Q values and one fewer number of variables.

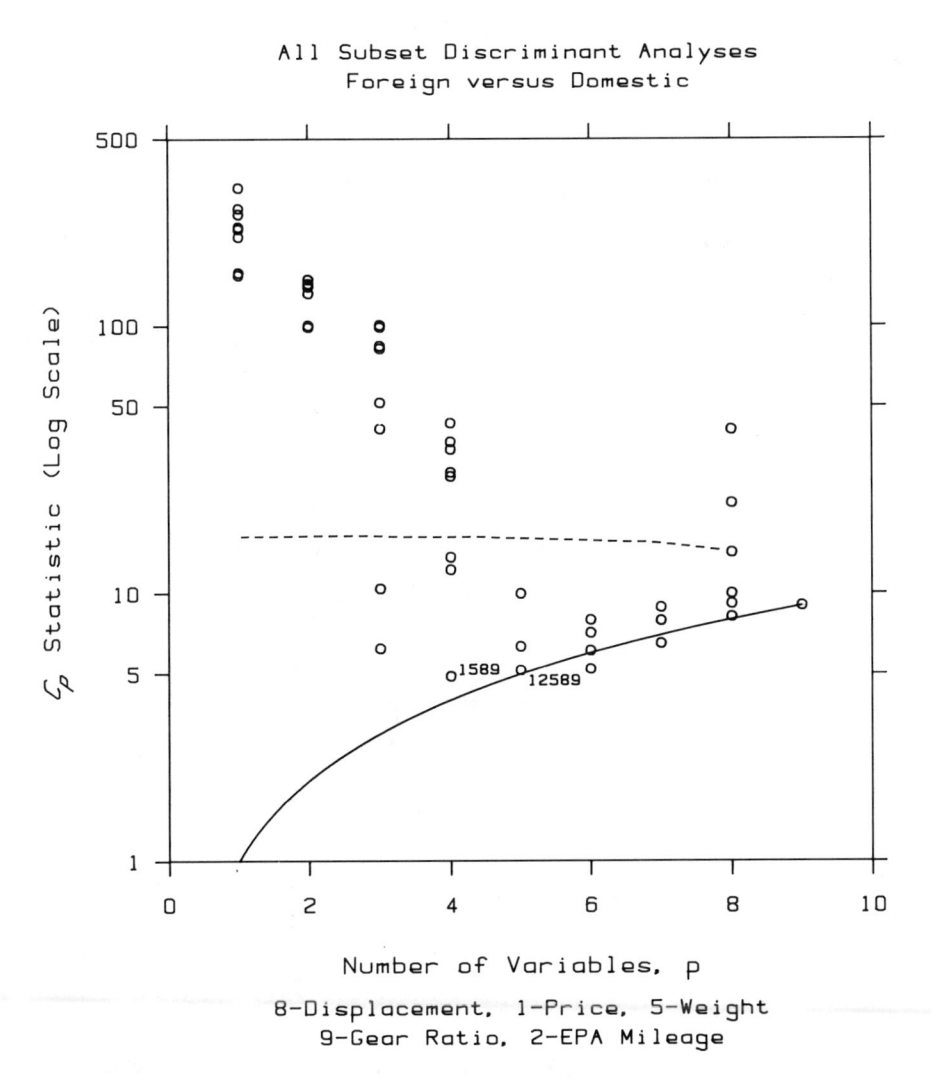

Figure 8. C_p plot for all subset discriminant analyses of foreign versus domestic autos.

32 VARIABLE SELECTION IN CLUSTERING AND OTHER CONTEXTS

The above analyses of the auto data in the three contexts have identified several common strands. For instance, while it need not have turned out that way, subset {1, 2, 5, 8, 9} figures prominently in discriminating between foreign and domestic autos are defining the most interesting cluster structure. Additionally, in the regression analysis, outliers and high leverage points corresponded approximately to certain clusters found in the hierarchical clustering.

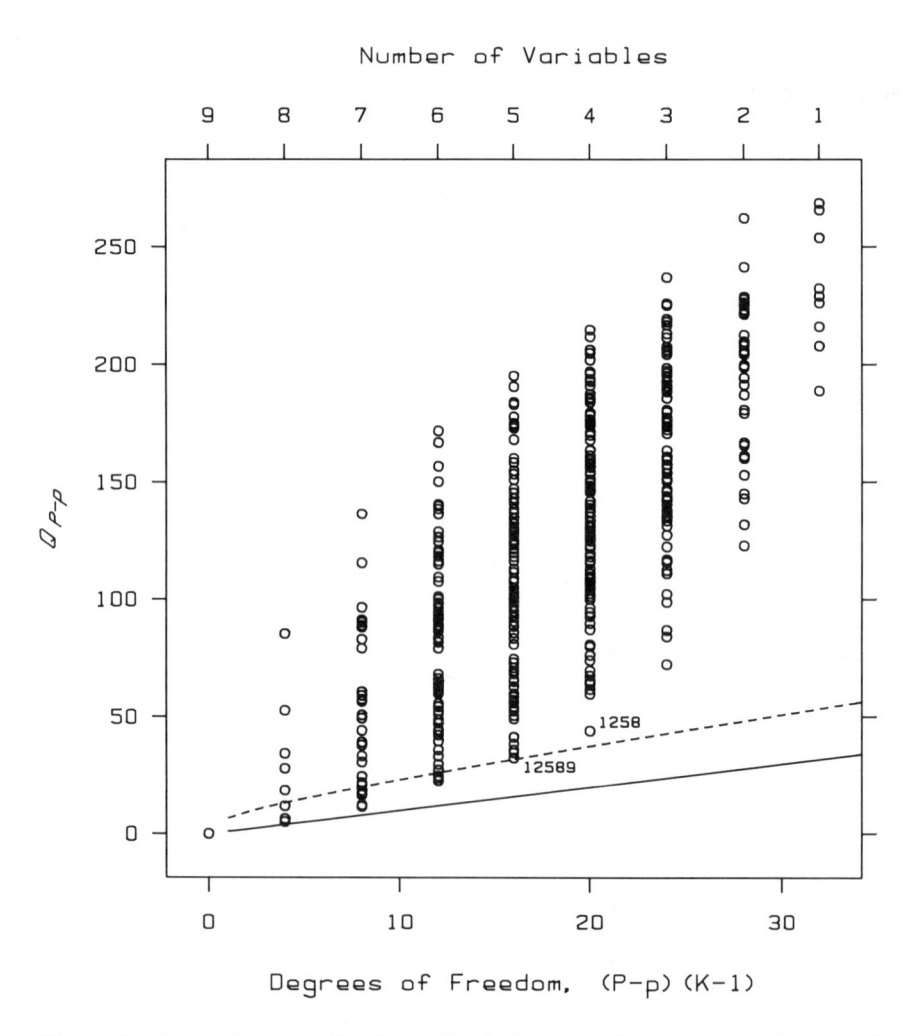

Figure 9. Q_{P-p} plot for all subset discriminant analyses of five clusters of autos.

4. CONCLUSION

Variable selection techniques provide a fundamentally important approach to the general problem of dimensionality reduction. Specific ones for multiple regression, discriminant analysis, and cluster analysis have been discussed and applied in this paper to a real set of data on automobiles. The data set is included so that others may experiment with it, too.

The strong theoretical underpinnings of regression and discriminant analysis make possible a variety of formal and informal approaches to variable selection for these problems. In the murky area of cluster analysis, where there is so little guiding theory, informal graphical approaches which can be used in a highly interactive manner are not only very useful but perhaps even essential for getting the job done. This is well illustrated in the automobile example.

REFERENCES

Belsley, D. A., Kuh, E., and Welsch, R. E. (1980). *Regression Diagnostics.* New York: Wiley.

Chambers, J. M., Cleveland, W. S., Kleiner, B., and Tukey, P. A. (1983). *Graphical Methods for Data Analysis.* Belmont, CA: Wadsworth.

Daniel, C. and Wood, F. S. (1980). *Fitting Equations to Data,* 2nd edition. New York: Wiley.

DeSarbo, W. S., Carroll, J. D., Clark, L. A., and Green, P. E. (1984). "Synthesized clustering: A method of amalgamating alternative clustering bases with differential weighting of variables," *Psychometrika,* 49, 57-78.

Draper, N. R. and Smith, H. (1981). *Applied Regression Analysis,* 2nd edition. New York: Wiley.

Fowlkes, E. B., Gnanadesikan, R., and Kettenring, J. R. (1985). "Some algorithms for the selection of variables in hierarchical cluster analysis." Bell Communications Research Technical Memorandum.

Gorman, J. W. and Toman, R. J. (1966). "Selection of variables for fitting equations to data," *Technometrics,* 8, 27-51.

Hand, D. J. (1981). *Discrimination and Classification.* New York: Wiley.

Hartigan, J. A. (1972). "Direct clustering of a data matrix," *Journal of American Statistical Association,* 67, 123-129.

Mallows, C. L. (1973). "Some comments on C_p," *Technometrics,* 15, 661-675.

McCabe, G. P. (1975). "Computations for variable selection in discriminant analysis," *Technometrics,* 17, 103-109.

McKay, R. J. (1977). "Simultaneous procedures for variable selection in multiple discriminant analysis," *Biometrika*, **64**, 183-190.

McKay, R. J. (1978). "A graphical aid to selection of variables in two-group discriminant analysis," *Applied Statistics*, **27**, 259-263.

McKay, R. J. and Campbell, N. A. (1982a). "Variable selection techniques in discriminant analysis. I. Description," *British Journal of Mathematical and Statistical Psychology*, **35**, 1-29.

McKay, R. J. and Campbell, N. A. (1982b). "Variable selection techniques in discriminant analysis. II. Allocation," *British Journal of Mathematical and Statistical Psychology*, **35**, 30-41.

Pillai, K. C. S. (1955). "Some new test criteria in multivariate analysis," *Annals of Mathematical Statistics*, **26**, 117-121.

Seber, G. A. F. (1984). *Multivariate Observations*. New York: Wiley.

Spjøtvoll, E. (1977). "Alternatives to plotting C_p in multiple regression," *Biometrika*, **64**, 1-8.

CHAPTER 3

Weighting Qualitative Data

Spencer M. Free
Newtown Square, Pennsylvania

Most people think of agricultural cash crops as coming from plants grown in the ground such as corn, potatoes and green vegetables. I would expect some to include livestock like chickens and pigs. Until I became active in this phase of the SmithKline Beckman Corporation, I did not think of young calves as a cash crop.

This example concerns two experiments designed to improve calf production. One of the major factors that determine the success and timing of a calving process is the health of the calf factory — the cow. If she is in really poor health she may not come into heat or become pregnant at the first mating, which is often artificial insemination. Or she may conceive but not carry the calf to full term. Farmers maintain an active interest in the health of their cows and calves. And, farmers continually cull cows that are problems in the reproductive process. Obviously, new cows are added to maintain the production capacity of the herd.

The success rate at first mating is not a lot more than 60% in a good operation. So farmers have accurate methods to detect pregnancy early. And, they expect to provide second and sometimes third matings. They do not like multiple matings because this increases costs and results in "late calving." This phenomenon causes all kinds of complications in the cash crop production.

One of the complications associated with the health status of a brood cow is a virus — in reality there are several viruses. A severe viral infection in a herd can markedly influence conception rates. A mild infection will have a measurable effect upon conception and late calving. When there is a problem, there is a solution. The solution is a vaccination for the virus.

The data in my example come from a "laboratory trial" designed to show the efficacy of a proposed vaccine for a specific virus that was known to affect cattle. This is a laboratory trial because the cows are exposed to a rather severe virus challenge. Maintaining and restraining the virus are complicated procedures, so sample sizes are a compromise between the power suggested by the statistician and the caution expressed by the animal husbandrymen.

Let's back up. When my data were collected, we had good reason to believe the vaccine would be effective. We wanted to know about potential benefits of one or two doses of the vaccine. Healthy cows tested to show no blood titer for our virus of interest were chosen and randomly assigned to three groups. One group was vaccinated twice at monthly intervals, one group received only the "second" vaccination. One group was the non-vaccinated control.

After an appropriate interval, the study cows were co-mingled with a small group of cows and bulls that were well infected with the virus. "Nature took its course within bounds." The study cows were periodically checked for pregnancy. Checking was to coincide with estrous cycles. The timing was needed to determine pregnancy after first, second or later mating. Some of the pertinent data look like this:

Estrous Pregnancy	Control Group	Vaccine One Dose	Vaccine Two Doses
First	6	14	14
Second	8	2	5
Not Pregnant	8	6	3
Total	22	22	22

Not much question about the efficacy of the vaccine in terms of better economics of first pregnancy. Of course, it is fun to ask how you might express this as a statistician. With programs like FUNCAT, it is easy. One can consider sets of weights for each pregnancy category. Here are some results using an academic choice (3,2,1) and a more economic choice (4,2,1) of weights (spacing).

| | Chi-Square | |
Comparison	Weights 3,2,1	Weights 4,2,1
Control vs. One Dose	3.24	4.55
Control vs. Two Doses	6.68	7.13
One vs. Two Doses	0.32	0.19

Note that the magnitude of the chi-square suggests the economic weights are more sensitive for the control versus vaccine discrimination than the academic weights.

I plead guilty to "showing" more than a set of orthogonal contrasts. My assignment was to get answers for my company and a regulatory agency.

The sample size was too small to provide any reasonable support for the hint that two doses is better than one. My experience in biological research indicates that it is relatively easy to support a measurable difference between something (vaccine) versus nothing (control). It is much harder to support a measurable difference between two actives (one versus two vaccinations).

Let me add that the results for the two vaccinated groups make it easy to consider a weak but unbiased comparison of results after the first estrous (2/8 versus 5/8) because both groups had 14 early successes. However, when the proportions of success after the first estrous are not equal, comparing only the subsequent counts is not appropriate. Success in the first estrous cycle is a selection process and not a random event. The ability to use all the data with the weights is one of the subtle benefits of the newer qualitative data analysis methodologies.

The hint of added benefits associated with two doses was followed up in a second laboratory challenge trial. The methodology was reasonably similar. The virus challenge was intentionally more severe. The sample size for the control group was deliberately smaller than the sample size for the vaccinated groups. Total sample size was again a compromise between the statistician and the animal husbandrymen. The control was only needed to measure the severity of the challenge and the sensitivity of the methodology. More estrous cycles were followed when it became obvious early in the data collection phase that the severe virus challenge was markedly influencing the pregnancy rate in all groups. Here are the data.

38 WEIGHTING QUALITATIVE DATA

Estrous Pregnancy	Control Group	Vaccine One Dose	Two Doses
First	1	6	9
Second	0	3	6
Third	2	6	6
Fourth	0	9	2
Not Pregnant	15	7	8
Total	18	31	31

For practical conclusions, the challenge was too severe. And yet, this provided a very stressful condition to compare one and two doses of the vaccine. Given the multiple options for weights, I will show you only two.

| One Dose versus Two Doses ||
Weight	Chi-Square
5,4,3,2,1	2.93
7,5,3,2,1	1.95

Since this is to be an example with real data, I leave to the reader the other options for data analyses. There is even the extension to consider combining the data from the first and second laboratory trial to see if you can develop a statistical comparison that will clearly support the difference between one and two vaccinations.

The industrial conclusion was that one dose was clearly effective and economically sound. Two doses are probably a little better in a practical situation. If a farmer was concerned about a severe virus challenge (and this is a real possibility) the added inconvenience and cost of two vaccinations would be worth it in terms of a cash crop with less late calving.

I want to add two notes that are unique to this opportunity to honor Cuthbert Daniel.

1. Among my many memories of Cuthbert's contributions is my appreciation for his normal plots for factorial designs. This reference provides all the data for such a plot of a fractional

factorial design. The authors have found the optimum pharmaceutical formulation for a two compound product. Yen, John K. C. and Free, S. M., Jr. (1967). "Using the fractional factorial experiment to evaluate related liquid formulations," *Canadian Journal of Pharmaceutical Science*, **2**, 19-21.

2. In his usual vocal and constructive style, Cuthbert contributed to the discussion of one of my presentations at the Gordon Conference on Statistics. Later that paper became a classic and the statistics internationally recognized as the Free-Wilson model. There is now a whole discipline including a Gordon Conference on *Quantitative Structure-Activity Relationships*. There is enough data in this paper to try some new analyses. Free, S. M., Jr. and Wilson, J. W. (1964). "A mathematical contribution to structure-activity studies," *Journal of Medicinal Chemistry*, **7**, 395-399.

CHAPTER 4

Explaining Experimental Design Fundamentals to Engineers: A Modern Approach

Gerald J. Hahn
General Electric Company

John L. Bemesderfer
Lebanon, Pennsylvania

Donald M. Olsson
General Electric Company

ABSTRACT

You have seven short sessions to tell engineers about planning experiments statistically. The major aim is to provide an understanding of the need for well-designed experiments, of the hazards of analyzing unplanned data, and of basic concepts of experimental design. The course should give participants the background to plan simple experiments, and an appreciation of when to get further help. Moreover, the material must be responsive to the national drive for quality improvement. What should such an abbreviated course contain?

We were faced with that question recently. The material we developed emphasizes major issues; provides many examples from our combined experiences; and stresses the graphical analysis of data. It de-emphasizes mathematical detail and formal statistical techniques. This chapter describes the course, which reflects the influence of Cuthbert Daniel.

1. INTRODUCTION AND SETTING

Quality improvement is now a major goal of Western industry. Japan's accomplishments have been an important driving force. One of the people who helped Japan achieve high quality is the eminent American statistician, W. Edwards Deming, and statistics is ONE important element of the new quality philosophy (see Hahn and Boardman, 1985). There is much emphasis on planning experimental investigations to assure that the information needed to produce high-quality products is obtained as validly and effectively as possible. This topic, often referred to as "the design of experiments," has aroused further interest recently through the publicity accorded to the work of Genichi Taguchi. Another important part of the new quality commitment is that of providing training in modern methods for quality improvement throughout the organization.

This chapter is concerned with both experimental design and training. It describes an introductory short course on experimental design for engineers, scientists, and managers. It is based upon material for one of a series of nine video-based courses, offered as part of the General Electric Company Quality Leadership Curriculum developed by GE Corporate Engineering and Manufacturing at the request of GE management. The course is now generally available.

There are many important tools for quality improvement with which engineers need to be familiar. Seven brief sessions, with exercises and discussion, are allotted to the course on experimental design. We, like everybody else, would wish more time. However, if we succeed, we will have planted some important seeds, and would expect that some participants will come back for a "second dose." The major purposes are to provide a basic appreciation of the need for and the power of well-planned experiments; to remove misconceptions about what can be achieved in analyzing historical data; and to give an understanding of the fundamental concepts of experimental design. The course should also help participants to plan simple experiments on their own, and to know when to call in an expert in more complicated situations.

There is a wide diversity in the backgrounds of the course participants. Some have had a course or two in statistics in the distant past, often leaving an unpleasant memory about such "obscure" topics as *t*-tests, chi-square tables, and analyses of variance, the details of which have long been forgotten. Others have more recently been exposed to some elementary concepts and to an introduction to statistical process control. Still others have had essentially no past training in statistics. Thus, we assume no previous statistical background. Fortunately, most engineers have an analytical bent, and a good appreciation of practical considerations. This results in greater homogeneity than one would expect from the diversity in backgrounds.

This environment is a great deal different from what one encounters in most academic situations, where, for example, the completion of two or more courses in statistics is generally a prerequisite to a course in experimental design. (The lack of discussion of how to obtain valid experimental data is, in our opinion, a major deficiency of most introductory statistics courses.) In any case, we do not have the luxury of providing much statistical background in the available time, even if we thought it desirable, and, therefore, rely almost exclusively on graphical methods. In so doing, we had to discard some of our past ideas, ingrained by more academically oriented courses.

The course is concerned with planning experiments to obtain valid data throughout the product life cycle. Long before manufacturing starts, designers must be responsive to the quality problems that they will face in making the product and that the customer will encounter in using it. They must, therefore, create designs and processes that will minimize problems and will make the product robust for use in various environments. This often calls for obtaining information on the impact of numerous material and process variables, using multi-variable plans as part of what many now refer to as "off-line quality control." As the process evolves, the need for proper planning continues and new challenges are encountered in obtaining valid data. In fact, as the process matures, the practical constraints of running a well-planned experiment tend to increase. Fortunately, the measurable payoff also increases.

The course described here consists of material proposed for seven videotaped sessions, each of approximately 15 minutes duration. (As we indicate later, the final course consists of only five sessions. Moreover, we have made some further modifications in writing this chapter.) Supporting text material and references were also prepared. The course is offered on-site under the leadership of a local moderator. This person promotes and leads discussion and assures that each of the topics is related directly to on-site applications. This includes challenging participants to show how the topics presented apply to their own problems.

We benefited from the work of many others in developing this material. Important groundwork was laid by the pioneering videotaped course developed by J. S. Hunter, some years ago, under the auspices of the Westinghouse Learning Center. Our course differs from Hunter's in that it is much briefer. As a result, we spend a lot less time on the analysis of the experimental data. Also, we emphasize "on-line," as well as laboratory-scale, experimentation. In many ways, our viewpoint has also been influenced by the efforts of Cuthbert Daniel, Jack Youden, and many others.

2. BASIC PHILOSOPHY

The following philosophy guided our preparation of the course.

- Stress the need for statistical planning

    We feel that the single most important objective in planning investigations statistically is to obtain information that responds to the real problem as meaningfully as possible. Also, it is imperative to correct the mistaken belief (sometimes resulting from introductory courses in statistics) that all one needs to do to evaluate the effect of process variables is to analyze historical data statistically, such as by stepwise multiple regression analysis. Thus, we stress both the importance of careful planning to get the right data, and the limitations of the analysis of historical data. We point out early and often that the information conveyed by a well-designed and executed experiment is often obvious, or can be readily appreciated, from simple plots. On the other hand, the world's most sophisticated statistical analysis is unlikely to rescue a poorly planned program. Statistical planning, on the other hand, not only helps assure proper data, but allows one to obtain such information as efficiently as possible.

- Emphasize basic concepts

    We emphasize that the selection of the matrix of experimental points represents only the proverbial tip of the iceberg. Therefore, we stress such matters as the need for clearly defining the goal of the test program, for enumerating all possible variables, and for deciding how to handle each one. We also consider, at some length, such basic concepts as randomization (and the associated practical constraints), blocking, replication, and the need for measuring experimental error.

- Avoid abstract ideas that might distract from the major goals

    As we have already suggested, a major aim is to maintain what some refer to as the principle of KISS: Keep it Simple and

Saleable! We wanted to avoid discouraging practitioners by refraining from a traditional and laborious exposition such as: "The effect due to treatments is evaluated in the following manner. Take each treatment total, square it, divide by the number of observations comprising each total, and then subtract the correction factor, obtained by finding the grand total, squaring it, and dividing by the total number of observations. Then take the resulting (treatment) sum of squares (weren't we comparing averages?), divide by this thing called the degrees of freedom (the discussion of which is beyond the scope of this course) to obtain a treatment mean-square, divide by the error (mistake?) mean-square and form an F-ratio. Now look up the critical F value to judge whether or not the treatments produce a statistically significant effect."

- Use graphical techniques for the analysis of experimental results

We agree with Cuthbert (and Yogi Berra) that "you can see a lot by just looking." Well-chosen plots of treatment averages that also exhibit possible interactions are much more appealing to most practitioners than formal analysis of variance techniques. They are easier to interpret, and generally are sufficient to draw the conclusions that are required to make decisions. Such plots also lend themselves nicely to analysis-of-means procedures for assistance in judging significance (see Schilling, 1973).

- Motivate the discussion by examples

Most sessions start with a specific example, around which the subsequent discussion is built. This seemed to be a better approach than the more common one of first presenting a concept and then illustrating it. The examples were drawn from our combined experience, totaling close to 100 years in planning industrial experiments, involving products that range from integrated circuits to major appliances and jet engines. (See Bemesderfer, 1979; Hahn, 1984 and Mueller and Olsson, 1971.) The studies are real, but the numbers and details were changed to protect the "innocent."

- Provide ample references

For those who wish to go further, we provide references, including the popular text by Box, Hunter, and Hunter (1978) and, at a slightly more advanced level, the book by Cuthbert Daniel (1976).

3. WHAT WE SELECTED AND WHY

The selected topics were:

Session 1: Basic concepts and simple comparative experiments

Session 2: Blocking designs and full factorial plans

Session 3: Fractional factorial plans

Session 4: Quantifying relationships using multiple regression

Session 5: Response surface experimentation and EVOP

Session 6: Estimating sources of variability and nested plans

Session 7: Taguchi concepts and course wrap-up

Session 1: Basic Concepts and Simple Comparative Experiments

In the first session we aim to lay the foundations for a well-planned experiment. Basic concepts are introduced by considering a simple experiment to evaluate the effect that a change of materials might have on a production process. The original proposal called for making a one-time process change, going from the old material to the new, and comparing the performance after the change with that before. The weaknessess of this plan are emphasized. Then, we show how a planned experiment, involving half-day paired comparisons of the new and old materials (a reasonable procedure in this case) conducted over a 24-day period, is much more likely to provide valid results (Hahn, 1982). The data are analyzed graphically and by a simple tabulation. This shows little difference between the yields for the two materials. It also suggests that if the comparison had been based upon running each material for one week, as originally proposed, whichever material would have been run during the first week would have come out worse.

This example provides the opportunity to:

- Describe the concept of random variation
- Indicate the pitfalls of making comparisons based upon what, in a sense, are samples of size one (i.e., subsequent to the change versus prior to the change) and show how a simple statistically planned experiment can provide a valid comparison.

- Outline the initial, and mainly non-statistical, steps in planning an experiment (define purpose, establish scope, identify variables, decide how to handle each type of variable, define constraints, document test protocol, etc.). The discipline required for these initial tasks is among the most important contributions of planning an experiment statistically.
- Stress the importance of making the experiment as broad as possible to assure that the conclusions are robust against possible subsequent attack on their relevance.
- Introduce, at an elementary level, basic concepts of experimental design, such as blocking, balance, randomization, and replication.
- Provide a simple example of analyzing experimental results graphically.

We elaborate on these concepts throughout the course and discuss some of them in more detail in the final session.

It turned out that the new material in our example resulted in a slightly higher yield, as compared to the old material. This invites questions about the precision and statistical significance of the results. It provides the opportunity to introduce the concept of a confidence interval to quantify statistical uncertainty. Such an interval is shown for the mean difference in percent yield between the two materials. We refer the participants to introductory statistics courses and computer packages for calculational details, but try to describe the practical meaning of this concept. Thus, we point out that:

- The difference in percent yield between the two materials was not "statistically significant," since the confidence interval on this difference overlapped the value zero (in most practical problems, a confidence interval is, in our opinion, much more useful to practitioners than a significance test).
- The lower bound of the confidence interval on the difference in percent yield suggests the potential worst case deterioration in quality associated with a switch to the new material.

Also we describe:

- The effect of sample size on precision (e.g., we need run approximately four times as many samples to reduce the length of the confidence interval in half).
- The opportunities of sequential experimentation.

Session 2: Blocking Designs and Full Factorial Plans

We expand the example of the previous session to consider blocking designs in general. Extraneous variables are discussed in some detail. Some of the major points are:

- The need to identify various types of extraneous variables, e.g., operators, material batches, day-to-day variation, and their relationship to the primary experimental variables.

- The desirability of including extraneous variables in the experiment to broaden the inferences that one can draw from the results, and to make the conclusions as robust as possible against subsequent attacks on their relevance. As Deming (1975) has emphasized, the vast majority of studies are "Analytical" or predictive; that is, one wishes to use the results of the experiment to draw conclusions about the future and/or about circumstances beyond those considered directly in the experiment. In contrast, classical statistical procedures apply strictly only to "enumerative" or descriptive studies; that is, studies in which one wishes to draw inferences under the specific set of circumstances under which the experiment has been performed.

- How blocking helps assure that the extraneous variables will not bias the evaluation of the effect on the response of the prime variables.

- How blocking, in contrast to randomization, permits one to remove the effect of extraneous variables from experimental error. We use the analogy of increasing the chance of detecting an electrical signal by reducing the background noise.

- The role of randomization in designs that involve blocking.

- The use of simple plots of the data to evaluate the effect of each of the primary variables, as well as, in many cases, those of the blocking variable(s).

Randomized complete block and incomplete block designs are given as examples of plans to control a single extraneous variable. Latin Square designs are used to show how to handle two extraneous variables. The three designs are illustrated by a problem involving the comparison of materials from different suppliers: see Tables 1, 2 and 3. Baking oven is the extraneous variable to be controlled by blocking. In the randomized block design, material from each of four suppliers is compared in four ovens, using a random assignment of oven positions. In contrast, oven position is used as the second extraneous variable in the Latin Square design. In the incomplete block design, we assume that there are seven materials that are to be compared, but that each oven has only three positions. References to tabulations of other incomplete block designs are provided.

TABLE 1. Randomized complete block plan for comparison of four material types.

	Oven Number		
1	2	3	4
A	C	B	C
C	B	A	B
D	A	D	A
B	D	C	D

Material Types: A, B, C, D

TABLE 2. Incomplete block plan for comparison of seven material types.

Oven Number	1	2	3	4	5	6	7
Materials	B	G	A	C	C	A	D
	F	F	E	D	G	B	G
	E	A	C	F	B	D	E

Materials Types: A, B, C, D, E, F, G.

TABLE 3. Latin Square plan for comparison of four material types.

Oven Position	Oven Number			
	1	2	3	4
1	D	D	A	C
2	A	C	B	D
3	B	D	C	A
4	C	A	D	B

Material Types: A, B, C, D.

We next turn to situations where one needs to evaluate the simultaneous effect of two or more process variables using full factorial plans. We illustrate such plans with a 2×2×3 design to assess the impact on "tanning measurement" of various process variables in painting a refrigerator door: see Table 4. This example lets us emphasize:

- The limitations of traditional one-variable-at-a-time experimentation.
- The concept of interactions between variables and the fact that many statistical plans allow one to evaluate these.
- The gain in efficiency realized by varying factors simultaneously.
- The use of randomization to neutralize the effect of variables that were not included in the experiment.
- The advantages of including a few repeats in the experiment (three factorial points were replicated in the example).

The results are again evaluated graphically, including a three-variable plot that clearly demonstrates:

- Possible outliers
- An interaction between two of the variables.

TABLE 4. 2×2×3 full factorial plan for paint bake study.

Run Number	Randomized Sequence	Oven Type	Oven Temperature	Paint Thickness
1	8	Gas	380°	8
2	3	Gas	380°	10
3	4	Gas	380°	12
4	2	Gas	405°	8
5	5	Gas	405°	10
6	1	Gas	405°	12
7	12	Electric	380°	8
8	6	Electric	380°	10
9	9	Electric	380°	12
10	7	Electric	405°	8
11	10	Electric	405°	10
12	11	Electric	405°	12

- The bottom-line conclusions (e.g., use an electric oven, instead of a gas oven, to reduce pollution; reduce the amount of paint to cut costs; vary oven temperature to achieve the desired tanning values).

Finally, a region for further verification tests is proposed.

Session 3: Fractional Factorial Plans

We have found more applications for fractional factorials than any other type of experimental plan. Two-level fractional factorials have been especially useful. Thus, we devote an entire session to this topic.

The discussion starts with the obvious: the need for reducing the number of test runs when all combinations of variables and levels leads to an unduly large number of runs, and how fractional factorials meet this need. We quickly turn to a specific example — a half fraction of a 2^4 factorial plan to help determine the impact of four process variables on the percent yield of useful product in making an engineering plastic material, using a scaled-down laboratory reactor: see Table 5. In addition to percent yield, there is also a second criterion: the need to maintain flammability below a specified upper bound.

TABLE 5. Fractional factorial plan for engineering plastics improvement program.

Test ID #	Test Sequence	Temperature (°F)	Pressure (PSI)	Catalyst (%)	Water (%)
FF1	7	120	15	6	0
FF2	9	120	15	10	4
FF3	3	120	25	6	4
FF4	4	120	25	10	0
FF5	2	150	15	6	4
FF6	8	150	15	10	0
FF7	10	150	25	6	0
FF8	5	150	25	10	4
Center	1	135	20	8	2
Center	11	135	20	8	2
Baseline	6	120	25	6	0

The rationale underlying fractional factorial plans is briefly described, and details are given to construct two-level designs for three to six variables. Plans involving variables at three or more levels and mixed fractional factorials are mentioned briefly. We refer participants to Box, Hunter and Hunter (1978) and Daniel (1976) for further details.

Concepts and practical considerations that are emphasized include:

- The situations that lend themselves most readily to fractional factorial plans and the price that we pay (frequently loss of information about some or all interactions).
- The importance of probing discussions with the experimenter to decide upon the variables and conditions, and to assure that we fully capitalize on all available physical understanding and insight. Thus, we build upon existing knowledge, rather than replace it.
- The need to make sure, at the outset, that the experimental setup (in our example, the small-scale reactor on which the experiment is to be performed) provides results that can be meaningfully scaled up to the manufacturing process.
- The importance of including a few repeat runs in the test plan.
- The desirability of using current plant operating conditions as one of the test conditions for the fractional factorial plan (this is achieved in the example by selecting the "right" fractional factorial).
- The advantage of including a point in the center of the test region to provide an overall (but not infallible) assessment of non-linearity in dealing with quantitative independent variables.
- The potential for building fractional factorial plans in stages (with proper care to handle possible differences between stages).
- The proper use of randomization at various levels, e.g., material selection, testing sequence, measurement sequence, etc.

We show how a fractional factorial plan can be an effective mechanism for scanning the response surface to identify those regions that seem most promising for further study. This is especially pertinent because of the confounding of interactions and the existence of more than one response variable. In fact, we have found this general scanning of the response surface, without necessarily fitting a model, to be one of the major advantages of the fractional factorial plans — and one often not sufficiently emphasized by texts.

We encourage setting up simple master sheets and considering other "nitty-gritty" details that can avoid confusion during the experiment. Plots are again suggested as the primary vehicle for analyzing and interpreting the experimental results. (Since in our example, two-factor interactions are confounded in pairs, we consider only those interactions that appear most credible from *a priori* physical considerations.)

It turned out that, in the actual experiment, no reaction could be obtained at two of the conditions — a situation that does occur in practice, even if not frequently found in textbook examples. Nevertheless, the graphical analysis provided useful results.

Session 4: Quantifying Relationships Using Multiple Regression

This is the only session that deals principally with data analysis. We devote it to multiple regression because of the wide use and misuse of this technique, the general lack of understanding of its limitations, and the fact that it provides a good lead-in to the discussion of response surface designs in the next session. Also, it allows us to make the point that when the data are unplanned (and, therefore, often non-orthogonal), simple graphical techniques often do not provide adequate insights. This is in sharp contrast to the case when one is dealing with the results of a well-designed experiment; in this situation, simple plots are frequently sufficient to obtain a good understanding of the results.

The session is built around an example dealing with data on sample material cut from 21 turbine wheels, built by a manufacturer over a period of years: see Table 6. Measurements of the transition temperature at which the material changes from ductile to 50% brittle are available on each sample. Also measured are:

- The composition of various raw materials, e.g., % carbon
- Various processing conditions, e.g., temperature
- Other background information, e.g., material supplier.

It is desired to use the past data to predict transition temperature. The stated long-term goal is to obtain relationships that will be helpful in learning how to build wheels with reduced transition temperature. To keep things simple, we limit most of the presentation to two predictor variables: % carbon and processing temperature.

The initial evaluations consist of simple plots of transition temperature versus % carbon and versus processing temperature. These plots show that transition temperature seems to increase with both % carbon and processing temperature. Also, both plots suggest one radical outlying observation and one moderate outlier. A further plot shows that the two predictor variables, % carbon and process temperature, are themselves negatively correlated.

We then introduce multiple regression analysis as a technique to use both predictor variables simultaneously to quantify the relationship. We show how this requires one to:

- Postulate a model.

We describe simple-linear, multiple-linear, and multiple-quadratic (including interaction terms) models, and the meaning

TABLE 6. Turbine wheel data for multiple regression analysis (after transformation).

Wheel Number	Percent Carbon	Process Temperature	Transition Temperature
1	47	1273	206
2	39	1251	213
3	33	1260	201
4	51	1284	212
5	34	1265	198
6	42	1284	209
7	38	1260	205
8	43	1285	207
9	45	1280	210
10	48	1277	216
11	44	1274	211
12	35	1267	203
13	52	1211	200
14	35	1260	199
15	54	1291	217
16	45	1278	221
17	40	1251	215
18	44	1264	208
19	43	1264	211
20	46	1264	211
21	49	1266	213

of the residual unexplained variation. We also comment briefly on the importance of using theoretical and/or physical knowledge of the system in selecting a reasonable model.

- Fit the model to the data

We describe, very briefly, the concept and mathematics of least squares and indicate that there are numerous "canned" statistical programs that do the calculations. One of these is used to fit various models for the example problem.

- Evaluate "usefulness" of alternative models

The residual standard deviation is described and compared to the initial standard deviation of the dependent variable, and the similarities are noted. We indicate briefly that the residual standard deviation is used by computer programs to calculate confidence intervals around the true coefficients of the model and the predicted values, but resist the temptation to say more. We also briefly describe the coefficient of determination as a frequently used, and often over-interpreted, measure in the interval (0,1) of "variation accounted for" by the regression (see Hahn, 1973). We provide further references to these topics, including Neter, Wasserman and Kutner (1983), Daniel and Wood (1980), and Draper and Smith (1981).

- Consider alternative models

We compare the results for the various fitted models for our example by displaying the fitted equations and comparing the residual standard deviations. The multiple linear model is selected over the two simple-linear models because its residual standard deviation is appreciably smaller (reduction of 20% and 30%, respectively). However, we reject the more complex multiple-quadratic model since its residual standard deviation is very close to that of the multiple-linear model. Emphasis is again placed on parsimony, i.e., trying to find the simplest model that adequately describes the data.

- Evaluate the chosen model

We now look more closely at the resulting fitted model. We note that transition temperature again appears to increase with increase in % carbon. However, in contrast to what was suggested by the plot of transition temperature against processing temperature, we now note that an increase in processing temperature seems to be associated with a decrease in transition temperature. We illustrate this further by partial residual plots — an approach that we have found quite useful in graphically portraying complex relationships. We describe partial residual plots as plots of the performance variable against one predictor variable, with each of the other predictor variables held constant statistically (see Larsen and McCleary, 1972). It is pointed out that partial residual plots can be readily obtained by some computer programs.

The basic point is that the simple plots and analyses were misleading. This is because of the correlation between the two predictor variables in the data. Thus, processing temperature serves as a proxy (or surrogate) for % carbon in the simple plot of transition temperature versus processing temperature; this led to the incorrect suggestion, from the simple plot, that an increase in processing temperature resulted in an increase in transition temperature.

- Assess the unexplained variability

    We examine the residuals around the fitted model and provide residual plots against (1) variables included in the regression, (2) variables that were excluded (both quantitative and qualitative), and (3) test sequence. These plots do not provide any important new results per se, but do show that the one observation that had previously been characterized as a radical outlier no longer appears as such. (Thus, if we had acted on the simple plots alone, we would have been misled into excluding what was incorrectly thought to be an outlying observation from the subsequent analyses.) On the other hand, the observation previously thought to be only a moderate outlier now appears as a prominent outlier.

We briefly indicate how the results can be generalized to situations involving more than two predictor variables. We conclude, however, on a cautionary note. We point out that our final analysis might be misleading, just like the initial simple evaluations, because the variables that were included in this analysis may be serving as proxies for some unmeasured, and possibly unknown, variables. Thus, regression analyses of historical data cannot provide cause and effect conclusions; it is unlikely that the earlier stated goal of these evaluations can be met by simply analyzing the data that happen to be on record. We point out that we can avoid these problems by a well-planned experimental investigation, thus reiterating our basic theme that proper design is more important than sophisticated data analysis. On this note, we return to the topic of the planning of experimental programs.

Session 5: Response Surface Experimentation and EVOP

The first part of this session is concerned with experiments to characterize response surfaces and optimization in reasonably conventional laboratory, or possibly, pilot plant environments. The second part deals with investigations to improve an ongoing manufacturing process.

We begin with an example dealing with machine tool optimization. We wish to assess the impact of (1) the speed of lathe rotation, (2) the insert feed-rate along the material surface, and (3) the depth-of-cut on the response variable: the life of a tool-insert. This example illustrates the following steps in planning a response surface experiment:

- Select an approximating statistical model

  A quadratic model is selected for the example, using log-life as the dependent variable.

- Select an experimental plan to fit the model

  A 3×3×3 full factorial plan is considered initially. However, a central composite plan is chosen, because of the smaller number of test points required (15 versus 27 prior to replication). The plan (see Table 7) is implemented in two stages, with random sequencing of the tests within each stage:

  — Stage 1: Eight factorial points plus two replicates of the center condition

  — Stage 2: Six prong points plus two further replicates of the center condition

  In general, we encourage stagewise experimentation moving from a fractional factorial to a full factorial to a central composite plan.

- Develop operational protocol

  This includes the variables to be held constant, the information to be recorded during the experiment, randomization, etc. What to do when some experimental conditions can not be attained or are of limited interest, is briefly discussed. Also, the need to clearly define the response variable(s) (in this case, what constitutes end of life?) is emphasized.

58 EXPLAINING EXPERIMENTAL DESIGN FUNDAMENTALS TO ENGINEERS

- Conduct the experiment

    Sometimes the experiment has to be redesigned after some initial results are obtained or some unexpected constraints are discovered.

- Plot the data and fit the statistical model

    The data and the fitted model are plotted at the end of each stage of the experiment; the interactions are again shown graphically. This time, the plots are supplemented by a statistical analysis — the fit of the data to the model (first-order after Stage 1; second order after Stage 2). Then a reduced model, excluding non-significant interactions and second order

TABLE 7. Response surface plan for machine tool optimization.

Lathe Speed (SFM)	Insert Feed Rate (IPS)	Depth (CM)	Randomized Sequence
\multicolumn{4}{c}{Stage 1}
700	0.010	0.030	7
1000	0.010	0.030	2
700	0.014	0.030	4
1000	0.014	0.030	5
700	0.010	0.060	9
1000	0.010	0.060	3
700	0.014	0.060	8
1000	0.014	0.060	6
850	0.012	0.045	1
850	0.012	0.045	10
\multicolumn{4}{c}{Stage 2}
600	0.012	0.045	4
1100	0.012	0.045	5
850	0.008	0.045	2
850	0.016	0.045	7
850	0.012	0.020	3
850	0.012	0.070	6
850	0.012	0.045	1
850	0.012	0.045	8

terms, is obtained. Various residual plots are shown. The results are examined to suggest an optimum region; further experimentation in this region is advised.

On-line process improvement, using evolutionary operation, is considered next. This topic was included because of its obvious relevance and the large potential payoffs — despite the fact that some of the original high expectations for this approach have, in our opinion, not been fully realized (see Hahn and Dershowitz, 1974).

We stress at the outset, the special characteristics of "on-line" investigations, and, following Box and Draper (1969), argue that a process, in addition to making a quality product today, should provide information to make an improved product tomorrow. An obvious advantage of on-line experiments is the fact that, unlike most off-line investigations, no scale-up assumptions are required. We repeat one of the major messages of the previous session — namely, that useful information generally cannot be gleaned from analyses of past process data [using George Box's admonition (1966) that to find out what happens to a process when you interfere with it, you have to interfere with it, rather than just passively observe it.]

We also stress the practical limitations of on-line investigations; e.g., we warn that some EVOP conditions are likely to result in a poorer, rather than an improved, product. In light of this, EVOP may involve introducing only minor perturbations to the process (in fact, we try to avoid the terminology of "conducting experiments on the process"). Since EVOP does not lend itself to all processes, one must be able to differentiate between situations for which EVOP is applicable from those where it is not. We also mention that one very elementary example of an EVOP application, dealing with the on-line comparison of two materials, was described in the first session.

Our specific EVOP example deals with a four-hour batch process. The objective is to improve the selectivity (the ratio of good stuff to bad stuff) by perturbing the reactant feed ratio and the percent of water in the feed. We use the example to indicate some of the characteristics that lend themselves to process improvement by EVOP, i.e.:

- High potential benefits from improvement
- Production of the same product under similar circumstances using the same performance criteria over reasonably long periods of time
- Clearly identified and easy-to-perturb process variables

- Rapid stabilization of the process after change
- Clear definition and rapid measurement of process performance
- Incomplete physical understanding and lack of a simpler approach
- Management support and active interest and participation by those responsible for, and involved in, the process

We point out that production people are often reluctant to tinker with a process when it seems to be running satisfactorily — much less make changes in several variables that could induce bad product or even lead to line shutdowns. Thus, it must be made clear that the tinkering that is to be done by EVOP is so slight that it is highly unlikely to have an appreciable harmful effect.

We use the example to describe both factorial and simplex EVOP and differentiate between the two approaches, pointing out their relative advantages and disadvantages. We conclude that, in this particular application (involving a 4-hour cycle), the dynamic nature of simplex EVOP gives it an edge over factorial EVOP, despite the fact that it is not as informative in helping one understand what is going on.

Finally, we show graphically the results of this particular simplex EVOP application. It resulted in an improvement in the selectivity from 9.57 to 11.96 in a series of nine cycles: see Figure 1.

Session 6: Estimating Sources of Variability and Nested Plans

Reducing variability, or, equivalently, achieving greater uniformity in product performance is a major objective of most quality improvement programs. Sometimes, a process capability study reveals that the inherent variability exceeds product specifications. In other cases, even though specifications are being met, a never-ending program of quality improvement calls for a continuing effort to reduce process variability. In both cases, we need to know what brought about the variability in order to reduce it. Often, this calls for special experimental investigations aimed at quantifying the major sources of process variation — the topic of this session.

We have found, as have others, that studies to quantify sources of variability often involve nested (or hierarchal) test plans and, therefore, we describe such plans in this session. We indicate, however, that experiments to quantify components of variability do not necessarily imply a nested data arrangement and vice versa.

The concepts are illustrated by an example dealing with the production of silicon crystals for integrated circuits. Each crystal is sliced into many wafers. Numerous circuits are built from each wafer. Measurements, subject to analytic error, are obtained on each circuit. A nested experiment is conducted to quantify the contributions to total variability of among-crystal variability, among-wafer (within crystal) variability, among-circuit (within wafer) variability, and measurement error: see Table 8. More generally, we show how nested experiments differ from factorial ones by examples of manufacturing processes involving three machines and three operators that lead to (1) a factorial data arrangement, (2) nesting of operators within machines, and (3) nesting of machines within operators. The concept of a partially nested plan is also briefly mentioned.

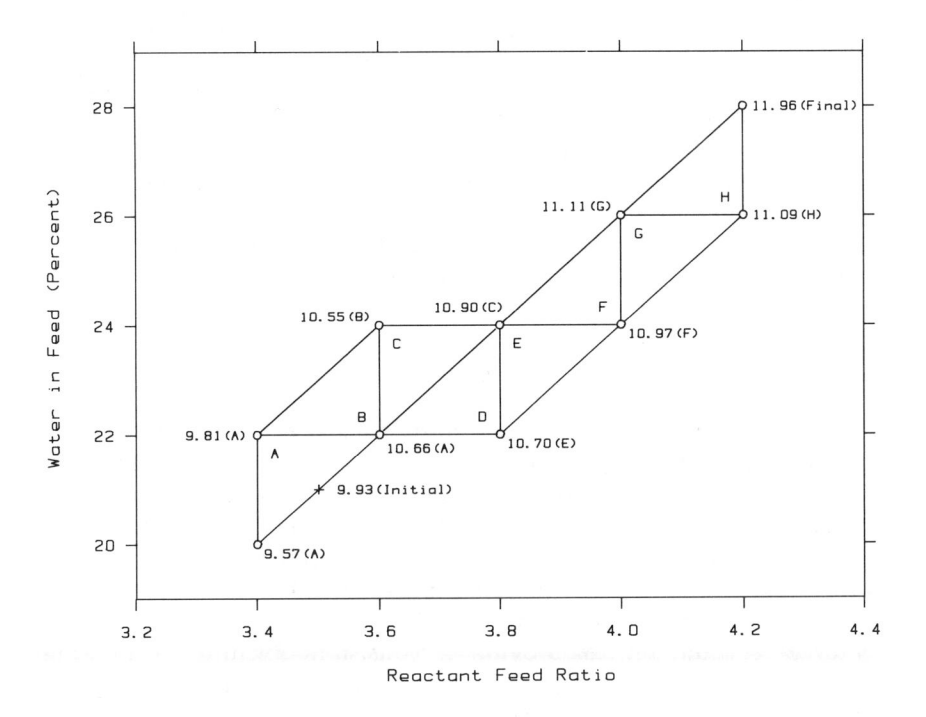

Figure 1. EVOP test plan to optimize chemical process.

TABLE 8. Nested test plan to assess sources of variability in integrated circuit performance.

- Select 5 crystals at random from year's production.
- Select 3 wafers at random from each crystal.
- Select 2 circuits at random from each wafer.
- Take 2 measurements on each circuit.

Again, the results of the experiment are analyzed graphically; this time using a simple approach suggested by Snee (1983). However, we also mention how an advanced statistical method, known as the "analysis of variance," available in various statistical computing packages, allows one to estimate separately the "sigmas" associated with each source of variability and give the results for our example. We then show how to evaluate the impact on total process variability of eliminating each of these sources. This allows one to rank sources of variability in order of importance, in a manner similar to a Pareto Chart (which ranks defect causes according to their relative importance). We also point out how this type of experiment, aimed at quantifying each of the contributors to total variability, differs from experimental programs, described in the preceding session, which are aimed at searching for the maximum of a response surface.

Session 7: Taguchi Concepts and Course Wrap-Up

We start with a brief description of some of the concepts of parameter design advocated by Genichi Taguchi and his associates. Taguchi has urged the use of multi-variable experimental design in process and product development. He has emphasized the importance of using experimental design to help identify conditions for which the variability in performance is minimized over a wide spectrum of product operating conditions; for example, we want a color television set to provide a consistent picture in different localities and terrains and at different times of day in different seasons. Achieving uniformity of performance under various operating conditions is especially useful for those products for which one can make a simple adjustment, like setting the time for a watch. One would then build the product at those conditions that minimize variability in performance and then adjust to reach the desired target value. Thus Taguchi stresses that learning how the design and process variables impact average performance, using the classical methods described in earlier sessions is not enough. One also needs to evaluate the variability in performance induced by variation in the environmental variables at different design and process conditions. To accomplish this, Taguchi proposes the use of fractional factorial experiments (in the form of orthogonal arrays, usually involving variables at three levels). The variables that impact mean response are treated separately from the environmental variables in two layers, identified as inner array and outer array variables, respectively.

We conclude with an overview of the course. The aim is to reemphasize important points, provide perspective, and make some additional comments. We reiterate the usefulness of statistically planned experiments in the entire cycle from gaining improvements in the design of the product to its manufacture. We point out that experiments run in a high-production manufacturing environment are generally much more challenging than evaluation engineering, design engineering, or R&D experiments. The experiments typically need to be smaller and simpler and must have the full support of everybody involved. Many things can go wrong or slip through the cracks without substantial planning and foresight. We must try to avoid problems such as:

- Someone couldn't get all the parts ready on time so we only ran this part of the experiment.
- We had difficulty controlling pressure.
- The first time we ran the short cure-time at the low temperature we couldn't get a complete part, so we didn't...
- We had to stop running after the fifth trial because the "so-and-so" failed.
- We hope to get to the experiment in several weeks but right now we have to...
- Oh, I thought you meant something else.

We emphasize that experimentation should supplement physical evaluations, not replace them, and again point out the frequent futility of analyzing historical data to gain insights about cause and effect relationships.

We next review the basic steps involved in planning an experiment. These were initially introduced in Session 1, and re-emphasized throughout the course. We indicate that limiting the scope of the experiment is likely to enhance the precision of the inferences given the limited conditions under which the experiment is conducted. In contrast, broadening the scope allows one to be more confident about drawing conclusions beyond these limited conditions and, thus, to project better to the conditions of future interest. How wide the scope of the experiment need be depends upon the broadness of the inferences that are to be drawn, the degree to which the variables interact, and the practical constraints and limitations on the test program.

An early step is to define all variables that might impact performance and then systematically choose for each variable among the following possibilities:

- Treat as full-fledged experimental variable
- Control the effect of the variable, and remove its contribution to experimental error, by blocking techniques
- Neutralize the effect of the variable by randomization
- Hold the variable constant
- Leave the variable uncontrolled, but keep records by measuring it (and potentially removing its effect in an after-the-fact statistical evaluation)
- Leave the variable uncontrolled, unmeasured, and, perhaps even undefined.

We also summarize different types of experimental plans that have been presented by a comprehensive tabulation (see Table 9) that shows both the applications and the limitations of each of the plans.

Some other topics in this wrap-up are:

- Further comments on randomization stressing
    - That randomization is a statistical insurance policy against bias.
    - That the need for randomization arises at many levels, e.g., the selection of lots, the preparation of samples, and final measurement.

— That all variables are not created equal; some can be varied more easily than others. This needs to be recognized in the planning of the test program so as to achieve a reasonable compromise between practical needs and protection from bias.

- The usefulness, in many experimental programs, of retaining materials to permit comparable runs to be conducted in the future.
- The need for careful documentation of the program protocol.
- The desirability of having the experimenter predict the results prior to conducting the experiment (to permit clear differentiation between the expected and the unexpected and to avoid "Monday morning quarterbacking"). Comparison with actual results, especially if they are dramatically different from those predicted, can be sobering and informative.
- The importance of understanding the various levels of repeatability (e.g., sample to sample variation versus variation in replicate measurements) and the need to quantify each.
- The usefulness of conducting some initial repeat runs to assure that a reasonable level of repeatability can be achieved, and the desirability of "sprinkling in" at least a few repeat runs at one or more experimental conditions.
- The importance of performing some initial pilot experimental runs and the desirability of conducting the experiment in stages whenever possible.

We conclude with some familiar themes stressed throughout the course:

- Plan ahead — experimentation costs money.
- A good test plan is one that is tailored to meet the needs of the investigation — and not the other way around.
- Graphical analyses often suffice to provide a first-cut evaluation of the results of a well-planned experiment and can, generally, be more readily understood than more complex statistical analyses; however, formal statistical analyses may provide some added frosting on the cake.

TABLE 9. Overview comparison of experimental plans.

Experimental Plan	Application	Limitations/Comments
Simple Comparative Experiment	Comparison of process alternatives or other evaluations on single main variables.	Applies for only one main variable. All extraneous variables randomized.
Randomized Block	Same as simple comparative experiment, while controlling for one extraneous variable.	Applies for only one main variable. Need to make all comparisons on main variable within block. Other extraneous variables randomized.
Incomplete Block	Same as randomized block, but do not need to compare all conditions of main variable within block.	Same as randomized block, except need not make all comparisons on main variable within block. Harder to analyze data due to lack of balance.
Latin Square	Same as simple comparative experiment, while controlling for two extraneous variables.	Applies for only one main variable. Block size for both extraneous for main variable. Other extraneous variables randomized. Assumes no interactions.

Full Factorial	Allows simultaneous evaluations of two or more main variables by running all test combinations.	Allows evaluation of interactions. Might require too many tests.
Fractional Factorial	Allows simultaneous evaluations of two or more variables by running fraction of all test combinations.	Allows evaluation of designated interactions only (depending upon degree of fractionation).
Response Surface	Applicable when functional relationship is desired between two or more process variables and response variable or optimum process conditions are sought.	Can be combined with fractional factorial to reduce number of tests (would then permit evaluation of only designated interactions).
Evolutionary Operation (EVOP)	Involves on-line perturbations for process improvement. Two major types: factorial and simplex. Major advantages is that no scale-up is required.	Sometimes not practical to do on-line evaluation. When practical, limited to what can be done on process. For example, limit allowable changes.
Nested Experiment	Applicable when test situation involves hierarchy of variables. Often involves evaluation of importance of different sources of variability.	Specialized plan that applies for specific type of situation only.

4. CONCLUDING REMARKS

What If We Had More Time?

We were faced throughout with the tough decision of carefully scrutinizing each of the topics to assure that we retained only what we regarded as most important to our audience in the limited time available. We challenge readers to suggest topics that they would have included and we did not — and to indicate what they would omit to make room.

If we had more time, we would have included

- Some discussion of Daniel half-normal plots — a technique which we have all found helpful in the analysis of the results of factorial and fractional factorial plans.
- Box-Behnken response surface plans.
- An example of a Taguchi parameter design experiment.
- Some discussion of computer programs to guide the design of experiments, and their limitations. A number of these programs have been developed for direct use by the experimenter.

If we were severely pressed for time, we might, reluctantly, shorten the discussion, at the beginning of Session 2, on blocking designs, perhaps omitting or reducing the already brief presentation of incomplete block and Latin Square plans.

What Actually Happened

We have described a seven-session course. Actually, we were originally asked to develop six sessions. We added the last session in this description to provide an introduction to the Taguchi concepts (of which we were not aware at the time we developed the material), and to provide a more detailed final overview (which had previously been included, in part, in Session 6).

It turned out that the course had to be reduced from six sessions to five. There was general agreement that Session 4 on "Quantifying Relationships Using Multiple Regression" should be dropped. This session was the one least in the mainstream of the presentation, and seemed most difficult to digest in this elementary course.

The omission of Session 4 impacted the first part of Session 5 on response surface plans as follows:

- We gave more emphasis at the beginning of the session to the hazards of drawing conclusions from the analysis of unplanned data.
- We briefly described first-order and second-order response surface models in this session, instead of the previous one.
- The discussion of the analysis of the response surface experiments had to be abridged, with more emphasis given to graphical evaluations.

It turned out that response surface plans were the part of the course that the participants have found most difficult. This was, perhaps, because we chose to retain some discussion of statistical models, despite the omission of the session on multiple regression analysis.

In contrast, the discussion of EVOP, later in the same session, came across very well, and did not appear intimidating. The discussion, in the first session, of the simple on-line experiment to compare two materials was also well received. This seems to suggest a strong interest in "on-line" manufacturing applications.

Our description has emphasized the contents of the videotaped material for this case. This lays the foundation and is supplemented by class notes and exercises. It is, however, critically important to relate the material to "on-site" interests and applications. This is achieved by application projects and class discussion, and presents an important challenge to the on-site moderator.

ACKNOWLEDGMENT

The development of the original course material was sponsored by General Electric Corporate Engineering and Manufacturing. It forms the basis of the video-based, five-session QLC-9 course: Designing Experiments.

REFERENCES

Bemesderfer, J. (1979). "Approving a process for production," *Journal of Quality Technology*, 11, 1-12.

Box, G. E. P. (1966). "Use and abuse of regression," *Technometrics*, 8, 625-629.

Box, G. E. P. and Draper, N. R. (1969). *Evolutionary Operation: A Statistical Method for Process Improvement*. New York: Wiley.

Box, G. E. P., Hunter, W. G., and Hunter, J. S. (1978). *Statistics for Experimenters.* New York: Wiley.

Daniel, C. (1976). *Applications of Statistics to Industrial Experimentation.* New York: Wiley.

Daniel, C. and Wood, F. S. (1980). *Fitting Equations to Data,* 2nd edition. New York: Wiley.

Deming, W. E. (1975). "On probability as a basis for action," *The American Statistician,* **29,** 146-152.

Draper, N. R. and Smith, H. (1981). *Applied Regression Analysis,* 2nd edition. New York: Wiley.

Hahn, G. J. (1973). "The coefficient of determination exposed!" *Chemtech,* **3,** 609-610.

Hahn, G. J. (1982). "Statistical assessment of a process change," *Journal of Quality Technology,* **14,** 1-9.

Hahn, G. J. (1984). "Experimental design in the complex world," *Technometrics,* **26,** 19-31.

Hahn, G. J. and Boardman, T. J. (1985). "The statistician's role in quality improvement," Forum Article, *Amstat News,* March 1985, 5-8.

Hahn, G. J. and Dershowitz, A. F. (1974). "Evolutionary operation to-day — some survey results and observations," *Journal of the Royal Statistical Society, Series C,* **23,** 215-218.

Larsen, W. A. and McCleary, S. J. (1972). "The use of partial residual plots in regression analysis," *Technometrics,* **14,** 781-790.

Mueller, F. X. and Olsson, D. M. (1971). "Applications of statistical design for the solution of industrial finishing problems," *Journal of Paint Technology,* **43,** 54-62.

Neter, J., Wasserman, W., and Kutner, M. H. (1983). *Applied Linear Regression Models.* Homewood, IL: Richard D. Irwin, Inc.

Schilling, E. G. (1973). "A systematic approach to the analysis of means, Part I. Analysis of treatment effects; Part II. Analysis of contrasts; Part III. Analysis of non-normal data," *Journal Quality Technology,* **5,** 93-108; 147-155; 156-159.

Snee, R. (1983). "Graphic analysis of process variation studies," *Journal of Quality Technology,* **15,** 76-88.

CHAPTER 5

Repeatability and Reproducibility: Some problems in applied statistics

Hugo C. Hamaker
Eindhoven, Netherlands

SUMMARY

When some test method has been standardized and is in general use, it is desirable to add to the standard some information concerning the precision of that test. Two measures of precision are in common use and known as the repeatability for the within and the reproducibility for the between laboratories variability. Numerical estimates of these two measures are derived from so-called interlaboratory or collaborative experiments. The analysis of the resulting experimental data is sometimes seen as an ANOVA problem, the interaction between laboratories and the level of the test property forming an essential element of the precision problem. It is pointed out that this is a mistake, that instead it is a regression problem in which the interaction does not play a part. Consequently some formulae current in the literature have to be corrected. Also a transformation sometimes applied in order to carry out an ANOVA on the transformed data turns out to be useless; the end result can be derived in a very simple way. The regression curve sought is one between standard deviations s_r (or s_R) and the mean level $\bar{x}$ of the property tested. Various ways of fitting a regression curve and associated problems, such as dealing with outliers, are discussed and illustrated by two numerical examples.

At the end the practical uses of the precision measures are considered, and it is pointed out that establishing such measures for a standard method is an entirely different problem from that of the standardization (or validation) of the method itself.

1. INTRODUCTION

In what follows a "test" will mean any measurement or observation — either chemical, physical, or technological — that ends up in a single numerical test result. Whether this result is obtained by a single instrument reading or deduced from a set of different such readings is immaterial.

Tests in this general sense play a predominant role in our daily lives, in checking our health, in controlling the quality of our foods, of the air we breathe, and of all sorts of industrial materials and products. No wonder therefore, that there exist national and international organizations that consider it part of their job to establish standards, so that a specific test will, in different laboratories, be carried out according to an identical protocol; and the test results will be intercomparable. And it is evidently of practical importance to add to such a standard some information concerning the precision of the test specified by it.

For obvious reasons the error variability is generally greater when the tests are reproduced in different laboratories than when repeated within a single laboratory. This has led to the introduction of two general concepts, that of the *repeatability* for the within, and of the *reproducibility* for the between laboratory variations; which are represented in theory by standard deviations σ_r and σ_R, and in practice by their estimates s_r and s_R respectively. As usual, variances will often be more convenient in analyzing experimental data.

The standard deviations are meant to measure the precision of the test method proper. As a rule the observations cannot be repeated on the same sample, as it is destroyed by the test. Hence, the batches of material from which these samples are drawn have to be carefully homogenized beforehand, and special precautions may sometimes be needed to ensure that the requisite homogeneity among the samples is maintained up to the moment the tests are performed.

σ_r and σ_R must be seen as two extremes; other measures in between are conceivable. Tests carried out in one laboratory on different days have, for example, been found to show a greater variability than when performed within a single day. Hence σ_r is specifically defined to hold under *repeatability conditions*; that is for tests carried out in quick succession within a single laboratory by one operator using the same equipment throughout.

The estimate s_r is usually obtained from tests carried out in duplicate within laboratories. It has been observed, however, that the values acquired in that manner are considerably smaller when the operators are aware of the fact that they are carrying out a duplicate test, than when they do not know this. Special instructions may be needed to make certain that the test results are mutually independent.

Further, it cannot be expected that σ_r will have the same value in all laboratories and an estimate s_r added to the standard of a test method will necessarily be an average; with which any laboratory can compare its own within laboratory precision if needed.

2. INTERLABORATORY OR COLLABORATIVE EXPERIMENTS

It has been found that the values of σ_r and σ_R often depend on the mean level, m, of the test results; for instance, on the concentration in the case of a chemical analysis. Hence, the ideal would be to establish a functional relation between these standard deviations and the level m; but in practice we have, of course, to be content with a regression of s_r and s_R on a mean $\bar{x}$.

The experiment then consists in selecting or preparing a set of batches of materials covering the range of levels of the test property encountered in practice; and, after careful homogenization, dispatch samples of these batches to a number of laboratories to be tested according to the test method under investigation. This is known as a collaborative or interlaboratory experiment.

The best design from a statistical point of view would be for each batch of material to use another group of laboratories drawn at random from those using the standard test method, in order to get mutually independent estimates s_r and s_R. But this would imply contacting a very large number of laboratories from a population that is, with a freely available standard, not clearly defined. Consequently, it is customary to have samples of all materials tested by one and the same group of laboratories, which greatly simplifies the organization of the experiment.

But this has its disadvantages. The estimates s_r and s_R for the different materials will be mutually dependent; and this may bring with it a systematic error in the resulting regression curve over its full length, the value of which cannot easily be assessed. This we have to accept. More important is, however, that by using one set of laboratories the pattern of the data obtained is such that the formulae of a two-way analysis of variance can be applied. This in turn has led to the misconception that a two-way ANOVA must be considered as *the* solution of the problem at hand (Steiner, 1975). To correct this view, and the theory and practices associated with it, is one of the main purposes of the notes which follow.

3. AN EXAMPLE

To keep the discussion as simple as possible, we first consider the example recorded in Table 1, where 10 laboratories carried out a single test on samples of 5 different materials.

TABLE 1. Giving the percentage Al in 5 different kinds of liming materials as determined by 10 different laboratories.

Material Laboratory	A	B	C x_{ij}	D	E
1	1.35	1.57	1.78	2.19	5.48
2	1.38	1.11	2.08	2.60	6.38
3	1.35	1.33	2.14	2.38	5.88
4	1.34	1.47	2.09	2.15	5.96
5	1.50	1.60	2.10	2.44	7.28
6	1.52	1.62	2.26	3.25	7.00
7	1.39	1.52	2.20	2.46	6.33
8	1.50	1.90	2.20	3.20	6.50
9	1.30	1.36	2.08	2.35	6.70
10	1.32	1.53	2.09	2.70	6.43
$\bar{\bar{x}}$	1.395	1.501	2.102	2.572	6.394
s_R	0.0814	0.2087	0.1293	0.3817	0.5324

Data from: Chichilo, P. (1964). *Journal of the Association of Official Agricultural Chemists*, **47**, p. 1019.

From a different point of view they were also discussed by W. J. Youden in the *Statistical Manual of the AOAC* published by the Association of Official Analytical Chemists in 1975.

The international standard ISO 4259 (ISO, 1978) defines the reproducibility as

> "The closeness of agreement between individual results obtained with the same method on *identical* test material but under different conditions (different operators, different apparatus, different laboratories, etc.)"

In keeping with this definition we can compute an estimate s_R of σ_R for each of the 5 materials as given in the bottom line of the table. And with these we can couple a statistical model

$$\sigma_R^2 = \sigma_L^2 + \sigma_r^2, \qquad (1)$$

where σ_L^2 and σ_r^2 are the between and within laboratory variance components.

On the other hand, those who see Table 1 as a problem to be solved by a two-way analysis of variance maintain that the statistical model should be

$$\sigma_R^2 = \sigma_L^2 + \sigma_{LM}^2 + \sigma_r^2, \qquad (2)$$

σ_{LM}^2 representing the interaction between laboratories and materials. And they hold that (1) must be in error because the interaction is not taken into account and has to be corrected for.

On closer inspection, it turns out that (1) and (2) are incompatible; according to (1) we have, in principle at least, separate values of the three parameters for each of the five materials, whereas in (2) we have only a single value for four parameters. In view of the definition quoted above the validity of (1) for each material can hardly be doubted; what then is wrong with (2)? To see this we have to go back to first principles.

Let

$$x_{ij}, \; i = 1 \ldots p, \; j = 1 \ldots q$$

be the test results on p materials by q laboratories; then an ANOVA is, as explained in text books, carried out by first computing

$$A = \sum_{ij} x_{ij}^2, \; B = \sum_i \left[\sum_j x_{ij} \right]^2 / q,$$

$$C = \sum_j \left[\sum_i x_{ij} \right]^2 / p, \; D = \left[\sum_{ij} x_{ij} \right]^2 / pq.$$

Now

$$A - B = \sum_i \left\{ \sum_j x_{ij}^2 - \left(\sum_j x_{ij}\right)^2 / q \right\} = SS_{L.M} = \quad (3)$$

the total sum of squares between laboratories within materials, with

$$\nu_{L.M} = p(q-1) \text{ degrees of freedom}; \quad (4)$$

and

$$ms_{L.M} = SS_{L.M}/p(q-1) = \sum_i s_{Ri}^2 /p = \overline{s_R^2} = \quad (5)$$

the mean value of the reproducibility variance estimates for the p materials.

Further, we have

$$C - D = SS_L \text{ with } \nu_L = (q-1), \text{ and} \quad (6)$$

$$A - B - C + D = SS_{LM} \text{ with } \nu_{LM} = (p-1)(q-1). \quad (7)$$

Now setting

$$A - B = (A - B - C + D) + (C - D); \quad (8)$$

inserting the various expressions presented above and switching to mean squares, we find

$$\overline{s_R^2} = ms_{L.M} = \{ms_L + (p-1) ms_{LM}\}/p. \quad (9)$$

From Table 1 we obtain for example

$$ms_L = 0.2220, \quad ms_{LM} = 0.0685,$$

and hence,

$$\overline{s_R^2} = (0.2220 + 4 \times 0.0685)/5 = 0.0992,$$

which, as can easily be verified, is equal to the mean square of the standard deviations in the bottom line of Table 1.

But (9) is a purely algebraic relation, applicable to any two-way table, whether the basic assumptions underlying an ANOVA apply or not. Moreover it is an unnecessarily complicated way of computing an average; only A and B are needed, as according to (8) the difference $(C-D)$ is first subtracted and then added again.

The ANOVA is also misleading, because it pools the variance estimates without looking at the individual values for each material. Whether such a pooled mean makes sense has to be judged by the differences between these individual values, and they have to be separately computed in the first place. Pooling them, if considered permissible, is then simple and straightforward.

Since (9) holds for a single ANOVA it will also hold when on each side of the equality sign we take expectations. This yields

$$E(\overline{s_R^2}) = \left\{ E(ms_L) + (p-1)E(ms_{LM}) \right\} / p, \tag{10}$$

but the meaning of the expectations will depend on the statistical model we adopt.

The most general model considers the p materials used as a random sample from a larger group of P possible choices. In that case

$$E(ms_L) = p\,\hat{\sigma}_L^2 + \frac{P-p}{P}\,\overline{\sigma_{LM}^2} + \overline{\sigma_r^2}, \tag{11}$$

and

$$E(ms_{LM}) = \overline{\sigma_{LM}^2} + \overline{\sigma_r^2}, \tag{12}$$

which inserted in (10) yield

$$E(\overline{s_R^2}) = \overline{\sigma_R^2} = \hat{\sigma}_L^2 + \frac{P-1}{P}\,\overline{\sigma_{LM}^2} + \overline{\sigma_r^2}. \tag{13}$$

Here $\overline{\sigma_R^2}$ and $\overline{\sigma_r^2}$ are mean values taken over the complete population of P materials, while $\hat{\sigma}_L^2$ and $\overline{\sigma_{LM}^2}$ are two parameters of that population.

In particular $\hat{\sigma}_L^2$ is a variance component that these P materials have in common and is essentially different from σ_L^2 in (1) which refers to a single batch of material. By combining (1) and (13) we find

$$\overline{\sigma_L^2} = \hat{\sigma}_L^2 + \frac{P-1}{P}\,\overline{\sigma_{LM}^2}, \tag{14}$$

a relation that can also be deduced from the expressions defining the different parameters. It is the failure to distinguish between σ_L^2 in (1) and $\hat{\sigma}_L^2$ in (14) that has led to the mistaken view that (1) underestimates the reproducibility variance because the interaction is not taken into account.

For $P = 1$ (14) reduces to (1), and for $P = \infty$ to a corrected version of (2), namely

$$E(\sigma_R^2) = \hat{\sigma}_L^2 + \sigma_{LM}^2 + E(\sigma_r^2). \tag{15}$$

(2) silently assumes that σ_R^2 and σ_r^2 have the same value for all materials.

Considerations similar to those above can be applied to the laboratories which can either be seen as a fixed set or as a random sample. But if, as explained in § 2, the analysis of an interlaboratory experiment is interpreted as a regression problem, these questions are no longer relevant. Our main purpose so far has been to correct the theory concerned with the reproducibility; because equations (1) and (2) jointly have led to a misinterpretation of the meaning and the role of the interaction between laboratories and materials; as is illustrated by the international standard ISO 4259 to be discussed in § 7.

4. A SECOND EXAMPLE

Before turning our attention to some further statistical problems we first consider a second numerical example presented by Table 2. It differs from that of Table 1 in that the laboratories have received two samples from each of the materials to carry out the tests in duplicate.

The arguments of the previous section now apply to the cell means, $\bar{x}$, for which

$$\sigma_{\bar{x}}^2 = \sigma_L^2 + \sigma_r^2 / n, \quad n = 2, \tag{16}$$

while from the within-cell differences we obtain a separate and independent estimate s_r^2 of σ_r^2. If, as usual, (1) is understood as the correct definition of σ_R^2 the corresponding estimate will be

$$s_R^2 = s_{\bar{x}}^2 + \frac{n-1}{n} s_r^2 = s_{\bar{x}}^2 + s_r^2 / 2. \tag{17}$$

TABLE 2. Duplicate determinations of the % ZnO by 10 laboratories in 6 kinds of rubber.

| | \multicolumn{6}{c}{Material} |||||| |
Lab.	A	B	C	D	E	F
1	1.84 1.86	2.42 2.42	4.78 4.81	6.64 6.63	12.34 12.41	20.50 20.45
2	1.86 1.86	2.39 2.41	4.86 4.89	6.47 6.56	12.28 12.28	19.60 19.75
3	1.87 1.84	2.36 2.38	4.71 4.69	6.54 6.42	12.13 12.22	20.18 20.09
4	1.89 1.91	2.42 2.42	4.97 4.93	6.68 6.65	12.30 12.60	20.60 20.50
5	1.90 1.90	.2.46 2.46	4.96 5.06	6.71 6.72	12.30 12.20	20.00 20.40
6	1.89 1.88	2.43 2.46	4.91 4.93	6.48 6.53	12.55 12.56	19.91 20.20
7	1.88 1.88	2.37 2.43	4.91 4.85	6.68 6.65	12.57 12.56	20.53 20.61
8	1.89 1.88	2.38 2.37	4.91 4.89	6.51 6.33	12.27 12.24	20.45 20.27
9	1.91 1.92	2.48 2.48	4.95 4.94	6.34 6.72	12.60 12.50	20.60 20.30
10	1.92 1.92	2.46 2.43	5.07 5.19	6.65 6.74	12.62 12.33	20.66 20.54
$\bar{\bar{x}}$	1.885	2.422	4.910	6.582	12.393	20.307
$s_{\bar{x}}$	0.0244	0.0361	0.1159	0.1037	0.1455	0.2924
s_r	0.0100	0.0177	0.0404	0.1029	0.1020	0.1467
s_R	0.0254	0.0383	0.1194	0.1267	0.1624	0.3103

Data taken from: Mandel, J. (1976). "Models, transformations of scale, and weighting," *Journal of Quality Technology*, **8**, p. 95.

5. THE REGRESSION PROBLEM

To solve the regression problem of § 2, we can start by plotting s_r or s_R against the mean $\bar{\bar{x}}$. For practical purposes, a regression curve drawn by hand through the set of points obtained may suffice. If instead it is preferred to construct such a curve by least squares, it may be best to plot ln s against ln $\bar{\bar{x}}$ for the following reasons.

In first approximation a functional relation $z = f(y)$ leads to

$$\sigma_z = f'(\bar{y}) \sigma_y, \tag{18}$$

which in particular yields for one material or level

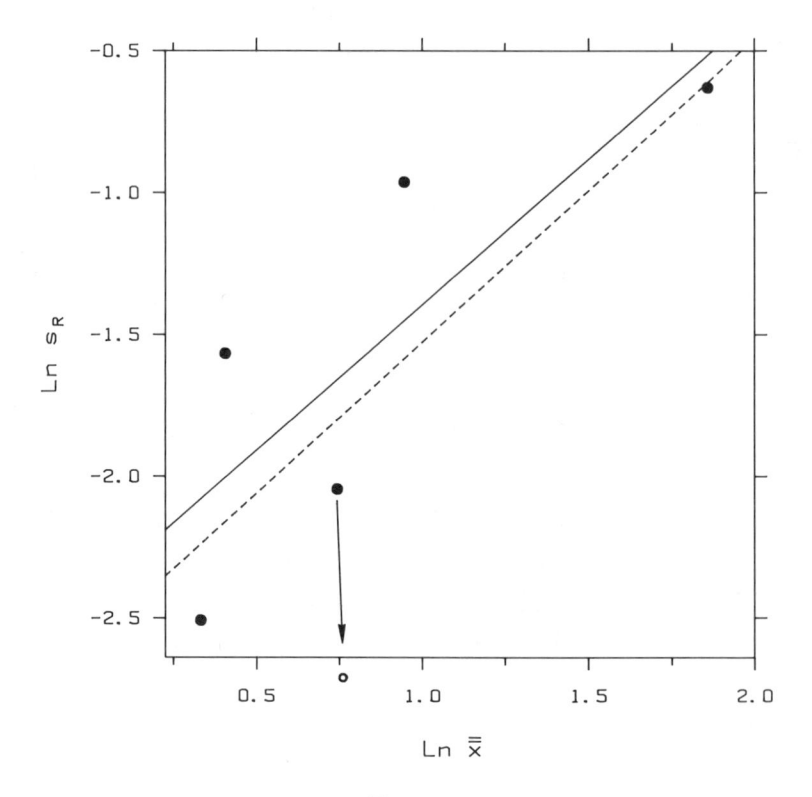

$$\sigma_{\ln s} = CV(s) = 1/\sqrt{2\nu}, \quad \sigma_{\ln \bar{\bar{x}}} = CV(\bar{\bar{x}}) = CV(\bar{x})/\sqrt{9}, \tag{19}$$

Figure 1. ln s_R plotted against ln $\bar{\bar{x}}$ for the data of Table 1; plus regression lines fitted by least squares.

Solid line: ln $s_R = -.2422 + 1.027$ ln $\bar{\bar{x}}$, $s^2_{\text{res}} = 0.260$
Dashed line: ln $s_R = -2.594 + 1.068$ ln $\bar{\bar{x}}$, $s^2_{\text{res}} = 0.560$

where q = number of laboratories, $\nu = q(n-1)$ n = number of replicates within laboratories. Hence $\sigma_{\ln s}$ is independent of $\bar{\bar{x}}$ and much larger than $\sigma_{\ln \bar{\bar{x}}}$ when, as usual, $CV(\bar{\bar{x}}) < 10\%$; so that the basic conditions for a least square regression are reasonably satisfied.

Plots of $\ln s$ against $\ln \bar{\bar{x}}$ are reproduced in Figures 1 and 2 and the fitted regression equations are given underneath. In both cases the regression coefficient b is for s_R close to 1.00, so that $\ln s_R = a + \ln \bar{\bar{x}}$ would be a reasonable approximation. This would be equivalent to assuming that the coefficient of variation is independent of the level $\bar{\bar{x}}$, which would be particularly convenient in practical applications. And this may hold as well for s_r in Table 2;

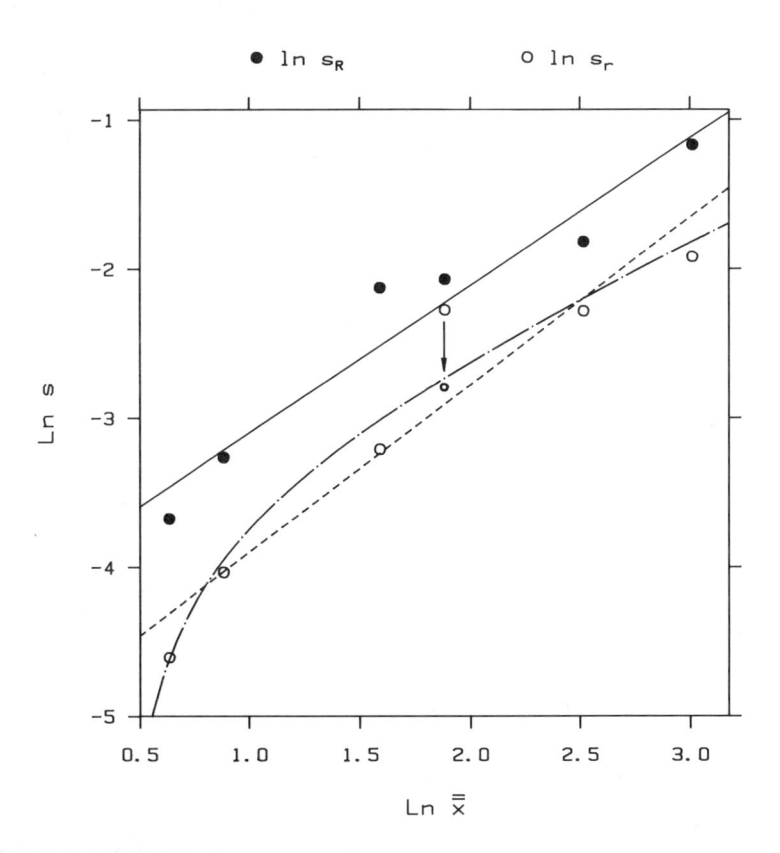

Figure 2. Plots of $\ln s$ against $\ln \bar{\bar{x}}$ for the data of Table 2, with least square fitted regression equations.

Solid line: $\ln s_r = -5.020 + 1.122 \ln \bar{\bar{x}}$, $s^2_{res} = 0.143$, $\gamma_{res} = 4$
Dashed line: $\ln s_R = -4.086 + 0.988 \ln \bar{\bar{x}}$, $s^2_{res} = 0.069$, $\gamma_{res} = 4$
Dash-dot line: $\ln s_r = -3.854 + 0.695 \ln(\bar{\bar{x}} - 1.55)$, $s^2_{res} = 0.090$ $\gamma_{res} = 3$

for if we make up the values of CV it turns out that there is not any convincing change as a function of $\bar{\bar{x}}$. Hence, in the case of Tables 1 and 2 we might be satisfied by

$$CV_R = 10\% \text{ and } CV_r = 0.9\%, \quad CV_R = 1.7\% \tag{20}$$

respectively, as the final results. It may then still be argued whether the CV's for the different materials should be pooled by taking their mean or their root mean square, but this makes too little difference to worry about.

Another point is that the general regression equation

$$\ln s = a + b \ln \bar{\bar{x}} \tag{21}$$

brings with it $s \to 0$ for $\bar{\bar{x}} \to 0$, and in situations where $\bar{\bar{x}}$ comes close to zero, as in determining residual amounts of insecticides, etc., this will not do. This defect might be remedied by replacing (21) by

$$\ln s = a + b \ln(\bar{\bar{x}} + c), \tag{22}$$

which can easily be fitted by least squares trying out different values of c and using a pocket computer.

This has been tried out for s_r in the case of Table 2 and has led to the last equation underneath Figure 2, which is presented by the interrupted curve. Though the residual degrees of freedom are reduced from 4 to 3, the residual variance diminishes from 0.143 to 0.090, indicating a closer fit. But the constant c turns out to be negative and the equation would lead to $s \to 0$ when $\bar{\bar{x}} \to 1.55$, which is not acceptable.

Alternatively the relation (22) can be used to construct a linear regression by searching that value of c which produces $b = 1.000$. For s_r and Table 2 this yields

$$\ln s_r = -4.659 + 1.000 \ln(\bar{\bar{x}} - 0.557), \text{ or} \tag{23}$$

$$s_r = 0.00948(\bar{\bar{x}} - 0.557) = 0.00948 \bar{\bar{x}} - 0.00528;$$

while a straightforward linear regression gave

$$s_r = 0.00713 \bar{\bar{x}} + 0.01232, \tag{24}$$

which is quite different from (23).

One possible explanation for this difference is that the variance of an estimate s is proportional to σ^2, and that therefore the regression between $\bar{\bar{x}}$ and s should be a weighted regression. To investigate this, values s'_r have been computed from (24) and the regression of s_r on $\bar{\bar{x}}$ recomputed with weights inversely proportional to s'^2_r, a procedure that can then be repeated.

Initially the weights derived in this manner are

$$w_0 = 1507 \quad 1142 \quad 446 \quad 285 \quad 99 \quad 40$$

leading to

$$s_{r1} = 0.00985 \,\bar{\bar{x}} - 0.00478, \tag{25}$$

a decided shift in the direction of (23).

After repeating the process four times the final outcome was

$$w_4 = 8213 \quad 3487 \quad 510 \quad 255 \quad 62 \quad 22$$

and

$$s_{r4} = 0.01102 \,\bar{\bar{x}} - 0.00983. \tag{26}$$

The situation is illustrated in Figure 3, which explains what is happening. The three lowest observed points lie almost perfectly on a straight line, and, coupled with the smallest set of standard deviations, are assigned the highest weights. Further, as we go from (25) to (26) the fixed term in the regression equation turns from positive to negative, and as a consequence the range of the weights increases enormously; initially the extreme weights differ by a factor 40, in the final state by a factor 400!

It might be thought that the regression line c is too extreme, but the standard deviations s_r are based on only 10 degrees of freedom; and a two-sided 95% confidence interval for σ_r given s_r is:

$$\text{Conf.}\,(0.70\,s_r < \sigma_r < 1.75\,s_r) = 95\%. \tag{27}$$

This yields such wide limits that all three regression lines in Figure 3 must be considered as possibilities.

84 REPEATABILITY AND REPRODUCIBILITY

Anyhow, this analysis seems to indicate that a linear regression fitted by (22) with $b = 1.00$ is a reasonable way of taking the differences in weights into account.

An unsatisfactory feature of several of the regression equations is that they lead to $s = 0$ for a positive $\bar{\bar{x}}$. From a mathematical point of view this may be acceptable, but from a technical point of view it is quite unacceptable.

On the basis of (19) one might be inclined to expect a residual variance of the order of $1/20 = 0.05$; the residual mean squares recorded underneath Figure 2 are all somewhat larger, while the fit in Figure 1 is a very poor one. Moreover, the residual variance predicted by (19) presupposes independent estimates of s_r, which those of Table 2 are not, being derived from data supplied by one and the same set of laboratories.

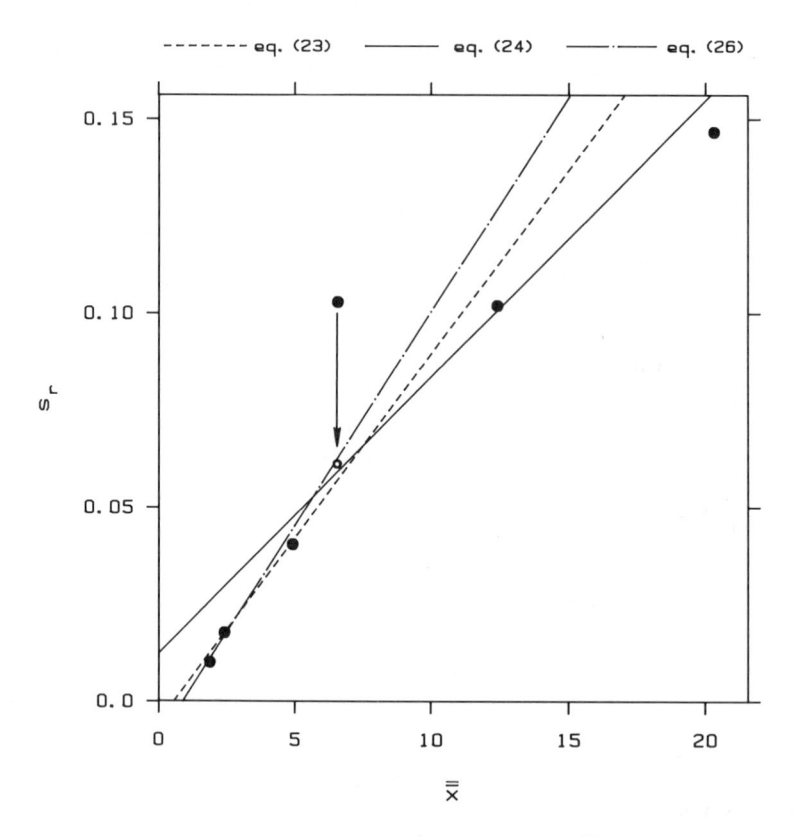

Figure 3. Different weighted regression lines of s_r on $\bar{\bar{x}}$ as given in Table 2.

The correlation coefficients between different columns in Tables 1 and 2 are all positive,, with an average value of about 0.5. As a consequence we may expect a residual variance of ln s somewhat less than expected in the case of mutual independence of the estimates, while the regression equation may be biased over its full length. It is difficult to say how much and we must leave it at that.

6. OUTLIERS

In the data resulting from interlaboratory, or collaborative, studies, such as those of Tables 1 and 2, outliers are a fairly common feature. One example is the datum 1.78 for Lab. 1 in Table 1, which, within material C, just reaches the 1% significant level with Grubbs' and easily exceeds that level with Dixon's outlier test. On the other hand rejection of this item would result in a much poorer fit of the data to the regression line in Figure 1, as indicated by an arrow; should it be discarded?

A second example is provided by material D, which in Figures 2 and 3 is presented by a point lying high above the regression lines. The differences between duplicates from which s_r was obtained were, in order of magnitude and multiplied by 100,

$$-38 \quad -9 \quad -9 \quad -5 \quad -1 \quad +1 \quad +3 \quad +3 \quad +12 \quad +18 \,,$$

and the first item lies between the 5 and the 1% level of significance both with Grubbs' and with Dixon's test. After rejecting the corresponding pair of observations, the data for material D become: $\bar{\bar{x}} = 6.588$, $s_r = 0.0612$, which, as indicated by an arrow in Figures 2 and 3, results in a much improved fit to the other points. With this correction the differences between the weighted regression lines in Figure 3 will be less extreme.

Closer inspection of Figure 2, after this correction, also suggested a curved regression, and this prompted another try by model (22); the result

$$\ln s_r = -4.057 + 0.7332 \ln(\bar{\bar{x}} - 1.41)\,, \tag{27}$$

$$s_{\text{res}}^2 = 0.00303\,, \quad \nu = 3\,.$$

These examples may suffice to show that fitting a regression curve and dealing with suspected outliers is a fascinating problem in applied statistics.

7. THE TWO INTERNATIONAL STANDARDS ISO 5725 AND ISO 4259

In recent years the ISO has, almost simultaneously, issued two international standards in order to standardize the organization, execution, and statistical analysis of interlaboratory experiments for obtaining acceptable estimates of σ_R and σ_r; ISO 5725 (ISO, 1981) is a general standard, ISO 4259 (ISO, 1978) is specially meant for use in the petroleum industry.

Up to a certain point both follow the same lines and establish a regression curve presenting s_R or s_r as a function of $\bar{x}$, say:

$$s_r = z(\bar{x}). \tag{28}$$

ISO 5725 stops there, while ISO 4259 goes on. Apparently the designers of that standard were so possessed of the idea that the interaction between laboratories and materials has to be taken into account, that on the basis of (28) they construct a transformation, $y(x)$, in order to homogenize the standard deviations. After applying this transformation to everyone of the original data, a full scale analysis of variance is carried out to find s_{ry} and s_{Ry}; and with these the transformation is inverted. This procedure involves a considerable amount of additional computations, which do not lead to any real improvement, and the result of which can very simply be predicted beforehand. This we proceed to show.

Given (28) the transformation needed is

$$y(x) = \int_a^x \frac{dv}{z(v)}, \tag{29}$$

as by applying (18) this yields

$$s_y = s_r / z(\bar{x}) = s_r / s_r', \tag{30}$$

where s_r are the original observed values and $s_r' = z(\bar{x})$ those computed from the regression equation. For example, using the first equation underneath Figure 2 we have

$$s_r' = 0.0066 \, \bar{x}^{1.122} \tag{31}$$

and the corresponding transformation would be

$$y = 151 \, x^{0.122}. \tag{32}$$

But from

s_r =	0.0100	0.0177	0.0404	0.1029	0.1020	0.1467
s'_r =	0.0135	0.0178	0.0394	0.0547	0.1127	0.1937
s_y =	0.741	0.994	1.025	1.881	0.905	0.809

we find

$$(\Sigma s_y^2 / 6)^{1/2} = 1.125 = \hat{s}_y .$$

According to the analysis in § 2 the ANOVA on the transformed data will result in a standard deviation $\hat{s}_y$ equal to the root mean square of the standard deviations s_y for the different materials; that is $\hat{s}_y = 1.125$ in the case above. And then, transforming backwards from y to x, we finally obtain

$$\hat{s}'_r = 1.125 \times 0.0066 \, \overline{x}^{1.122} = 0.00742 \, \overline{x}^{1.122} , \tag{33}$$

and the root mean square of the ratio's $s_r / \hat{s}'_r$ will now be equal to 1.00. Whether and in what respect (33) must be considered as a real improvement to (31) seems open to question.

It will be noted that the factors 0.0066 in (31) and 151 in (32) are not essential; if they are omitted they will automatically be taken into account in the values of s_y. Further, the exponent 1.122 in (31) is not corrected by the transformation.

It may be useful to illustrate the procedure with a further example borrowed from the standard ISO 4259.

Tests were performed in duplicate by 9 laboratories on samples of 8 different materials. After rejecting one flagrant outlier evidently due to a sample from a wrong material, the means and standard deviations were as recorded in the first three columns of Table 3. The regressions of ln s on ln $\overline{x}$ yielded:

$$s'_r = 0.0550 \, \overline{x}^{0.577} \quad \text{and} \quad s'_R = 0.0918 \, \overline{x}^{0.714} . \tag{34}$$

To avoid the use of two different transformations, ISO 4259 then assumes, without adequate proof, that both standard deviations can satisfactorily be considered proportional to $\overline{x}^{2/3}$. The corresponding transformation, $y = x^{1/3}$, is applied to everyone of the 144 test results, and followed by a full scale analysis of variance to find the estimates s_{ry} and s_{Ry} for y. Using these in inverting the transformation finally produced:

$$s'_r = 0.0523 \, \overline{\overline{x}}^{2/3} \quad \text{and} \quad s = s'_R = 0.1096 \, \overline{\overline{x}}^{2/3}, \tag{35}$$

while by the simpler procedure described above and without the use of a transformation, we obtained from Table 3:

$$s'_r = 0.0514 \, \overline{\overline{x}}^{2/3} \quad \text{and} \quad s'_R = 0.1086 \, \overline{\overline{x}}^{2/3}. \tag{36}$$

Actually the end results given in ISO 4259 are $r = 2\sqrt{2} \, s'_r$ and $R = 2\sqrt{2} \, s'_R$, for reasons explained in the next section.

This example may suffice to show that, at least for finding estimates s_r and s_R from such data as those of Tables 1 and 2, a transformation combined with analysis of variance involves a considerable amount of computations, which serves no useful purpose.

Moreover, for the range of values of $\overline{\overline{x}}$ in Table 3, replacing the exponents in (34) both by 2/3 introduces systematic errors that are by no means negligible; and that are not corrected by the use of a transformation.

TABLE 3. Simplified procedure for applying the transformation $y = x^{1/3}$; to the data of ISO 4259.

$\overline{\overline{x}}$	s_r	s_{yr}	s_R	s_{yR}
0.756	0.0500	0.0602	0.0668	0.0805
1.22	0.0572	0.0500	0.159	0.1393
1.91	0.1247	0.0810	0.154	0.1000
3.64	0.1155	0.0488	0.211	0.0892
10.90	0.0942	0.0192	0.291	0.0592
48.21	0.526	0.0397	1.496	0.1129
65.42	0.818	0.0504	2.218	0.1366
114.2	0.935	0.0397	2.933	0.1246
	$\hat{s}_{yr} =$	0.0514	$\hat{s}_{yR} =$	0.1086

$s_{yr}, s_{yR} = s_r, s_R$ divided by $\overline{\overline{x}}^{2/3}$.

$\hat{s}_{yr}, \hat{s}_{yR} =$ root mean squares of s_{yr}, s_{yR}

8. THE PURPOSE OF INTERLABORATORY STUDIES

Interlaboratory or collaborative experiments such as illustrated by Tables 1 and 2 are nowadays quite common. They are meant to serve a practical purpose.

Suppose a supplier and a customer have both tested a sample taken from a batch of material delivered by the one to the other; it is then important to know how far a difference in the test results can be explained as due to errors in the test method or must be interpreted as indicating a real difference. As an answer to that question the results of an interlaboratory experiment are, in the standards discussed in the previous section, not stated as standard deviations but as the *repeatability* $r = 2\sqrt{2}\, s_r$ and the *reproducibility* $R = 2\sqrt{2}\, s_R$; with the additional specification that the probabilities are approximately 5% that, as a result of errors in the test method, two test results in one laboratory will differ by more than r, or two test results obtained in different laboratories by more than R.

In case of doubt, a single laboratory can always carry out some additional tests, but between laboratories one has to rely on an estimate s_R as supplementary tests cannot rapidly or easily be carried out. It is then of interest to know what an approximate probability of 5% really means.

It has sometimes been suggested that the factor $2\sqrt{2}$ should be replaced by $1.96\sqrt{2}$, but that only holds when σ_r or σ_R are known. Alternatively, it has been proposed that that factor should be set at $t\sqrt{2}$, the value of t being taken from the t-distribution for a two-sided t-test with the number of degrees of freedom associated with s_r or s_R. But this again is not an acceptable solution, because the t-distribution presupposes that each time it is applied we use a fresh and independent estimate s. If instead we use a single estimate s repeatedly, the associated probability will systematically differ from 5%; sometimes larger, sometimes smaller.

An interlaboratory study requires quite an effort to organize, and often the number of laboratories taking part is about 10, each laboratory carrying out tests in duplicate. The number of degrees of freedom associated with s_r and s_R will be of the same order. The probabilities α that $r = t\sqrt{2}\, s_r$, or $R = t\sqrt{2}\, s_R$, will be exceeded will vary from case to case, because s_r and s_R are only estimates based on a limited number of degrees of freedom. For three situations the cumulative distributions of α are presented in Figure 4; these were derived as follows.

Assuming normality, $\text{Prob}(|x_a - x_b| > t\sqrt{2}\, s) = \alpha_o = 10\%$ when $ts < 1.645\,\sigma$ or $s/\sigma < 1.645/t$, where 1.645 is the abscissa of a standard normal distribution corresponding to a two-sided exceedance probability of 10%. Given t and ν, the probability that the second inequality holds good is then obtained from the chi-square distribution; for $\alpha_o = 10\%$ they were found to be 26.9, 20.0, and 14.6% for curves A, B, and C in Figure 4, in that order. By starting from different values of α_o the full curves were obtained. The expectations, $E(\alpha)$, underneath Figure 4, were derived by numerical integration. For $t = 2.00$ they turn out to be considerably larger than the intended 5%, which is due to the skew distribution of α; for $\nu = 9$ an $E(\alpha) = 5\%$ can be achieved by $t = 2.26$. Further, with such limited numbers of degrees of freedom as in Figure 4 values of α as low as 1

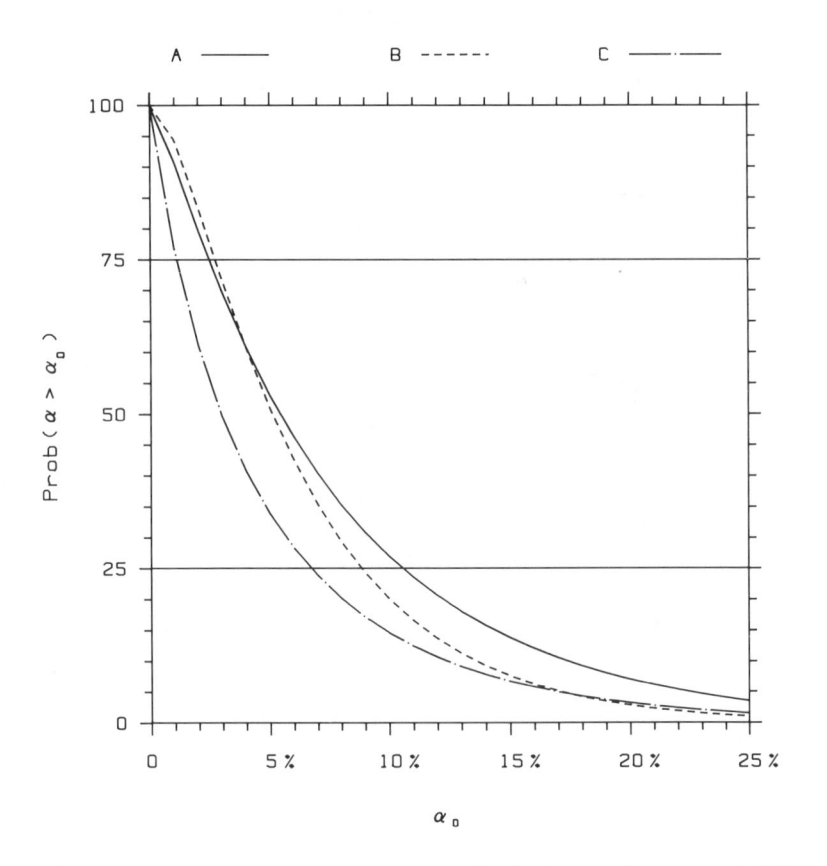

Figure 4. Some distribution functions of the exceedance probabilities associated with critical differences of the type $t\sqrt{2}\, s_r$ or $t\sqrt{2}\, s_R$.

Solid line A: $n = 10, \gamma = 9, t = 2.00\ E(\alpha) = 7.7\%$
Dashed line B: $n = 15, \gamma = 14, t = 2.00, E(\alpha) = 6.6\%$
Dash-dot line C: $n = 10, \gamma = 9, t = 2.26, E(\alpha) = 5.0\%$

or 2%, or as high as 15 or 20%, do occasionally occur. These must be interpreted as systematic, because for a given test method r and R are estimated only once and then applied repeatedly.

Within a single laboratory this lack of precision can easily be mended, for instance by keeping a record of differences between duplicate tests and plotting these in a control chart. But with regard to s_R this lack of precision has to be accepted, because the number of laboratories included in an interlaboratory study is usually limited by the organizational difficulties.

As a consequence statements concerning the use of r and R in practice must of necessity be vague. In *Standard Methods for Testing Tar and Its Products* (1967), for instance, the following phrases are systematically used:

Repeatability: Duplicate results by the same operator should be considered suspect if they differ by more than r.

Reproducibility: Single results submitted by each of two laboratories should be considered suspect when they differ by more than R.

Numerical values of r and R are given for many test methods described in that handbook.

Despite the uncertainties in the values of the exceedance probabilities associated with r and R, these criteria perform a useful function in practical applications, and the standards ISO 4259 and ISO 5725 are frequently used. This illustrates the gap that exists between applied and theoretical statistics, where the theoreticians go to great lengths to establish tests corresponding to significance levels of exactly 5 or 1%. In practice we need criteria by which all parties concerned are willing to abide, the exact significance level being of very secondary importance.

To conclude it may also be useful to point out that establishing numerical values for the repeatability and reproducibility is an entirely different problem from that of the standardization (or validation) of a test method. In this last process the interaction between laboratories and the level of the test property is of interest. A pronounced interaction may indicate that further improvements of the test method are required, and may lead to a detailed investigation of the structure of the data, as described in many papers by John Mandel (Mandel, 1964; 1967). Once a test method has been standardized, its practical applications are usually concerned with some specific level of the test property, and interactions with different levels are no longer of interest.

REFERENCES

ISO (1978). *Petroleum Products — Determination and Application of Precision Data in Relation to Methods of Test*, ISO 4259. Geneva, Switzerland: International Organization for Standardization.

ISO (1981). *Precision of Test Methods — Determination of Repeatability and Reproducibility by Interlaboratory Tests*, ISO 5725. Geneva, Switzerland: International Organization for Standardization.

Mandel, J. (1964). *The Statistical Analysis of Experimental Data*. New York: Wiley.

Mandel, J. (1969). "A method for fitting empirical surfaces to physical or chemical data," *Technometrics*, **11**, 411-429.

Standard Methods for Testing Tar and Its Products, 6th edition. The Standardization of Tar Products Tests Committee.

Steiner, E. H. (1975). "Statistical analysis." In W. J. Youden and E. H. Steiner (Eds.), *Statistical Manual of the Association of Official Analytical Chemists*. Arlington, VA: Association of Official Analytical Chemists, pp. 72-83.

CHAPTER 6

Design, Modelling, and Analysis of Some Biological Data Sets[1]

Frank R. Hampel
ETH Zürich, Switzerland

Personal Preface and Dedication

When I heard about the plan to produce a book on data-analytic examples in honor of Cuthbert Daniel — sometime between his $(2^2)^2 \cdot 5$th and 3^{2^2}nd birthday — I was extremely pleased. I met Cuthbert for the first time in 1968 in Berkeley, where he had been invited by his friend Henry Scheffé to teach two courses, and I had the privilege of hearing 1½ of them. (It was unfortunate that what were for me the two most fascinating personalities in the department gave courses at the same time, but since I had decided that my future would lie more in data analysis than in probability theory, I switched fully to Cuthbert's courses.) His courses were a revelation for me: he did data analysis the way I had always dreamt of doing it. It was remarkable that there were four professors sitting in his lectures. I also remember the toast at the "High Tea" for the four guest professors of the Statistics Department that David Blackwell brought out to Cuthbert: "You are worth ten of us. Not because you are any better, but because you are different." Later, I met Cuthbert again in Princeton and noticed the great mutual respect and admiration between him and John Tukey. I also had the pleasure of enjoying the

---

[1] Work for this paper was done mainly at the University of Zürich, and partly also at Universities of Göttingen, California at Berkeley, and ETH Zürich.

warm hospitality of Cuthbert and his wife Janet at their home in Rhinebeck, and still recently, shortly before his 80th birthday, I could revel in his marvelous spirit and wit. I would be happy if, with this article, I could give him back, in deep gratitude, just a little bit of what he gave to me.

ABSTRACT

Eight examples of data sets from biology are analyzed in some depth.

CONTENTS

1.	Introduction	95
2.	Marriage Data: Several Layers of a Data Structure	95
3.	Sucking Rates of Young Fallow Deer (Cervus dama): Statistical and Social Interactions	101
4.	Grooming Rates of Monkeys: A Nonstandard Analysis of Variance With Incomplete Triangular Data	104
5.	Crowding Data: A 4 × 3 With Diagonal and Winsorized Variances	107
6.	Resting Periods of Migrating Birds: Modelling the Connection Between Observed and Actual Distribution	109
7.	Home Ranges of Mice: Traps of Systematic Errors	115
8.	Desperado Designs: The Utmost in Super-Saturated Designs	120
9.	Scale-Split Factorials: Measuring Curvature in Response Surface Exploration	123

References

1. INTRODUCTION

The following article treats several examples of data analysis which the writer came across in consulting and/or through his private interests, except for the first and last example, which were studied for teaching purposes. They discuss aspects of design, modelling and statistical analysis in reverse order. They are hoped to contain something of the spirit of Cuthbert Daniel, unforgettable for those who know him and which, by the others, can still be found in his books (Daniel and Wood 1971, Daniel 1976).

The data were analyzed as they came in. The idea was to do what was required by the data (and their scientific background), no less and no more. Doing no less implies that there was hardly any interesting data set in consulting which the writer could treat by mere routine methods; almost all contained some peculiarities which required some ad hoc methodological improvisation. The article hopes to show the spirit of such improvisations, by giving several examples. Doing no more implies, for example, that many approximations could be improved or generalized, but this was not deemed necessary for the particular data at hand (and not well feasible because of lack of time). The examples are all special in their ways, though some readers may find some germs of general "theories" or "methods" in some of them. Other readers (hopefully) may find everything obvious (as was remarked by N. Wermuth in a similar context, and as indeed should be so); but experience has taught the writer that not everything is obvious to everybody, even in simple data analysis. It is therefore hoped that every reader can pick out whatever is of the greatest interest to him or her, and that the examples are at least of some value for some readers.

2. MARRIAGE DATA: SEVERAL LAYERS OF A DATA STRUCTURE

The Data and the Design Structure

Our first example is taken from Pfanzagl (1968), where it serves to illustrate the χ^2-test in contingency tables. The data are the numbers of marriages in Vienna 1957 classified according to religion of bridegroom and religion of bride (Table 2.1). Four categories of religion are distinguished; since they are the same for rows and columns, we have a square contingency table with a natural diagonal. There is no natural *a priori* order (or even quantitative scale) among the rows and columns (however, we shall later mention some aposteriori orders, given the data). The data are a complete census for Vienna 1957; however, they may be regarded as a sample (not necessarily random) of one year for Vienna, or, for example, as a sample of one year and one Austrian or central European city. The observation units ("independent," under some models to be tested) are the bridal pairs, which makes sense if there were no mass weddings of certain faiths. The question to be analyzed is the structure of the (direct or indirect) preferences (if any) for the religion of the spouse.

The First Coarse Analysis

The first question we may ask is whether the couples marry without any (direct or indirect) regard to religion or, more precisely, whether we can speak of "random mating" with regarding to religion, given the total numbers of bridegrooms and brides in each of the four categories. When we carry out the χ^2-test of independence in Table 2.1, we obtain $\chi_9^2 = 3,168$*** which needs no comment (apart from a warning regarding the interpretation that the "effect" of religion could be entirely and is probably partly due to indirect causes, such as preferences of the same social circle, which itself may be correlated with religion).

A comparison of Table 2.1 with the expected values under independence (Table 2.2) reveals as a striking feature that the observed diagonal is much higher than the expected one, indicating a strong preference for the same religion of both partners. We could leave the analysis at that point. But we may also raise two new questions: Is there any interesting structure left in the off-diagonal numbers? And how can we measure and perhaps differentiate the strength of "self-preference" in the four diagonal values?

The Structure of the Off-Diagonal Elements

In order to assess the deviations from independence in individual cells, we may compute several other tables from the data, such as the table of the components of χ_9^2, the table of χ_1^2-values computed for the 2 × 2 tables consisting of each cell and the sums of the remainders in its row and column and in the remaining table (both showing significance, not size of deviations), the table of ratios of observed and expected values (namely of Tables 2.1 and 2.2), and the table of observed values divided by the values expected from the remaining data table if the respective observed values were missing. However, since we have discovered a strongly different behavior of the diagonal, we ought to take out all diagonal elements simultaneously and treat them (and the margins) as missing. We can imagine filling the diagonal with artificial values such that their χ^2-components are zero. Then we can compute the ordinary χ^2-statistic for independence with this artificial diagonal, but because of the four artificial zeros, we have to subtract four degrees of freedom. This was the obvious thing to do; as it turned out later, the method had already been published by Goodman (1968). The resulting expected

TABLE 2.1 Marriages in Vienna 1957 by religion of bridegroom and bride. Observed data.

	Bride				
Bridegroom	Catholic	Protestant	Other	None	Total
Catholic	9,919	693	97	293	11,002
Protestant	782	344	22	44	1,192
Other Religion	248	27	134	22	431
No Religion	812	108	31	197	1,148
Total	11,761	1,172	284	556	13,773

Source: *Statistisches Handbuch der Stadt Wien*. Jahrgang 1957, p. 30.

TABLE 2.2 Marriages in Vienna 1957. Expected values under independence.

	Bride			
Bridegroom	Catholic	Protestant	Other	None
Catholic	9,395	936	227	444
Protestant	1,018	101	25	48
Other Religion	368	37	9	17
No Religion	980	98	24	46

values are given in Table 2.3. The χ^2-test for quasi-independence (to use Goodman's terminology) of the off-diagonal elements yields $\chi_5^2 = 16.3**$, still significant on the 1%-level. Hence, even among religiously mixed marriages, there are still deviations from random pairing of religions, and we have to dig further.

The largest contribution to χ^2 comes from cell (4,3) with its 31 observed marriages. Treating it also as missing, in addition to the diagonal, yields an artificial value of 17.2 in (4,3), with very small changes for the other expected values, and a nonsignificant $\chi_4^2 = 8.4$. Hence there is a significantly too large number of bridegrooms without religion marrying brides with "other" religions, and in the remaining off-diagonal elements we cannot find any further significant structure.

Can't we? The χ_4^2-value, though nonsignificant, is about twice its expected value under quasi-independence, which may cause us to raise an eyebrow. But the main point is that so far we have neglected to check one important aspect of the data, namely their symmetry about the diagonal, or rather, what would be symmetry if the margins were equal.

How can we reasonably transform the data table to equal margins? If we just want to preserve "interactions" (deviations from the model of independence) defined by the cross-product ratios of all sets of four cells in two rows and two columns, we may multiply all rows and all columns by arbitrary constants, and thus achieve any prescribed margins, that is, we may use the technique of iterative proportional fitting described in Bishop et al. (1975), which has long been used in survey sampling (Deming and Stephan 1940, cf. also Mosteller 1968). If we also prescribe constant margins of 100, the result, rounded to integers, is Table 2.4. It is striking how close to symmetry this otherwise heterogeneous table is. In particular, there is no visible difference between cells (4,3) and (3,4). Going back to Tables 2.1 and 2.3, we notice roughly the same relative *size* of deviation, namely ratio of observed to expected number in both cells, of about 1.5, and only their *significance* is different because of the different margins and hence different absolute cell numbers.

Instead of *estimating* (visually) the degree of asymmetry under equal margins, we may also *test* for quasi-symmetry, for example, as described in Bishop et al. (1975). A more naive method (which may or may not be equivalent to this test and which was invented on the spot just to yield some quick crude indication of the statistical significance) gave a χ_3^2 of about 4. Even if the test came out significant, it is clear from Table 2.4 that we have quasi-symmetry in very good approximation.

Combining the evidence for (at least approximate) quasi-symmetry with the significance of cell (4,3), we thus come to the conclusion that both cells (4,3) and (3,4) deviate clearly and equally from an otherwise quasi-independent background of non-diagonal cells, indicating a certain preference between partners with "other" and without religion.

The Sizes of the Diagonal Elements

How can we reasonably measure the deviations of the four diagonal elements from independence? The simple idea of dividing the observations by the expectations under independence (yielding 1.06, 3.4, 14.9, 4.3) is misleading if, as in our case, the margins are extremely variable. It is easy to see that with our margins the first ratio can at most reach 1.17, leaving no Catholic bridegroom for any non-Catholic bride. It is more reasonable to treat each diagonal value in turn as missing, calculate the expectation for this situation (which

TABLE 2.3 The values expected under independence from the data without diagonal.

Bridegroom	Bride			
	Catholic	Protestant	Other	None
Catholic	4,785	678	113	296
Protestant	781	111	18.4	48
Other Religion	247	35	5.8	15.2
No Religion	817	116	19.2	50

TABLE 2.4 The data table standardized to have constant margins.

Bridegroom	Bride			
	Catholic	Protestant	Other	None
Catholic	51	22	7	19
Protestant	21	56	8	15
Other Religion	9	6	74	10
No Religion	18	15	10	56

can be done simply and in closed form: just collapse the table to the 2 × 2 table determined by the cell considered, rest of row, rest of column, and rest of table) and take the ratio of the observed value to this expectation. The values are 4.6, 5.8, 39.6, 7.1, and their (natural) logarithms (which are more natural for comparisons than the ratios themselves) are 1.5, 1.7, 3.7, 1.9. However, even if the observation studied is taken out, the other diagonal elements may still disturb the picture to some extent. Since in our case the off-diagonal table is practically quasi-independent (with the deviations in two rare cells having very little effect on estimation of other cells), we may contrast the diagonal with this background, that is, compute the expectations while treating the whole diagonal as missing, as done in Table 2.3. The ratios of observed to expected without diagonal are now 2.1, 3.1, 23.0, 3.9, and their logarithms are 0.7, 1.1, 3.1, 1.4. We see that the "self-preference" is very strong among "other" religions and is less strong and about evenly decreasing among those with no religion, Protestants, and Catholics. Next, and again about equally distant would come the mixed marriages "other" with no religion.

In passing, we note that the χ_1^2-values of each cell versus the remaining condensed 2 × 2-table, namely 990, 690, 1840, 550, (as well as the "standardized" $(\chi_1^2/n)^{1/2}$) again measure significance rather than size of the deviations; thus, the sequence of the "non-others" is reversed because of the differences in the marginals.

It is remarkable that the "self-preference" is stronger among Protestants than among Catholics. Apart from the fact that the "preferences" may be partly or even largely due to indirect reasons, such as same social circle or layer, this particular result is probably a diaspora effect. It could be interesting to compare the results with those for other central European cities, such as Zürich, where there are more Protestants than Catholics (and where indeed the "self-preference" among Protestants is much lower), but we shall terminate this analysis here.

Looking back, we realize that we discovered a second layer of the data structure (in cells (4,3) and (3,4)) only after taking away a first, dominant layer (the diagonal); and that even such a small table did contain enough structure so that we could "borrow strength" (to use Tukey's term) from quasi-symmetry for judging deviations from quasi-independence, and that we could do a number of numerical studies and comparisons. Some idiosyncrasies of extremely heterogeneous (and different) margins also showed themselves. There are suggestions for further numerical studies, such as the monotone relation between "self-preference" and sum of the two marginals, but such studies, as well as other techniques like scoring and correspondence analysis, are more interesting for larger data sets.

3. SUCKING RATES OF YOUNG FALLOW DEER (CERVUS DAMA): STATISTICAL AND SOCIAL INTERACTIONS

The Data Background

The following data were observed by Erwin Meier (1971) in the Tierpark (animal park) Langenberg near Zürich. He studied, among other things, the sucking (drinking) rates of four calves of fallow deer in dependence on age and time of the day. The data, including the length of observation for each time period, are given in Table 3.1. The sucking rates are the responses in a 4^3 design (3 factors at 4 levels each: one factor linearly ordered, one factor circular, one factor unordered). Originally only the averages over the four calves were presented; however, it proved more revealing to refrain from premature data lumping and to study the complete three-way structure.

The Analysis

We shall try to fit a main-effects model to the 4^3. For simplicity, we treat it as balanced, although the numbers have different accuracy, depending on the observation time (which we only shall use later qualitatively). Neither is it of high priority here to try out transformations.

The analysis of variance table (with pooling of all interactions) yields a very highly significant effect of time of day (with $F_{3,54} = 9.6$), a barely significant effect of age ($F_{3,54} = 2.8$) and no significant effect of individual ($F_{3,54} = 1.3$). The relative sequence of F-values is of course more meaningful than the absolute values, since one might argue against the pooling of all kinds of interactions into the mean squared error. But we shall now analyze the "interactions" in a different way.

It turns out to be very instructive to study the location of the largest absolute residuals from the least squares fit of a main effects model in the 4^3. There is a certain concentration at the first and last time of day and a very even spread over the animals, but the most striking feature is the concentration at the first age period. Four of the five largest and nine of the eleven largest absolute residuals (larger than about three and two median deviations, respectively) occur during the first age period, cf. Table 3.2. A closer look reveals that the other two larger residuals occur during periods with very short observation times, hence have a larger random error, while the first age period is very well observed.

(Note that we are not talking about outliers. Only one observation looks like a clear outlier at first glance, but the sizes of most large residuals are roughly what one would expect from the small ones. A more refined analysis would also take into account the correlations between the residuals, which would diminish the evidence for a special structure slightly, but we are just trying to find quickly the essentials of the data structure.)

TABLE 3.1 Sucking rates of fallow deer (number of events in 4h).

	Time of Day			
Age (Days)	20:00–08:00	08:00–12:00	12:00–16:00	16:00–20:00
Calf 1				
4– 20	0.50	0.94	1.51	2.77
21– 50	0.86	0.86	1.11	2.11
51– 80	0.56	0.77	0.64	1.33
81–120	1.60	1.25	0.95	1.28
Calf 2				
4– 20	2.10	1.43	1.88	0.62
21– 50	1.10	1.29	1.11	1.78
51– 80	0.87	0.60	0.76	1.60
81–120	0.53	0.83	1.33	1.92
Calf 3				
4– 20	0.40	1.86	1.70	0.97
21– 50	0.71	0.43	0.74	1.68
51– 80	0.61	0.80	0.40	1.60
81–120	0.80	0.74	0.48	1.37
Calf 4				
4– 20	1.28	1.25	1.19	1.28
21– 50	0.81	0.46	1.48	1.27
51– 80	1.08	0.51	0.88	1.67
81–120	0.35	0.70	0.72	2.43
Length of Observation in Hours and Minutes				
4– 20	71.20	46.50	78.50	70.40
21– 50	59.40	37.00	43.10	37.30
51– 80	72.15	47.45	41.30	15.30
81–120	19.30	57.50	60.00	27.30

We obtain a similar result if instead of least squares we use median polishing, as described in Tukey (1970/71). After several iterations, three of the four largest and nine of the twelve largest absolute residuals belong to the first age period.

This finding suggests leaving out the first age period and trying to fit a main effects model again. Using least squares, the mean squared error is now halved, and the F-values are $F_{2,39} = 1.8$ for age, $F_{3,39} = 23$ for time of day, and $F_{3,39} = 2.0$ for individual. Only time of day is significant, even very highly so (though the other F-values still leave room for guesses of slight differences); the mean square for time of day is even larger than for the full data set. The estimated effects show a clear preference of the last time of day for all four animals, while during the first age period we find preferences for the fourth, the first and third, and second and third time of day, and no preference at all.

When these findings were discussed with E. Meier, he was not at all surprised. He explained that during the first age period, the calves lived fairly hidden in different parts of the enclosure and had no social contacts with each other. Obviously, each one developed its own drinking habits. Starting with the second age period, they played with each other, and, importantly, they showed social stimulation with their sucking behavior: when one started drinking, the others also wanted to drink. In this way, they built up a common pattern of drinking habits; that is, the social interactions made the

TABLE 3.2 Location of largest (×) and second largest (•) absolute residuals.

Age (Days)	Time of Day			
	20:00–08:00	08:00–12:00	12:00–16:00	16:00–20:00
4 – 20	• × •	×	•	× × • •
21 – 50				
51 – 80				
81 – 120	•			×

statistical "interactions" (nonadditivities) disappear. It is quite possible that the preference for the last time of day is only a "random effect" of this group and would come out differently with a different group of animals; but to be sure about this, one would need additional data. The main point of this data set is that the location of the largest deviations from a main effects model provided the clue for a very simple interpretation, and for an even better fit of a main effects model for three quarters of the data.

4. GROOMING RATES OF MONKEYS: A NONSTANDARD ANALYSIS OF VARIANCE WITH INCOMPLETE TRIANGULAR DATA

The Design and Model

We shall now discuss an example about the social interaction of monkeys (hamadryas baboons, *Papio hamadryas*). This is one of the small earlier data sets in a much larger study by H. Kummer and coworkers (Hinderling 1976, see also Stammbach and Kummer 1982). The problem was to analyze the strength of interaction between two individuals who saw each other for the first time (later to be contrasted with the behavior among "familiar" animals and in larger groups). Was the behavior determined by the individual features of each monkey in a pair, or were there personal interactions

TABLE 4.1 Observed grooming rates Y_{ij} among pairs of baboons.

	Tk	Td	Ad	Sa	Wa	Wi
Tk						
Td	30.8					
Ad	23.0	71.7				
Sa	0.0	52.7	—			
Wa	0.0	—	14.3	—		
Wi	—	—	18.0	1.9	6.5	

(corresponding, for example, to "sympathy" or "friendship" among humans)? The data were the grooming rates (in some time scale) among pairs formed from six captive male baboons (identified here by the abbreviations of their names) put together in a cage for the first time. Since grooming can be mutual, the direction of the social interaction was not noted in this data set. For some technical reasons, not all of the $\binom{6}{2} = 15$ possible pairs were formed. The data can thus be described in form of a lower triangular matrix (without the diagonal of the 6^2 constructable from the six individuals) with some values missing (see Table 4.1).

When we try to model the data, we may add a contribution ("main effect") A_i and A_j from each individual and an interaction term R_{ij} between each two individuals. To make them unique, we make their averages equal to zero and take out a grand mean M. The error terms are clearly confounded with the interactions and blow them up to an unknown extent. We thus obtain the model $Y_{ij} = M + A_i + A_j + R_{ij}$ with $\Sigma A_i = \Sigma R_{ij} = 0$ and $\Sigma^{(k)} R_{ij} = 0$ for all k, where $\Sigma^{(k)}$ means the sum over those R_{ij} where $i = k$ or $j = k$. This model is a simple linear model with only zeros and ones in the design matrix, but it is not a customary analysis of variance model. An additional problem is the missing values. Clearly, we cannot identify the R_{ij} for the missing combinations, but fortunately we have enough redundancy to estimate all main effects, and we may estimate the missing values from a main effects model; that is, we may put those R_{ij} artificially equal to zero. This remark suggests a simple iterative way for estimating all effects: instead of making a complicated matrix inversion based on the actual design, we fill some arbitrary starting values into the gaps, estimate all parameters from simple averages (analogously to a one-way layout, using the balance of the completed design), refit the missing values, and iterate the last two steps until convergence.

The Results

The estimated grand mean and main effects $\hat{A}_i$ are: $\hat{M}$: 22.5; Tk: -16.0, Td: 33.1, Ad: 10.4, Sa: -6.0, Wa: -9.7, Wi: -11.9. The residuals $\hat{R}_{ij}$ from the main effects model are given in Table 4.2. The residual mean square is 73.1. The analysis of variance test of main effects against residuals yields an $F_{5,4} = 13.4$, which is very large and despite the low numbers of degrees of freedom, significant on the 5%-level

TABLE 4.2 Residuals $\hat{R}_{ij}$ from main effects model for grooming rates.

	Tk	Td	Ad	Sa	Wa	Wi
Tk						
Td	−8.8					
Ad	6.1	5.7				
Sa	−0.5	3.1	—			
Wa	3.2	—	−8.8	—		
Wi	—	—	−3.0	−2.7	5.6	

(and almost on the 1%-level). This result was quite surprising. It means that a main-effects model fits very well; that is, the actual grooming activity is essentially the sum of the grooming predilections of the two individuals, without regard to the partner. It was particularly surprising to find a significant result with only six individuals and only four degrees of freedom for error. On the other hand, it must also be noted that a very large contribution comes from a single individual, namely Td.

The example shows a way to try to analyze similar data about social interactions. If the main effects are so clearly dominant, we can also treat the individuals as independent data sources and use the jackknife for assessing the significance of more complicated statistics (e.g., the rank correlation between grooming rate and sum or difference between the social ranks of the two individuals) by leaving out one individual in turn. (The rank pairs in such a situation clearly cannot be considered as stemming from independent data, although in the psychological literature apparently these were sometimes treated as independent, presumably mainly because of lack of knowledge of another method.) On the other hand, we cannot always hope for such a clear main-effects model, and in fact under different social circumstances (other than first encounters) further experiments show the interactions ("personal relationships") usually clearly dominant over the main effects. Compare Stammbach and Kummer (1982) for a number of other experiments going beyond the simple and basic example discussed here.

5. CROWDING DATA: A 4 × 3 WITH DIAGONAL AND WINSORIZED VARIANCES

Background and Data

In the sixties, Berger (1964 and later work) discovered that the common green frog Rana esculenta of central Europe, in many school books the classical example of a frog species, is not a species but a hybrid between Rana ridibunda and Rana lessonae, which practically cannot propagate itself in isolation. However, in the area around Zurich Rana ridibunda is almost completely absent, and this situation gave rise to a number of different studies by local specialists, both in the field and laboratory, about the properties and relations between these three forms; see for example Blankenhorn et al. 1971. One such study (Heusser and Blankenhorn 1973) consisted of raising the larvae (tadpoles) of all three forms in water "polluted" by all three forms, as well as clean water for control, and watch their growth, in order to investigate whether the concentrated presence of another (or the same) form inhibited or stimulated the growth. The data we shall consider are the weights (averaged as discussed below) after some time period for larvae of each of the three forms under each of the four kinds of water. They are given in Table 5.1. (Again, the data form only a small part of much larger experiments.) We have the structure of a two-way layout; however, in addition we have a natural diagonal, namely a form living in water contaminated by the same form, even though the data matrix is not square. The corresponding question is: Does water from the same form, on the average, have a positive or negative effect on the growth, compared with water from different forms? This question can be answered with an F-test as easily as the classical one, namely, whether there are noticeable differences between the average effects of the four types of water.

TABLE 5.1 Growth of rana larvae in "crowded" water.

Water Polluted By	Larvae		
	Rid	Les	Esc
Ridibunda	2	3	8
Lessonae	3	5	9
Esculenta	2	2	8
Control	3	2 2/3	6 1/3

There was another complication. For each combination of water and animal form, 10 larvae were raised, however in some groups several larvae did not grow well and died before the end of the observational period, apparently for genetic causes. It would have been unfair against the other groups to use the simple arithmetic means of the weights of the survivors, since in the smaller groups presumably they would have included only the strongest and heaviest individuals of the original groups of ten. A way out was to use in *all* groups only the mean of the same number of heaviest tadpoles, that is, to use an asymmetrically trimmed mean. The lower trimming proportion was determined by the largest number of missing values in any cell (which was five). In addition, the largest value in each cell was trimmed off, just for safety in case it was an outlier. (It should be recalled that trimming is not the same as rejecting (cf. Hampel 1974) and causes hardly any efficiency loss; and even rejecting (cf. also Hampel 1985) is not the same as discarding a random selection of the data and thereby wasting an equal proportion of information.) The data in Table 5.1 are thus the means of the weights of the sixth smallest to ninth smallest tadpoles, putting the missing values (by death) equal to zero (or, e.g., $-\infty$). It is clear that the grand mean (and the absolute scale) have not much meaning, since they are affected by an unknown bias; however, we were only interested in the relative comparisons.

The Analysis

First, we can make the usual analysis of variance of the data in Table 5.1 and test the main effects against the interaction. The residuals from the main-effects model do not show any peculiarities, and (with somewhat rounded data) the test for effect of water yields $F_{3,6} = 2.8$ (nonsignificant), and the test for effect of animal form yields $F_{2,6} = 51***$. Almost all of the latter effect is due to the fast growth of the (eventually lethal) esculenta larvae. (This effect is not what we were looking for in the present context, but it turns out to be interesting from an ecological viewpoint, cf. Blankenhorn 1974.)

In order to test the diagonal, we can allow for an effect 2D in the diagonal and $-D$ outside the diagonal and the control water. In this way we can take out one degree of freedom orthogonal to the main effects, that is, from the residuals. The difference of the means of the diagonal values and the off-diagonal values (outside control water) estimates 3D, whence (with somewhat rounded data) $\hat{D} = 1/6$. The sum of squares of 2D and D over these cells equals 1/2, which is also the mean square for the test of the diagonal. The remaining sum of squares for residuals of about 3.5 (with only 5 d. f.) yields a new error mean square of 0.7; hence, the effect of the diagonal (with $F_{1,5} = 0.5/0.7$) is clearly nonsignificant.

What about testing the interactions? We do have replicates, though we have summarized them with a rather unfamiliar statistic. In order to get a *rough* indication for the variability of the asymmetrically trimmed mean, we may use a result for the variability of the *symmetrically* trimmed mean; namely, that it is estimated by the Winsorized variance of the sample. (Recall that Winsorizing means putting fixed numbers of extreme values onto the first unaffected value on the same side, respectively.) This result was first found empirically for small samples by Tukey and McLaughlin (1963), and later it was shown to hold also asymptotically (in a nonparametric sense) by Huber (1970). In our case, the more extreme values in each group of ten are replaced by the sixth smallest and second largest value, respectively, the squared deviations of this modified sample from the trimmed mean are added, and the sum is divided by $4 \cdot 3 = 12$ (or, perhaps, $10 \cdot 9 \cdot (4/10)^2 \approx 14$) to yield the (crudely) estimated variance of the trimmed mean (with roughly 48 d. f.). The ratio of interaction and error mean square is about 1.9, which is nonsignificant. This result is rather crude, and it could be that a more refined analysis would produce a weakly significant result, but there are certainly no strong interactions besides the random variability, so we can now terminate this analysis.

6. RESTING PERIODS OF MIGRATING BIRDS: MODELLING THE CONNECTION BETWEEN OBSERVED AND ACTUAL DISTRIBUTION

Quantitative Assessment of Bird Migration

How many ducks (or reed warblers) ("mDZ") pass through a certain lake during a migration season? What is the total sum of days all individuals spend there (the number of "bird-days"; for example, of interest for the food demand) ("IT")? What is the mean number of individuals (often the size of a flock) ("mBS") on a randomly selected day, given there are any birds (and what is the unconditional average number ("mIZ"))? What is the probability ("AH") of finding a certain species at a certain time of the year (and what is the somewhat to much higher probability that it is there)? What is the average resting period or lingering period ("Verweildauer") ("mVD") of a bird in a stopping place during migration?

All these quantities, as well as some others, are connected in simple ways (Hampel 1967). We have, within a suitable framework, $mIZ = mBS \times AH$, and $IT = mIZ \times L = mDZ \times mVD$, where L is the length of the migration season. Details are described in Hampel (1967). These formulas are so simple that they seem hardly worth a publication. One of their main virtues is that they allow a statistical extrapolation from the days (or areas) where excursions took place, to the days (or areas) where no excursion took place. Unfortunately, the idea of such an extrapolation, so natural for a statistician, seemed rather odd to many ornithologists, and in fact, frequently the days and areas without excursions were (at least implicitly) treated as if they had no birds at all. True, some ornithologists also made bold extrapolations, but as a rule these had to be merely qualitative since there was no usable quantitative data basis available. Often only the conditional numbers of birds, given that they are positive ("mBS") are available, although it would be easy to obtain also the unconditional numbers and the total "bird-days" by means of an "excursion card-file" or "excursion list" if such a list would exist.

(Some ornithologists have gone so far as to demand that an area has to be covered daily, otherwise the data are considered "unscientific" and worthless. It is true that daily data are simpler to evaluate, but instead of developing methods for data with gaps, as they arise without special effort by many good hobby ornithologists, these scientists are simply wasting a tremendous amount of information. Moreover, even if they reach permanent surveillance of a few places, they are never able to fill the gaps between such places, which for them are complete blanks. It seems absurd to circumvent the necessity for an excursion list or something equivalent by demanding daily excursions and dumping all other information, which is often the overwhelming majority of information, or even the only one available.)

In order to obtain also the total number of individuals during a migration season, one either has to mark all individuals (which is usually impossible), or one has to know something about the distribution of their length of stay, or resting period. Again, extrapolations will be needed. There are several possibilities for estimating the mean and the distribution of the lengths of stay, some of which are rather fallible. One of the most reliable methods uses recaptures of banded birds at the place and during the season considered. It turns out that the naive use of such data is misleading, and that there are interesting problems and results of stochastic modelling. This method will therefore be treated in some more detail.

The Relation Between True and Observed Distribution of Resting Periods

Let us consider a closed habitat, such as a reed area, and mist nets capturing the migrants in this area with a certain probability. They are then banded and thus marked individually. Some of them will be caught a second time before continuing their migration, while negligibly few are caught three or more times. Those caught exactly twice provide a distribution of observed (minimum) resting periods. How is this distribution related to the distribution of true resting periods?

On the one hand, the time difference between the two capture dates is never longer and often much shorter than the whole period of stay: in the simplest model, that of constant chance of being caught, it is on the average only one third of the actual length of stay, being equivalent to the distance between two points chosen randomly and independently according to the uniform distribution on some interval. On the other hand, the chance of a bird being caught exactly twice increases the longer it lingers (as long as its chance of being caught three times is still low); it increases even quadratically with the length of stay in the simplest model, namely that of a Poisson point process of capture dates with constant low intensity. Therefore, birds which stay longer are overrepresented in the data. The two effects work in opposite directions, and the outcome is not even qualitatively clear without a more detailed mathematical study.

We shall derive the connection between the two distributions for the simplest imaginable model; namely, that of a constant chance of the bird being caught in the next hour (or day) independently of what happened before, and a chance so low that certain higher order terms become negligible. We shall not make any assumptions about the distribution of the true resting periods t, except that it has a smooth density $h(t)$ vanishing at infinity. The time points of capture then form a Poisson process with rate λ, say; hence given t, the number of captures is Poisson distributed with parameter λt. We shall assume that λ is so low that even for the longest times occurring $\exp(-\lambda t) \approx 1$ (or $\lambda t \ll 1$). To this approximation the density of the true resting periods of the birds being caught exactly twice is $g(t) = t^2 h(t)/c$, with $c = \int t^2 h(t) dt$ (cf. the remark above). Given t, the distribution of the time span Δ between the two captures is known to have a triangular distribution with density $i(\Delta|t) = 2(t - \Delta)/t^2$; hence the joint distribution of t and Δ has density $f(t, \Delta) = g(t) \cdot i(\Delta|t) = 2(t - \Delta)h(t)/c$. From there we obtain the density of the observed time spans between the two captures

$j(\Delta) = \int_\Delta^\infty f(t, \Delta)dt$ or $\int_\Delta^\infty (t-\Delta)h(t)dt - cj(\Delta)/2 = 0$. This Volterra-type integral equation of the first kind can be solved for h by differentiation: $-\int_\Delta^\infty h(t)dt = cj'(\Delta)/2$ and finally

$$h(\Delta) = cj''(\Delta)/2,$$

with $c = 2(\int j''(\Delta)d\Delta)^{-1} = -2/j'(0)$.

Hence, we have to differentiate the empirical density of the observed time differences twice in order to obtain an estimate of the density of the actual times of stay! This task needs a large amount of data; it is facilitated by the observation that j has to be convex (from above) since h is also a density.

The first moment ET of the true durations of stay can be obtained with partial integration as

$$ET = \int_0^\infty th(t)dt = c\int_0^\infty tj''(t)dt = cj(0)/2 = -j(0)/j'(0).$$

This leads to certainly one of the more unusual estimates of an expectation. The corresponding estimate says: put the tangent at the estimated convex curve of j in zero and read off the expectation on the time axis. Similarly the variance Var T can be obtained as Var $T = c - (ET)^2 = -2/j'(0) - j^2(0)/j'^2(0)$.

The equation for the expectation (as well as the variance) has important consequences for the data collection. It says that the shortest time spans between captures (say, a few hours) are most relevant. Unfortunately, these short time spans, which theoretically carry all the information, often were not noted at all in the capture records, as being "uninteresting".

It is possible to incorporate the higher order terms which are needed for Poisson processes with higher intensity; but the formulas become more complicated. From $g(x) = h(x)x^2\exp(-\lambda x)/k$ we obtain $h(x) = (k/2)j''(x)\exp(\lambda x)$ with $k = \int h(x)x^2\exp(-\lambda x)dx$, and $ET = (k/2)(j(0) + \int j(x)(\lambda^2 x + 2\lambda)\exp(\lambda x)dx)$. These formulas are exact for Poisson processes with arbitrary intensity λ. They need, however, an estimate of λ in addition. As λ is typically small, they may serve often just to give an indication of the error committed by using the simplified first model.

Analysis of Some Recapture Data

Several data sets of the kind described in the previous subsection were kindly provided by E. Bezzel (1963a, 1963b, and especially in litt. 1965). They contain about 15 to 20 recaptures each of four species of Old World Warblers (Sylviidae), namely Sedge Warbler (Acrocephalus schoenobaenus), Blackcap (Sylvia atricapilla), Chiffchaff (Phylloscopus collybita), and Garden Warbler (Sylvia borin). Among them were ten triple and three quadruple captures. In total there were about 300 to 600 birds caught of each of the three larger species. These data were obtained in the course of several years near Munich. A summary of the observed periods between captures of the birds caught exactly twice is given in Table 6.1. A crude estimate for λET, obtained by equating the ratio of the numbers birds caught exactly once and twice, respectively, with the ratio of the corresponding terms of the Poisson distribution, yields values between about 0.05 and 0.1 for the three larger species (and two others which were otherwise too uncommon to be considered here). These values are decently small, though they would not be quite negligible for more refined calculations.

The (discretized) empirical distributions for j in Table 6.1 look all but convex. This is partly due to random effects (possibly enhanced by partial lack of independence), but partly probably to the negligence with recording "quick" recaptures. Some very long stays are remarkable. It is clear from the small sample sizes that we cannot determine h in a reasonable way. However, we may try to estimate ET in a crude way by fitting a convex curve (e.g., by eye) and putting a tangent to it. The results for all four species are about 4 to 5 days as estimated mean true resting times (somewhat undetermined for Blackcap, though). These values are probably biased upward, because of the systematic lack of small values in the sample. The estimated standard deviations of the true resting period distributions are of the same order of magnitude, though probably somewhat smaller (probably roughly between 2 and 4 days).

It is interesting to compare the above estimates of the true average resting periods with the results of the "naive" method of taking the arithmetic means of the observed times between captures. In two cases the biasing effects mentioned in the second paragraph on page 111 happen to cancel out, and we get virtually the same results. In the other two cases, however, the arithmetic means of the observed time spans are about twice to three times as large as the proper estimates (10 for Blackcap, 11.5 for Chiffchaff). Clearly, these high values are mainly caused by a few "long stays" which have a much larger chance of being caught twice than "ordinary" birds and therefore give a distorted picture if treated naively.

114 DESIGN, MODELLING, AND ANALYSIS OF SOME DATA SETS

TABLE 6.1 Periods between two captures in days.

Days	0	1	2	3	4	5	6	7	8	9	10	11	12	13	14	15	16	17	18	19	20	More
Acrocephalus schoenobaenus	–	4	4	2	3	1	1	1	–	1	1	–	1	–	–	–	–	–	–	–	–	–
Sylvia atricapilla	1	2	2	2	1	–	–	–	–	2	–	–	–	–	–	–	1	–	1	–	–	2(25,45)
Phylloscopus collybita	–	–	2	3	–	–	1	–	1	–	1	–	–	1	–	–	–	–	2	2	–	2(21,27)
Sylvia borin	–	2	5	4	1	2	1	–	1	4	–	–	–	–	–	–	1	–	–	–	–	
Total	1	8	13	11	5	3	3	1	2	7	2	–	1	1	–	–	2	–	3	2	–	4

In passing, it may be noted that one can also estimate the number of passing birds not caught at all, most simply (and crudely) by using the terms of the Poisson series. One may also try to estimate conditional means, given a certain minimum stay, or to incorporate the information from the threefold and fourfold captures. Another mathematical problem is the fitting of a "smooth" convex curve to data of this kind. So far, we have only considered the simplest stochastic model (partly with a further approximation in the derivation of the final formulas). It would be nice to incorporate further features such as varying chances for different birds of being caught, different intensity of catching, lack of independence of the birds due to flocking, weather, etc., nonconstant chances for a single bird due to its spatial pattern of moving around, and possibly to "net-shyness" or similar properties after being first caught, and so on. However, with data of the size given here — which were already hard to obtain — we are unlikely to be able to do much more than the simple and crude analysis given here.

7. HOME RANGES OF MICE: TRAPS OF SYSTEMATIC ERRORS

A Study of Altitudinal Distribution of Rodents

The author was confronted with the much-discussed problem of the statistical estimation of the sizes of home ranges (regions of regular activity) of rodents in the course of the statistical analysis of data obtained by Jürg Paul Müller (1972). The data are too numerous to be given here, but their analysis is published in the above reference, so we can restrict ourselves to a brief description of some interesting points.

The set-up in Müller's study was atypical for home range determinations, because the main purpose of the study was not home range or density estimation, but a relative comparison of the altitudinal distribution of the rodents in different habitats on a mountain slope in the Swiss Alps near Chur. Ordinarily, for home range estimation one sets up a square grid of (e.g., 10×10) life traps over some area, where the rodents are trapped alive and marked the first time, so they can be identified at later captures, and the distribution of the trapping localities (including multiple trappings at one locality) can then be studied. Müller instead used groups of three parallel rows of ten traps each (in distances of 10m within rows), one row within the forest, one row along the forest edge, and one row in the meadow. Thereby he also obtained information about the distribution of different species over different habitats. It turned out that the three most important forest species never went into the meadow, and two of them were very uniformly distributed over forest and forest edge, so that for purposes of home range determination one could essentially condense the data into a one-dimensional row of traps.

How can one extrapolate from the traps visited by a mouse to the range of its activity? Clearly, the more often a mouse is caught, the further apart tend to be its most distant trapping locations, so we should correct for the number of captures n. If we tentatively work with the simple model of a rectangular or uniform distribution of the locations of the mouse, with the trapping locations as randomly selected points within this range, the correction factor for the distance between the most distant trapping locations (in one dimension, as mentioned above) is $(n+1)/(n-1)$. However, this yields only an unbiased estimate of the length r of the part of the home range that overlaps with the row of traps. Obviously, the observed length r can never be larger than the length ℓ of the row of traps (or three times that value, after the above correction). If the true home range a is not small compared with the length of the trap field, we have to apply another correction. A simple (and crude) formula is $a = r/(\ell - r)$. For small r/ℓ, it gives the order of magnitude of the necessary correction, and for r/ℓ near 1 it shows that the trap field is far too small to allow a decently accurate estimation of the home range; all we can say is that the latter is probably much larger than the trap field. (In order to obtain areas, we can square the above lengths.)

With this methodology, we obtained home ranges of about 4400 m^2 for Clethrionomys glareolus and of about 14000 m^2 for Apodemus flavicollis. For Eliomys quercinus, the second correction factor is so large and undetermined that we can only say that its home range is much larger than the (squared) dimension of the trap field.

These numbers were much larger than the values in the literature at that time (by a factor 2 to 8 in the first case, by a factor 3 to 10 in the second case). How can these discrepancies be explained?

We have to consider the various statistical methods proposed for the determination of the home range (cf., e.g., Jennrich and Turner 1969 for a partial survey). As said before, the basic data are the trapping locations in a square (or similar) grid. One method consisted of connecting the outermost trapping locations by a polygon and using the area of that polygon. To this it was objected that the polygon is rather arbitrary and not uniquely defined, and it was proposed to use the smallest convex polygon containing all trapping points. Later it was observed that the general polygon method could be made unique by the restriction to polygons which are star-shaped with respect to the center of gravity. A proposed refinement of all these methods was the addition of a boundary strip around the polygon with width equal to half the minimum distance between two traps. Another group of methods used the mean (squared) radius of all the trapping locations to their center of gravity, with a circular bivariate normal distribution as model in the background, and with the arbitrary choice of, e.g., a 95% or a 99% home range. Since home ranges are often non-circular, the use of the covariance matrix of the capture points was proposed, with the general (elliptical) bivariate normal distribution as model. The trace of the covariance matrix leads to the length of way travelled by the mouse ("trace of the mouse"), while the determinant leads to the area visited. In order to avoid boundary effects, sometimes all mice caught at least once or twice in a certain boundary strip of the trap field were excluded from the further analysis; moreover, sometimes only mice caught a certain minimum number of times (such as 5 or 10 times) were considered, in an attempt to diminish the effect of the number of captures on the estimates of home range by some of the above methods.

There was much discussion of the relative merits and disadvantages of these methods. However, as soon as the size of the home range is comparable with or even surpasses the area of the trap field, all these methods suffer from a severe bias which is much bigger than the differences between the methods. In fact, some of the intended improvements even increase the bias by enhancing a selection effect towards mice with small home ranges. It is surprising that nobody seemed to have noticed that all larger home ranges were forcibly made to appear smaller than the trapping area (and be it by selection of those mice whose trapping localities randomly happened to be concentrated in a central subfield of the trapping area). Ironically, there existed already older data (before these systematic designs and evaluation methods became fashionable) indicating that some mouse species travelled over much larger distances than the diameter of a usual trap field; but these data had been obtained by irregularly putting some traps here and there (including some large distances); they were therefore considered as "unscientific" or "prescientific" and were simply ignored.

In fairness to the literature it should be added that one author at least noticed some hints pointing towards larger home ranges, and another author used an ingeniously simple method of reading tracks with the result of finding out that the values obtained by trapping methods were far too low (cf. Müller 1972 for this and other literature).

(Incidentally, it is possible to give a "canonical" choice for the percentile or contour of the normal distribution (such as 95% or 99%) which defines the "size" of the home range. We can simply use the uniform distribution with the same second moment(s). In the one-dimensional case, a normal with standard deviation σ corresponds to a uniform with half-width $3^{1/2}\sigma$, or a one-dimensional home range of about 3.5σ, covering almost 92% of the normal curve. In the two-dimensional case, the corresponding circular uniform has radius 2σ, containing about 86.5% of the circular normal. If for some reasons of simplicity we prefer a square uniform, the factor of σ is again $3^{1/2}$, which is not much different from 2, but leaves slightly more than 17% of the normal mass outside.)

Let us now briefly return to the study of altitudinal distribution. There were several other statistical aspects, one of them connected directly with the main purpose of the study. It was assumed that the number of captures of a species was a direct relative measure of the frequency of that species at the given altitude. However, apart from assumptions which were plausible and hard to check, there was also a danger of systematic errors by the statistical method used. Each life trap could catch only one animal, and then it was closed until the next trap control. In areas with many rodents, most would find many traps already filled and therefore had a lower chance of getting caught in the few remaining open traps. Therefore, high frequencies are underestimated and need a correction factor. If F is the total number of traps and B the number of traps occupied at the control, the average number of available traps between controls is not F but roughly $F-B/2$, and therefore a simple correction factor is $F/(F-B/2)$. Again, for small B/F it should be quite accurate (apart from sampling variation), and for B/F closer to 1 (say, larger than 1/2) it becomes inaccurate and essentially indicates that the true relative numbers are much higher than the observed captures. For Müller's data, the correction went up to about 15%, which is noticeable but did not require a more refined correction method. The potential problem of different activity periods for different species, which could change the correction factor between 1 and $F/(F-B)$, is also discussed in Müller (1972).

Home Ranges of an African Mouse

In the year 1972/73, Müller (1977) studied a population of Arvicanthis abyssinicus in the grasslands of the Semien Mountains National Park (Ethiopia). A large part of the data were recapture data of marked individuals from a regular network of traps. The analysis of these extensive and highly structured data, which was done by Müller and the author jointly with J.-D. Tacier, was a rewarding experience for a statistician. Both the spatial and the time structure of the recaptures were analyzed, under different aspects and with different methods. One of the pleasant surprises was the discovery of families and the social structure by purely statistical means, namely with an (informal) cluster analysis of the centers of the home ranges together with the analysis of their sizes. Also the mortality was studied. There were results, for example, on the probability of capture for the mice, on the spatial distribution of the places of capture and on the distribution of the number of captures in the traps. Also the number of mice never caught at all could be estimated (using, inter alia, mixtures of binomials).

Let us now only consider briefly the estimation of the home range, which forms also an important basis for the estimation of the density and biomass of the mice. The basic trap field was a regular grid with 10 × 10 traps. To use many more traps was not feasible. On the other hand, it was feared that the trapping area was too small to yield accurate estimates of the home ranges, and therefore several times all traps were moved to cover first one half and then the other half of a fringe around the inner square to form altogether an 18 × 18 square. In addition, there were some more qualitative controls even further out from the inner square.

The estimation of the home ranges was done in three steps: first the "naive" home range based only on the inner square was computed, using the root determinant of the covariance matrix of the capture places; then all data of the full square were used; and then the results were extrapolated to take into account that some home ranges (especially those with apparent centers near the edge of the trapping area) overlap only partly with the trapping area. For this purpose, a regression was made of the apparent size of the home range on the apparent location of the center, and the result was compared with the curves for various true home range sizes.

It turned out that both the temporary extension of the inner trap field and the extrapolation were important. For example, the linear dimension of the home range (in trap distance units) during June to

September for others than adult males was about 5.3 from the inner square, 7.0 from the large square, and 8.3 extrapolated. For adult males, the numbers are 6.4 from the inner square, 10.5 from the large square, and roughly 14 (already somewhat shaky) from the extrapolation. The corresponding areas differ by a factor of more than 4 in the last case. For more details see Müller (1977).

8. DESPERADO DESIGNS: THE UTMOST IN SUPER-SATURATED DESIGNS

Introduction To Desperado Designs

During a study in the early seventies of the possible reasons for the somewhat mysterious decline of the number of hares in large parts of Switzerland (cf. also Pfister 1984), H. Pfister tenaciously insisted on testing many more factors than he had observations (be it in an analysis of variance or a contingency table), since there were so many possible causes to be tested, although he was told that with, say, eight observations there were only eight degrees of freedom, at most enough for one grand mean and seven main effects (if one assumed no interactions). Finally, it dawned on the writer that it is indeed possible to test more factors than one has observations, namely if one makes some additional strong assumptions. The strongest assumption one can make is that there is only *one* clear main effect, and all other main effects, interactions, and random errors are practically zero, so that even their sums are small compared with the dominating main effect. Then n observations are sufficient to search for the one dominating main effect among $2^{n-1} - 1$ potential effects. For example, eight observations are enough to test 127 factors on two levels each in this way. This could be helpful in screening experiments with a large number of factors and one suspected dominating cause (e.g., in quality control). However, already a second main effect could completely spoil the interpretation. Since these designs are a measure of despair, they are called desperado designs.

The construction is simple. One considers all nontrivial splits of the n planned runs (decompositions into two nonempty sets) and identifies each split with the two levels of a factor. This fixes the experimental conditions. Since there are $2^n - 2$ proper nonempty subsets of n points, and each one and its complement forms a split, we have $2^{n-1} - 1$ different splits. If the basic assumption is true, the responses fall into two groups which uniquely identify the split and hence the dominating factor.

To give some numbers: with 2, 3, 4, 5 runs we can investigate 1, 3, 7, 15 factors, with 12 runs already 2047 factors. In a way, the desperado designs are the counterpart to complete factorial designs. The naive scientist who thinks that with eight runs he can estimate seven effects, will be surprised when the statistician tells him that he can estimate only $\log_2 8 = 3$ effects because there are also many interactions. The statistician may comfort him that if he "assumes away" the interactions, he may again estimate his seven main effects. But then he may also "assume away" all main effects except one, and pick and estimate that one out of 127.

The analogy goes further. Experience often shows that all higher order interactions are practically zero, and only some low order interactions may stick out. This is the empirical justification for a certain confounding and fractional factorials. Experience also shows that (especially in pilot studies) often most main effects are zero, and only a few are large, except we do not know beforehand which ones. This suggests study of designs which are intermediate between desperado designs and fully saturated designs, in the sense that a certain fixed number (between 1 and $n-1$) of main effects can be safely identified if all other effects are equal to zero. Some preliminary thoughts about such designs are given in the sequel.

Some Aspects of Super-Saturated Designs

The paradigm we are considering now, in its mathematical idealization (to be approximated by reality), is the following: We put many factors, each at two levels, on n experimental runs by identifying each factor with a certain split of the runs (to be selected informatively), and we assume that only one or a few (or not all) of the factors have main effects different from zero, all other main effects, all interactions and random errors being exactly zero. Then we observe our responses, which under our assumption take on only a few different values (with k nonzero factors at most 2^k different values, possibly fewer). These values possess a certain pattern, namely that of the (complete or incomplete) set of responses of a main-effects model with k factors, except that we do not know the design. It is our task to deduce from these numbers to which levels of which factors they belong, and thereby identify the relevant splits and their factors (as well as estimate the effects of the factors). It is remarkable that this task is the same as that (in a more realistic setting) of the sequence of estimators beyond the "shortdth" first defined in Hampel (1975) (cf. also Hampel et al., 1986, p. 431). The task is possible for k factors when we have 2^k different responses. It is an open question how many different responses we actually need.

For example, with two nonzero factors we can obtain 2, 3 or 4 different responses, for the following reasons. The number of responses is diminished below 2^k either when two effects are equal (or, more generally, when an algebraic sum of the effects is zero), or when the intersection of two sets from different splits (or, in general, an intersection of k sets, each from a different split) is empty. With two nonzero factors, we get at least three different responses (under the four possible combinations of levels, which may not all occur in the design) and at least three nonempty intersections of sets from different splits, that is, occurring treatment combinations; hence, we obtain at least two different observed responses. Now, even with three responses, we cannot identify the splits anymore; all we know is a warning that we have at least two nonzero factors, but we do not know which ones. In order to identify two factors, we therefore need four different responses. It is presently not clear whether for three factors we can get along with fewer than eight different responses.

We cannot avoid being unlucky with the sizes of the effects, so that some combinations of effects are zero ("mean effects"); but we can avoid having empty intersections of sets from different splits and hence missing treatment combinations. This is a design problem.

For example, one way of ensuring that each two sets from different splits have a nonempty intersection is for even n to consider only the splits into $n/2$ points each. (For odd n, we may identify two points.) This yields $\binom{n}{n/2}/2$ splits or factors which can be incorporated so that the dominant two factors can be picked out (unless their absolute effects are equal). (Note that such a design may also make their interaction estimable if it is small compared with the main effects.)

It is also clear that we need at least 2^k runs if we want all treatment combinations of k factors. This demand increases quickly with k and makes the question whether and when incomplete designs are sufficient more urgent. We note that (for $k \geq 2$) we can incorporate a $(k + 1)$st factor into the 2^k (by alternating levels along edges) so that each k of them possess all level combinations.

There appear to be many research questions connected with the construction and properties of such and similar supersaturated designs. They all lead up to the question: how much, and what kind of information can we extract from n data points (within the framework of prior knowledge and under auxiliary assumptions)? An additional side issue can be efficiency; for example, we may demand that all intersections of 2 or of k sets from different splits contain at least m points for some $m \geqslant 2$. This property can also be useful from the robustness point of view (especially for $m \geqslant 3$); robustness considerations are clearly also important.

It is surprising that there seems to exist hardly any literature on a systematic treatment of super-saturated designs, with the partial exception of random balance designs, and this despite, for example, the statement by Box (in the discussion of Satterthwaite 1959) that "the only thing wrong with random balance is random balance." Perhaps staking the claims up to desperado designs has helped clarifying the scope and the prerequisites of such designs.

9. SCALE-SPLIT FACTORIALS: MEASURING CURVATURE IN RESPONSE SURFACE EXPLORATION

The Reconsideration of a Published Example

The following considerations were inspired from a reanalysis of Example P in Cox and Snell (1981). The data are an unbalanced and highly incomplete factorial on the yield of bacteria under different compositions of a nutritive medium. There were ten factors on two levels each, but only 16 runs. Only two factors and their interaction were dominant, though some other factors were also significant (compared with an independent estimate of error). These data are an excerpt from Fedorov et al. (1968), who make a response surface exploration trying to optimize the yield. While retracing the path of the response surface exploration, the present writer was disappointed that, with so many points in the factorials and only two dominant factors, still there was no information on their interaction, that is, the curvature above their plane. All points collapsed just to a square in that plane. It would have been much more helpful if they had collapsed into two concentric squares, for example.

This suggested the idea of splitting a factorial and running its halves on two different scales. The natural, simplest and most informative halves are fractional factorials, of course. In this way, one can do the standard analysis for each half and then only has to combine the results with different weights. The price is a loss of efficiency, but the gain is that more terms become estimable and confounding patterns are broken. If the random error is small compared with curvature, efficiency is of minor importance anyway; and this situation may often be reached by enlarging the design, which can be done because curvature is to some extent under control.

DESIGN, MODELLING, AND ANALYSIS OF SOME DATA SETS

Another aspect is that two half-replicates on different scales can fill the design space more evenly than a single factorial, even than a single factorial with center point; and there is no additional point needed. We shall exemplify these statements now by studying the 2^3 in more detail.

Scale-Splitting the 2^3

Let us assume we have three quantitative factors in the design space, and instead of running an ordinary 2^3, we blow up the 2^{3-1} containing (1) by a factor 2. The expansion of the response function is

$$y = M + Ax_1 + Bx_2 + Cx_3 + A_2x_1^2 + B_2x_2^2 + C_2x_3^2 + ABx_1x_2$$
$$+ ACx_1x_3 + BCx_2x_3 + ABCx_1x_2x_3 + \cdots$$

where the x_i are ± 1 or ± 2. Define $Q = A_2 + B_2 + C_2$. Note that we should be interested in Q, as a second order term (and if possible even in its components), while the usual 2^3 only gives us the third-order term ABC. By the scale split we obtain

$$(1) = M - 2A - 2B - 2C + 4AB + 4AC + 4BC + 4Q - 8ABC ,$$

$$bc = M - 2A + 2B + 2C - 4AB - 4AC + 4BC + 4Q - 8ABC , \text{ etc.,}$$

while

$$a = M + A - B - C - AB - AC + BC + Q + ABC , \text{ etc.,}$$

as before the scale split. Note that we have left ABC in to facilitate comparison with classical evaluation; from a logical viewpoint it should be dropped. From the inner 2^{3-1} we obtain the estimates

$$\hat{M}^{(1)} = (a + abc + b + c)/4 = M + Q + ABC ,$$

$$\hat{A}^{(1)} = (a + abc - b - c)/4 = A + BC , \text{ etc.,}$$

from the outer 2^{3-1} we obtain

$$\hat{M}^{(2)} = M + 4Q - 8ABC , \quad \hat{A}^{(2)} = A - 2BC , \text{ etc.}$$

We now can combine the corresponding estimates in order to break the confounding patterns (except for ABC).

Thus,

$$\hat{\hat{M}} = (4\hat{M}^{(1)} - \hat{M}^{(2)})/3 = M - 4ABC, \hat{\hat{A}} = (2\hat{A}^{(1)} + \hat{A}^{(2)})/3 = A, \text{ etc.,}$$

$$\hat{\hat{BC}} = (\hat{A}^{(1)} - \hat{A}^{(2)})/3 = BC, \text{ etc., } \hat{\hat{Q}} = (\hat{M}^{(2)} - \hat{M}^{(1)})/3 = Q - 3ABC.$$

If we postulate independent random errors with variance 1 for all observations, then Var $\hat{\hat{M}}$ = 17/36, Var $\hat{\hat{A}}$ = 17/144, Var $\hat{\hat{BC}}$ = 5/144, Var $\hat{\hat{Q}}$ = 1/18. From these variances we can also compute efficiencies relative to the classical procedure, but it is not clear what scale the comparison 2^3 should have: 2? 3/2? 1? The efficiencies of the estimate for A in this sequence are 9/34, 8/17, 18/17, and those for BC are 9/40, 32/45, 18/5, while those for M are always 9/34 and those for Q clearly infinite. Perhaps the 8/17 for a main effect, compared with an intermediate classical design, can be picked out. But if we can assume there are only linear (and constant) terms, without interactions, we can find more efficient estimates: $\hat{\hat{A}} = (4\hat{A}^{(2)} + \hat{A}^{(1)})/5$ etc., with Var $\hat{\hat{A}}$ = 1/20 and relative efficiencies 5/8, 10/9, 5/2, and $\hat{\hat{M}} = (\hat{M}^{(1)} + \hat{M}^{(2)})/2$, with Var $\hat{\hat{M}}$ = 1/8 and efficiencies clearly equal to 1. (Note: The results for other main effects and interactions are naturally obtained by exchanging letters.)

What can we do with these results? We have Q as a global check on curvature. But the main advantage comes when only one main effect, say A, is large (or, in a bigger design, a few main effects). For then most likely $Q \approx A_2$. We can then even project the design onto the x_1-axis and fit a cubic polynomial in x_1, with 4 d.f. left for error. The tentative assumption is of course that factors with large main effects have relatively large interactions, while those with small main effects have negligible interactions and may be entirely uneffective. The data are ambiguous, to be sure; but some interpretations make more sense than others.

If only the A and B main effects are big, we may fit a second degree polynomial on the two lines $x_1^2 = x_2^2$, with 3 d.f. left for error, but clearly the ambiguity is larger. Yet, if we project the design into the x_1-x_2-plane, we obtain eight different design points instead of only four from an ordinary 2^3, hence a much more detailed picture of the response surface.

There is another aspect under which we can consider the scale-split factorials, namely: how densely or evenly is a cube filled by a design? We may ask for the largest distance of any point in a cube, say $|x_i| \leqslant 2$ ($i = 1, 2, 3$), from the nearest design point. Again it is not clear which 2^3 to compare with the scale-split design, and the results are somewhat reciprocal to those for efficiency. If we start with the 2^3 on $|x_i| = 2$, the largest distance is $2 \cdot 3^{1/2} = 3.46$, and even if we add a center point, it is still $5^{1/2} = 2.24$ (if these and the following computations are correct). However, if instead of adding one point, we put a half-replicate on the smaller cube $|x_i| = 1$, the largest distance of any point is only $(121/32)^{1/2} = 1.94$. We may now ask for the minimum of the largest distance if we vary the scale of the inner half-replicate; according to some unchecked calculations, this seems to be $(121/36)^{1/2} = 1.83$, hence hardly smaller. Overall, we have a reasonably dense packing with a simple design which retains almost all the simplicity, beauty, and elegance of ordinary factorial designs.

Some Additional Remarks

Which scales should be chosen for the scale-split design? While ordinary factorials try to avoid the curvature occurring on a larger scale, the scale-split designs can be enlarged until curvature becomes noticeable, since it can be better estimated. In this way also the efficiency is increased. Another question is the choice of the relative scale for the two half-replicates. It seems that for the 2^3 the factor 2 is a numerically simple and also very reasonable choice, but it may well be that for other 2^k designs the factor should tend to 1 as k increases (because of the "curse of dimension"). Still another question is whether one should also consider splits on 4 or 8 different scales, etc. It seems presently that the simple splits into two parts are the most useful ones, but there may well be occasions where multiple scale splits are called for.

It may be noticed that scale-split factorials may be regarded as highly incomplete 4^k-designs (with unequal spacing) or also as 5^k-designs (with equal spacing, if the factor 2 is used). But they contain very special patterns, and the description as a combination of two 2^k-designs appears to be simpler.

Another point is the relation to second-order designs. These latter designs need more points, but on the other hand they are able to and meant to estimate a full second order equation if all factors are effective. The scale-split designs may also be able to estimate full second order equations (and even third order equations) if some factors have dropped out. But their main purpose is to replace first-order designs and provide a better coverage of the design space with the same experimental effort, the same technology of statistical evaluation and just a minimally increased effort of evaluation.

REFERENCES

Berger, L. (1964). "Is Rana esculenta lessonae Camerano a distinct species?" *Annales Zoologici Warszawa*, 22, 45-61.

Bezzel, E. (1963a). "Der Durchzug des Schilfrohrsängers (Acrocephalus schoenobaenus) bei München nach Fangergebnissen," *Anz. orn. Ges. Bayern*, 6, 459-462.

Bezzel, E. (1963b). "Zum Durchzug und zur Brutbiologie von Grasmücken (Sylvia) nach Fängen und Ringfunden im Ismaninger Teichgebiet, Oberbayern," *Die Vogelwarte*, 22, Heft 1, 30-35.

Bishop, Y. M. M., Fienberg, S. E., and Holland, P. W. (1975). *Discrete Multivariate Analysis: Theory and Practice*. Cambridge, MA: The MIT Press.

Blankenhorn, H. (1974). "Soziale Organisation einer Mischopopulation von Rana Lessonae Camerano und Rana esculenta Linnaeus." Ph.D. Thesis, University of Zürich, Switzerland.

Blankenhorn, H., Heusser, H., and Vogel, P. (1971). "Drei Phänotypen von Grünfröschen aus dem Rana esculenta - Komplex in der Schweiz," *Revue Suisse De Zoologie*, 78, 1242-1247.

Cox, D. R. and Snell, E. J. (1981). *Applied Statistics: Principles and Examples*. London and New York: Chapman and Hall.

Daniel, C. (1976). *Applications of Statistics to Industrial Experimentation*. New York: Wiley.

Daniel, C. and Wood, F. S. (1980). *Fitting Equations to Data*, 2nd edition. New York: Wiley.

Deming, W. E. and Stephan, F. F. (1940). "On a least squares adjustment of a sampled frequency table when the expected marginal totals are known," *Annals of Mathematical Statistics*, 11, 427-444.

Fedorov, V. D., Maximov, V. N., and Bogorov, V. G. (1968). "Experimental development of nutritive media for micro-organisms," *Biometrika*, 55, 43-51.

Goodman, L. A. (1968). "The analysis of cross-classified data: independence, quasi-independence, and interactions in contingency tables with or without missing entries," *Journal of the American Statistical Association*, 63, 1091-1131.

Hampel, F. (1967). "Ein statistisches Modell zur quantitativen Erfassung des Durchzuges." Unpublished manuscript.

Hampel, F. (1974). "The influence curve and its role in robust estimation," *Journal of the American Statistical Association*, 69, 383-393.

Hampel, F. (1975). "Beyond location parameters: Robust concepts and methods (with discussion)." In *Proceedings of the 40th Session of the ISI*, Vol. 46, Book 1. Warsaw, Poland: Central Statistical Office, pp. 375-391.

Hampel, F. (1985). "The breakdown points of the mean combined with some rejection rules," *Technometrics*, 27, 95-107.

Hampel, F. R., Ronchetti, E. M., Rousseeuw, P. J., Stahel, W. A. (1985). *Robust Statistics: The Approach Based on Influence Functions*. New York: Wiley.

Heusser, H. and Blankenhorn, H. (1973). "Crowding-Experimente mit Kaulquappen aus homo- und heterotypischen Kreuzungen der Phänotypen esculenta, lessonae und ridibunda (Rana esculenta-Komplex, Anura, Amphibia)," *Revue Suisse De Zoologie*, 80, 543-569.

Hinderling, R. (1976). "Die Entwicklung von Zweierbeziehungen bei Mantelpavianen." Diplomarbeit, Zoologie Institut der University Zürich.

Huber, P. J. (1970). "Studentizing robust estimates." In M. L. Puri (Ed.), *Nonparametric Techniques in Statistical Inference*. Cambridge, England: Cambridge University Press, pp. 453-463.

Jennrich, R. I. and Turner, F. B. (1969). "Measurement of non-circular home range," *Journal of Theoretical Biology*, **22**, 227-237.

Meier, E. (1971). "Beiträge zur Geburt, zur Mutter-Kind-Beziehung und zum Jugendverhalten von Cervus dama L." Diplomarbeit, Zoologie Institut der University Zürich.

Mosteller, F. (1968). "Association and estimation in contingency tables," *Journal of the American Statistical Association*, **63**, 1-28.

Müller, J. P. (1972). "Die Verteilung der Kleinsäuger auf die Lebensräume an einem Nordhang im Churer Rheintal," *Z. f. Säugetierkunde*, **37**, 257-286.

Müller, J. P. (1977). "Populationsökologie von Arvicanthis abyssinicus in der Grassteppe des Semien Mountains National Park (Aethiopien)," *Z. f. Säugetierkunde*, **42**, 145-172.

Pfanzagl, J. (1968). *Allgemeine Methodenlehre der Statistik, Band II*. Berlin: De Gruyter.

Pfister, H. (1984). "Raum-zeitliche Verteilungsmuster von Feldhasen (Lepus europaeus Pallas) in einem Ackerbaugebiet des schweizerischen Mittellandes." Ph.D. Thesis, University of Zürich, Switzerland.

Satterthwaite, F. E. (1959). "Random balance experimentation," *Technometrics*, **1**, 111-137. Discussion, 157-193.

Stammbach, E. and Kummer, H. (1982). "Individual contributions to a dyadic interaction: An analysis of baboon grooming," *Animal Behavior*, **30** 964-971.

Tukey, J. W. (1970/71). *Exploratory Data Analysis*. (Preliminary edition.) Reading, MA: Addison-Wesley.

Tukey, J. W. and McLaughlin, D. H. (1963). "Less vulnerable confidence and significance procedures for location based on a single sample: Trimming/Winsorization I.," *Sankhyā*, **A25**, 331-352.

CHAPTER 7

Analytical Representation of Dielectric Constants: A Complex Multiresponse Problem

Stephen Havriliak, Jr.
Rohm and Haas Company

Donald G. Watts
Queen's University, Canada

ABSTRACT

The parameters in the expression proposed by Havriliak and Negami to represent the complex dielectric constant behavior of polymers with frequency were determined for polycarbonate and syndiotactic poly(methylmethacrylate) using multiresponse estimation techniques. The parameter estimates for polycarbonate are in good agreement with those obtained using graphical methods, but the estimates for syndiotactic poly(methyl methacrylate) are quite different from the graphical estimates. In both cases the residuals are not well-behaved, and mechanisms are proposed to account for their behavior. Confidence limits for the real and imaginary components are estimated and found to be similar in size to the manufacturer's statements of equipment accuracy.

Key words and phrases: multiresponse estimation; dielectric constants; complex plane plots; Cole-Cole plots.

130 ANALYTICAL REPRESENTATION OF DIELECTRIC CONSTANTS

1. INTRODUCTION

Detailed understanding of the complex dielectric constant can provide valuable insights into the structure-property relationships of polymers. To gain such understanding, the complex dielectric constant should be measured over a wide range of frequencies and temperatures, and the data should be represented by one of the analytical expressions which have been developed for such phenomena. The parameters can then be interpreted in terms of one of the several molecular models which exist.

Physically, a disk of the polymer is inserted between the two metal electrodes of a dielectric cell which forms one arm of a four-armed electrical bridge. The bridge is powered by an oscillating voltage whose frequency (f, in Hertz) can be changed over a wide range (say 5 to 500,000 Hz). Bridge balance can be achieved with and without the polymer in place by substitution or by direct methods using capacitance and conductance standards. The complex dielectric constant is then calculated, using changes from the standards relative to the cell dielectric constant. Measurements are made by simultaneously adjusting the capacitance (real) and the conductance (imaginary or loss) arms of the bridge when it is excited at a specific frequency and temperature. The complex dielectric constant is written $\epsilon^* = \epsilon' + i\epsilon''$, where $i = \sqrt{-1}$, and $'$ denotes the real component and $''$ the loss component.

As recommended in Cole and Cole (1941), complex dielectric constants at a constant temperature should be plotted in the complex plane. We do this in Figures 1 and 2, where we plot the imaginary or loss component of the complex dielectric constant, y_{imag}, versus the real component of the dielectric constant, y_{real}, for polycarbonate at 164 °C, and syndiotactic poly(methylmethacrylate), (s-PMMA) at 86.7 °C. The data are listed in Appendix 1.

For some polar liquids, the locus of the data in a complex plane plot is a semicircle (provided the axis scales are equal) with theoretical representation

$$\epsilon^* = \epsilon' + i\epsilon'' = \epsilon_\infty + (\epsilon_0 - \epsilon_\infty)/(1 + (i2\pi f/f_0)). \qquad (1.1)$$

In (1.1), the parameter ϵ_0 is the equilibrium dielectric constant obtained as $f \to 0$, ϵ_∞ is the instantaneous dielectric constant obtained as $f \to \infty$, and f_0 is the critical, or relaxation, frequency. For other polar liquids, Cole and Cole, 1941, found empirically that the complex plane plot could be better represented as

$$\epsilon^* = = \epsilon_\infty + (\epsilon_0 - \epsilon_\infty)/(1 + (i2\pi f/f_0)^\alpha). \qquad (1.2)$$

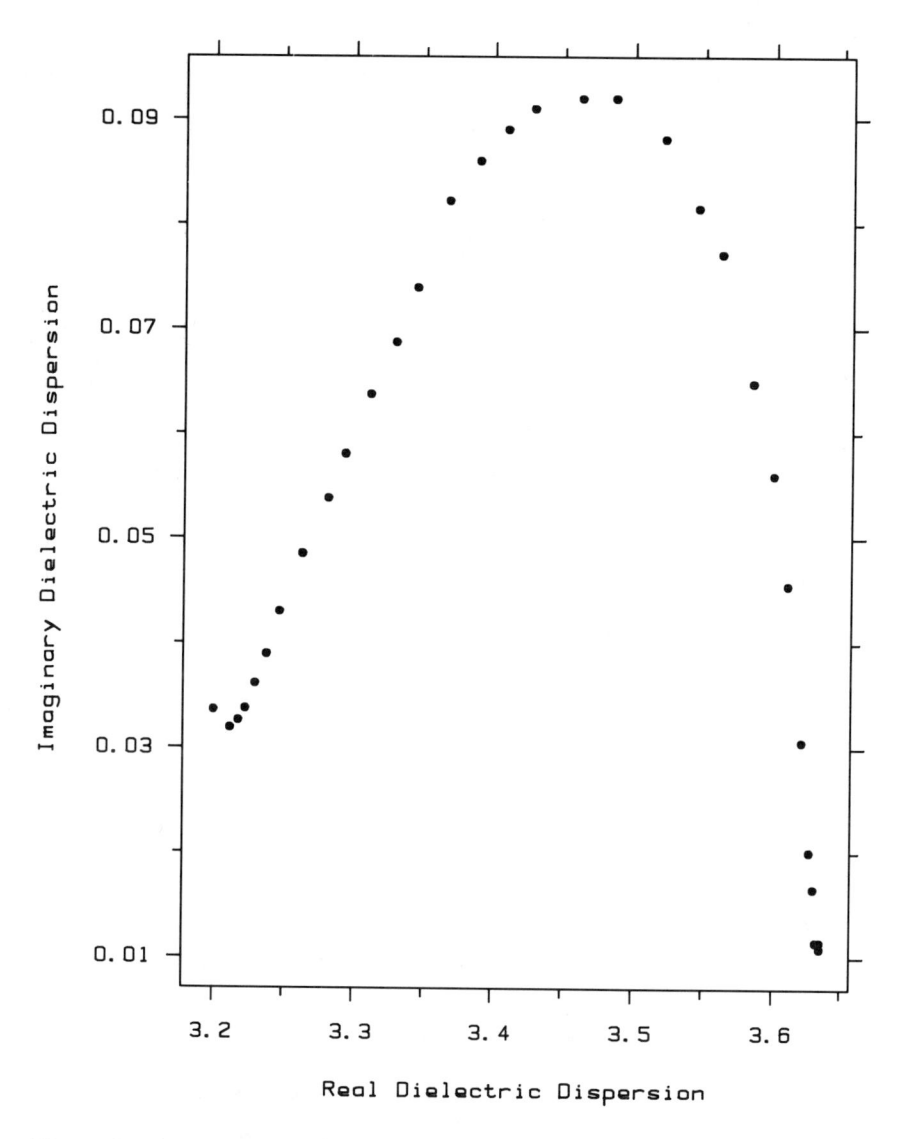

Figure 1. A complex plane plot for polycarbonate at 163.9° C is given here. In this plot the imaginary part is plotted against the real part of the complex dielectric constant. Each point represents a measurement at a specific frequency.

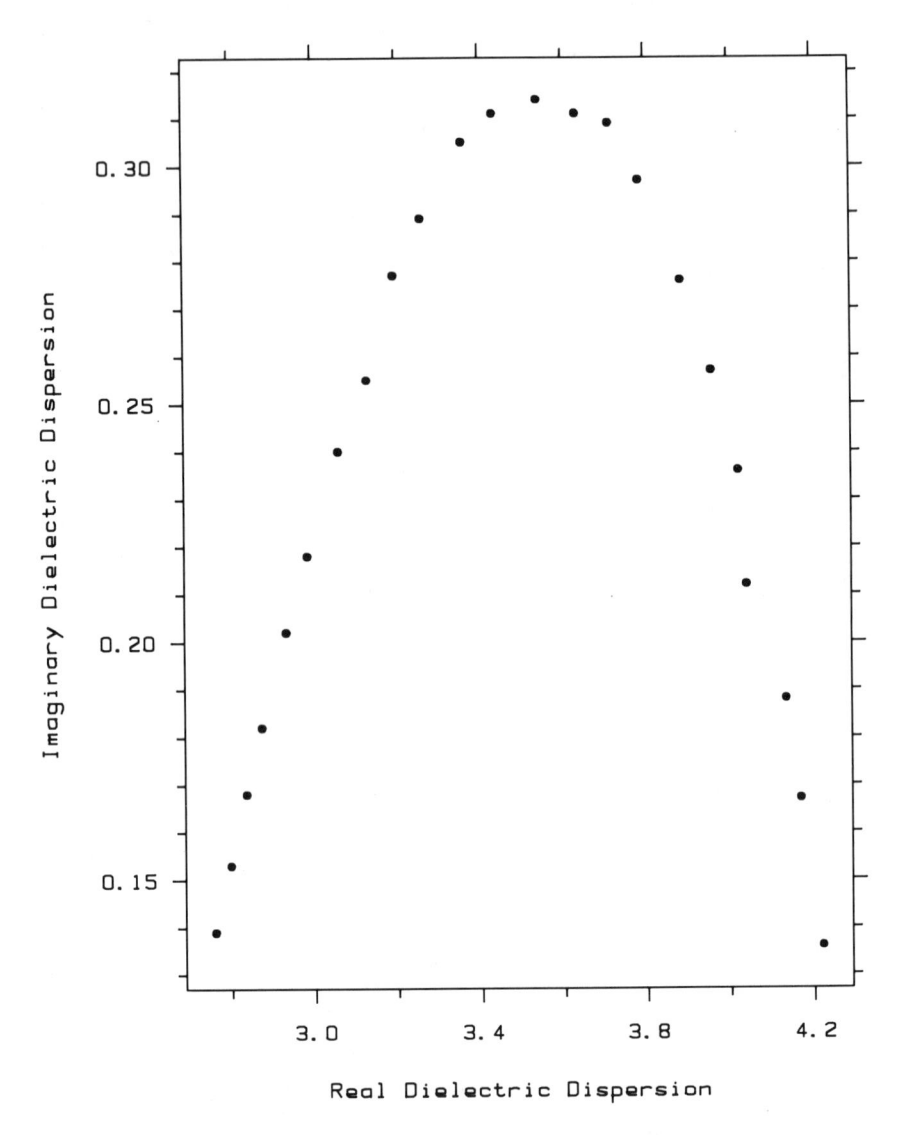

Figure 2. A complex plane plot for syndiotactic PMMA at 86.7° C is given here. In this plot the imaginary part is plotted against the real part of the complex dielectric constant. Each point represents a measurement at a specific frequency.

The parameter α, which has the range $0 < \alpha \leqslant 1$, produces a circular arc, not a semicircle. That is, the locus in a complex plane plot is a circle with center $((\epsilon_0 + \epsilon_\infty)/2, -(\epsilon_0 - \epsilon_\infty)(\cot \pi \alpha /2)/2)$ and radius $(\epsilon_0 - \epsilon_\infty)(\mathrm{cosec}\pi \alpha /2)/2$. In Figure 3 we plot the semicircle ($\alpha = 1$) as a solid line and a circular arc ($\alpha = 0.5$) as a (short) dashed line.

Later, Davidson and Cole, 1950, found that for strongly hydrogen-bonded liquids the data could be modelled as

$$\epsilon^* = \epsilon_\infty + (\epsilon_0 - \epsilon_\infty)/(1 + (i2\pi f/f_0))^\beta \quad (1.3)$$

where $0 < \beta \leqslant 1$. This produces a skewed semicircle, as illustrated by the (long) dashed line in Figure 3 ($\beta = 0.5$). Subsequently, Havriliak and Negami, 1967, studying the dielectric properties of 21 polymers, found that the locus in the complex plane could be represented by

$$\epsilon^* = \epsilon_\infty + (\epsilon_0 - \epsilon_\infty)/(1 + (i2\pi f/f_0)^\alpha)^\beta \quad (1.4)$$

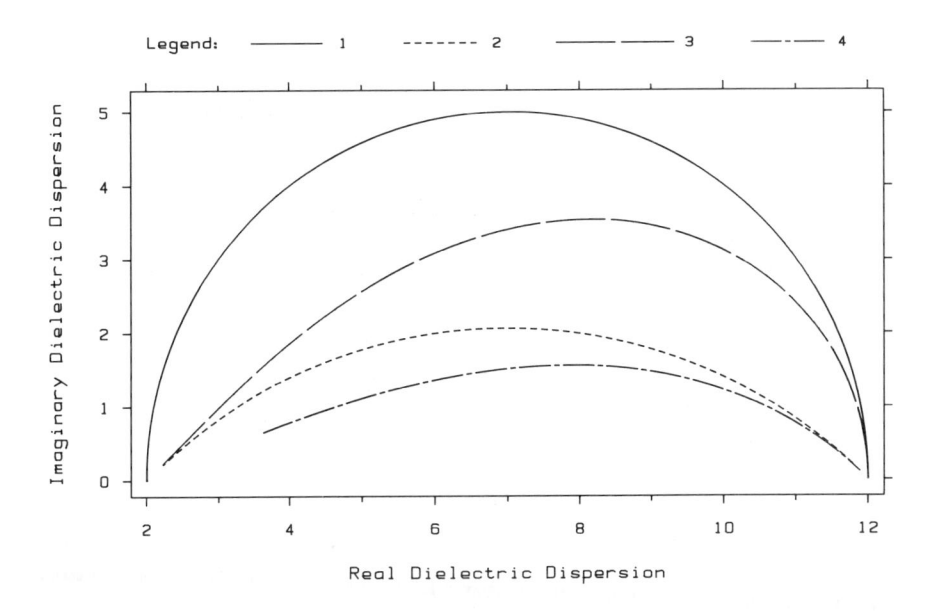

Figure 3. Different complex plane plots are given here to represent different parameter choices in the Havriliak-Negami expression. The examples are cited in the text.

which includes all the previous models. In Figure 3, we plot this locus for $\alpha = \beta = 0.5$ as the (short-long) dashed line. Recently, Mansfield, 1983, has shown that the complex plane locus of dielectric dispersions of polymers is determined by the nature and relative magnitudes of inter- and intra-chain barriers that restrict polymer chain rotation. His loci, when plotted in the complex plane, are similar to those calculated from (1.4) for real experimentation studies.

Analysis of such data has been primarily by graphical methods. Havriliak and Negami, 1967, showed that the real and imaginary components can be written

$$\epsilon' = \epsilon_\infty + (\epsilon_0 - \epsilon_\infty) R^{\beta/2} \cos \beta \Phi \tag{1.5}$$

and

$$\epsilon'' = (\epsilon_0 - \epsilon_\infty) R^{\beta/2} \sin \beta \Phi \tag{1.6}$$

where

$$R^2 = [1 + (2\pi f / f_0)^\alpha \cos \pi \alpha / 2]^2 + [(2\pi f / f_0)^\alpha \sin \pi \alpha / 2]^2$$

and

$$\Phi = \arctan[(2\pi f / f_0)^\alpha \sin \pi \alpha / 2] / [1 + (2\pi f / f_0)^\alpha \cos \pi \alpha / 2].$$

Graphical estimates of the parameters ϵ_0, ϵ_∞, f_0, α and β were obtained by Havriliak and Negami (1967) who showed that ϵ_0 and ϵ_∞ are the limiting high and low frequency intercepts of the locus with the real axis. Furthermore, the limiting angle the high frequency locus makes with the real axis is $\psi_L = \alpha \beta / 2$, and the angle bisector of ψ_L from ϵ_∞ intersects the locus at the frequency for which $2\pi f / f_0 = 1$. Finally, they showed that α is related to ψ_L through

$$\psi_L = -\pi \alpha \, \ell n(R^* / (\epsilon_0 - \epsilon_\infty)) \, / \, \ell n(2 + 2\cos \pi \alpha / 2)$$

where R^* is the length of the line from ϵ_∞ to $\epsilon^*(f_0)$.

Using estimates obtained from these graphical relations and complex plane plots, values of ϵ' and ϵ'' were calculated for each frequency and the fitted values were plotted in the complex plane together with the observed dielectric values y_{real} and y_{imag}. Visual assessments of the quality of the fit were then made. Residuals were not analyzed and measures of precision, such as parameter standard errors, were not determined.

On the statistical front, in 1965 Box and Draper derived an expression for the posterior density of a vector of unknown parameters when several responses are measured. Subsequent papers (Box et al., 1973; Boag, Bacon, and Downie, 1976, 1978; McLean, Pritchard, et al., 1979; McLean, Boag, et al., 1979; Stewart and Sorensen, 1981; Ziegel and Gorman, 1980) discussed applications and problems associated with the analysis of multiresponse data. More recently, a generalized Gauss-Newton procedure was proposed using the gradient and Hessian of the determinant, Bates and Watts, 1985a,b and an algorithm for multiresponse estimation was presented in Bates and Watts, 1984.

In this contribution, we use multiresponse parameter estimation techniques to estimate the parameters in the Havriliak-Negami model. In Section 2 we present a summary derivation of the determinant criterion and in Section 3 we analyze the two polymer systems.

2. MULTIRESPONSE ESTIMATION

In multiresponse situations where there are M measured responses and the errors have unknown variances and covariances, but are assumed uncorrelated from case to case, the likelihood or Bayesian approach leads to minimization of the $M \times M$ determinant (Box and Draper, 1965)

$$|V(\underline{\theta})| = |\sum_{n=1}^{N} (\underline{y}_{(n)} - \underline{\eta}_{(n)})(\underline{y}_{(n)} - \underline{\eta}_{(n)})'|$$

$$= |\sum_{n=1}^{N} \underline{z}_{(n)} \underline{z}_{(n)}'| = |\sum_{n=1}^{N} V(n)| \quad (2.1)$$

$$= |Z'Z|.$$

In (2.1) $\underline{y}_{(n)}$ represents the $M \times 1$ vector of responses on the nth case, $n = 1, 2, \ldots, N$, $\underline{\eta}_{(n)}$ the $M \times 1$ vector of expected responses, $\underline{z}_{(n)}$ the $M \times 1$ residual vector $\underline{y}_{(n)} - \underline{\eta}_{(n)}$, and Z the $N \times M$ matrix of residuals. The vertical bars denote a determinant, and the expected responses η are assumed to depend on P parameters $\underline{\theta}$. The ' indicates a transpose of a vector.

As shown in Bates and Watts, 1985b, the terms in the gradient $\underline{\gamma}$ and the (approximate) Hessian Γ can be written

$$\gamma_p = \partial |V| / \partial \theta_p = |V| tr[U_p] \quad p = 1,2,...,P \tag{2.2}$$

and

$$\Gamma_{pq} = \partial^2 |V| / \partial\theta_p \partial\theta_q \simeq \tag{2.3}$$

$$|V|tr(U_p)tr(U_q) - |V|tr(U_p U_q) + |V|tr(V^{-1}[Z'_p Z_q + Z'_q Z_p])$$

where $U_p = V^{-1}(Z'Z_p + Z'_p Z)$, and the subscript p denotes differentiation with respect to the pth parameter. Note that second derivative terms Z_{pq} have been omitted in (2.3), and that $Z_p = -H_p$, H denoting the $N \times M$ matrix of expected responses. The increment from any point $\underline{\theta_i}$ can then be calculated using

$$\underline{\delta} = -\Gamma^{-1}\underline{\gamma}.$$

TABLE 1. Summary statistics for polycarbonate.

		Data		
Parameter	Graphical	Original	Edited	Offset
ϵ_0	3.64	3.64 (0.0021)	3.64 (0.0034)	3.64 (0.0015)
ϵ_∞	3.13	3.12 (0.0066)	3.12 (0.0076)	3.12 (0.0041)
$\ell n f_0$	6.81	6.85 (0.072)	6.90 (0.082)	6.85 (0.043)
α	0.80	0.79 (0.024)	0.76 (0.025)	0.77 (0.013)
β	0.29	0.28 (0.019)	0.30 (0.022)	0.29 (0.011)
scaled determinant		3.87×10^{-9}	2.19×10^{-10}	2.19×10^{-10}
real std. dev.		0.0031	0.0026	0.0023
coeff. of var.(%)		0.09	0.08	0.07
imaginary std. dev.		0.0045	0.0051	0.0014
coeff. of var.(%)		8.0	8.3	2.3

An alternative derivation incorporating efficient numerical procedures is given in Bates and Watts (1985a) and an algorithm for the calculations appears in Bates and Watts (1984).

For dielectric coefficients, $M = 2$ corresponding to the real and imaginary components, and $P = 5$, corresponding to the parameters ϵ_0, ϵ_∞, f_0, α and β. A multiresponse estimation program was written using SAS PROC MATRIX, Ray, 1982, incorporating the expressions (1.5), (1.6), (2.2) and (2.3). For reference, we give expressions for the derivatives of the expectation functions with respect to the parameters in Appendix 2. It should be noted that the parameter f_0 was incorporated into the model in the form $\theta = \ell n f_0$ because it is suggested from theory that the relaxation frequency depends on temperature according to an Arrhenius relationship. The logarithmic form is then especially simple for dealing with data at several temperatures. Furthermore, plots of $\epsilon'(f)$ or $\epsilon''(f)$ versus log-frequency are much more symmetric than when plotted versus frequency.

3. ANALYSIS OF POLYCARBONATE AND S-PMMA

The two data sets discussed above were analyzed using multiresponse estimation techniques. Starting values for the parameters were taken from the graphical analyses, Havriliak and Negami, 1967, and are listed under the column headed "graphical" in the Tables. It is necessary to have good starting values to obtain convergence, and fortunately the graphical procedure provides excellent estimates.

Polycarbonate

For the polycarbonate data, convergence was obtained to the parameter values listed in the column headed "original" in Table 1. In this and subsequent tables, the scaled determinant is $|Z'Z|/df$, where $df = N - 5$, the real and imaginary standard deviations are the square roots of the diagonals of the scaled determinant, and the coefficients of variation are the standard deviations divided by the average dielectric value. The terms in parentheses are the parameter approximate standard errors.

The residuals from the real and imaginary components are plotted versus $\log_{10}$ frequency in Figures 4 and 5. The residuals are not well-behaved: several outliers are evident, almost all of the imaginary residuals are negative, and there is some periodicity. The outliers at the extreme frequencies are evidence of secondary relaxation processes, which can be detected from a careful examination of the complex plane dielectric plot, Figure 1. The two highest and two lowest frequencies were deleted, along with the wild case at 1000 Hertz, and a second fit made. The parameter estimates for this fit are listed in the column headed "edited" in Table 1. The residuals were slightly improved, but the periodic tendency persisted and the imaginary residuals were all negative.

The frequency dependence of the residuals is most likely due to inaccuracies in the dielectric measuring equipment. For example, the fine tuning and decade switches on the oscillator powering the bridge may not be perfectly linear, which could cause periodicities in the frequency settings. Or the decade switches in the bridge, used to change conductance or resistance ranges, could introduce stray impedances. This could be the source of the apparent offset in the imaginary component.

To account for the offset of the residuals, a constant equal to the average of the imaginary residuals was added to the imaginary values, and convergence to the values in the column headed "offset" in Table 1 was obtained. The residuals, plotted in Figures 6, 7 and 8, show a slight tendency for the real residuals to have increasing variance with frequency, and both sets of residuals have a periodic tendency, but otherwise they are well behaved.

Although the residuals are not perfectly random, their magnitude is so small that further analysis is not deemed worthwhile, as evidenced by the complex plane plot of the observed and fitted values shown in Figure 9. Note the excellent agreement between the original graphical results and the current statistical results.

4. s-PMMA

For the s-PMMA data, convergence was obtained to the parameter values listed in the column headed "original" in Table 2. The residuals, plotted versus natural logarithm radian frequency in Figures 10 and 11, show marked nonrandom behavior. There is a strong trend with superimposed periodicities and steps. There is also a bad observation at 100 Hertz, and so this case was deleted in subsequent analyses.

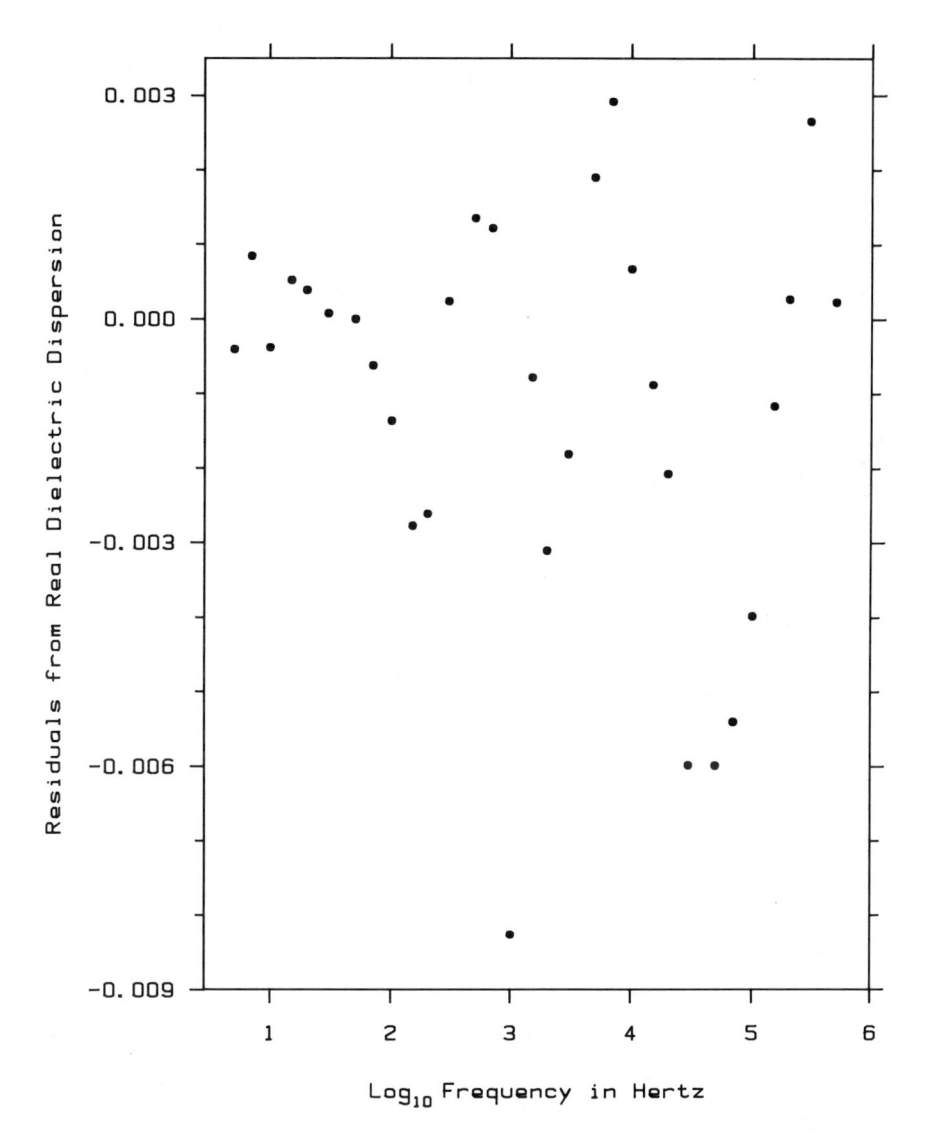

Figure 4. A plot of the real residuals with log frequency is given here for polycarbonate at 163.9° C.

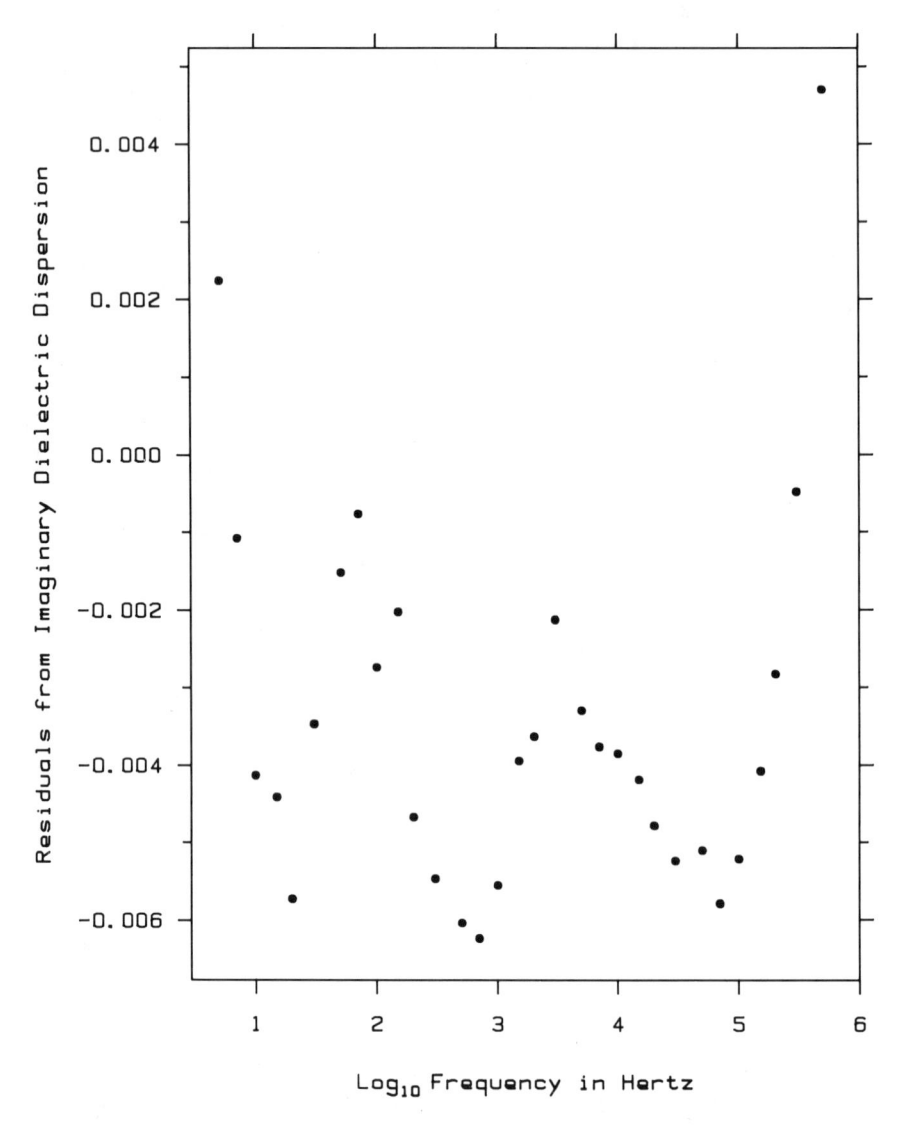

Figure 5. A plot of the imaginary residuals with log frequency is given here for polycarbonate at 163.9° C.

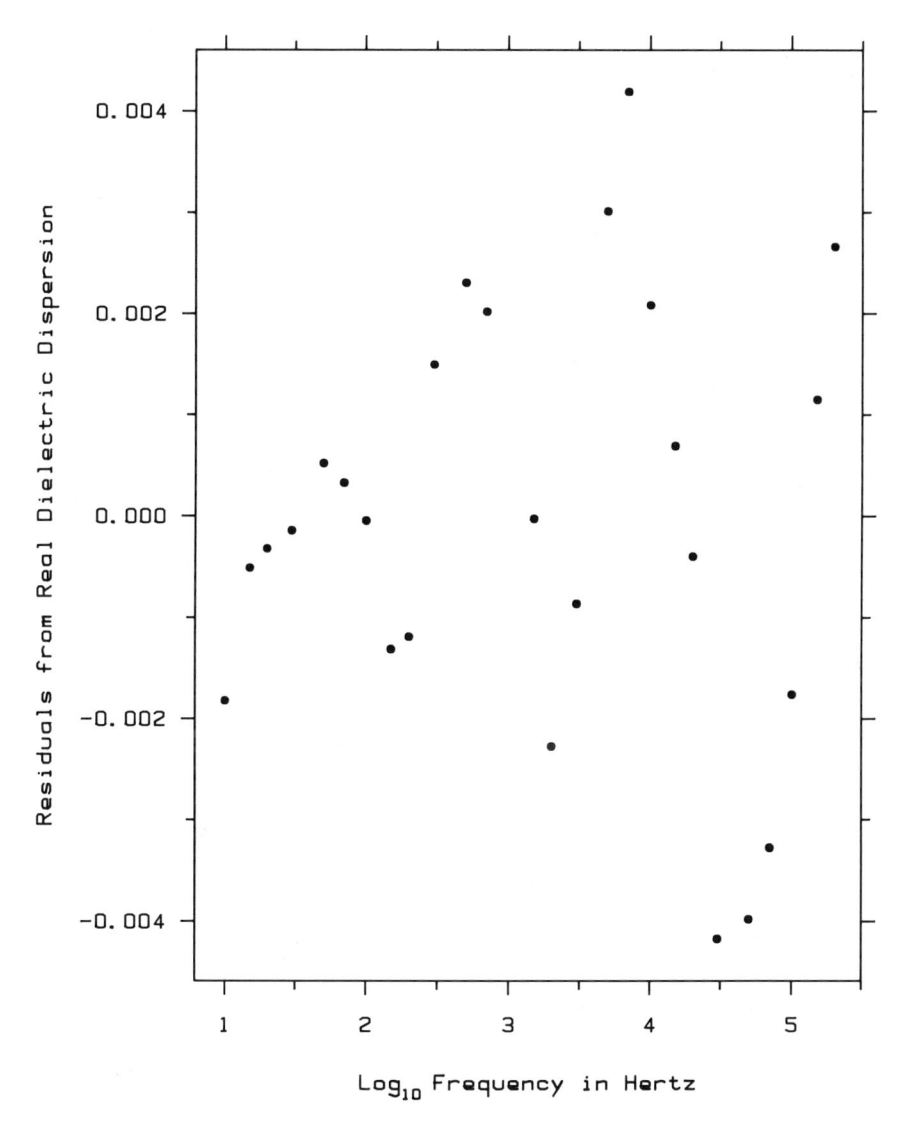

Figure 6. A plot of the real residuals with log frequency is given here for polycarbonate at 163.9° C. Experimental data at 5, 7, 1,000, 300,000 and 500,000 were deleted. In addition, an offset of 0.0045 was added to the imaginary dielectric.

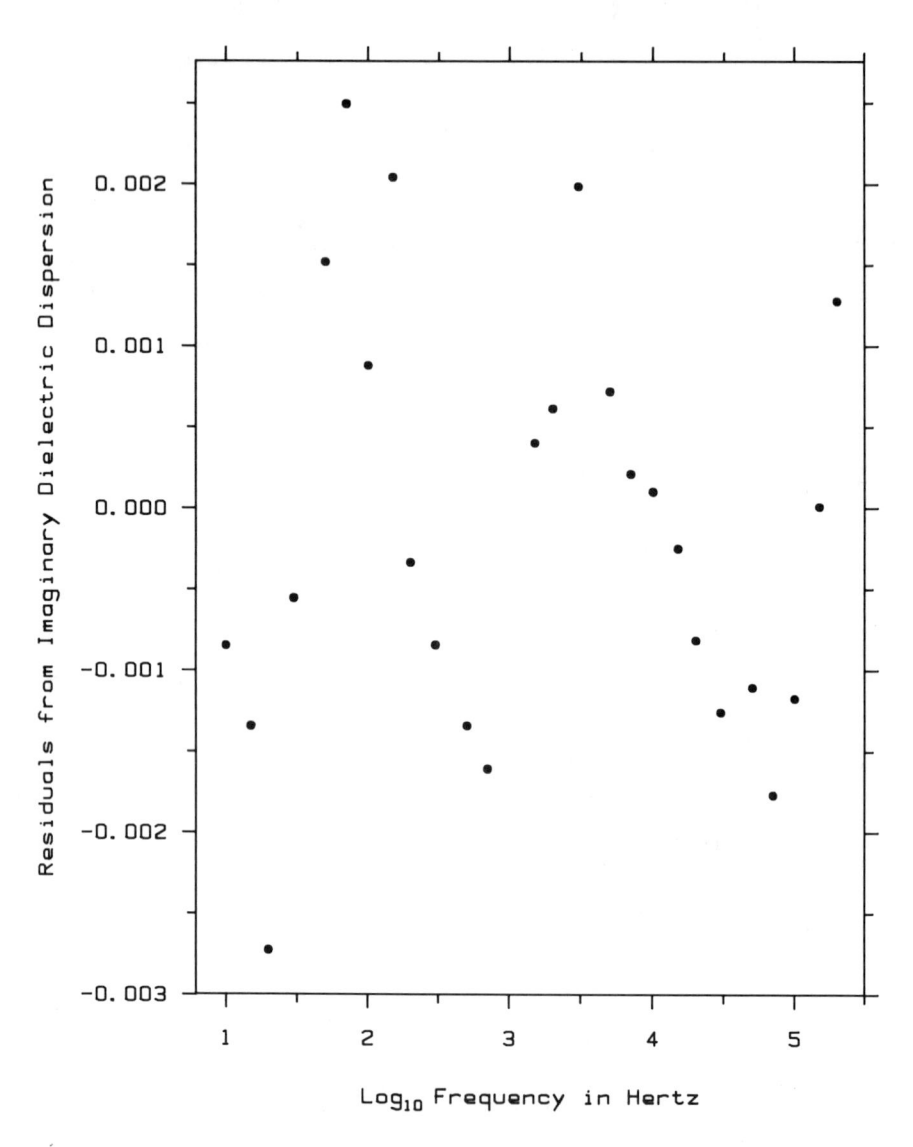

Figure 7. A plot of the imaginary residuals with log frequency is given here for polycarbonate at 163.9° C. The conditions of calculation are the same as those in Figure 6.

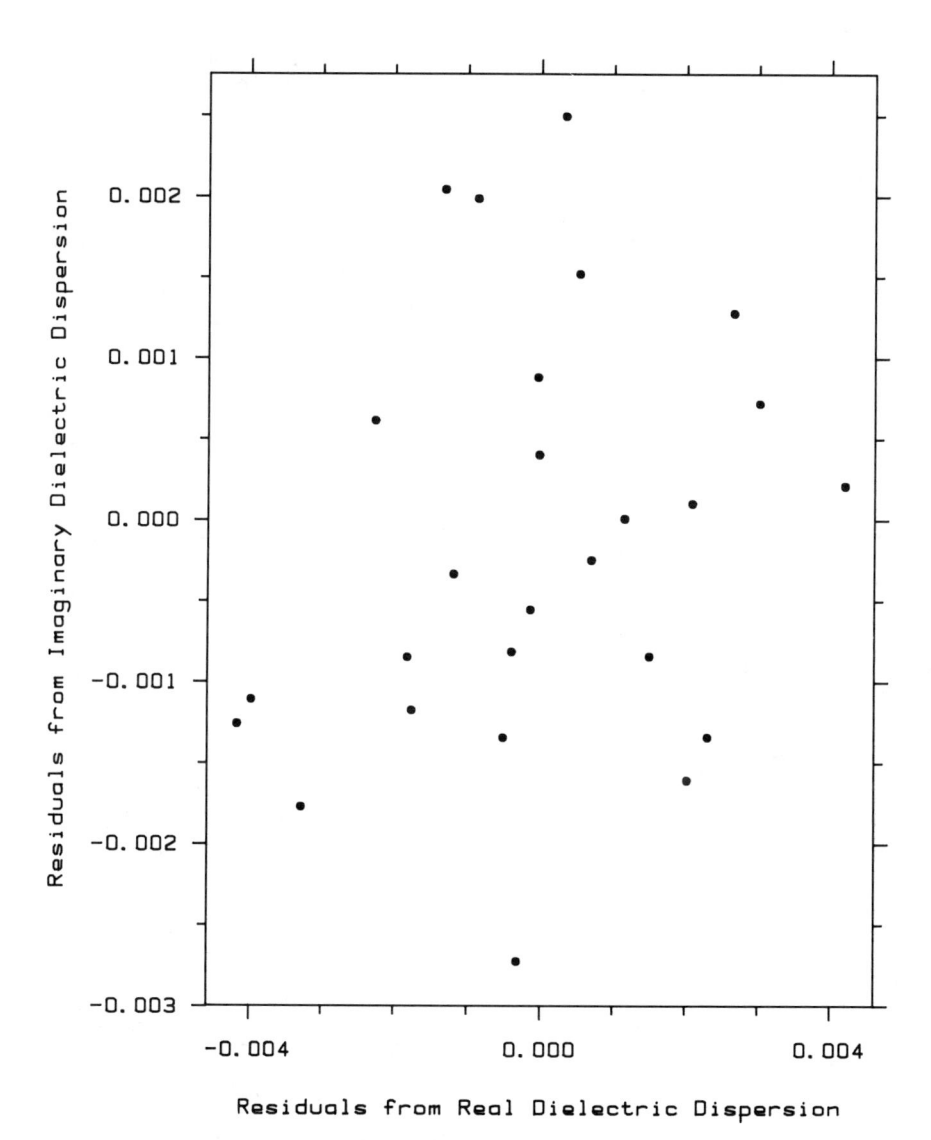

Figure 8. A complex plane plot of the residuals is given here for the conditions of calculation given in Figure 7.

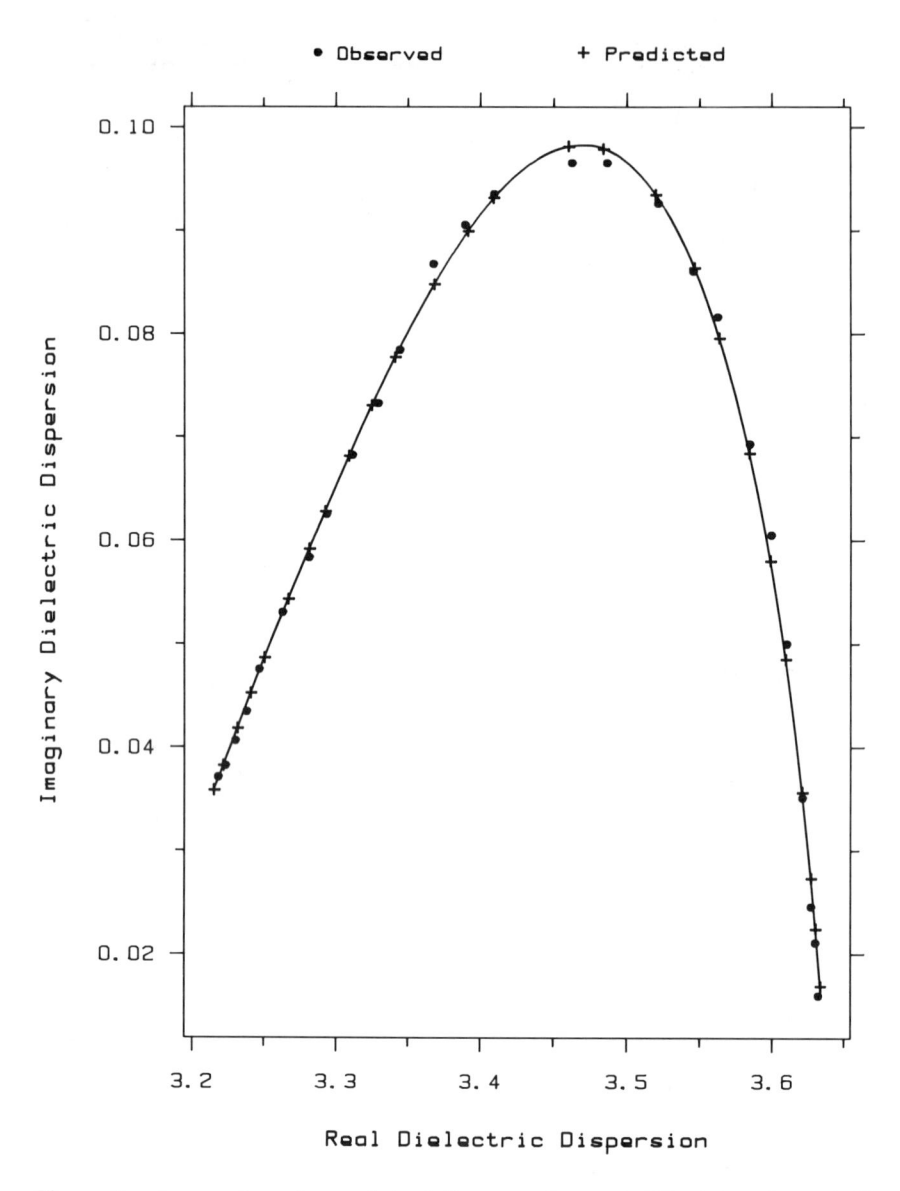

Figure 9. A complex plane plot of the experimental (+) and estimated (•) values using the conditions in Figure 7 are given here.

The behavior of the residuals is probably due to nonlinearities in the oscillator or bridge, although the trend could be accounted for by temperature drift. Nonlinearity within a decade could account for the periodicities and trend, and nonlinearities between decades could account for the trend and steps. We therefore introduced a decade factor K, such that when a decade increase is made the frequencies are multiplied by $10 \times K$. For the s-PMMA data, K must be greater than 1, since the real residuals are positive for low frequencies and negative for high frequencies, and so the fitted curve lies inside the data on a complex plane plot.

A series of values for K was used, with the minimum scaled determinant found at a decade factor $K = 1.25$. The residuals were markedly reduced, and a second outlier detected at 150 Hertz. This case was deleted and the results recorded in the column headed "decade" in Table 2 were obtained. The scaled determinant and the real component variance were reduced by a factor of about 100.

TABLE 2. Summary statistics for s-PMMA.

		Data Set		
Parameter	Graphical	Original	Nonlinearity Decade	Corrected Decade & Dial
ϵ_0	4.48	4.32 (0.012)	4.40 (0.006)	4.40 (0.006)
ϵ_∞	2.55	2.52 (0.018)	2.45 (0.010)	2.45 (0.010)
$\ell n f_0$	9.28	7.96 (0.084)	8.24 (0.074)	8.24 (0.074)
α	0.04	0.53 (0.010)	0.49 (0.007)	0.49 (0.007)
β	1.00	0.55 (0.030)	0.57 (0.021)	0.57 (0.021)

scaled determinant	1.89×10^{-7}	1.49×10^{-9}	8.52×10^{-10}
real std. dev.	0.041	0.004	0.003
coeff. of var.(%)	1.2	0.1	0.1
imaginary std. dev.	0.0025	0.0023	0.0024
coeff. of var.(%)	1.1	1.0	1.0

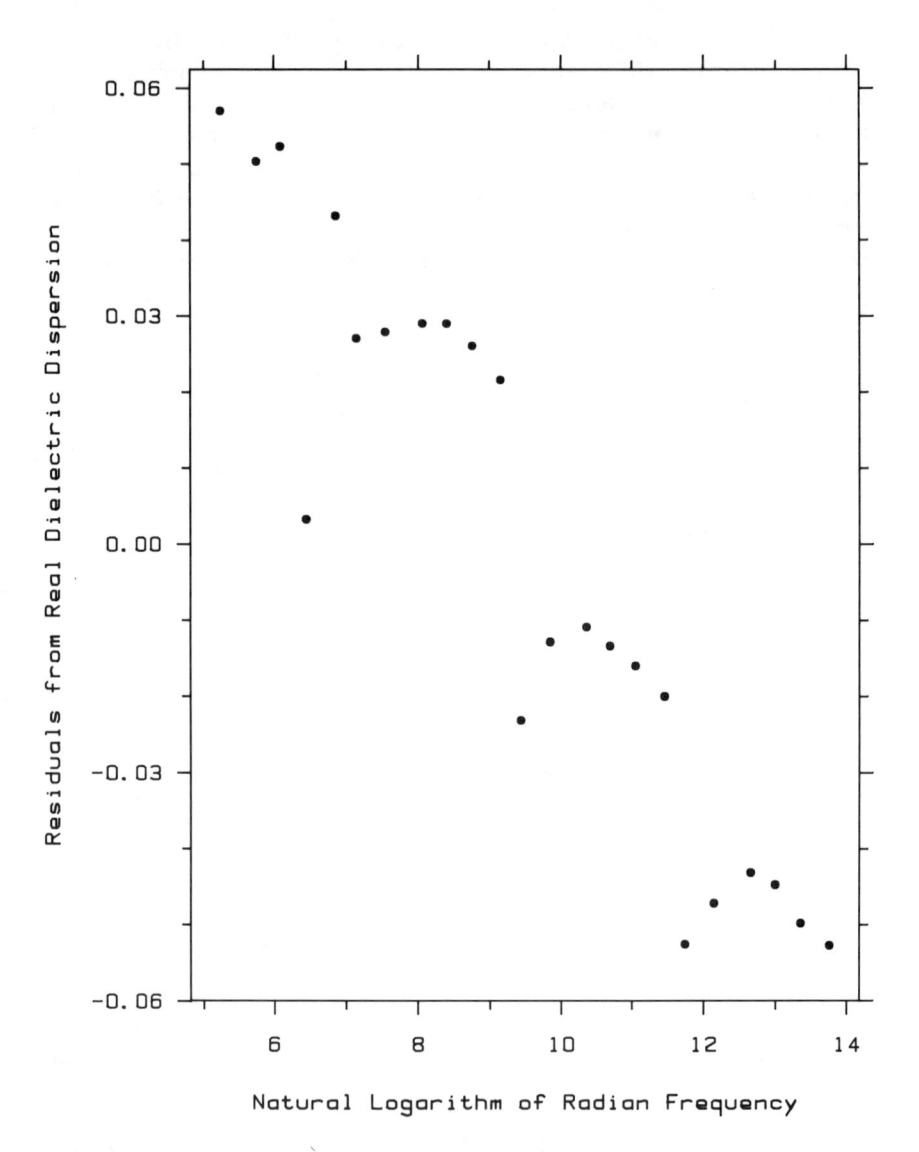

Figure 10. The real residuals for s-PMMA are plotted against natural log frequency in (radians) using the original parameter estimates in Table 2.

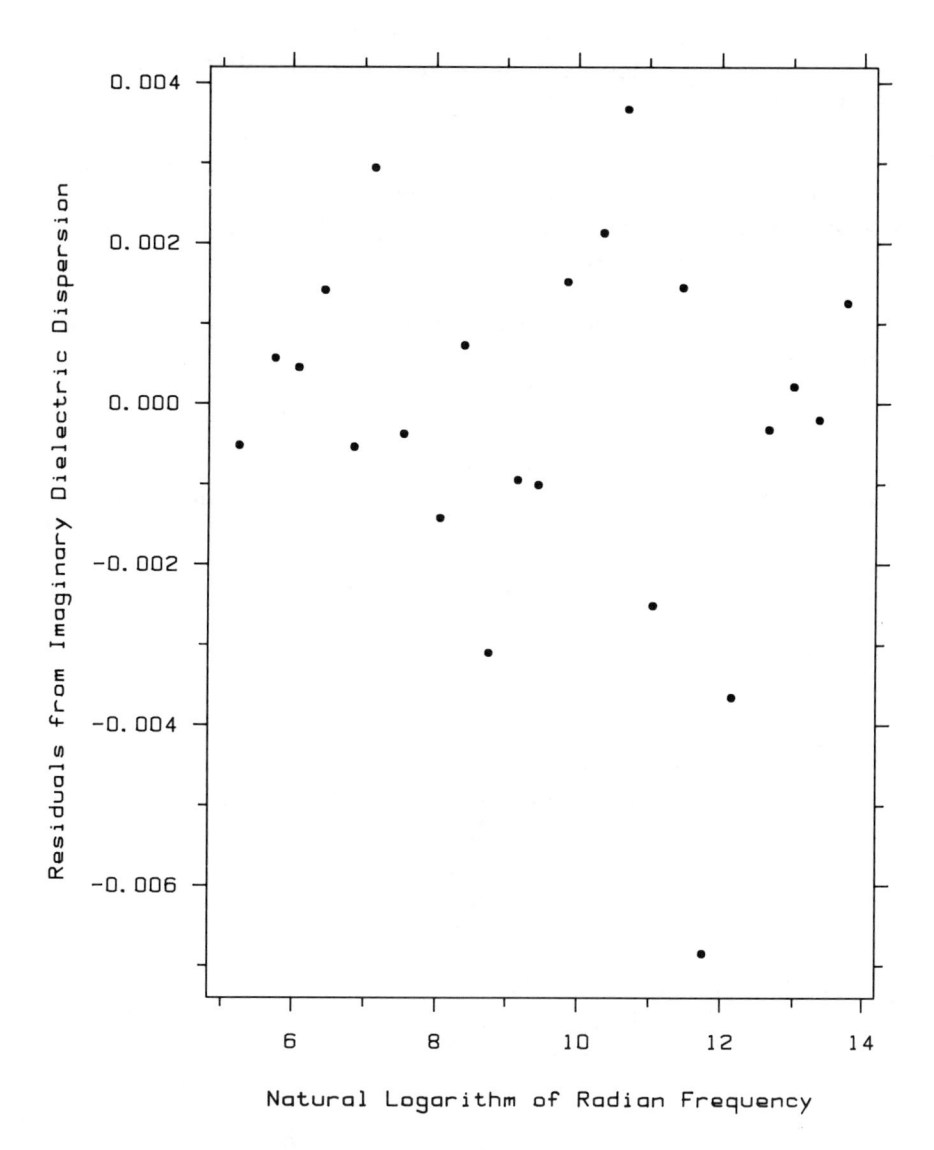

Figure 11. The imaginary residuals for s-PMMA are plotted against natural log frequency in (radians) using the original parameter estimates in Table 2.

It is also possible to account for the nonlinearity within decades, which we term the dial nonuniformity. From Figure 12, where the real residuals are plotted versus frequency, it can be deduced that the dial nonuniformity is such that low and high range recorded frequencies are high while the middle range recorded frequencies are low. Incorporating a dial correction produces the results shown in the column headed "decade and dial" in Table 2, and the residuals in Figures 13 and 14. Clearly the fit is excellent, as judged from the behavior of the residuals, from the summary statistics, and from the plots of the observed and fitted values in Figures 15 and 16. The decade factor, 1.25, is surprisingly high.

Note that in the graphical analysis of s-PMMA, the parameter β was specified to be 1.0, which is not plausible according to the statistical analysis. Because of inherent interactions between the parameters, such a misspecification induces changes in the other parameters, especially α and $\ell n f_0$.

5. DISCUSSION

Application of modern statistical techniques provides several important benefits in the analysis of dielectric coefficients of polymers. First, objective estimates of the parameters are produced, together with measures of their uncertainty. In the case of s-PMMA, for example, in the original graphical analysis the parameter β was judged to be unity, which is clearly inappropriate according to multiresponse estimation. Second, examination of the residuals provides valuable insights into the experimental procedure by revealing important sources of variation. Both decade and dial effects can be detected and corrected for, thereby improving the sensitivity of the analyses and pointing to possible improvements in the experimental equipment and technique.

ACKNOWLEDGMENTS

The authors are grateful to Rohm and Haas Company for support and for permission to publish this paper. Support from the Natural and Engineering Sciences Research Committee of Canada is also gratefully acknowledged by D. G. W.

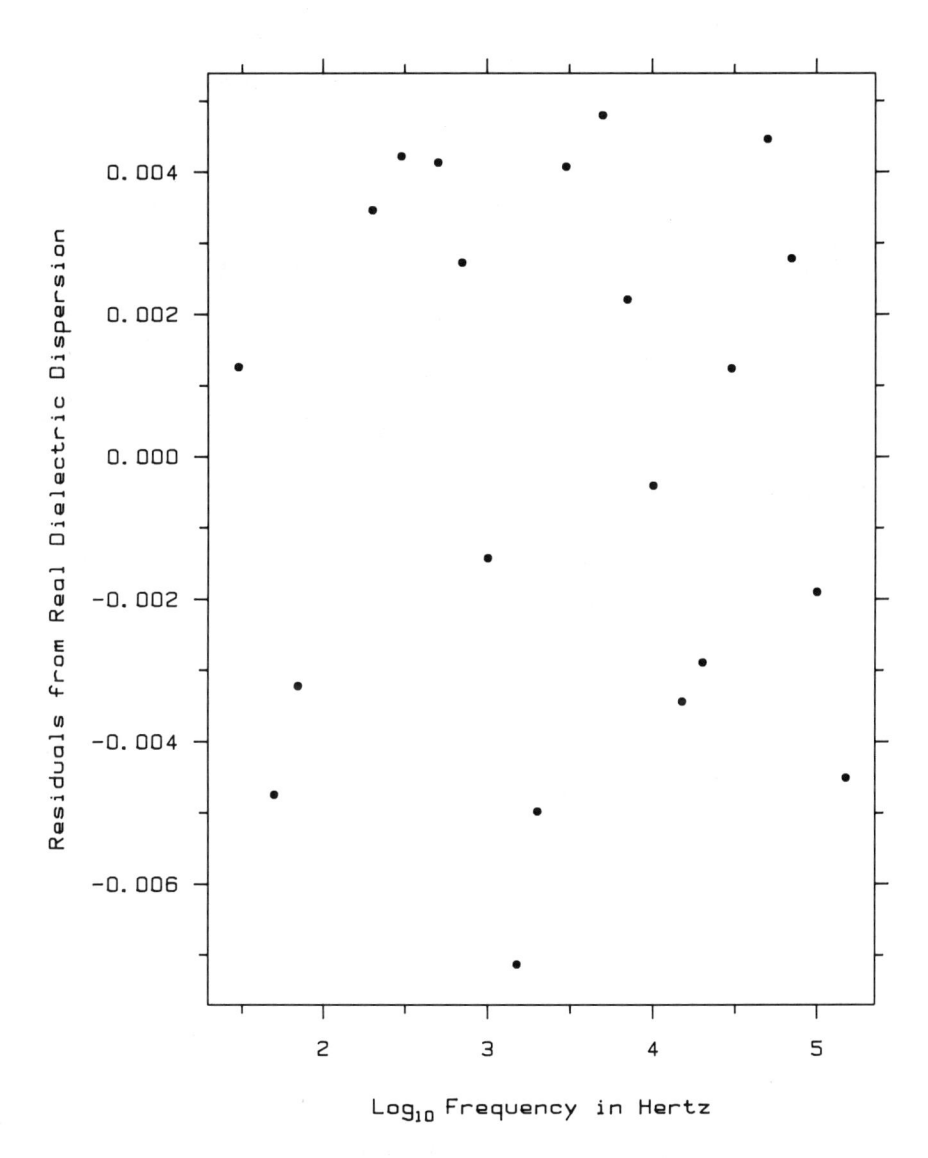

Figure 12. The real residuals are plotted here as a function log frequency for s-PMMA. Data at 100 and 150 Hz. have been deleted. Also a decade multiplier of 1.25 was included.

150 ANALYTICAL REPRESENTATION OF DIELECTRIC CONSTANTS

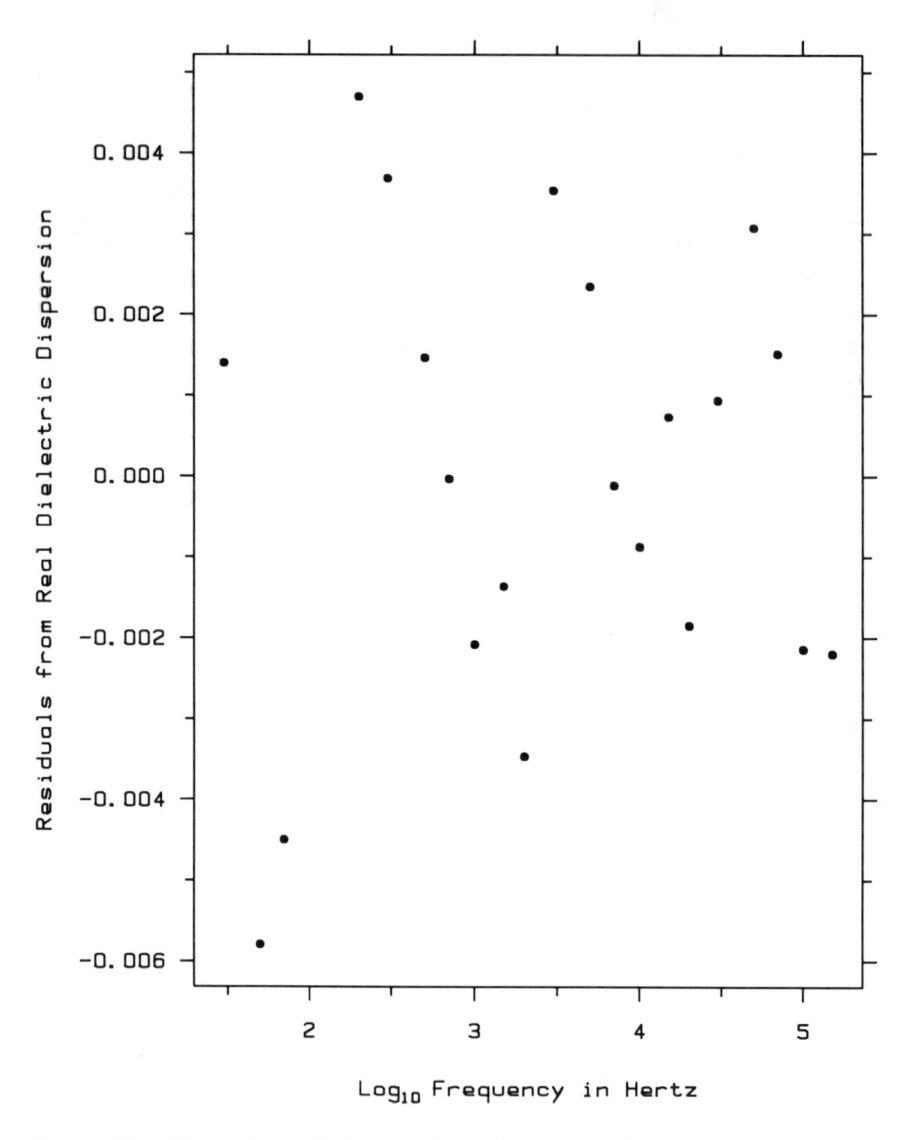

Figure 13. The real residuals are plotted here as a function log frequency for s-PMMA. The estimation conditions are those of Figure 12 as well as the inclusion of the dial correction.

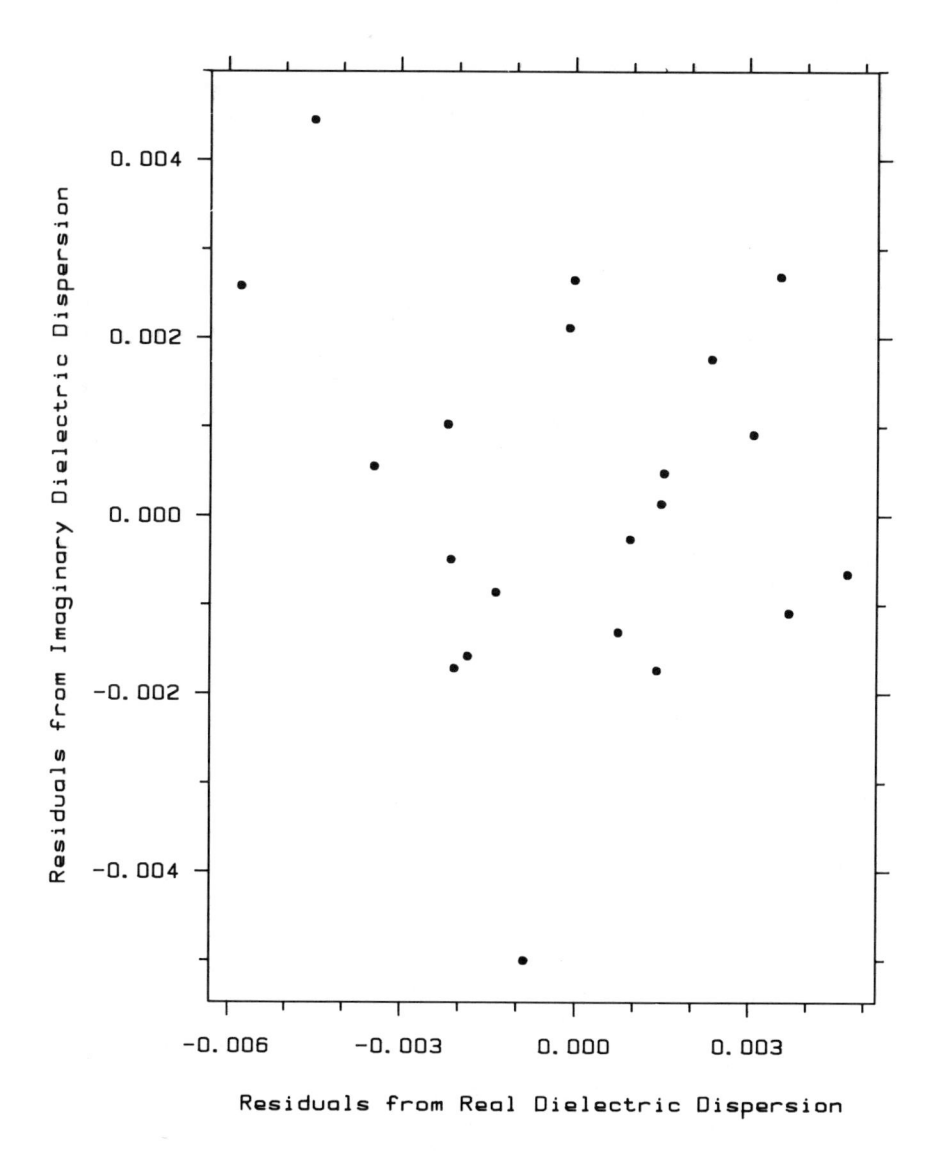

Figure 14. A complex plane plot of the fully corrected residuals is plotted here for s-PMMA.

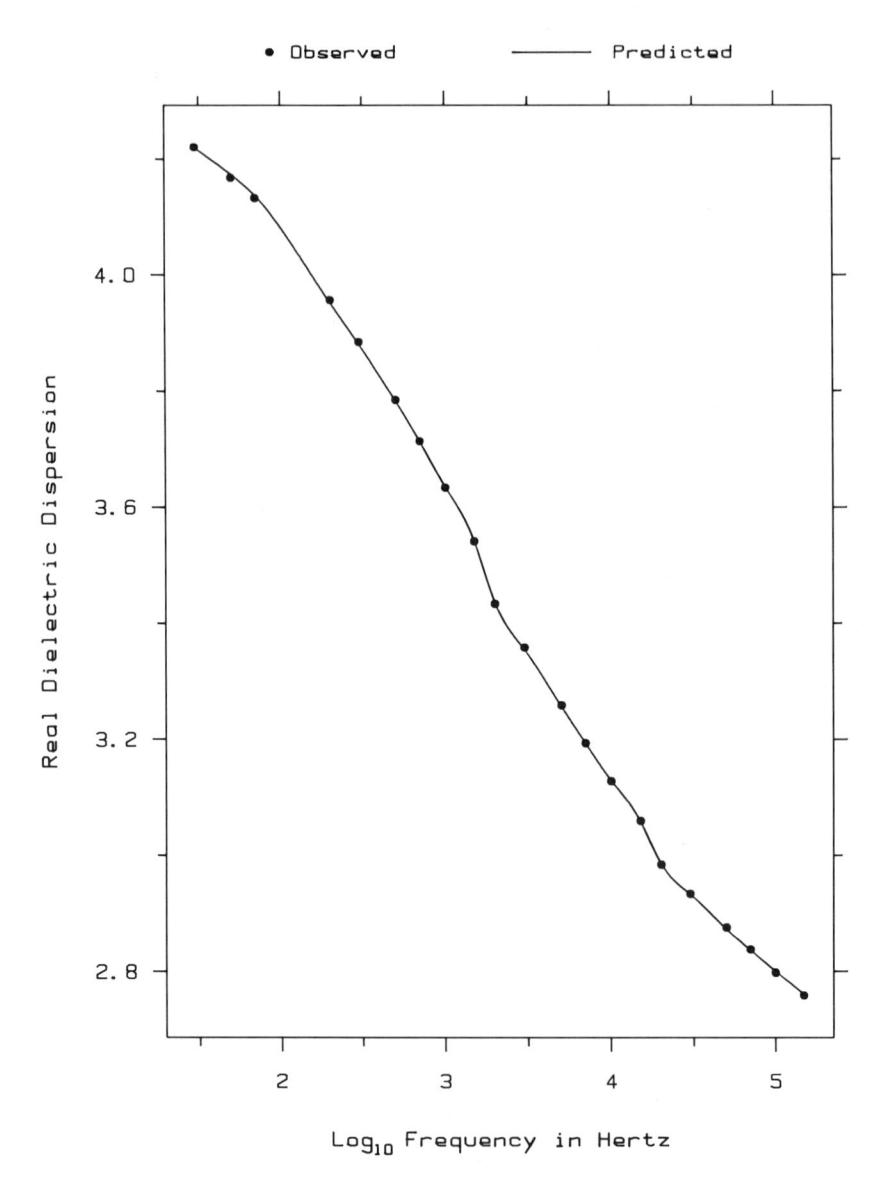

Figure 15. The experimental (•) and predicted (solid line) values of the real dielectric constant are plotted against frequency in Hz.

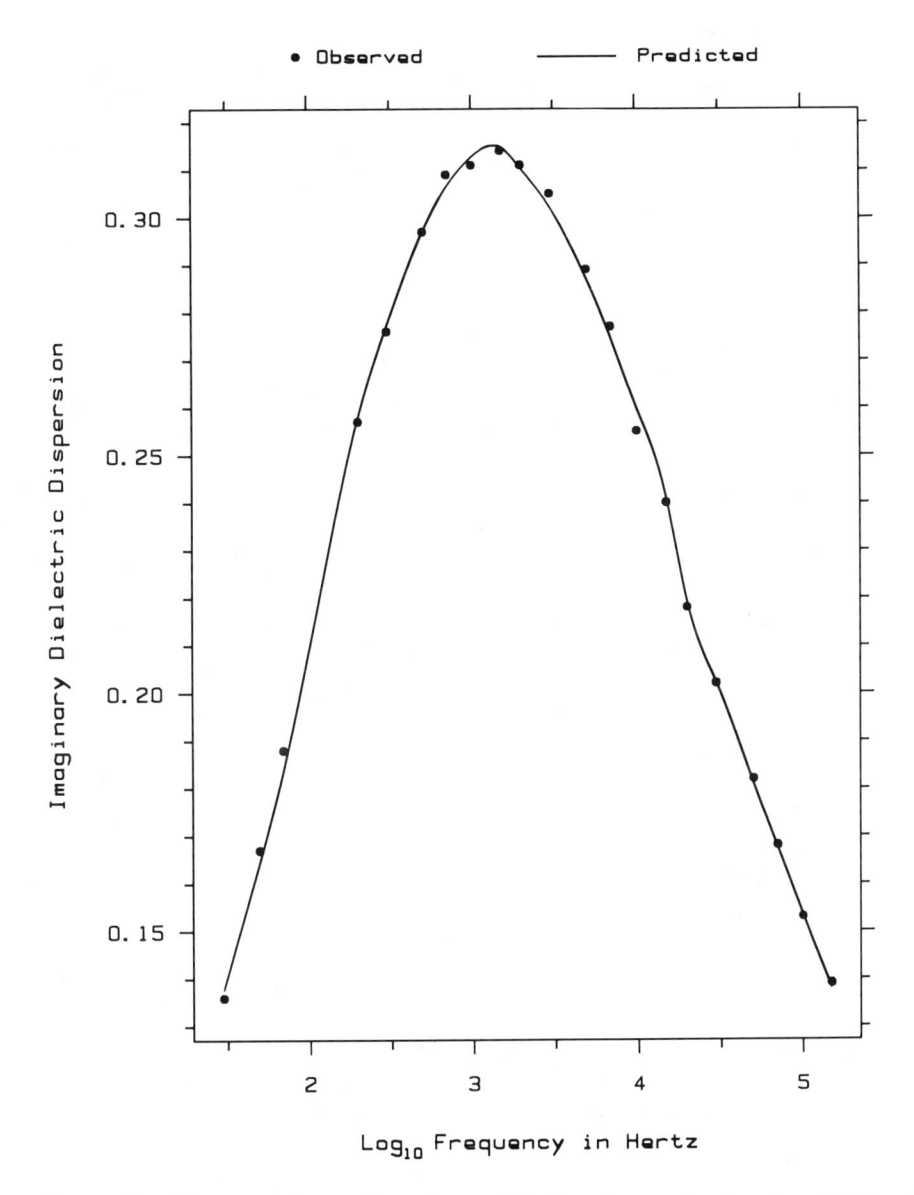

Figure 16. The experimental and predicted values of the imaginary dielectric constant are plotted against frequency in Hz.

REFERENCES

Bates, D. M. and Watts, D. G. (1984). "A multi-response Gauss-Newton algorithm", *Communications in Statistics Part B — Simulation and Computation*, **B(13)**, 705-715.

Bates, D. M. and Watts, D. G. (1985a). "A generalized Gauss-Newton procedure for multi-response parameter estimation," *SIAM Journal on Scientific and Statistical Computing*. To appear.

Bates, D. M. and Watts, D. G. (1985b). "Multiresponse estimation with special application to systems of linear differential equations, (with discussion)" *Technometrics*, **27**, 329-360

Boag, I. F., Bacon, D. W., and Downie, J. (1976). "The analysis of data from recirculation reactors, *Canadian Journal of Chemical Engineering*, **54**, 107-110.

Boag, I. F., Bacon, D. W., and Downie, J. (1978). "Using a statistical multiresponse method of experimental design in a reaction network study," *Canadian Journal of Chemical Engineering*, **56**, 389-395.

Box, G. E. P. and Draper, N. R. (1965). "The Bayesian estimation of common parameters from several responses," *Biometrika*, **52**, 355-365.

Box, G. E. P., Hunter, W. G., MacGregor, J. F., and Erjavec, J. (1973). "Some problems associated with the analysis of multiresponse data," *Technometrics*, **15**, 33-51.

Cole, K. S. and Cole, R. H., (1941). "Dispersion and absorption in dielectrics I: Alternating current characteristics," *Journal of Physical Chemistry*, **9**, 341-351.

Davidson, D. W. and Cole, R. H., (1950). "Dielectric relaxation in glycerol propylene glycol and n-propanol," *Journal of Chemical Physics*, **19**, 1484-1490.

Havriliak, S. and Negami, S. (1967). "A complex plane representation of dielectric and mechanical relaxation processes in some polymers," *Polymer*, **8**, 161-210.

Mansfield, M. L., (1983). "One-dimensional models of polymer dynamics. II: A Dashpot-Spring model, *Journal of Polymer Science — Polymer Physics Edition*, **21**, 787-806.

McLean, D. D., Boag, I. F., Bacon, D. W., and Downie, J. (1979). "Solution of SSAM or REDOX equations," *Canadian Journal of Chemical Engineering*, **57**, 605-608.

McLean, D. D., Pritchard, D. J., Bacon, D. W., and Downie, J. (1979). "Singularities in multiresponse modelling," *Technometrics*, **21**, 291-298.

Ray, A. A., ed (1982). *SAS User's Guide: Statistics*. Cary, NC: SAS Institute.

Stewart, W. E. and Sorensen, J. P. (1981). "Bayesian estimation of common parameters from multiresponse data with missing observations," *Technometrics*, **23**, 131-141.

Ziegel, E. R. and Gorman, J. W. (1980). "Kinetic modelling with multiresponse data," *Technometrics*, **22**, 139-151.

APPENDIX 1

Data Sets

| | POLYCARBONATE AT 164°C || s-PMMA at 86.7°C ||
Frequency (Hertz)	Dielectric Real	Dispersion Loss	Dielectric Real	Dispersion Loss
5	3.635	0.0115		
7	3.635	0.0109		
10	3.632	0.0115		
15	3.630	0.0166		
20	3.627	0.0201		
30	3.621	0.0306	4.220	0.136
50	3.610	0.0455	4.167	0.167
70	3.599	0.0560	4.132	0.188
100	3.584	0.0648	4.038	0.212
150	3.562	0.0771	4.019	0.236
200	3.545	0.0815	3.956	0.257
300	3.521	0.0881	3.884	0.276
500	3.486	0.0920	3.784	0.297
700	3.462	0.0920	3.713	0.309
1000	3.428	0.0910	3.633	0.311
1500	3.409	0.0890	3.540	0.314
2000	3.389	0.0860	3.433	0.311
3000	3.367	0.0822	3.358	0.305
5000	3.344	0.0739	3.258	0.289
7000	3.329	0.0687	3.193	0.277
10000	3.311	0.0637	3.128	0.255
15000	3.293	0.0580	3.059	0.240
20000	3.281	0.0538	2.984	0.218
30000	3.263	0.0485	2.934	0.202
50000	3.247	0.0430	2.876	0.182
70000	3.238	0.0389	2.838	0.168
100000	3.230	0.0361	2.798	0.153
150000	3.223	0.0337	2.759	0.139
200000	3.218	0.0326		
300000	3.212	0.0319		
500000	3.200	0.0336		

156 ANALYTICAL REPRESENTATION OF DIELECTRIC CONSTANTS

APPENDIX 2

Gradient of the Havriliak-Negami Function

To use Gauss-Newton minimization techniques, it is useful to have the derivatives of the function with respect to the parameters. In this appendix, we give a coding of the function and of the derivatives. Liberal use is made of temporary functions and the chain rule for derivatives.

Parameter	Code
ϵ_0	THETA1
ϵ_∞	THETA2
$\ell n f_0$	THETA3
α	THETA4
β	THETA5
$2\pi f$	OMEGA
π	PI
ϵ'	REAL
ϵ''	IMAG

Temporary functions
```
    THETAD = THETA1 - THETA2
     MULT = (OMEGA*EXP(-THETA3))**THETA4
     COS4 = COS(PI*THETA4/2)
     SIN4 = SIN(PI*THETA4/2)
      ORD = MULT*SIN4
      ABS = MULT*COS4
    ANGLE = ATAN(ORD/ABS)
    RADSQ = ABS**2 + ORD**2
    RMULT = RADSQ**(THETA5/2)
   COSINE = COS(THETA5*ANGLE)
     SINE = SIN(THETA5*ANGLE)
    REAL1 = RMULT*COSINE
    IMAG1 = RMULT*SINE
```

Function η:
  real   REAL = THETA2 + THETAD*REAL1
  imaginary   IMAG = THETAD*IMAG1

APPENDIX 157

Derivatives $\partial \eta / \partial \epsilon_0$:
    real   REAL1
    imaginary   IMAG1

Derivatives $\partial \eta / \partial \epsilon_\infty$:
    real   1 − REAL1
    imaginary   − IMAG1

Temporary functions
    MULT3 = −THETA4*MULT
    ORD3 = MULT3*SIN4
    ABS3 = MULT3*COS4
    ANGLE3 = (ORD3*ABS − ABS3*ORD)/RADSQ
    SINE3 = THETA5*COSINE*ANGLE3
    COSINE3 = −THETA5*SINE*ANGLE3
    RADSQ3 = ABS*ABS3 + ORD*ORD3
    RMULT3 = −THETA5*RMULT*RADSQ3/RADSQ

Derivatives $\partial \eta / \partial \ell n f_0$:
    real   THETAD*(RMULT3*COSINE + RMULT*COSINE3)
    imaginary   THETAD*(RMULT3*SINE + RMULT*SINE3)

Temporary functions
    MULT4 = MULT*(THETA3 + LOG(OMEGA))
    ORD4 = MULT4*SIN4 + (PI*MULT*COS4)/2
    ABS4 = MULT4*COS4 − (PI*MULT*SIN4)/2
    RAD4 = ABS*ABS4 + ORD*ORD4
    RMULT4 = −THETA5*RMULT*RAD4/RADSQ
    ANGLE4 = (ABS*ORD4 − ORD*ABS4)/RADSQ
    COSINE4 = −THETA5*ANGLE4*SINE
    SINE4 = THETA5*ANGLE4*COSINE

Derivatives $\partial \eta / \partial \alpha$:
    real   THETAD*(RMULT4*COSINE + RMULT*COSINE4)
    imaginary   THETAD*(RMULT4*SINE + RMULT*SINE4)

Temporary functions
    SINE5 = COSINE*ANGLE
    COSINE5 = SINE*ANGLE
    RMULT5 = −LOG(RADSQ)*RMULT/2

Derivatives $\partial \eta / \partial \beta$:
    real   THETAD*(RMULT5*COSINE + RMULT*COSINE5)
    imaginary   THETAD*(RMULT5*SINE + RMULT*SINE5)

CHAPTER 8

Indirect Measurement of Work

Mary B. Hovik
Zionsville, Pennsylvania

Sutton Monro
Coopersburg, Pennsylvania

We are concerned with work measurement in an office or shop. The estimates are to come from analysis of accounting data rather than from time study or work sampling. The data are summary figures for a standard time period an eight hour day in our example, and are of two kinds: the total number of paid man-hours for the office, say, and the total number of units produced in each of the mutually exclusive and, except for slack or non-productive time, jointly inclusive work categories. We want to estimate the average number of man-hours per unit spent now in each category though there is no breakdown of the total man-hours into categories. The problem is common and interesting for groups of workers who are salaried or who are reimbursed for whole blocks of time, like a shift, and who individually produce, or contribute to, units in more than one category.

Table I contains data collected in an office processing the paper work for six kinds of orders. The usual work force there was ten women, and the data represent five successive weeks of five days each, starting on a Monday. The data were provided by Professor W. J. Richardson of the Lehigh University Department of Industrial Engineering and were published on page 221 of his book *Cost Improvement, Work Sampling, and Short Interval Scheduling*, 1976, Reston Publishing Company.

Some authors (see, for example, D. D. Martin, "Instant Time Standards," *Industrial Engineering*, November 1971, pages 24-27) have used multiple linear regression, taking the paid man-hours, y, to be the dependent variable, the number of units produced in the various categories to be the predictors, the desired estimates to be the coefficients and the slack to be the intercept. This approach, while arithmetically feasible, suffers the two disadvantages that it cannot be justified in principle and does not produce useful estimates in practice. The number of paid man-hours is less a distributed random

TABLE 1.

Day	Man-Hours	\multicolumn{6}{c}{Job Categories}						
		A	B	C	D	E	F
1	80	197	155	211	360	171	17
2	80	187	113	194	236	196	71
3	80	394	125	204	113	128	53
4	80	187	61	191	407	181	70
5	80	121	25	193	317	210	86
6	72	136	67	140	329	210	18
7	64	187	24	169	402	174	69
8	80	133	122	216	259	104	84
9	80	172	97	273	329	100	0
10	72	214	55	231	406	114	69
11	78	383	100	178	396	67	69
12	80	325	115	212	381	162	36
13	80	321	100	152	82	195	74
14	80	216	30	203	335	299	67
15	80	96	32	282	514	130	34
16	80	221	25	204	96	133	68
17	80	218	50	221	404	225	47
18	80	170	94	151	621	188	58
19	80	247	83	282	175	124	76
20	80	266	52	199	396	203	74
21	80	279	75	192	419	76	47
22	74	160	17	160	263	281	85
23	80	315	49	219	122	324	40
24	80	245	91	199	546	89	24
25	94	330	116	184	86	192	128

variable than a nearly constant limiting condition, as seen in the given data. This leads to an over-estimate of the intercept and under-estimates in general for the coefficients. In fact, published accounts (see Martin, op. cit.) contain negative coefficient estimates.

Common experience shows slack time to be a random variable, and that suggests considering productivity, or productive time, to be the distributed variable. We chose to represent that effect by a proper fractional multiplier of the paid man-hours, y, the fraction, p, being the proportion of the man-hours used productively. If we had known the appropriate p-value for each day, we might have let $p_j y_j$ be the dependent observation for the j-th day in the time order and used a regression model without intercept. Since we did not know, we undertook to create an artificial set of p-values, to assign them with some rationale to the days and then to modify both their values and their assignments in view of the effect. We proceeded as follows.

Using a beta density $f(p; a, b)$ we created p_i such that $F(p_i) = i/(n+1)$, where $n = 25$ for our data. Professional judgment of the office led to setting $E(p) = .7$, initially, and $V(p) = .01$, inducing an $a = 14$, $b = 6$ and yielding p_i roughly from .5 to .9. We used the residuals of the ordinary least square multiple linear regression for y_j to create an initial rank order of the days from the least to the most productive, and then assigned p_i to the i-th least productive day. (It might have been preferable, since the office appeared to be productive, to use a model with no intercept.) Then, letting $p_i y_i$ play the role of the dependent observation, we again fitted the multiple linear regression by least squares. Again, we did leave the intercept in the model, hoping that its estimate would be nearly zero.

There were two searches to be carried out: one to find a and b, and the other to find the order for the days. An F-ratio was used for comparison purposes during the searches.

Since the original order of the days derived from method inappropriate to the problem, the first search steps involved reorder. In the example, the 25th day had appeared to have the most slack and its man-hours were modified by p_1. This led it to have the smallest (largest absolute) residual, -13.52, when the $p_i y_i$ were first fitted. The corresponding F-value was 1.93. Without changing a or b, the 25th day was alternated with days further down the list, one at a time, until it no longer had the largest absolute residual. At that point it was in the 13th position and F was 6.26.

Interchanges of other days could have continued, but a crude search for new a and b was undertaken, leading to $a = 30$ and $b = 5$, with $F = 45.54$. The two searches were arbitrarily alternated until F reached 1045, $a = 25$ and $b = 5.25$. Then with the order left alone, a careful search for a and b led to $a = 24.756$, $b = 5.959$ and $F = 1694$. This process appeared to stop with $F = 2387$, $a = 24.4$ and $b = 5.65$.

That the three least productive days appeared at this point to be numbered 16, 6 and 21, all Mondays, was a source of some practical satisfaction. Moreover, the residuals were substantially normally distributed. The seven estimates were, in order from b_0 to b_6, -2.304, .028, .103, .150, .015, .069 and .088. The b_0 was small as was hoped.

Since busy days can be expected to decrease the estimates of the coefficients, we went back and ran the same analysis on the first fifteen days to see if the estimates were larger. Each of the estimated coefficients was larger, the biggest difference being less than 15%. Although the estimated (a, b) became (16.36, 1.92) the practical nature of the model and the order of the fifteen days both remained the same.

We have evidence, however, that the problem is not easily solved. Starting over again, we drove the interchanges of the days in the order until there was no improvement in the criterion. Then we optimized (a, b) for that order, and repeated the process. This produced $F = 2909$, with $(a, b) = (14.74, 9.71)$ and the seven estimates, -6.59, .03, .14, .092, $-.004$, .0376 and .223. The larger F-value merely emphasizes that everything else seems less satisfactory. Only one Monday was at the low end of productivity; the intercept was larger and the negative estimate was unusable.

Comments

1. For a given (a, b) there may well be a unique order maximizing F but we have no evidence that systematic reordering based on reducing maximum residuals will achieve it. We suspect the surface of maximum F-values over the domain of (a, b) has local maxima.

2. Given enough data, days in our case, it might be advantageous to estimate unique (a, b)'s for each day of the week.

3. Since the workers are engaged in more than one category, the question should arise whether, as has been described at the Volvo works, this raises productivity beyond what it would be if all of one's work were in one category. This still might imply a model linear in the coefficients but with powers slightly higher than one on the predictors.

4. Having an intercept in the model was not helpful.

CHAPTER 9

Are Some Latin Squares Better Than Others?

J. Stuart Hunter
Princeton, New Jersey

This paper assumes that an experimenter is interested in investigating the role of three factors under his control upon some measured response. Thus

$$\eta = f[x_1, x_2, x_3],$$

where η is the response of interest and the x's three controlled factors. An experimental design sometimes employed in such investigations is the Latin Square in nine runs, the design's rows, columns, and letters used to identify each of the factors x_1, x_2, and x_3.

The Latin Square design for $k = 3$ can be written down in a total of twelve different ways as shown in Table 1. If each three-version factor is identified as R = rows, C = columns and L = letters, or equivalently as x_1, x_2, and x_3, each Latin Square can be considered as a fraction of a complete 3^3 factorial design. Letting (−, 0, +) indicate the three versions of the factors, the design matrix for the complete 3^3 factorial is displayed in Table 2, along with the design matrices for two representative Latin Squares.

The (−, 0, +) notation may now be used to identify each experimental design in three-space as illustrated in Figure 1.

Except for reflections, the twelve Latin Square designs provide only two distinguishable configurations of points identified as Type A and Type B and illustrated in Figures 1b and 1c. The Latin Squares

164 ARE SOME LATIN SQUARES BETTER THAN OTHERS?

numbered (3), (6), (7) and (10), all having the letter b on a diagonal, or equivalently the run (0, 0, 0), are of Type A. The remaining eight Latin Squares are of Type B.

In investigating an unknown response function, some experimenters require from the start the use of three equally spaced settings for each factor. It is argued that three levels for each factor is required in order to provide some measure of response curvature over the range of each factor. The $k = 3$ Latin Square in nine runs is thus a fraction of the 3^3 factorial that would be required if all factor combinations were employed.

TABLE 1. The twelve 3-factor Latin Squares.

(1)	a b c b c a c a b	(2)	a b c c a b b c a	(3)	a c b c b a b a c	(4)	a c b b a c c b a
(5)	b a c a c b c b a	(6)	b a c c b a a c b	(7)	b c a a b c c a b	(8)	b c a c a b a b c
(9)	c a b b c a a b c	(10)	c a b a b c b c a	(11)	c b a b a c a c b	(12)	c b a a c b b a c

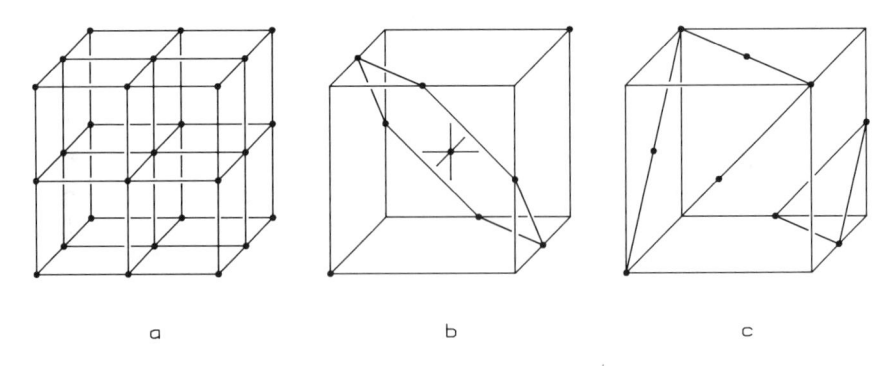

      a   b   c

Figure 1. The 3^3 factorial and two Latin Squares.

Figure 1a: The 3^3 factorial
Figure 1b: The Type A Latin Square
Figure 1c: The Type B Latin Square

TABLE 2. The 3^3 factorial and associated Latin Squares.

		3^3	Factorial	Observation		Latin Square (3) Type A			Latin Square (2) Type B	
	R	C	L	\multicolumn{2}{c	}{Observation}	R	C	L	R	C	L
1	−	−	−	945,	961	−	−	−	−	−	−
2	0	−	−	969,	960	0	−	+	0	−	0
3	+	−	−	964,	964	+	−	0	+	−	+
4	−	0	−	905,	897	−	0	+	−	0	+
5	0	0	−	936,	946	0	0	0	0	0	−
6	+	0	−	940,	924	+	0	−	+	0	0
7	−	+	−	842,	845	−	+	0	−	+	0
8	0	+	−	868,	790	0	+	−	0	+	+
9	+	+	−	845,	880	+	+	+	+	+	−
10	−	−	0	933,	968						
11	0	−	0	944,	882						
12	+	−	0	949,	964						
13	−	0	0	969,	927						
14	0	0	0	925,	985						
15	+	0	0	905,	943						
16	−	+	0	848,	872						
17	0	+	0	981,	989						
18	+	+	0	993,	1020						
19	−	−	+	962,	950						
20	0	−	+	942,	958						
21	+	−	+	965,	974						
22	−	0	+	908,	892						
23	0	0	+	892,	904						
24	+	0	+	950,	917						
25	−	+	+	851,	881						
26	0	+	+	872,	879						
27	+	+	+	890,	902						

(The data in Table 2 are from the paper "Partially replicated Latin Squares," by W. J. Youden and J. S. Hunter, (1955), *Biometrics*, **11**, 399-405.)

In these circumstances, the model postulated is:

$$y = \beta_0 + \beta_1 x_1 + \beta_2 x_2 + \beta_3 x_3 +$$
$$\beta_{11} x_1^2 + \beta_{22} x_2^2 + \beta_{33} x_3^2 +$$
$$\beta_{12} x_1 x_2 + \beta_{13} x_1 x_3 + \beta_{23} x_2 x_3 + \epsilon$$

where

y = an observed value,

x_1, x_2, and x_3 are independent variables,

β_0 = constant term,

β_i = first order coefficients, $i = 1,2,3$,

β_{ii} = quadratic (curvature) coefficients,

β_{ij} = cross product (interaction) coefficients, $i \neq j$,

ϵ is an "error" assumed to be normally and independently distributed with mean zero and constant variance σ^2.

The model is a second order approximation of the unknown function.

If a first order approximation to the unknown response proves reasonable,

$$y = \beta_0 + \beta_1 x_1 + \beta_2 x_2 + \beta_3 x_3 + \epsilon$$

then the estimates of the first order coefficients β_1, β_2, and β_3 for any one of the Latin Square designs are given by:

$$[\bar{y}_+ - \bar{y}_-]/2$$

where $\bar{y}_+$ and $\bar{y}_-$ are the average responses at the high and low settings respectively of the separate factors x_1, x_2, and x_3, and the variance of each estimated coefficient will be

$$V(b_k) = \sigma^2 / rk,$$

where here $k = 3$ and r is the number of times the design has been replicated.

It is seldom wise to assume a postulated first order model to represent an unknown response function exactly. For Latin Square designs the estimates of the quadratic coefficients in a second order approximating model are easily obtained. However, all the two-factor interaction coefficients can not then be estimated. The second order model contains ten coefficients and the design has only nine distinctly different experiments. In this situation, common practice is to estimate only the quadratic coefficients β_{ii} and to assume the coupled influences as represented by the crossproduct coefficients β_{ij} to be zero, or very small. The model fitted is thus an incomplete order model. With this model the Latin Square can be called a "main effect clear" design since, for the quantitative factors x_1, x_2, and x_3, the contribution of each factor upon the response is separable.

When the crossproduct coefficients are required in the approximating polynomial, the unestimated β_{ij} coefficients bias the estimates of the coefficients in the fitted incomplete order model. The nature of this bias is given by the alias matrix where it can be shown that the β_{ij} coefficients bias the estimates of the first order coefficients only for the Latin Squares of Type B. The crossproduct coefficients do not bias the estimates of the first order terms if the data are secured from Latin Squares of Type A.

When fitting a second order model, the magnitude and signs of the second order terms β_{ii} and β_{ij} depend upon the orientation of the response surface with respect to the axes x_i, x_2, and x_3 defining the design factor space. These axes are of course determined by the experimenter. If the response function is thought to be non-planar, it would seem reasonable always to search for both the curvature and coupled influences of the three factors. The best design to employ would then be the Box-Behnken three-level second order design illustrated in Figure 2a, and not the Latin Square.

If a Latin Square design is initially planned, then the designs of Type A are to be preferred over Type B. If a Type A Latin Square is first used, it can be augmented by six points to give a Box-Behnken design containing only two extra points. If a Type B Latin Square is employed, ten additional points are required before a Box-Behnken configuration can be obtained. Some Latin Squares do appear to be better than others.

To provide an opportunity for the reader to enjoy a bit of data analysis, the second order model was first fitted using the data from the replicated 3^3 factorial given in Table 1, and again using only the data from the augmented Latin Square Type A.

168 ARE SOME LATIN SQUARES BETTER THAN OTHERS?

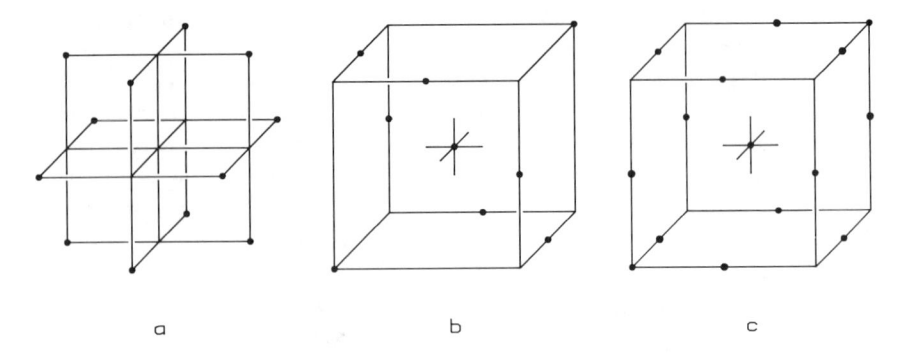

a   b   c

Figure 2. Augmenting the Type A Latin Square.
Figure 2a: The Box-Behnken design
Figure 2b: The Type A Latin Square
Figure 2c: The augmented design

The fitted second order model based upon the fifty-four observations obtained from the replicated 3^3 factorial is:

$$y = 946.630 + 14.806x_1 - 30.722x_2 + 3.000x_3 +$$
$$0.028x_1^2 - 3.556x_2^2 - 31.222x_3^2 +$$
$$13.750x_1x_2 + 1.333x_1x_3 + 9.042x_2x_3.$$

The associated analysis of variance table is:

Sy^2	120095.43	53	
Model	60585.986	9	
Residual	59509.440	44	1352.49

The design matrix, observations and fitted second order model for the augmented Latin Square Type B are as follows:

x_1	x_2	x_3	Observation	
−	−	−	945,	961
0	−	+	942,	958
+	−	0	949,	964
−	0	+	908,	892
0	0	0	925,	985
+	0	−	940,	924
−	+	0	848,	872
0	+	−	868,	790
+	+	+	890,	902
−	−	0	933,	968
+	+	0	993,	1020
−	0	−	905,	897
+	0	+	950,	917
0	−	−	969,	960
0	+	+	872,	879

The fitted second order model is:

$$y = 964.30 + 23.07x_1 - 35.37x_2 + 0.01x_3$$

$$-5.69x_1^2 - 17.56x_2^2 - 44.31x_3^2$$

$$+30.48x_1x_2 - 4.02x_1x_3 + 10.60x_2x_3.$$

The associated analysis of variance table is:

Sy^2	67842.80	29	
Model	48024.17	9	
Residual	19818.63	20	990.93

REFERENCES

Youden, W. J. and Hunter, J. S. (1955). "Partially replicated Latin Squares," *Biometrics*, **11**, 399-405.

CHAPTER 10

Graphical Exploratory Analysis of Variance Illustrated on a Splitting of the Johnson and Tsao Data [1]

Eugene G. Johnson
Educational Testing Service

John W. Tukey
Princeton University

INTRODUCTION

Since our main purpose is to illustrate how a combination of graphic display and simple arithmetic can be used to enhance the effectiveness of Daniel's half-normal plots, we shall focus on an analysis of a 2 × 4 × 7 data set provided by the responses of person IB1 in the "methodological experiment" presented by (Palmer) Johnson and Tsao (1944) and also analyzed by Palmer Johnson (1949) and by Green and Tukey (1960). The full data set involves 8 persons. We will return below to a fuller description of the data set and a discussion of how it might be analyzed, and elsewhere to a discussion of how the analysis might be carried further, with special attention to the identification and sterilization of exotic values.

We need to make clear our overall prejudices and purposes — a (well-founded) prejudice that most analyses of variance with 3 or more factors are used for exploration rather than confirmation, with a

---

[1] Prepared in connection with research at Princeton University sponsored by the U. S. Army Research Office (Durham).

clear description of the apparent behavior being much more important than formal significance tests, and a clear purpose to reach as simple and complete description of the data behavior, in the instance before us, as we know how, taking reasonable account of questions of multiplicity, but not overemphasizing precise significance. We want a description of the *appearance* of our data, even though more data might not confirm that appearance.

Since we further believe that good techniques come from the accretion of many ideas, not just from a single brain wave, we are not dismayed by the appearance of at least 12 conceptual ingredients (3 old, 1 due to Daniel). Rather we wonder where the 13th and 14th will come from. To tease the reader's imagination, we list the 12 ingredients so far at hand (the later ones need not be as large or important as the earlier):

1) classical analysis of variance
2) aggregation
3) half-normal plotting
4) horizontalized plotting
5) scission into bouquets of contrasts
6) pretrimming by nomination
7) post-trimming by election
8) nominated bouquets
9) 2nd order trimming (super-election)
10) reformulating a response
11) rethinking a scission
12) refactoring an analysis

We believe that these ingredients can be used in any factorial analysis of variance — and in many others of different form.

The basic elements underlying all this are:

(A) basic ANOVA concepts of decomposition — of separating of each number into parts, each part coming as purely as we can arrange from its specified "source,"

(B) anticipation of revision in the light of the data, not only of numbers but also of the style and form of separation,

(C) use of long-term insight to select specifics for trial,

(D) use of pictures to see what may need special treatment or modification,

(E) use of arithmetic to conduct modifications,

(F) ultimately a combination of (a) numerical summaries, hopefully depictable, and (b) pictorially apparent absence of what else might plausibly be present.

We now discuss the ingredients, and explain their concatenation and mixing, in terms of the single $2 \times 4 \times 7$ data set mentioned above, showing how they lead to a reasonably compact description of the 56 numbers.

CONTENTS

PART A:	ANALYZING IB1'S PERFORMANCE IN GRAMS	
A1.	Looking at the Data Overall	174
A2.	Bouquets of Contrasts	178
A3.	Horizontalizing Plots	178
A4.	Display Ratios in the Example	180
A5.	The Largest of the Three-Factor Contrasts	183
A6.	Pretrimmed Bouquets; Nomination	184
A7.	Trimmed Bouquets in the Example	188
A8.	Dragging Upward	190
A9.	The Effect of Aggregation	193
A10.	Aggregation in the Example	196
PART B:	DATA-GUIDED TRIMMING OF BOUQUETS	
B1.	Scales and Ratios-to-Scale	199
B2.	Null Behavior of "Ratio-to-Scale"	200
B3.	Post-Trimmed Bouquets; Election	203
B4.	Election (Post-Trimming) in the Example	204
B5.	The Final Outcomes for the First 56 Numbers	206
PART C:	ANALYZING IB1'S PERFORMANCE IN OTHER TERMS	
C1.	Reformulating the Response	208
C2.	A First Analysis of Log Response Time	211
PART D:	RETHINKING A SCISSION INTO CONTRASTS	
D1.	Spreading of Contributions across Contrasts	213
D2.	Some Useful Bouquets of Contrasts	214
D3.	Alternative Descriptions of the (Log-Response) Rate Effect	217
D4.	The Example after Rescission	223
D5.	Refactoring	225
D6.	Recapitulation	233
PART E:	A LOOK AT THE OTHER 7 PEOPLE	
E1.	All 16 of the Person-Date Units	234
E2.	Reassembly	239
PART F:	SUMMARY	242

REFERENCES

PART A: ANALYZING IB1's PERFORMANCE IN GRAMS

A1. Looking at the Data Overall

The 2 × 4 × 7 data set for person IB1 (one of the two blind males in the full experiment) involves 2 dates (1,2), four rates (50, 100, 150 and 200 grams per 30 seconds), and seven (initial) weights (100, 150, 200, 250, 300, 350 and 400 grams). The experimental procedure involved attaching a pail by a lever system to a ring on the subject's finger. One of the seven initial weights was placed into the pail, and then water was allowed to flow into the pail at one of four constant rates until the subject reported a change in pull on the finger. The intended response, the difference limen (D.L.), was measured by the amount of water added by time of report. Five determinations were made for each of the 28 rate-weight combinations, and the average of these values was used as the response. The entire experiment was conducted, for each person, at each of two dates, one week apart.

The full experiment consisted of 8 persons, two persons in each cell of a 2 × 2 design for male vs. female and sighted vs. blind. In their analysis of the complete data set, Green and Tukey noted that person IB1 had a pattern of response that was considerably different from that of the other persons (including the other blind male) and designated him as the "eccentric blind man." For this very reason, we have selected person IB1 for our initial (within person) analysis.

TABLE 1. Average difference limen in grams for person IB1 — male, blind.

Rate (gm/30 sec)	Date	\multicolumn{7}{c}{Initial Weight (Grams)}
		100	150	200	250	300	350	400
50	1	24.2	25.3	25.1	17.6	20.7	19.4	17.3
	2	41.2	29.8	28.5	23.8	20.9	17.8	13.4
100	1	48.1	41.2	31.4	30.4	39.9	36.7	35.5
	2	59.1	59.7	48.7	38.1	30.7	28.4	27.2
150	1	60.9	52.0	58.2	60.6	57.1	57.9	49.5
	2	75.8	79.9	69.1	64.4	42.2	53.1	36.3
200	1	69.9	76.7	82.4	76.4	71.4	76.9	79.6
	2	148.3	123.1	73.5	61.9	77.8	56.0	53.2

PART A: ANALYZING IB1's PERFORMANCE IN GRAMS   175

As a first step in the analysis of the performance of IB1 to the experiment, we display his responses. The actual values appear in Table 1; a graphical display of the responses is shown in Figure 1. Figure 1 consists of a series of 7 plots, one for each level of weight (indicated on the horizontal axis). Each of the seven plots shows the relationship between the response (D.L. in grams) and rate for both dates. The responses for each date are connected by a broken line. In considering Figure 1, the first thing that strikes the eye is the strong linear relationship between D.L. and rate. In fact, such a relationship, which was also found by Johnson and Tsao and by Green and Tukey, holds for each person. In Part C, we will consider an analysis of the data for person IB1 which uses a different dependent variable (log(response time)) and which produces a particularly simple interpretation of the relationships between level of response and the various factors. For the moment, however, we will press forward with an analysis of person IB1 with response in the original units — D.L. in grams.

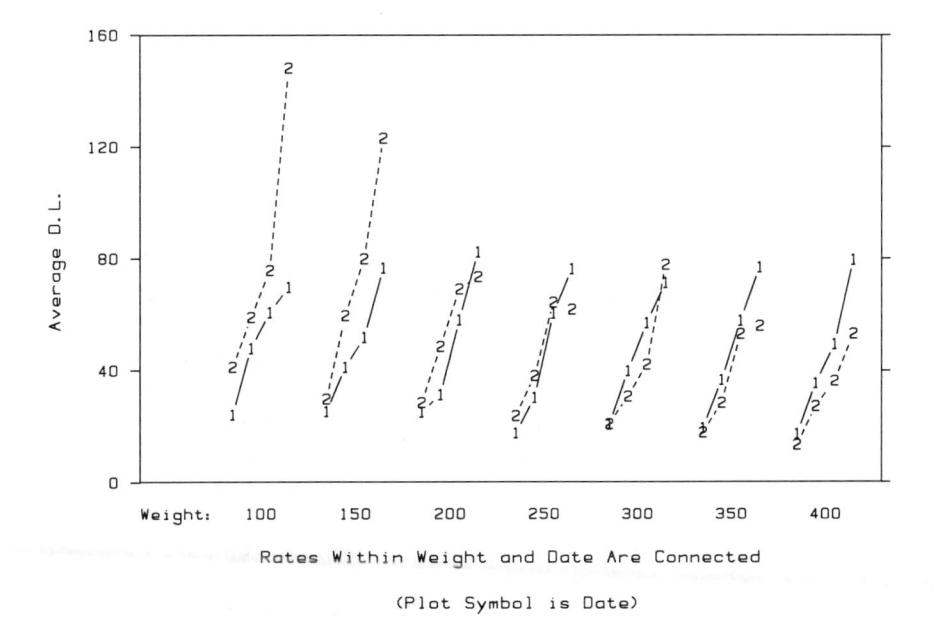

Figure 1. Person IB1: male, blind. Average difference limen (grams).

Crude Classical Analysis of Variance

A standard analysis of variance table of the 2 × 4 × 7 factorial design for person IB1 with difference limens in grams as the dependent variable is given in Table 2. In the table, we have denoted the independent variables as R for rate, W for weight and D for date. In determining the values for "F" and the significance levels, the line of the table corresponding to the three-factor interaction DRW was (naively) taken as measuring appropriate error for each of the other lines (extreme model 1).

Given the strong linear relationship between D.L. and rate within each date-by-weight combination noted from Figure 1, it is not at all surprising to find that the largest mean square is that associated with rate. The only other "significant" lines in Table 2 are the weight main effect and (somewhat less strongly) the date × weight two-factor interaction.

Crude Aggregated Analysis of Variance

Using the sort of aggregation proposed by Green and Tukey (and described in section A9), the result would be as in Table 3.

We shall consider more refined analyses starting from (analogs) of these two tables. The results are similar to those for the classical analysis, although the 2 × 7 date and weight table is reassembled (from D, W and DW).

Single df's

A (traditional) [aggregated] analysis would now proceed to pull apart from the various (significant) [remaining] lines one or more single-degree-of-freedom components, comparing the magnitudes of each of the constituent contrasts with that of (the three-factor interaction mean square) [an appropriate aggregated denominator] taken to represent error. Rather than beginning with such an approach, we will cut up each of the lines of the (full) [aggregated] analysis of variance table (including the DRW line) into single degree-of-freedom components — contrasts — and compare the sizes (absolute values) of these contrast components graphically by a technique related to Daniel's half-normal plots.

In such an analysis, to be described shortly, we do not assume that any prechosen line of any analysis of variance table is necessarily solely measuring error. Rather, we assume that any of the selected contrasts which combine to constitute some line (i.e., a main effect, a two-factor interaction, ..., a n-factor interaction) might have mean values different from zero, but that most of the totality of them will serve for error estimates. That is, we assume the bulk of the (properly defined) single-degree-of-freedom components are actually measuring error — or come close to doing so — but we do not *a priori* specify which ones, or which error.

We selected our 2 × 4 × 7 subset of the data in such a way as to avoid major complications with multiple error terms, which arise when the whole data set is considered. Similar techniques will apply to factorial data sets deserving more error terms.

TABLE 2. Standard analysis-of-variance table for person IB1 (dependent variable is difference limen in grams).

Source	df	MS	DEN	F	Sig
D	1	348	149	2.33	not
R	3	8514	149	57.06	0.01%
W	6	772	149	5.18	0.5%
DR	3	21	149	0.14	not
DW	6	545	149	3.65	2.5%
RW	18	74	149	0.50	not
DRW	18	149	—	—	—

TABLE 3. Aggregated analysis-of-variance table for person IB1.

Label	df	MS	DEN	F	Sig*
Rate	3	8514	105**	81.10**	0.01%
Date and Weight	13	635	105	6.05	0.01%
Residual	39	105	—	—	—

* Notice that (a) significance levels of F-values require a large, rather unspecified multiplier for multiplicity and (b) 0.01% is the most extreme level considered.

** Would have been 635 and 13.4, respectively, had any rate interaction appeared in the following (date and weight) aggregation.

A2. Bouquets of Contrasts

Since we are going to focus on single degrees of freedom, we need to break up each factor into a bouquet of contrasts, each a single degree of freedom. We expect to use the natural combinations (outer products) of these one-factor contrasts to also break up the two-factor and three-factor interactions into single-degree-of-freedom contrasts.

Because the two factors to be broken up (date is already a single contrast) are scales with equispaced versions (levels), it is perhaps natural to consider the classical orthogonal polynomials as a possible first choice for the basic bouquet. Besides these contrasts there are other types of orthogonal contrasts which, depending on circumstances, may have greater utility. We shall return to some of these in section D2.

If the versions of our factors had been only ordered, not measured, we might have followed Abelson and Tukey (1963) in selecting an initial contrast, or conceivably, have separated the response into monotone increasing and monotone decreasing parts. Unordered versions can often be sensibly partitioned, although we may have to be somewhat arbitrary in some or all of our choices of contrasts.

Various bouquets of contrasts have their place in the analysis of data. We will use a number of different bouquets in our analysis of our 2 × 4 × 7 data set. Given a collection of bouquets of single-degree-of-freedom contrasts, one for each line of the standard analysis of variance table, the next step in the continued analysis of the data is the assessment of what the values of the contrasts are trying to tell us about the relationship within and between the various factors. This assessment will be done graphically via a procedure related to Daniel's half-normal plots.

A3. Horizontalizing Plots

The classic "half-normal plot" relates the sizes (absolute values) of the normalized contrasts, ordered by size, with typical values of order-statistics of the half-Gaussian distribution by plotting (ordered) size of contrast versus typical order-statistic. The corresponding natural reference is a line *through the origin*, whose *slope* corresponds to an estimate of the underlying scale σ. To make internal comparison much easier, we shall instead plot

$$\frac{\text{size of contrast}}{\text{typical order statistic}} \text{ versus (typical order-statistic)}$$

PART A: ANALYZING IB1's PERFORMANCE IN GRAMS

thus making the natural reference a *horizontal line*, whose *height* corresponds to an estimate of σ.

Display Ratios

While classical probability plots often use the unit deviates corresponding to $\dfrac{i}{d+1}$ or $\dfrac{i-\frac{1}{2}}{d}$ as the typical order statistics for a sample of d values, we shall work very close to the order-statistic medians by using deviates corresponding to $\left(i - \dfrac{1}{3}\right) / \left(d + \dfrac{1}{3}\right) = (3i-1)/(3d+1)$. For the half-Gaussian (the distribution of the positive square root of any chi-square on one degree of freedom), this means using the half-Gaussian working values, the ith such (of d) being

$$c(i:d) = \Phi^{-1}\left[\tfrac{1}{2} + \tfrac{1}{2}\left(\frac{3i-1}{3d+1}\right)\right] = \Phi^{-1}\left(\frac{3i+3d}{6d+2}\right)$$

where Φ is the unit Gaussian cumulative distribution function.

Thus, we shall plot the

$$\text{display ratio} = \frac{|C(i:d)|}{c(i:d)}$$

versus the typical order statistic $= c(i:d)$ where $|C(i:d)|$ is the ith largest size of our contrasts. Under the simple (null) model that the sizes of contrast $|C(1:d)|, ..., |C(d:d)|$ represent a set of order statistics from a sample of size d from a half-Gaussian distribution with scale σ and location 0, each of the d display ratios provides an estimate of σ.

We compute the display ratios separately for each bouquet of contrasts, one bouquet for each line of a conventional analysis of variance table. A plot of display ratio versus working value for a particular bouquet shows:

1) the general level of variability, hopefully background noise, captured by a typical defining contrast of the bouquet and measured by a horizontal line, and

2) the relative magnitude of the various sizes of contrast in terms of the general level for that bouquet and in terms of what would be expected under a simple (null) model.

We tend to focus on the display ratios for the largest sizes of contrasts, interpreting relatively large display ratios as indicating potentially meaningful contributions, likely to be worth separate description.

A plot of display ratio versus working value for a bouquet will sometimes produce slightly confusing appearances, when granularity, arithmetic errors, or other causes of individual exotic values keep the contrasts of smallest size from being as small as a simple model suggests they ought to be. Thus, relatively high values of the display ratio for quite small working values should often be ignored. If considered, they should usually be regarded as suggesting isolated errors, exoticities or granularities. (We turn later (elsewhere) to looking for such isolated phenomena.) A general downward trend (to the right) invites similar interpretation and treatment.

Although we compute the display ratios separately for each bouquet, ordinarily we will overlay the plots for each bouquet of a given type (main effects, 2-factor interactions, etc.) on the same figure, connecting the points for contrasts in each bouquet by a broken line. This allows both for internal comparison of the sizes of contrast within a bouquet and comparison with the sizes of contrasts of the other bouquets of that type. By using the same vertical scale for all of the plots, we can also compare the sizes of contrasts across the various types. The latter comparison allows the assessment of the relative importance of a given contrast in the experiment as a whole and also, by comparing the general level of one bouquet with that of the others, indicates if the set of defining contrasts for a given factor might be replaced by another set of defining contrasts to produce a simpler account of the data. Such a possibility exists if the general level of a particular bouquet, particularly a main effect bouquet, is above the levels of the other bouquets. We will discuss the possible causes of this in Part D.

A4. Display Ratios in the Example

We now return to subject IB1 and apply the above procedure, using the polynomial contrasts. The result is shown in Figure 2, where we have grouped the bouquets into three sets, plotting the three main-effect bouquets together in the first panel, the three two-factor-interaction bouquets together in the second, and the three-factor interactions in the third panel. The vertical scale for the three plots is the same, allowing for the comparison of magnitude of the display ratios for all bouquets.

PART A: ANALYZING IB1's PERFORMANCE IN GRAMS   181

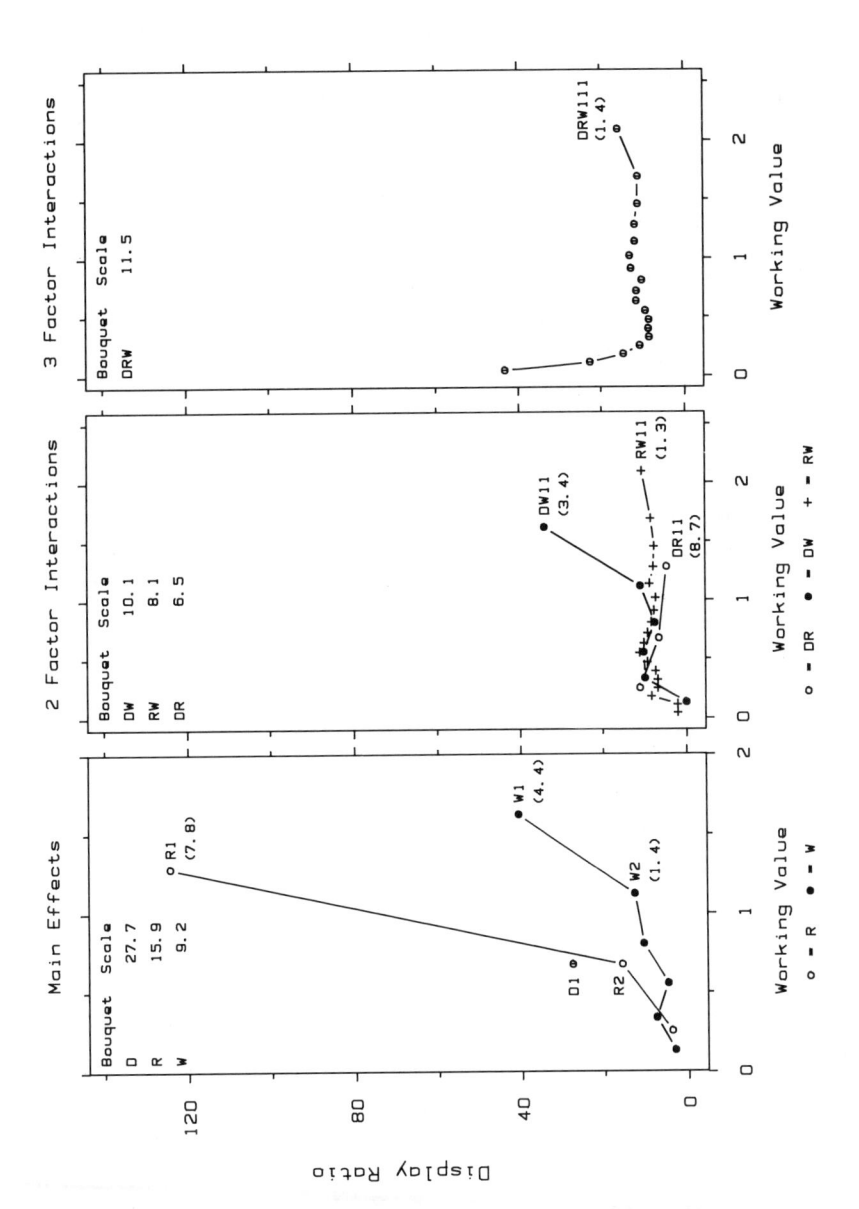

Figure 2. Person IB1 — D.L.in grams. Polynomial contrasts.

The points for contrasts within each bouquet are connected by a broken line, and the largest size of contrast within each bouquet is labeled. Occasionally, other contrasts of large size will be labeled. The notation for the various bouquets is as in the initial analysis of variance (Table 2); the order of polynomial contrast is indicated by a number following the bouquet label. For example, $R1$ is the linear contrast for rate, $W2$ is the quadratic contrast for weight, $DW12$ is the linear (in date)-by-quadratic (in weight) two-factor contrast, and $DRW123$ is the linear (date)-by-quadratic (rate)-by-cubic (weight) three-factor contrast. (We shall return to the various numbers attached to the bouquets and to the high individual points in section B1.)

The first thing to note from the plots is that the bulk of the contrasts have display ratios at a level of about 10 grams. In light of this background level, we have to recognize the contrasts with the largest display ratios — $R1$ (linear in rate), $W1$ (linear in weight), $DW11$ (linear in date by linear in weight), $D1$ (linear in date), and $DRW111$ (linear by linear by linear three-factor interaction), in decreasing order — as worth careful consideration. The values of these display ratios, along with those for certain of the next largest contrasts within each bouquet, are given in Table 4.

In view of the proportional relationship between D.L. and rate suggested by Figure 1, it is not surprising that $R1$ is the strongest observed relationship. It is striking that the five largest contrasts in

TABLE 4. Values of display ratio for the largest contrasts within each bouquet for the polynomial decomposition of IB1 (D.L.).

Contrast	Display Ratio
$R1$	124
$W1$	41
$DW11$	34
$D1$	28
$DRW111$	16
$R2$	16
$W2$	13
all others	< 11

terms of display ratio are solely composed of linear (straight-line) contrasts and their products. In fact the linear (or linear by linear, etc.) comparisons have the largest size of contrast within every bouquet. We will return to this in the next section.

For the three-factor-interaction contrasts, the display ratios for the contrasts of smallest size are relatively larger than might be expected. As mentioned previously, this phenomenon might be indicating granularity due to rounding or small arithmetic mistakes (one deviant observation tends to contribute similar amounts to each single degree-of-freedom contrast).

Another phenomenon to notice is associated with the R, W and DW bouquets. In each of those bouquets, the largest size of contrast is relatively much larger than the remaining sizes of contrast within the bouquet. Notice, in each of those three bouquets, that the next-to-largest size of contrast is also somewhat high in terms of display ratio, the point for the contrast appearing above the display ratios of all the remaining contrasts of the bouquet. We call the underlying phenomenon "dragging upward" and will discuss it in section A8.

A5. The Largest of the Three-Factor Contrasts

The right-most point for DRW requires careful discussion. It seems to continue, and enhance, a general upward trend for the ratios plotted for the contrasts in this bouquet. However, it does not rise far above the others. Had this, for instance, been a linear-by-quadratic-by-quartic three-factor interaction, or some other nondescript contrast among the $1 \times 3 \times 6 = 18$ in this bouquet, we would not have been likely to attend to it. It is, however, the linear-by-linear-by-linear contrast, *a priori* the most distinctive and most likely (however unlikely) to contain something meaningful. To have it come out as the highest absolute value of all 3-factor contrasts is thus, by itself, significant at $1/18 = 5.56\%$, so that it needs at most a little extra push to be worth our honest attention.

Granting, then, that it may include a real effect, how should we interpret it? It is, after all, a three-factor contrast in a situation where the constituent single-factor contrasts are all large. For the present, then, we may not be too wrong to think of it as "probably real, but likely to be a spill-over from the large main effects because of something resembling not-quite satisfactory expression of the response."

A6. Pretrimmed Bouquets; Nomination

Having found linear, linear-by-linear and linear-by-linear-by-linear contrasts outstanding in our example, we must ask ourselves: "In such a situation, where a few contrasts are distinguished above all others in their respective bouquets, why did we not plan to treat them separately in the beginning — not only in this example but in general?" No good answer is available. So let us trim our bouquets — and even pretend that we pretrimmed them in this example — moving the linear contrast out of each single-factor bouquet, the linear-by-linear ("linear-to-the-2") contrast out of each two-factor bouquet, and the linear-by-linear-by-linear ("linear-to-the-3") contrast out of the three-factor bouquet.

Each original bouquet, corresponding to a line in the analysis of variance table and consisting of d contrasts, has now been partitioned into two bouquets:

- a nominated contrast consisting of the single linear-to-the-j contrast; nominated *a priori* as likely to be interesting

- a trimmed bouquet consisting of the $d-1$ remaining contrasts, which collectively are telling us about the contribution of the corresponding line of the analysis of variance table after eliminating variation describable by the linear-to-the-j contrast.

In our example this creates 13 bouquets from the original 7 (since D is already linear-to-the-1, there is no trimmed bouquet for D). (For a related use of the word "nominated" see S. C. Pearce, 1953 or 1976.)

By nominating $D1$, $R1$, $W1$, $DR11$, $DW11$, $RW11$, and $DRW111$ as *a priori* interesting contrasts we have agreed to treat each of these contrasts not as one of the d members of the original effect bouquet, but rather as a separate thing unto itself. As such, we display them using the working value $c(1:1) = .674$ to compute the display ratios for each of the nominated contrasts.

By pretrimming our bouquets, removing the nominated contrast from the initial bouquet with d members, and producing a trimmed bouquet with $d-1$ members, we have agreed to treat the contrasts in the trimmed bouquet as collectively separate in impact from the nominated contrast. As such, we assess the magnitudes of the sizes of contrast for the $d-1$ members of the trimmed bouquet in terms of what would be expected from a sample of size $d-1$ from a half-Gaussian distribution and so use the working values $c(1:d-1)$, ..., $c(d-1:d-1)$ to compute the display ratios.

PART A: ANALYZING IB1's PERFORMANCE IN GRAMS   185

Results in the Example; Nominated Contrasts

Proceeding in this manner with our example data, we produce Figure 3. In order to better show the detail for the trimmed bouquets, we have truncated the vertical axis of the plots at 50 and thus do not show directly the display ratios for the three largest nominated contrasts: $R1$, $W1$ and $DW11$, each of which should be plotted at working value $c(1:1) = .674$.

On examining the plots, we see first of all that the display ratios of all the nominated contrasts, with the exception of $DR11$, are notably larger than the display ratios of any of the contrasts remaining in the trimmed bouquets (with the exception of the display ratio of the smallest size of contrasts in the trimmed three-factor bouquet, corresponding to the (small) contrast $DRW133$ — possible reasons for this large display ratio have been previously mentioned).

The display ratios for the 7 nominated contrasts are shown in Table 5, both for the nominated contrasts plotted in Figure 3 and, for comparison, as parts of the original effect bouquets plotted in Figure 2.

We can see from the table (and from the plots) how much the display ratios for 6 of the nominated contrasts have each increased when treated as single-contrast bouquets over the display ratios for the same contrasts when treated as the largest member of one of the original bouquets. (The median display ratio, a natural background level, has fallen from 10 to 9.) The ratio of nominated display ratio to original display ratio appears as the last column of Table 5. We also see that, in terms of size of display ratio, the ordering of the display ratios for the nominated contrasts is essentially the same as before, with the exception of $D1$, which has moved down from the 4th largest to the 6th largest (after nomination).

These increases in the values of the display ratios reflect the sizes of the working value used to compute the display ratios, which have decreased from $c(d:d)$ to $c(1:1)$. The ratio of $c(d:d)$ to $c(1:1)$ is exactly equal to the proportional increase in display ratio due to pretrimming. We can see from the table that the ratio of increase grows somewhat as the size d of the original bouquet grows. This growth explains the increase in relative importance of $DRW111$ and $RW11$, both of which belonged to bouquets with 18 members. This also helps to explain why $DR11$, whose display ratio is inflated by a factor of only 1.9, remains at the level of background variability. The plot of display ratio vs. working value for the full DR bouquet in

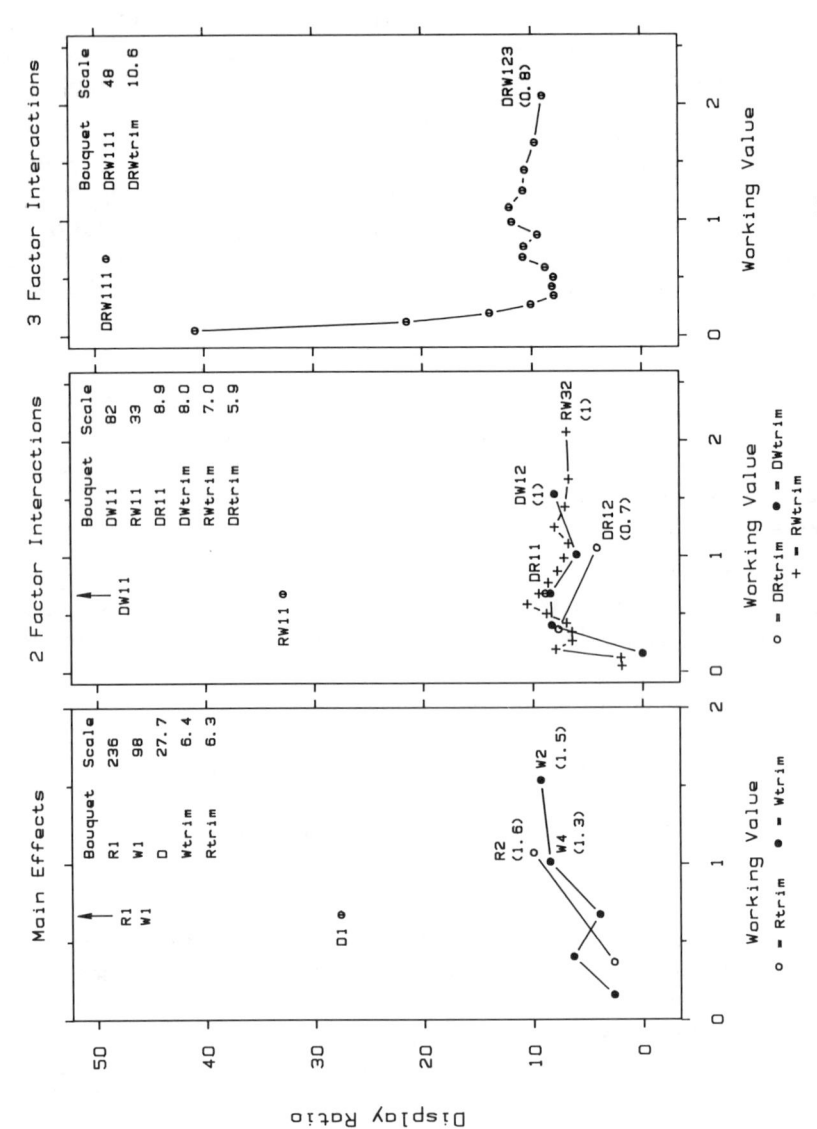

186　GRAPHICAL EXPLORATORY ANALYSIS OF VARIANCE

Figure 3. Person IB1 — D.L. in grams. Polynomial contrasts — pretrimmed bouquets.

PART A: ANALYZING IB1's PERFORMANCE IN GRAMS 187

TABLE 5. Display ratios and reference working values for the nominated contrasts when trimmed out and when left in the original effect bouquets.

	Nominated Contrast		(In Figure 2)			Ratio Of Display Ratios
Contrasts	Display Ratio	Working Value $c(1{:}1)$	Bouquet Size d	Display Ratio	Working Value $c(d{:}d)$	
R1	237	(.674)	3	124	(1.282)	1.9
W1	98	(.674)	6	41	(1.620)	2.4
DW11	82	(.674)	6	34	(1.620)	2.4
DRW111	49	(.674)	18	16	(2.093)	3.1
RW11	33	(.674)	18	11	(2.093)	3.1
D1	28	(.674)	1	28	(.674)	1.0
DR11	9	(.674)	3	5	(1.282)	1.9
Median Display Ratio Over All 55 Contrasts	9			10		.9

Figure 2 shows $DR\,11$ at the end of a general decline; $DR\,11$ is relatively smaller than might be expected for the largest order statistic of a sample of size 3.

Before examining the trimmed bouquets in Figure 3, we should reiterate that we are, in this section, discussing only pretrimming. By coincidence (perhaps), the nominated contrasts in our example all were the largest representatives of their respective bouquets. Since the linear-to-the-j contrasts are the most easily interpretable (and in general the strongest in many experiments), we should have nominated them *a priori*, in any event. The increase of display ratio on nomination will, of course, be less when the nominated contrast is not the largest in its bouquet.

Other Alternatives

If we had used a different set of orthogonal contrasts other than the orthogonal polynomials to define a bouquet, we could, and probably should, still pretrim whenever one of the contrasts is naturally *a priori* distinguished above all others. It is, or course, also possible to post-trim a bouquet, electing for removal the largest (or largest few) contrasts which attract our attention because of their relatively large display ratios. We discuss this possibility in section B3.

188 GRAPHICAL EXPLORATORY ANALYSIS OF VARIANCE

A Nominated Bouquet?

We have nominated 7 contrasts, one from each line of the basic analysis. So far we have treated them as 7 one-contrast bouquets. But why should we not treat them as 1 seven-contrast bouquet, the nominated bouquet? Table 6 shows the display ratios for the nominated bouquet; the first panel of Figure 4 is the corresponding horizontalized plot.

Both Table 6 and Figure 4 show $R1$ as standing out. It might be reasonable to super-elect (see section B3) $R1$ and post-trim the nominated bouquet, separating $R1$ into its own 1-contrast bouquet and leaving the remaining contrasts in a 6-contrast bouquet. The result of this is shown in the last two columns of Table 6 and the second panel of Figure 4. We observe that, whether we post-trim or not, the display ratios of the other 6 nominated contrasts are surprisingly similar. We will return to this point below.

A7. Trimmed Bouquets in the Example

We now return to the trimmed bouquets to consider the effect of nomination and trimming on their display ratios. A consequence of pretrimming can be seen by comparing the plots of the display ratio versus working value for the trimmed and original bouquets. Considering, for example, the three-factor bouquet, we can see from

TABLE 6. Display ratios for the nominated contrasts as members of the seven-contrast nominated bouquet.

Contrast	7-Contrast Bouquet Display Ratio	7-Contrast Bouquet Working Value	After Super-Electing $R1$ and Post-Trimming Display Ratio	After Super-Electing $R1$ and Post-Trimming Working Value
$R1$	94	(1.691)	237	(.674)
$W1$	55	(1.208)	41	(1.620)
$DW11$	61	(.908)	49	(1.119)
$DRW111$	49	(.674)	41	(.804)
$RW11$	47	(.472)	40	(.555)
$D1$	64	(.288)	56	(.336)
$DR11$	52	(.114)	45	(.132)

PART A: ANALYZING IB1's PERFORMANCE IN GRAMS 189

Figure 2 that the display ratio of the second largest contrast, *DRW* 123, appears at essentially the same level as that of the third largest contrast *DRW* 112. Turning to Figure 3, we now see that the display ratio of *DRW* 123 (now the largest size of contrast) is noticeably lower (by .7 units) than that of *DRW* 112 (now the second largest size of contrast). Looking further, comparing the plots of the trimmed bouquets with the original bouquets, we can see a general tendency for the slopes of the lines between adjacent points to become more negative.

Both this and the reduction in the general level of the display ratios for the trimmed bouquets are consequences of a reduction in the "dragging upward" phenomena to be discussed in the next section.

The Changing Typical Size of Residuals

Starting to act as if we had nominated all linear-to-the-*j* contrasts will change the typical sizes of the display ratios, decreasing such sizes when the nominated contrasts are large, as in this example, and

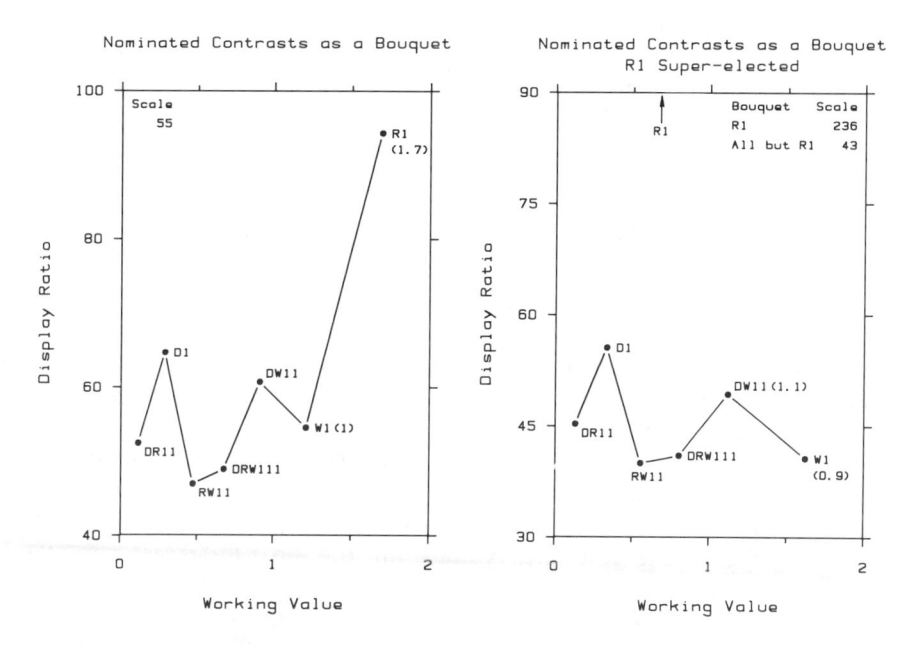

Figure 4. Person IB1. D.L. in grams.

fluctuating them irregularly when the nominated contrasts appear similar in size to the others in their bouquet. The most interesting summary sizes of the display ratios seem to be:

--- before nomination ---	
median for all 55 initial contrasts =	9.9
median for 45 initial non-main-effect contrasts =	9.3
--- after nomination ---	
median for all 55 contrasts with nomination =	8.5
median for all 48 unnominated contrasts =	8.1
median for all 41 unnominated, non-main-effect contrasts =	8.1

Roughly speaking, nomination reduced the median size of display ratio by 13%. (The effect would have been larger if we had not used the median, a highly resistant summary. It is here neither important nor wholly negligible.)

A8. Dragging Upward

In our example (section A4) we saw that retaining the largest contrast in each bouquet tended to make the second-largest contrasts look more distinctive than need be. Do we expect this in general?

We need only look at the divisors, at the order-statistic typical values, to see how this occurs. For $d = 7$ (say before setting the largest apart) and $d = 6$ (after) we have the values in Table 7. On a relative basis, the divisor for what was initially the second largest size of contrast was about ¾ as large before setting aside the largest one as it was after this. It is, in fact, always the case that the typical value of the ith order statistic of a sample of size d, $c(i:d)$, is smaller than $c(i:d-1)$, the typical value of the ith order statistic of a sample of one less. The relative difference is most pronounced for smaller bouquet sizes and is largest for the next-to-largest contrast of a bouquet. Table 8 shows the reference values for the next-to-largest contrast within an original bouquet both before and after trimming out the largest contrast, for the bouquet sizes of our example. The table also includes their ratios $c(i:d)/c(i:d-1)$, and the median value of these ratios.

PART A: ANALYZING IB1's PERFORMANCE IN GRAMS   191

If we have pretrimmed our bouquets, then the various display ratios for the trimmed bouquets will be reduced from what they would otherwise have been in the original bouquets by fractions indicated by Tables 7 and 8. If the nomination was done in advance of seeing the data — and, also, to a practical approximation, if it was done before any detailed analysis of the data was made — then the after-trimming display ratios will almost surely be more appropriate. (True post-trimming requires somewhat more careful thought.) The larger display ratios before trimming were "dragged upward" by being taken as less exalted order statistics than they deserved to be — because the even higher contrast, deserving of nomination, unfairly seized the highest position. By trimming, we have prevented this dragging upward, restoring the display ratios to what they ought to be.

TABLE 7. Illustration, for $d = 7$, of dragging upward via denominators.

i	$d=7$ $c(i:7)$	$d=6$ $c(i:6)$	Ratio	Ratio to Median
7	1.691	—	—	—
6	1.208	1.620	.745	.882
5	.908	1.119	.812	.961
4	.674	.804	.838	.992
3	.472	.555	.852	1.008
2	.288	.336	.859	1.017
1	.114	.132	.863	1.021
			median = .845	

TABLE 8. Dragging upward via denominators of the next-to-largest contrast.

d	$c(d-1:d)$	$c(d-1:d-1)$	Ratio	Median Ratio*
3	.074	1.058	.631	.661
6	1.119	1.534	.729	.823
18	1.691	2.070	.817	.937

* Median is of $c(i:d)/c(i:d-1)$ for $i = 1, ..., d-1$.

A Possible Initial Plot

We could try to reflect this dragging upward effect in an initial plot, at the cost of making things rather "busy" looking. Figure 5 shows the three-factor sizes of contrast with

$$\frac{|C(i:d)|}{c(i:d)} \quad \text{plotted as 0}$$

$$\frac{|C(i:d)|}{c(i:d-1)} \quad \text{plotted as 1}$$

and

$$\frac{|C(i:d)|}{c(i:d-2)} \quad \text{plotted as 2}$$

with the three for each *i* connected by broken lines. The vertical axis has been truncated at 20 to show the main detail. We see a consistent

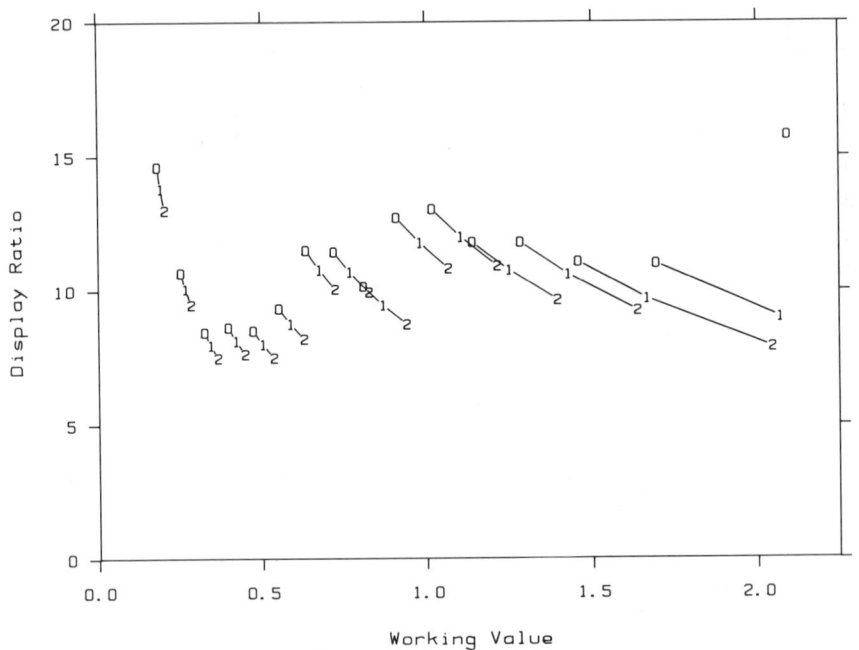

The *i*th size of contrast within bouquets of 18, 17, 16 are connected. Plot symbol is the number of largest contrasts set aside.

Figure 5. Effect of undragging for the three-factor contrasts. IB1 — D.L. in grams — polynomial contrasts.

PART A: ANALYZING IB1's PERFORMANCE IN GRAMS 193

decrease in the value of the display ratio as we move from a bouquet of all 18 to a bouquet of the smallest 17 to a bouquet of the smallest 16 sizes of contrast. The horizontal spread in the plot of each size of contrast, indicated by the pair of lines connecting a 0, 1 and 2, shows the relative change in value of the reference value as the bouquet size is reduced. The change in working value versus bouquet size is the most pronounced for the largest size of contrast, as is the decline in the value of the display ratio.

Since we must expect some such effect, even if the largest contrast did not deserve to be nominated, it is not easy to argue cogently from such a plot. We shall not pursue its possible use further.

A9. The Effect of Aggregation

Sections A2 to A8 have been concerned with either (a) choosing a general approach or (b) illustrating the consequence of using the approach starting from Table 2 or an analog. It is time to ask what changes we expect when we start from an analog of Table 3, if we aggregate before going to the individual contrasts.

Opening Analysis

If we are to pretrim, we should choose the nominees before any detailed analysis of the data. So it is natural for us to begin with a conventional post-nomination analysis-of-variance table, involving 13 lines. Table 9 sets out the numbers. We will use the notation "$X(n)$" for the nominated portion of the bouquet labeled by "X".

A striking thing to note from the post-nomination analysis-of-variance table is that the value of the mean square for DRWtrim, the three-factor interaction after removing the linear-to-the-3 component, is larger than the values of the mean squares for any of the other "trimmed" lines in the table.

The Notion of "Above"

In a general context, one line of an analysis-of-variance table is "above" another line if variability in the "lower" line inevitably penetrates into the "upper" line, a situation often formalized (usually satisfactorily) as: "the expected mean square of the former ("upper") line contains all the terms in the expected mean square of the other ("lower") line."

In doing aggregation after nomination, we need to be somewhat careful in defining what is above what. We will take the view here that "$X(n)$" is above "Xtrim" and also above anything that "Xtrim" is above (using the conventional definition to decide the partial orderings for the "trim" lines). Whether any nominated contrast can be above any other nominated contrast is a consequence of the particular sets of orthogonal contrasts used for the various bouquets. In our particular situation, where we are using sets of orthogonal polynomials (and their outer products) to define the various bouquets, Interpretation One holds that no nominated contrast can be above any other nominated contrast. Thus, for example, $R1$ is not above $RW11$ because $R1$ contains the mean of the W effect while $RW11$ contains the slope (but not the mean).

The situation is perhaps easier to understand if we use a less familiar notation. Write x_0 if we have taken a mean over x, and x_1 if we have taken a slope over x, and X or X_t for having done neither, without or with trimming. Then

$$R1 \rightarrow d_0\ r_1\ w_0$$

TABLE 9. Analysis-of-variance table after nomination and before aggregation. (Labels for all nominees (i.e., linear, linear-by-linear, etc.) are marked (n).)

Label	df	MS	DEN	F	Sig
$R(n)$	1	25426	94	270.5	0.01%
$D(n)$	1	348	94	3.70	10%
$W(n)$	1	4338	94	46.1	0.01%
$DR(n)$	1	36	94	.38	not
$RW(n)$	1	492	94	5.23	5%
$DW(n)$	1	3041	94	32.4	0.01%
$DRW(n)$	1	1089	94	11.6	0.5%
Rtrim	2	58	94	.62	not
Wtrim	5	59	94	.63	not
DRtrim	2	14	94	.15	not
RWtrim	17	49	94	.52	not
DWtrim	5	46	94	.49	not
DRWtrim	17	94	—		
(Total)	(55)	689			

PART A: ANALYZING IB1's PERFORMANCE IN GRAMS

$$RW\,11 \rightarrow d_0\ r_1\ w_1$$

while

$$R \rightarrow d_0\ R\ w_0$$

$$RW \rightarrow d_0\ R\ W$$

or

$$R_t = d_0\ R_t\ w_0$$

$$R_t\ W_t = d_0\ R_t\ W_t$$

so that the 3 basic questions are: Is w_0 above w_1? (No, but!) Is $\overset{\smash{\prime}}{w_0}$ above W? (Yes!) Is w_0 above W_t? (Yes!) Where the parenthesized answers are for Interpretation One.

The issue is that a real (non-zero) slope *need not* — but is very likely to — imply a real (non-zero) mean. If the exact location of the mean for a factor is not any meaningful value, then the likelihood of a mean-free slope is small, so we may want to move away from Interpretation One.

It is far from clear when we ought to move all the way from Interpretation One to Interpretation Two and say "x_0 is over x_1". For the present, we recommend, in such circumstances, accepting Interpretation Two as a *possible alternative*, not an exclusive choice. One reason for this caution is the absence of any standardized way for x_1 to contribute to x_0 that is at all analogous to the standard contribution

$$\frac{\sigma^2}{\text{number of terms}}$$

of X to x_0.

Rules for Aggregation

Aggregation (as detailed by Green and Tukey) is the combination of lines in the analysis-of-variance table according to the values of their mean squares, using a rule of thumb (in philosophical contrast with significance testing, where non-significance is followed by pooling). The procedure is to start with the lowest remaining line (in terms of "above" with ties broken by value of mean square) and aggregate any other line with it which

a) is "above" the basic line and has mean square less than twice that of the basic line;

b) is NOT "above" any other line which does not satisfy (a).

A10. Aggregation in the Example

We start the aggregation with *DRW*trim, the lowest of the low, as we should. Since the line for each of the trimmed bouquets is above *DRW*trim and since each of the mean squares is less than (twice) that of *DRW*trim, the entire set of trimmed bouquets will be aggregated together. Additionally, since the nominated contrast *DR*11 is above *DR*trim, it is also above *DRW*trim; and since the mean square of *DR*11 is also less than (twice) that of *DRW*trim, *DR*11 is also aggregated in with the trimmed bouquets. No other nominated contrasts have mean squares less than twice that of *DRW*trim, and so this step of aggregation ceases. We will identify the aggregated collection of all trimmed bouquets and *DR*11 as "residual".

No other aggregations are possible, and so we are led to an aggregated analysis-of-variance table with 7 lines: 6 lines corresponding to the 6 largest nominated contrasts and a seventh line called residual with 49 degrees-of-freedom.

TABLE 10. Display ratios for the six largest nominated contrasts as members of 6-contrast and 5-contrast bouquets.

	6-Contrast Bouquet		After Super-Electing $R1$ and Post-Trimming	
Contrast	Display Ratio	Working Value	Display Ratio	Working Value
$R1$	98	(1.620)	237	(.674)
$W1$	59	(1.119)	43	(1.534)
$DW11$	68	(.804)	55	(1.009)
$DRW111$	59	(.555)	49	(.674)
$RW11$	65	(.336)	55	(.402)
$D1$	141	(.132)	119	(.157)

PART A: ANALYZING IB1's PERFORMANCE IN GRAMS

We can choose to treat the 6 remaining nominated contrasts as a single bouquet of 6. In this case, we form the display ratios shown in the first two columns of Table 10. If we were "splitters," we might make a separate bouquet of $R1$, leaving the other 5 nominees in a single bouquet, which we will call "middle 5" (since the largest and smallest of the original 7 have been removed). The last two columns of Table 10 show the resulting display ratios.

The striking thing in Table 10, when compared with Table 6, is the proportionally large increase in the display ratio for $D1$. The suggestion, in view of the relative constancy of the display ratio of the next 4 contrasts, is that the size of the date main effect is larger than might be expected for the smallest of the unaggregated contrasts, possibly because part of one of the dates was "different".

The analysis-of-variance table after aggregation, collecting the 6 largest nominated contrasts into a bouquet and then electing (separating) out $R1$, has three lines, given in Table 11. The horizontalized plots for the three bouquets corresponding to Table 11 are shown in Figure 6. The essential difference between the first panel of Figure 6 and the second panel of Figure 4 is that we have now put the smallest nominated contrast, $DR11$, into the residual before constructing the nominated bouquet. (The size of contrast for $DR11$ is, in fact, exactly the median size of contrast of the 49 members of the residual poly-bouquet.) The main result of this exclusion of $DR11$ from the nominated bouquet is to inflate the size of the display ratio of the now-smallest member, $D1$.

TABLE 11. Analysis-of-variance table after nominating, aggregating, collecting all remaining nominated contrasts into a bouquet and electing out the largest.

Label	df	MS	DEN	F	Sig*
$R(n)$	1	25426	64	397	0.01%
middle 5	5	1862	64	29	0.01%
Residual	49	64			
Total	(55)	689			

* Notice that (a) significance level of F-values requires a large, rather unspecified multiplier for multiplicity and (b) 0.01% is the most extreme level considered.

198 GRAPHICAL EXPLORATORY ANALYSIS OF VARIANCE

Turning to the second panel of Figure 6, the horizontalized plot of the residual bouquet of 49, we see that our aggregation has eliminated the high values of display ratios for the smallest of the three-factor contrasts that we have become used to seeing. Instead, the smallest four contrasts within the residual bouquet (in order: $DW13$, $RW33$, $RW24$ and $W6$) have smaller display ratios than might be expected. This seems unlikely to mean anything. (The smallest three-factor contrasts, $DRW133$ and $DRW116$, are now the 8th and 11th smallest contrasts of the 49 and are in the bump seen on the left-hand side of the plot). The largest three contrasts are the three-factor contrasts $DRW123$, $DRW112$, $DRW122$, in decreasing order, each of which has a display ratio very slightly smaller than might be expected. In general, the display ratios of the contrasts in the residual bouquet are almost precisely what we would expect for random Gaussian noise with homogeneous variability.

Results after Aggregation

At the end of our aggregated analysis we have come to the following overall phenomenological picture:

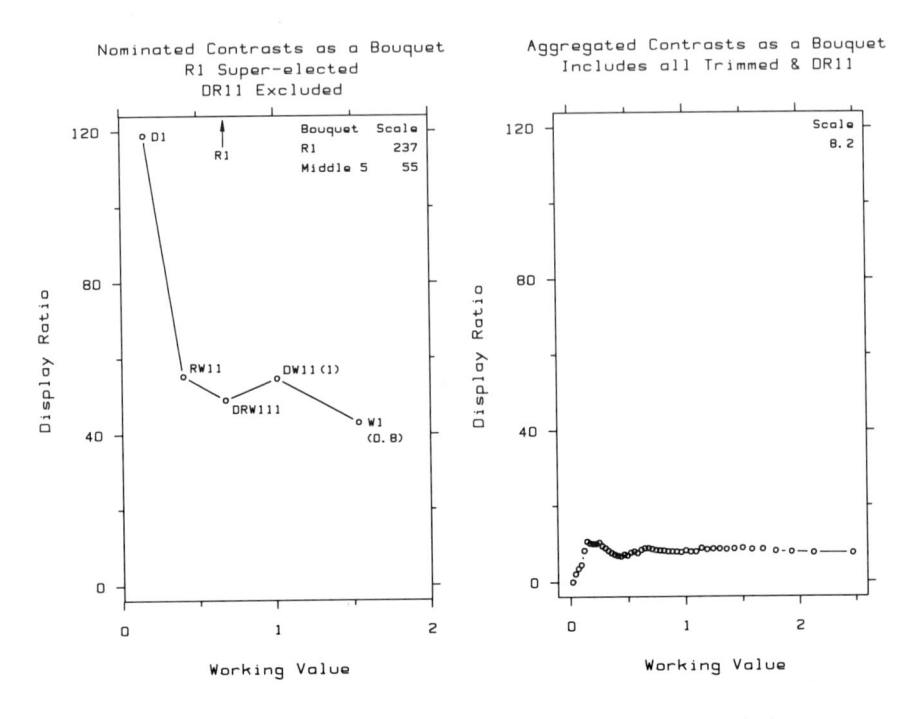

Figure 6. Person IB1 — D.L. (grams). Result of aggregation and election.

- large linear rate effect
- moderate linear-to-the-j contrasts for each of 5 other lines
- perhaps a few small exotics, calculation errors, etc. that remain unflagged
- a featureless "error body"

This is, of course, except for the small exotics, just what we saw when we didn't begin by aggregating, an encouraging agreement. All these choices of analysis can, and often should, lead to the same report (see section B5).

And under Interpretation Two?

Almost as an aside, we note that if we had considered the various nominated contrasts to be above each other, as might seem reasonable after aggregation (i.e., $R1$ is above $RW11$, $DR11$ and $DRW111$ but not above $DW11$), then the resulting aggregation would produce 4 lines rather than 3, namely:

- $R1$
- $D1$, $DW11$ and $W1$ (linear date and weight involving a mean on R)
- $DR11$, $RW11$ and $DRW11$ (linear date and weight involving a slope on R)
- all trimmed bouquets

This, too, gives an analysis worth looking at and thinking about.

PART B: DATA-GUIDED TRIMMING OF BOUQUETS

B1. Scales and Ratios-to-Scale

We are now used to plotting display ratios of the form

$$\frac{\text{size of contrast}}{\text{typical order statistic}}$$

in various ways. The general picture is that most ratios are estimating a residual variability (possibly differing from one bouquet to another), but that some, hopefully a few, are trying to reveal consistent contributions of some sort. To assess the size of the residual variability, it is thus natural to turn to the median (or conceivably the midmean) of these display ratios. It is this median that is shown as "scale" next to the bouquet labels in the horizontalized plots (Figures 2, 3, 4, 6). Because of the "dragging upward" phenomena we are not surprised to see this scale decrease somewhat as we trim the bouquets, removing opportunities for dragging upward.

Ratio-to-Scale

We have been judging the sizes of the display ratios both externally — looking across bouquets — and internally — within either the entire or a trimmed bouquet. For internal comparison, it is convenient to have numbers, and the natural number to look at is the

$$\text{ratio-to-scale} = \frac{\text{display ratio}}{\text{median display ratio}}.$$

(In other contexts, but not here, we may want to refer to this as an assassination or sterilizability ratio.) It is these ratios that are attached (in parentheses) to individual high points in the horizontalized plots (Figures 2, 3, 4, 6).

B2. Null Behavior of "Ratio-to-Scale"

It is helpful to know how large values of ratio-to-scale we are likely to see in a null situation, particularly how large a value we are likely to see for that contrast of largest size (in the bouquet at hand). The distribution of

$$\frac{\text{display ratio (for largest-size contrast)}}{\text{median display ratio (for all contrasts in the bouquet)}}$$

is easily simulated, starting with a sample of d "sizes" from a half-Gaussian. The resulting % points are given in Table 12.

Simulation Details

Each row of Table 12, corresponding to a bouquet of size d, was computed from the empirical distribution of the ratio-to-scale for the largest order statistic from a sample of size d from a half-Gaussian distribution. This empirical distribution was based on 2048 replicates. The half-Gaussian random variates were generated using the random normal generator of Kinderman and Monahan (1976), that generator using the McGill universal uniform generator (see Chambers, 1977), a combination of a 32-bit congruential with an independent 32-bit shift-register generator.

Simulation Error

To obtain an estimate of the variability of these simulated percent points, a method akin to balanced repeated replications (the multi-halving jackknife) was used. Based on the parity of the ith digit in the binary representation of the replication number (1-2048, in the order of generation), the collection of 2048 values of ratio-to-scale can be divided into 11 pairs of mutually orthogonal, interpenetrating

TABLE 12. Percent points from the distribution of the ratio-to-scale of the largest size of contrast for a sample of size d from the half-Gaussian (from simulations of 2048 replicates each — standard errors in parentheses).

Sample Size d	\multicolumn{10}{c}{Probability of Larger Value}
	20%		10%		5%		1%		0.5%	
2	1.40	(.02)	1.67	(.01)	1.83	(.01)	1.95	(.01)	1.98	(.01)
3	1.22	(.03)	1.75	(.06)	2.48	(.15)	5.25	(.67)	6.71	(1.0)
4	1.30	(.03)	1.65	(.04)	2.12	(.08)	3.86	(.32)	4.80	(.40)
5	1.30	(.03)	1.70	(.05)	2.14	(.06)	3.86	(.25)	4.61	(.43)
6	1.30	(.01)	1.60	(.04)	1.95	(.04)	3.22	(.18)	3.90	(.27)
7	1.28	(.02)	1.56	(.03)	1.91	(.06)	2.98	(.12)	3.70	(.30)
8	1.28	(.02)	1.53	(.02)	1.80	(.05)	2.64	(.08)	3.19	(.24)
9	1.24	(.01)	1.53	(.02)	1.80	(.04)	2.58	(.11)	3.01	(.17)
10	1.27	(.03)	1.51	(.03)	1.78	(.04)	2.61	(.09)	2.88	(.10)
15	1.24	(.02)	1.46	(.02)	1.65	(.02)	2.27	(.11)	2.54	(.13)
20	1.22	(.01)	1.39	(.01)	1.55	(.02)	2.01	(.03)	2.17	(.03)
30	1.18	(.01)	1.30	(.02)	1.44	(.02)	1.74	(.04)	1.88	(.05)
approx. (for $d > 2$)	$1.20 + \frac{.36}{d}$		$1.30 + \frac{1.4}{d}$		$1.38 + \frac{3.24}{d}$		$1.42 + \frac{10.7}{d}$		$1.43 + \frac{15}{d}$	

half-samples. From each pair of half-samples, two estimates (one for each half-sample) of the percentage points can be obtained, and an estimate of the variance of the (full-sample) percent point, worth perhaps 1 df, comes from ¼ the squared difference of the half-sample estimates. The standard errors, shown in parentheses in Table 12, are the square roots of the average of the 11 separate variance estimates and each is worth (optimistically) perhaps 11 df.

$d = 2$ is Special

The anomalous appearance of the percent points for $d = 2$, relative to the general pattern exhibited for the larger bouquet sizes, is due to the special constraint placed on the maximum size of the ratio-to-scale for a sample of size 2. Since we have defined the denominator of the ratio-to-scale as the median of the two display ratios, the values of the ratio-to-scale for a sample of size 2 are bounded above by 2.

Some Approximations

Approximations for the values of these percent points, valid for $d > 2$, are given at the bottom of Table 12. These approximations were derived by fitting a linear dependence of the percent point on $1/d$, a column at a time, by a simple resistant regression. To preserve monotonicity between columns for large values of d, the last two approximations were modified by -.02 and +.02, respectively. The approximations have relative errors of less than 8% throughout the pertinent ($d \geq 3$) entries of the table.

In terms of the estimated standard errors, 30 of the 55 approximations were within 1 standard error of the simulated percentage point, and 44 of the 55 approximations were within 2 standard errors. (The null comparison calls for 36 and 51, respectively.) In these terms, the approximations were relatively better for the columns for 5%, 1% and 0.5% probabilities of a larger value (P), where 31 of the 33 approximations were within two standard errors.

The maximum absolute estimated error for the approximations is, by column, .10 for $P = 20\%$, .12 for $P = 10\%$, .11 for $P = 5\%$, .30 for $P = 1\%$ and .36 for $P = 0.5\%$.

B3. Post-Trimmed Bouquets; Election

The value of the ratio-to-scale of the largest size of contrast within a bouquet (which may be either already pretrimmed or an original bouquet) provides us with a criterion for use in assessing the amount of attention that should be paid to that particular contrast in terms of describing the data. The largest size of contrast within the bouquet can be considered as indicating an interesting, potentially credible, component of the total information collectively imparted by the bouquet if the value of its ratio-to-scale is larger than some selected threshold value, where the threshold value can be selected in view of our Table 12 and probably should depend on the number of contrasts in the bouquet.

Having found such a display ratio, we can *elect* it for special attention and post-trim the bouquet, creating two new bouquets: one consisting solely of the elected contrast — designated as potentially interesting — and the other, post-trimmed bouquet consisting of the remainder. We then proceed as we did for nomination and pre-trimming, recomputing the display ratios, standing ready to assess the relative importance of the elected contrast in the experiment as a whole in terms of its relative standing in terms of display ratio.

We can, and may need to, repeat the election process before doing anything else, comparing the ratio-to-scale of the (now) largest size of contrast within the post-trimmed bouquet with an appropriate threshold value and proceeding as above if the threshold value is exceeded. (Experience will show, we believe, to what extent such recursive calculation is wise.) At some stage, which might very well be the assessment of the largest size of contrast within the initial (not post-trimmed) bouquet, the ratio-to-scale of the largest size of contrast within the current bouquet will not exceed the threshold value. The interpretation is that this contrast, and hence all remaining contrasts of smaller size, does not appear individually to be capturing a significant amount of the information embodied in the bouquet beyond that expected by the simple (null) half-Gaussian model. At this stage, post-trimming certainly ceases.

We will end up splitting the initial bouquet into two sets of contrasts: the first set, which may be empty, consists of the elected contrasts, the largest in the initial bouquet, each of which individually appears to account for an important amount of the information embodied in the bouquet. The second set is the post-trimmed bouquet and consists of the remaining (smaller) contrasts, which are deemed not to be *separately* providing significant information. We return later to the possibility of extracting additional information from the post-trimmed bouquet.

Treating the Elected Contrasts

The elected contrasts can be treated either individually, source bouquet by source bouquet, or as members of a single bouquet, the elected bouquet, analogously to our treatment of the nominated contrasts. They could even be combined together with the nominated contrasts into a single bouquet, the nominated-plus-elected bouquet. In considering the elected contrasts, some attention should be paid to issues of multiplicity.

We can apply the post-trimming procedure to the nominated bouquet itself (as well as to the elected bouquet and the nominated-plus-elected bouquet). Contrasts flagged as too large in terms of their ratio-to-scale within such a bouquet will be referred to as being *super-elected*, since they have distinguished themselves above the other contrasts, already distinguished by nomination or election.

B4. Election (Post-Trimming) in the Example

Although we have advocated pretrimming (nominating) the $D1$, $R1$, $W1$, $DR11$, $DW11$, $RW11$ and $DRW111$ linear-to-the-j contrasts as a general maxim, it is interesting to consider what would have been the effect if instead we had retained the full bouquets and elected large contrasts exceeding some threshold value(s), probably less than or equal to 2.5. Returning to Figure 2, we have $R1$, $W1$ and $DW11$ as the three most obvious candidates for election, having ratios-to-scale of 7.8, 4.4 and 3.4, respectively, each of which is above the corresponding 1% point for the appropriate bouquet size from Table 12. These, of course, had the highest display ratios after pretrimming, substantially exceeding the levels of all other contrasts. A horizontalized plot of the result of electing $R1$, $W1$ and $DW11$, post-trimming the R, W and DW bouquets and leaving the other bouquets alone, is shown in Figure 7.

The vertical axis of the plot has been truncated at 50 to show detail, and so the display ratios of the elected contrasts, which we are treating as individual bouquets, are off scale. These ratios are the same as in Table 5 and also correspond to the values of "scale" shown in the inserts of the horizontalized plot. This plot is, of course, a middle ground between the horizontalized plot of the original bouquets (Figure 2) and the horizontalized plot of the pretrimmed bouquets (Figure 3). Depending on the values of threshold selected, we could have also considered electing $DRW111$, $RW11$ and $W2$, in that order. Since the threshold values for suggesting this do not reach the 10% points of Table 12 in each case, we shall not do so, but instead will turn to Figure 3.

PART B: DATA-GUIDED TRIMMING OF BOUQUETS 205

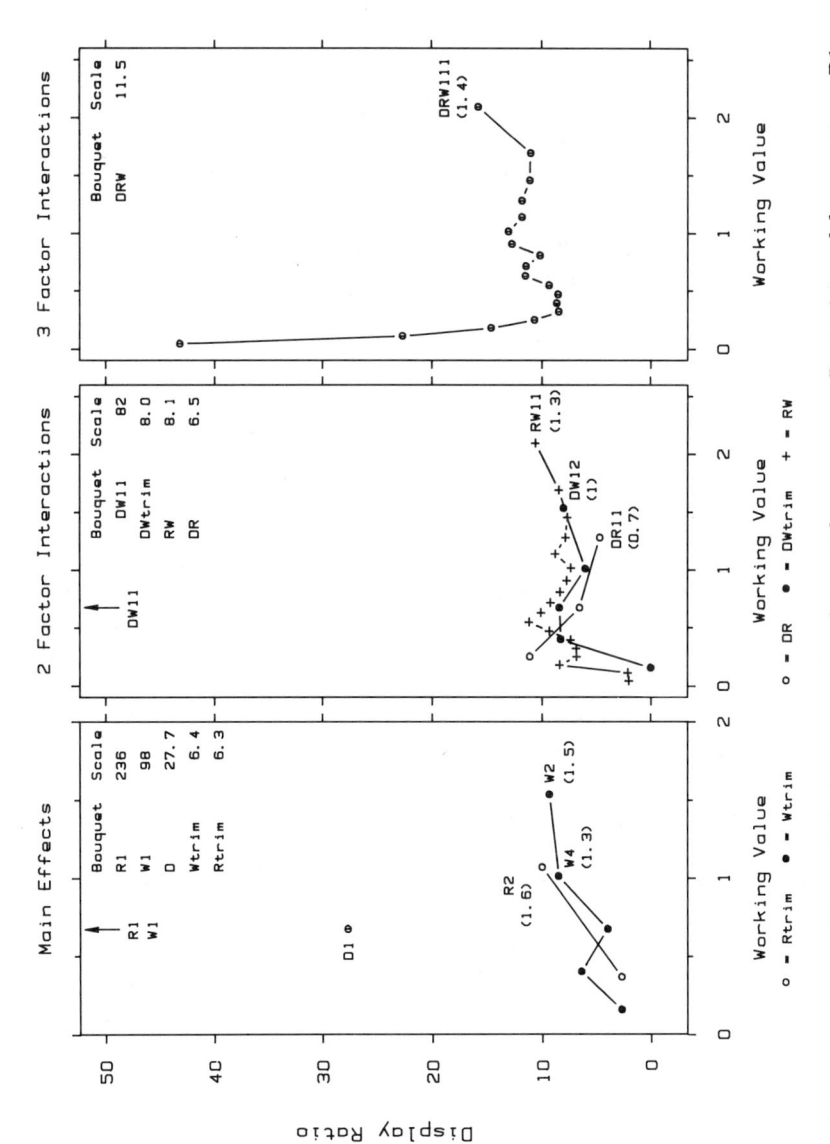

Figure 7. Person IB1 — D.L. in grams — polynomial contrasts . Post-trimmed bouquets — R1, W1 and DW11 elected.

On looking at the values of ratio-to-scale for the largest contrasts in the pretrimmed bouquets in Figure 3, we see that $R2$ and $W2$ may be of marginal interest and that no other contrasts distinguish themselves.

Clearly, a large part of the story is being told by the six largest nominated contrasts: $R1$, $W1$, $DW11$, $DRW111$, $RW11$ and $D1$, in apparent order of importance. Of these, we have already super-elected $R1$ as the single contrast displaying the most information about the experiment.

It is possible to push the analysis of the responses for person IB1 further, but in order to do so more readily, and to demonstrate more clearly certain other characteristics of our horizontalized plots, we will reformulate the response. First, however, we summarize what we have found so far about IB1's responses.

B5. The Final Outcomes for the First 56 Numbers

The previous sections have indicated that, as far as difference limen in grams is concerned, the relationship between the responses of IB1 and the various factors is largely captured by the nominated contrasts $R1$, $W1$, $DW11$, $DRW111$, $RW11$, $D1$ and $DR11$. Let us model, with $i =$ date, $j =$ rate and $k =$ (initial) weight, the response in terms of the linear-to-the-j contrasts as

$$y_{ijk} = a_0 + b_D d(i) + b_R r(j) + b_W w(k) +$$
$$+ b_{DW} d(i)w(k) + b_{RW} r(j)w(k) + b_{DR} d(i)r(j) + b_{DRW} d(i)r(j)w(k) + z_{ijk}$$

where, for convenient comparison of coefficients, we have taken

$$\Sigma d(i) = \Sigma r(j) = \Sigma w(k) = 0$$
$$\Sigma d(i)^2 = 1$$
$$\Sigma r(j)^2 = 3$$
$$\Sigma w(k)^2 = 6 \ .$$

Then we can summarize our results by

$$a_0 = \text{centercept} = 50.4$$

$$b_R = \text{rate slope} = 24.6$$

and by the other linear-to-the-h ($h = 1, 2, 3$) contrasts in the $2 \times 2 \times 2$ table:

	No D		D	
	No R	R	No R	R
No W	a_o	b_R	$b_D = 3.5$	$b_{DR} = 1.3$
W	$b_W = -9.5$	$b_{RW} = -3.7$	$b_{DW} = -11.3$	$b_{DRW} = -7.8$

The residuals are

Rate (gm/30 sec)	Date	\multicolumn{7}{c}{Initial Weight (Grams)}
		100	150	200	250	300	350	400
50	1	−1.3	1.5	3.0	−2.8	2.0	2.3	1.9
	2	8.5	0.3	2.1	0.5	0.8	0.8	−0.4
100	1	6.2	0.4	−8.4	−8.4	2.2	0.0	−0.1
	2	−3.2	3.8	−0.8	−4.9	−5.9	−1.8	3.5
150	1	2.6	−5.9	0.7	3.5	0.4	1.6	−6.4
	2	−16.2	−2.4	−3.4	1.6	−10.9	9.8	2.7
200	1	−4.8	1.8	7.2	0.9	−4.3	0.9	3.4
	2	26.6	14.5	−22.1	−20.7	8.2	−0.5	9.7

The various horizontalized plots show us that, so far as orthogonal polynomial contrasts go — simple or multiple — there is no appreciable evidence of needing a more detailed description.

We are coming out as we should; using numbers to describe our results and pictures to show no need to go further in the terms we have considered.

PART C: ANALYZING IB1's PERFORMANCE IN OTHER TERMS

C1. Reformulating the Response

It is often the case that the original response variable, the values of which were recorded (or calculated) in the process of the experiment, is not the best variable to use in the analysis. It is sometimes possible to find a reformulation of the response data which yields a simpler, clearer set of relationships between the dependent variable and the factors of the experiment. This is achieved when there are fewer important interactions and when the important main effects become more pronounced in reference to the background level. This can sometimes be achieved by a more trenchant change in the definition of the response which involves the values of one or more factors as well as the response, one that may largely remove the impact of a previously important main effect.

Besides seeking to simplify the relationships necessary to adequately describe the data, we shall be delighted if we can also make the variability of the response variable approximately homogeneous.

In considering the results of our initial analysis of the response data (as D.L. in grams) for our example person IB1, we noticed that the linear contrast for the rate main effect, $R1$, was far and away the most important single contrast in the experiment. A look at Figure 1 suggests that the relationship between difference limen in grams and rate might be close to being a proportional one; Table 13 confirms this. In this table we show the average of the difference limen values (in grams) for IB1 for each level of rate, averaging across all levels of data by weight within each rate level. The second line of the table is

TABLE 13. Average difference limen in grams by rate and its ratio to rate for person IB1.

	\multicolumn{4}{c}{Rate (grams/30 seconds)}
	50	100	150	200
Average D.L. (in grams)	23.2	39.7	58.4	80.5
$30(\frac{\text{average D.L}}{\text{rate}})$ (in seconds)	13.9	11.9	11.7	12.1

the ratio of this average level in grams to the rate. To produce simple units, since rate is measured in grams per 30 seconds, we multiply by 30 so that the response is now in seconds of time. Since the original response variable, D.L., was the number of grams of water added to a pail at a constant rate until the person could detect a difference in pull, the new response (given in the second line of Table 13) is a response time.

The relatively constant response time (relatively constant compared to a change from 23 grams to 80 grams) for the various levels of rate implies that the relationship between response and rate can be largely explained by assuming that the person responds after a constant time, regardless of the rate. (This was found by Green and Tukey to hold in a collective analysis of all 8 persons.)

Since the large rate effect can be substantially explained in the above manner, we can obtain a simpler analysis by changing our response from difference limen (in grams) to

$$\text{response time} = \frac{\text{difference limen}}{\text{rate}} \times 30 \text{ (in seconds)}.$$

Re-Expressing the Reformulated Response

We shall, in fact, go slightly farther. In their analyses of the entire experiment, Green and Tukey found, when the dependent variable was re-expressed as response time, that the standard deviations were approximately linearly related to the means. This can be seen most clearly by comparing persons. However, a plot of the residuals versus predicted values for a linear-to-the-j fit of the response time for our example person also shows an increase in the variability as the predicted response time increases. In order to produce more homogeneous variability, Green and Tukey re-expressed the reformulated response on the log scale. We will do the same, and so our new response is

log(response time),

the natural log of the response time as defined above.

Figure 8 shows the relationship between our new response variable and rate within each combination of weight and date levels. The actual data values appear in Table 14.

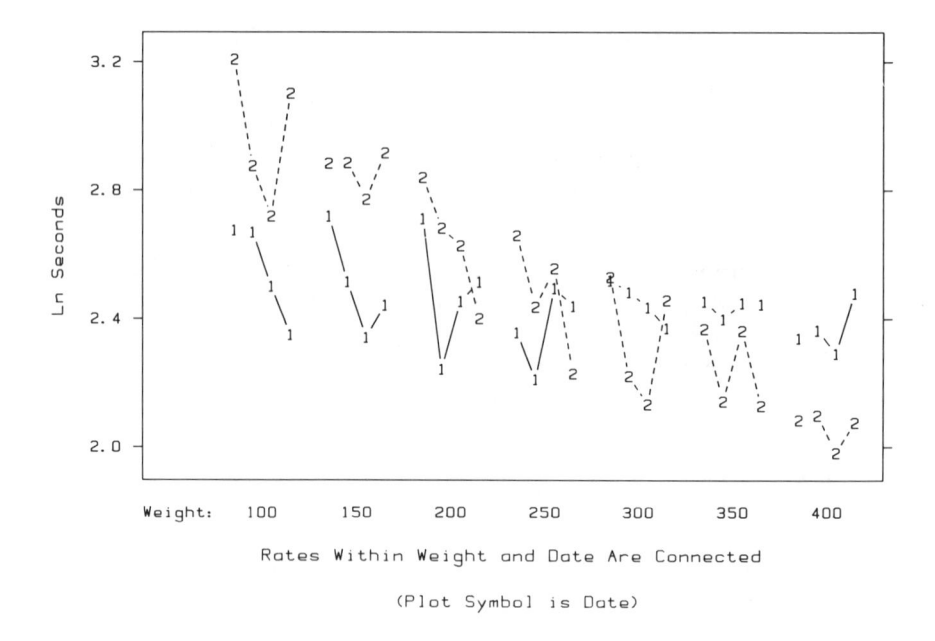

210 GRAPHICAL EXPLORATORY ANALYSIS OF VARIANCE

Figure 8. Person IB1: male, blind. Log response time (Ln seconds).

TABLE 14. Log response time in log seconds for person IB1.

| Rate (gm/30 sec) | Date | \multicolumn{7}{c}{Initial Weight (grams)} |
		100	150	200	250	300	350	400
50	1	2.68	2.72	2.71	2.36	2.52	2.45	2.34
	2	3.21	2.88	2.84	2.66	2.53	2.37	2.08
100	1	2.67	2.51	2.24	2.21	2.48	2.40	2.37
	2	2.88	2.89	2.68	2.44	2.22	2.14	2.10
150	1	2.50	2.34	2.45	2.49	2.44	2.45	2.29
	2	2.72	2.77	2.63	2.56	2.13	2.36	1.98
200	1	2.35	2.44	2.51	2.44	2.37	2.45	2.48
	2	3.10	2.92	2.40	2.23	2.46	2.13	2.08

PART C: ANALYZING IB1's PERFORMANCE IN OTHER TERMS   211

C2. A First Analysis of Log Response Time

Having reformulated our response from D.L. (in grams) to log response time (in log seconds), we proceed with an analysis of the apparent relationships involving the various factors (data, rate and weight, as before) via the horizontalized plotting techniques. As an initial step, we will use the orthogonal polynomials, as before, to produce the single-degree-of-freedom contrasts which define our various bouquets. As in the analysis of D.L. in grams, we nominate the linear-to-the-j contrasts $D1$, $R1$, $W1$, $DR11$, $DW11$, $RW11$ and $DRW111$ as *a priori* important and pretrim our bouquets. Going through the same steps as in the analysis for D.L., we reach the plots of Figure 9. (We note, in passing, that $RW11$ and $DRW111$ are now *not* the largest contrasts in their original bouquets — we had already nominated them anyway.)

In our plots of the display ratios (in units of log seconds) in Figure 9, we have truncated the vertical axis at 0.6 in order to better show the detail. This truncation has put the two largest display ratios, $W1$ and $DW11$, off scale. The display ratios for the nominated contrasts, which we are treating as 7 separate bouquets, are listed in Table 15. Also included in Table 15, for comparison purposes, are the display ratios (in units of grams) from the pretrimmed analysis of the original response (in grams), as well as the median display ratio across all 55 contrasts for both responses and the ratio of display ratio to these medians.

TABLE 15. Display ratios (in units of $\log_e$ seconds) for the polynomial analysis of log response time for person IB1 (display ratios for D.L. in grams included for comparison).

Contrast	Log Response Time Display Ratio ($\log_e$ Seconds)	Log Response Time Ratio To Median	D.L. In Grams Display Ratio (Grams)	D.L. In Grams Ratio To Median
$W1$	1.97	16.4	98	10.9
$DW11$	1.42	11.8	82	9.1
$R1$	.54	4.5	237	26.3
$D1$	.34	2.8	28	3.1
$RW11$	.33	2.8	33	3.7
$DRW111$	.24	2.0	49	5.4
$DR11$	.16	1.3	9	1.0
Median Display Ratio Over All 55 Contrasts	.12		9	

Comparison of Analyses

We can see that the relative importance of the $R1$ contrast has been considerably reduced by the reformulation but that, in comparison to the median display-ratio, it still merits appreciable attention. The relative apparent importance of the weight and date-by-weight linear contrasts remains high and has, in fact, been increased by going to log response time. The relative importance of the remaining four nominated contrasts has generally been decreased.

Table 16 shows the display ratios and ratios-to-scale for the nominated contrasts when they are treated as the 7-contrast nominated bouquet. Based on the sizes of their ratios-to-scale, we might conceivably consider super-electing $W1$ and $DW11$ as the most important contrasts, but their relative importance over the remainder of the nominated contrasts seems somewhat slight.

Examining the ratios-to-scale for the largest sizes of contrasts within the trimmed bouquets, we find these to be generally small, the largest being 1.4 for $RW32$, the cubic-by-quadratic interaction for rate-by-weight, and also for $DW16$, the linear-by-6th-degree interaction for date-by-weight. Because of the relatively small sizes of these ratios-to-scale and because of the unpromising nature of the contrasts associated with them, we will not elect either one.

General Levels

In looking at the general level of the display ratios for the trimmed bouquets (also reflected by their value of "scale" indicated on the plots), we feel that for the most part these display ratios are measuring noise. There are two exceptions — the first being the relatively large value of the display ratios of the smallest size of contrast within the three-factor bouquet — which we again take as measuring some type of isolated error or granularity and accordingly ignore. The other exception corresponds to the trimmed rate bouquet, measuring the quadratic and cubic contributions of rate, and is of more interest. The levels of the display ratios for both the contrasts in this bouquet are nearly the same and are noticeably above the general level ("scale") of the other trimmed bouquets and above the levels of two of the nominated contrasts. This type of general inflation of all levels of a trimmed bouquet, with no contrast indicated as individually important, could be indicative of a particular phenomenon, the discussion of which we turn to next.

PART C: ANALYZING IB1's PERFORMANCE IN OTHER TERMS   213

TABLE 16. Display ratios (in units of $\log_e$ seconds) for the nominated contrasts, treating them as a 7-contrast nominated bouquet.

	Log Response Time For Person IB1		
Contrast	Display Ratio	Working Value	Ratio-to-Scale
W 1	.79	(1.691)	1.42
DW 11	.80	(1.208)	1.43
R 1	.41	(.908)	.73
D 1	.34	(.674)	.61
RW 11	.48	(.472)	.86
DRW 11	.55	(.288)	1.00
DR 11	.97	(.114)	1.74
	scale = .55		

PART D: RETHINKING A SCISSION INTO CONTRASTS

D1. Spreading of Contributions across Contrasts

We have previously stated that each trimmed bouquet, at the end of post-trimming, where the ratios-to-scale of the remaining contrasts are not sufficiently large, is deemed to consist of contrasts which *individually* are not imparting significant information about the relationships between the response variable and the collective components of the factor(s) embodied in the (trimmed) bouquet. This need not mean that the trimmed bouquet is certain not to be telling us anything of importance about the data.

The elected contrasts from post-trimming are each, potentially, individually representing systematic relationships in the data (of varying degrees of strength depending on their sizes of trimmed-out display ratios). It is possible that there are other, real, systematic relationships within the data which are not individually captured by any of the various contrasts which have been selected to define the (original untrimmed) bouquets. Such a systematic relationship is then jointly indicated by a number of contrasts, and its actual size is spread across those contrasts.

The effect of such a situation might be a bouquet (trimmed or untrimmed) where the general level of the display ratios (the scale) is at the background noise level and where the largest few sizes of contrast correspond to the contrasts jointly indicating the systematic relationship. Because this relationship is spread among a number of the contrasts, it is possible that not all, or even none, of these contrasts will be flagged in post-trimming as individually indicating an interesting contribution.

If the systematic relationship is spread across enough of the defining contrasts for a bouquet, the scale for that bouquet will be inflated, and the plot of the display ratios for the bouquet will be at a general level above the background noise level, although no individual contrasts in the bouquet may be flagged as individually interesting.

It is sometimes possible — either in these two circumstances or, better, initially — to select a different bouquet of defining contrasts for the line of the analysis-of-variance table which will more nearly isolate the systematic contributions, each into a single (different) contrast, and result in a potentially simpler account of the interrelationships in the data.

D2. Some Useful Bouquets of Contrasts

Some interesting bouquets of orthogonal contrasts emphasize the ordering of the versions of a factor. A classical example of those using only order are the Helmert contrasts, which, for example, may be formulated to compare the response value of the first version with the average of the remaining versions, the value of the second with the average of all but the first two, and so on, the last such contrast comparing the response value of the next-to-last version with that of the last version. We will call these Helmert SFP contrasts, for "Starting with First Point." There are also Helmert SLP contrasts, starting with the last point. In our situation, however, we would like to use both order *and* value. In particular, we will often want to include *the* linear contrast.

LPO's and FPO's

An interesting alternative was recently considered by Daniel (1985), who notes that if a set of m responses at equally spaced versions of a factor are nearly linear in that factor, then a commonly

PART D: RETHINKING A SCISSION INTO CONTRASTS 215

observed deviation from linearity is localized at one end, the remaining $m-1$ points falling close to a straight line. He defines the contrast LPO_m, for Last Point Off of m, which measures the deviation of the mth point in the sequence from its predicted value based on a least squares line through the previous $m-1$ points. Table 17 shows these Last Point Off contrasts for $m = 3, ..., 7$. Given n equispaced versions of a factor, the collection $\{LPO_n, LPO_{n-1}, ..., LPO_3, L\}$ defines a set of orthogonal contrasts, where L is the ordinary linear contrast and LPO_i compares the observed value at the ith level with the predicted value from the line through the values for the first $i-1$ levels.

General coefficients for LPO_m, $m \geq 3$:

ith value $= m + 1 - 3i$, $i < m$

end (mth value) $= \frac{1}{2}(m-1)(m-2)$

Sum of Squares $= \frac{1}{4}(m-2)(m-1)m(m+1)$.

If we use the last column, labeled "(j)", in Table 17 as our ordering, we get Daniel's First Point Off contrasts. Ordinarily, in those circumstances where LPO or FPO contrasts are likely to be helpful, either advance insight or data behavior will make it clear which to select. But there may be doubt.

TABLE 17. Last Point Off contrasts for equally spaced levels illustrated for m from 3 to 7 (* marks special point).

i	LPO_3	LPO_4	LPO_5	LPO_6	LPO_7	(j)
1	1	2	3	4	5	7
2	−2	−1	0	1	2	6
3	1*	−4	−3	−2	−1	5
4		3*	−6	−5	−4	4
5			6*	−8	−7	3
6				10*	−10	2
7					15*	1
SSq	6	30	90	210	420	

EPO's

In such doubtful cases, the *EPO* contrasts, for End Point Off, which treat both ends more nearly symmetrically, may be in order. These can be easily made up from *FPO*'s and *LPO*'s. Table 18 shows examples for $n = 7$ and $n = 6$, where the slight "preference" has been given to *LPO*'s. (In the world as a whole, we believe there is at least as much curvature near the upper end of the range as near the lower end.)

TABLE 18. Double-ended (EPO) contrasts for equally spaced levels for $n = 7$ and $n = 6$ (* marks special point — note slight preference for LPO).

$n = 7$ Rank	L	$m = 7$	$m = 6$	$m = 5$	$m = 4$	$m = 3$
1 of 7	−3	5	10*	—	—	—
2 of 7	−2	2	−8	3	3*	—
3 of 7	−1	−1	−5	0	−4	1
4 of 7	0	−4	−2	−3	−1	−2
5 of 7	1	−7	1	−6	2	1*
6 of 7	2	−10	4	6*	—	—
7 of 7	3	15*	—	—	—	—
SSq	28	420	210	90	30	6
Identity	L	LPO_7	FPO_6	LPO_5	FPO_4	LPO_3

$n = 6$ Rank	L	$m = 6$	$m = 5$	$m = 4$	$m = 3$
1 of 6	−5	4	6*	—	—
2 of 6	−3	1	−6	2	1*
3 of 6	−1	−2	−3	−1	−2
4 of 6	1	−5	0	−4	1
5 of 6	3	−8	3	3*	—
6 of 6	5	10*	—	—	—
SSq	70	210	90	30	6
Identity	L	LPO_6	FPO_5	LPO_4	FPO_3

SEPO's

If it is really important to have symmetry, to the extent that we do not mind irrational coefficients, we can arrange for it by combining pairs of *LPO*'s and *FPO*'s. We will call these *SEPO* contrasts, for Symmetric End Point Off. For $n = 7$, for example, we can use L, $FPO_7 + FPO_6 \sqrt{2}$, $LPO_7 + LPO_6 \sqrt{2}$, $FPO_5 + FPO_4 \sqrt{3}$, $LPO_5 + LPO_4 \sqrt{3}$, $LPO_3 = FPO_3$. In these contrasts, both FPO_7 and FPO_6 treat the first data point (of the 7) as special, LPO_7 and LPO_6 the last data point, FPO_5 and FPO_4 treat the second data point (of the original 7) as special and compare it with the next 4 and 3 points respectively, and so on. For either initial or intermediate values of $m \geq 4$, the First Point SEPO combination is $FPO_m + FPO_{m-1} \left(\dfrac{m+1}{m-3}\right)^{1/2}$, which has sum of squared coefficients $\dfrac{m(m+1)(m-2)}{2}[(m-1) + \sqrt{(m+1)(m-3)}\,]$.

Double-Ended Helmert Contrasts

We can also define a double-ended set of Helmert-type contrasts, as illustrated in Table 19.

General coefficients for m non-zero entries ($m \geq 3$):

$$\text{end values} = \frac{m-2}{2} \pm \frac{\sqrt{m(m-2)}}{2}$$

$$\text{inner values} = -1,$$

$$\text{Sum of Squares} = m(m-2).$$

D3. Alternative Descriptions of the (Log-Response) Rate Effect

We have noted that the trimmed rate bouquet (consisting of $R3$ and $R2$) has display ratios which are nearly equal and which appear high relative to the assumed background level. From Figure 9 we can see that the general level for the trimmed rate bouquet, as measured by its scale, .285, is 3 times that of the apparent background level (.092) as measured by the median scale of the 6 trimmed bouquets. A pattern of display ratios such as this, given its high level relative to the background, is suggestive of the spreading of a systematic relationship across contrasts.

TABLE 19. Double-ended Helmert-type contrasts for equally spaced levels illustrated for $n = 4$ and $n = 7$ (* marks special point).

$n = 4$

	$m = 4$	$m = 2$	$m = 4$
1 of 4	2.414*		-.414
2 of 4	-1	+1*	-1
3 of 4	-1	-1	-1
4 of 4	-.414		2.414*
SSq	8	2	8

$n = 7$

	$m = 7$	$m = 5$	$m = 3$	$m = 3$	$m = 5$	$m = 7$
1 of 7	5.458*					-.458
2 of 7	-1	3.436*			-.436	-1
3 of 7	-1	-1	1.366*	-.366	-1	-1
4 of 7	-1	-1	-1	-1	-1	-1
5 of 7	-1	-1	-.366	1.366*	-1	-1
6 of 7	-1	-4.36			3.436*	-1
7 of 7	-.458					5.458*
SSq	35	15	3	3	15	35

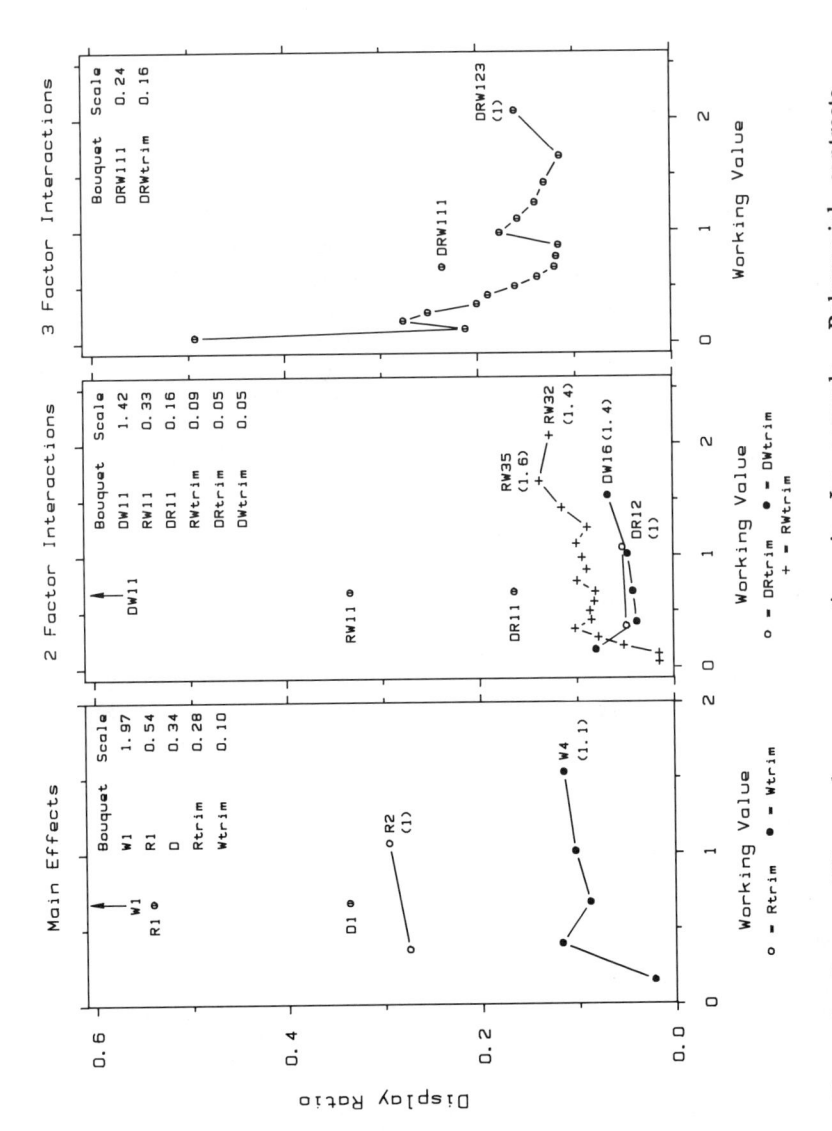

PART D: RETHINKING A SCISSION INTO CONTRASTS 219

Figure 9. Person IB1 — log response time in Ln seconds. Polynomial contrasts — pretrimmed bouquets.

In fact, looking at the values of the size of contrast for the polynomial decomposition of the rate main effect, given in Table 20, we see that the linear and quadratic contrasts are both relatively large and of roughly the same magnitude.

Since the rate main effect has only three degrees of freedom, this near equality of the two largest sizes-of-contrast suggests that another orthogonal decomposition might produce a simpler description of the relationship between log response time and rate. To help understand if this is possible, we consider Figure 10, the plot of average values of log response time by rate for each date (averaging across weight within each combination of rate and date). The plot firstly shows a similar relationship between average log response time and rate within date, with a minor difference in the slopes of the simple linear fits of log response time vs rate — accounting for the moderate $DR\,11$ display ratio. More importantly, within a given date the levels of the response variable for the latter three rates (100, 150 and 200) are all at roughly the same value and notably lower than the level of log response time for the rate of 50 grams/30 seconds.

Results for Various Bouquets

This latter observation suggests that a different bouquet of orthogonal contrasts might usefully be considered in defining the rate effect. Specifically, we want a set of contrasts which emphasize the ordering of the levels of the factor, such as those given in the last section.

Table 21 shows the results of applying a number of different bouquets of contrasts to the average values of the log response time

TABLE 20. Values of the size of contrast for the polynomial decomposition of the rate main effect for IB1 (log response time).

Contrast	Size of Contrast ($\log_e$ Seconds)
$R\,1$	.365
$R\,2$	.315
$R\,3$	.100

PART D: RETHINKING A SCISSION INTO CONTRASTS   221

for each of the rates. These averages are shown as the first line of the table. The remainder of the table consists of the sizes of contrast and display ratios that would be obtained if each of the bouquets given in the exhibit were used in defining the rate main effect. The sizes of contrast are those which would be obtained from a full analysis (and are $\sqrt{14}$ times the normalized values which would be obtained by applying the contrasts to the averages by rate). The display ratios are for the original three-contrast bouquet (with working values 1.282, .674, and .253). We have arranged the terms in each set of contrasts so that the resulting sizes of contrast come out in descending order. (Notice that *EPO* and *LPO* are identical for $n = 4$.) Clearly, in view of the display ratios, if spreading is occurring with the polynomial bouquet, then it is also occurring with the *EPO*, *LPO*, *FPO*, and *SEPO* bouquets of contrasts. The common element is, of course, the inclusion of the linear contrast.

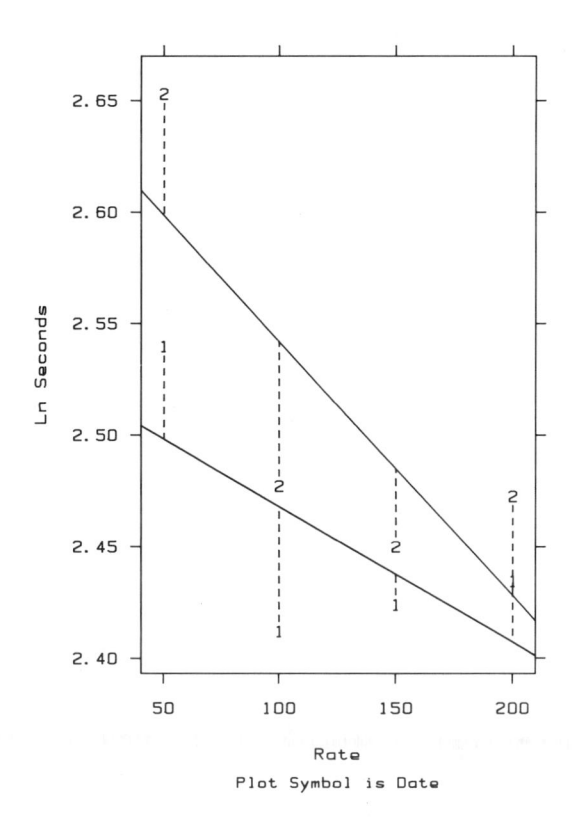

Figure 10. Person IB1 log response time vs rate, by date (lines are the linear fit).

TABLE 21. Values of size of contrast and display ratio for various bouquets of orthogonal decompositions of rate effects (person IB1 — log response time).

Bouquet		Rate 50	Rate 100	Rate 150	Rate 200	Size of Contrast	Display Ratio
Average Response By Rate		2.596	2.445	2.437	2.454		
Polynomial	L	−3	−1	1	3	.365	.284
	Q	1	−1	−1	1	.315	.470
	C	−1	3	−3	1	.100	.400
EPO (=LPO)	L	−3	−1	1	3	.365	.284
	LPO_4	2	−1	−4	3*	.250	.373
	FPO_3	1*	−2	1	0	.220	.880
FPO	L	−3	−1	1	3	.365	.284
	FPO_4	3*	−4	−1	2	.329	.491
	FPO_3	0	1*	−2	1	.037	.148
SEPO	L	−3	−1	1	3	.365	.284
	$FPO_4 + \sqrt{5}FPO_3$	5.236*	−8.472	1.236	2	.294	.439
	$LPO_4 + \sqrt{5}LPO_3$	2	1.236	−8.472	5.236*	.152	.608
Helmert	50 vs rest	3*	−1	−1	−1	.490	.382
SFP	150 vs 200	0	0	1*	−1	.044	.065
	100 vs 150, 200	0	2*	−1	−1	.002	.009
Double-ended	50 vs rest	2.414*	−1	−1	−.414	.490	.383
Helmert	200 vs rest	−.414	−1	−1	2.414*	.044	.066
	100 vs 150	0	1*	−1	0	.020	.081

* Marks special point, contrasts arranged in order of size of contrast, display ratios are for bouquets of 3 contrasts.

If we consider the display ratios for the Helmert *SFP* bouquet, we see that the majority of the information about the effect of rate on log response time is captured in the first contrast, the one comparing the response at rate 50 with the average of the other responses. While it is difficult to justify nominating this contrast, we can assuredly elect it, as its ratio-to-scale is 5.7. (According to Table 12, 5.7 is beyond the 0.5% level. Thus if we make an allowance for multiplicity of between 6 — the number of alternative bouquets in Table 21 — and 8 — the largest number of alternative bouquets we might reasonably have considered, we are still well beyond 5%.) The double-ended Helmert contrasts also produce much the same result.

D4. The Example after Rescission

Adopting the Helmert *SFP* contrasts as our scission of rate, and appropriately adjusting the definitions of all two- and three-factor contrasts which involve rate, will produce the horizontalized plots shown in Figure 11.

In the plots we use the following notation: $r1$ is the Helmert *SFP* contrast comparing the first rate (i.e., 50 gms/30 seconds) with the average of the remainder, $r2$ compares the second rate with the average of 3rd and 4th, and $r3$ compares the third rate with the fourth. The two-factor interactions involving rate are obtained as the outer product of the Helmert contrasts for rate and the polynomial contrasts for the other factor. Thus, $rW11$ is the interaction involving the first Helmert contrast for rate and the linear polynomial contrast for weight. Similarly, the factor contrast, $DrW123$, combines the day-to-day difference, the second Helmert contrast for rate, and the cubic-polynomial contrast for weight.

As we have been doing all along, we have nominated the linear-to-the-j contrasts which *do not* involve rate (i.e., $D1$, $W1$ and $DW11$) as *a priori* potentially important contrasts. As mentioned above, it is difficult to justify nomination of any of the Helmert contrasts, which is why no contrasts involving rate have been nominated. We have, however, elected $r1$ as an *a posteriori* important contrast in view of its ratio-to-scale within the full three-contrast Helmert *SFP* bouquet. No other contrasts involving rate can be elected for any reasonable threshold value.

Using the Helmert contrasts as our scission of rate has produced a simplification in the apparent relationship between the response and the three factors. This rescission has eliminated the apparent importance of any interaction involving rate in an adequate

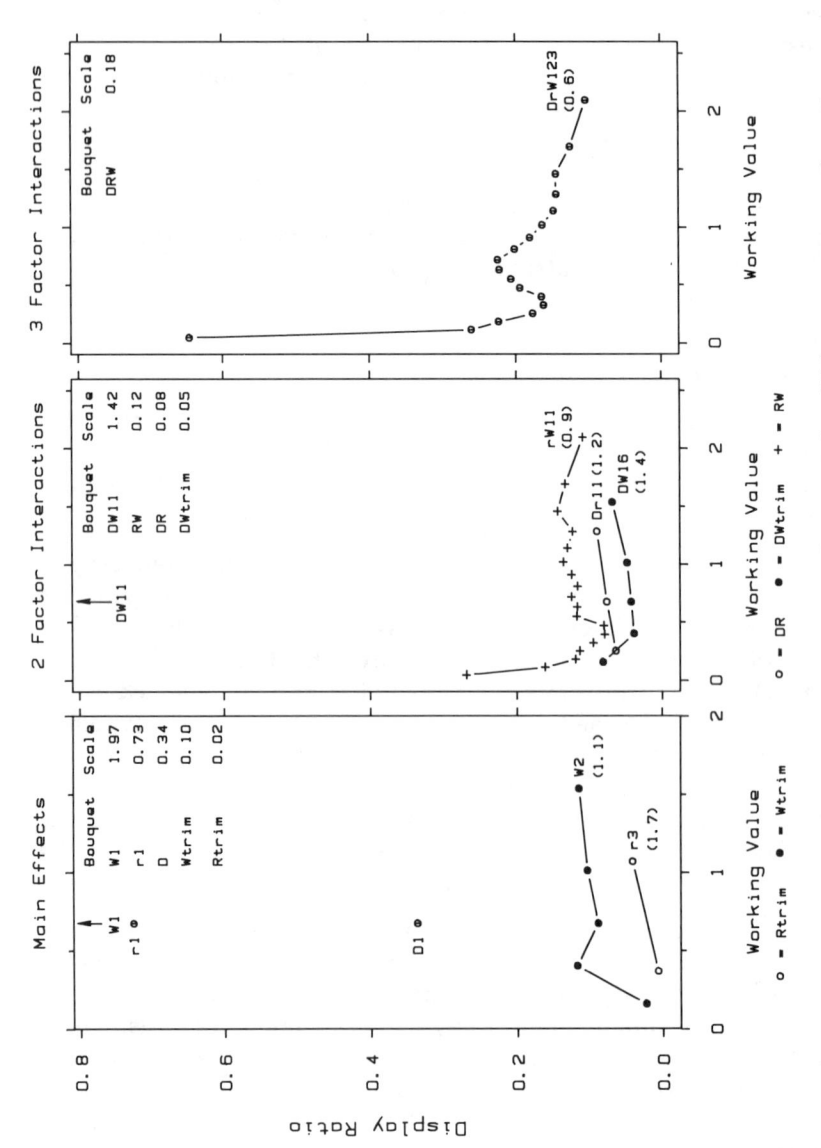

224 GRAPHICAL EXPLORATORY ANALYSIS OF VARIANCE

Figure 11. Person IB1 — log response time in Ln seconds. Helmert contrasts for rate — polynomial contrasts for weight. W1,DW11 nominated — r1 elected.

description of the data and has isolated the (main) effect of rate into the comparison of the response at the lowest rate with the average of the responses at all other rates.

D5. Refactoring

Our general attitude of "redoing anything that seems to deserve it, at least on a trial basis" should by now be clear. We have considered, in increasing order of drasticness: rescission into contrasts, re-expression of our response, (by implication at least) re-expression of our factors, and reformulation of the response. Well along in this order we should also consider another redo, refactoring of the pattern of analysis. Actually, as we shall soon see, our example already illustrates this.

Splitting

The earliest approach to the simplest sort of refactoring seems to be that of Brownlee's (1947) World War II concise book *Industrial Experimentation*, which was heavily concerned with 2^k designs with $k = 4$, 5 or 6 factors. Brownlee rightly, we feel, emphasized the frequent advantages of "splitting the experiment" and then analyzing and discussing the halves separately. This is particularly likely to help when the two versions of a factor were "do Q" and "don't do Q," and somewhat less likely to help when the versions were "the high level of Y" and "the low level of Y."

Brownlee decided whether or not to split in terms of the appearance of a significant interaction, which was not, for this purpose, compared with the mean square above it. We would feel that the proper reason for splitting is having something just above, the size of whose effect (or mean square) is not much larger than the interaction (which does itself need to appear not to be pure error). This formulation makes it much clearer what is to be split — those factors in the substantial interaction which do not appear in the label of the similar-sized mean square above.

In Brownlee's case — 2^k for small k, high-order interactions for error — it was not easy for an interaction to be significant, and if significance was reached, it was not easy for the main effects to be considerably still larger (unless they were known about all the time). Thus, for 2^k, his approach usually led to decisions to split that would also be made on the basis of what we assert to be appropriate reasons.

226 GRAPHICAL EXPLORATORY ANALYSIS OF VARIANCE

The fact that this would not be true for designs whose factors have several versions may account for the disappearance of the idea of splitting, both from Brownlee's later books and from the literature generally.

Splitting into Persons

The experiment from which our example is drawn was designed as a crossing of the sort of 2 × 4 × 7 treatment pattern we have been analyzing for a single person by a pattern involving 8 subjects. The subject pattern involved 2 persons in each cell of a 2 × 2 for male vs. female and seeing vs. blind. (The original failure to make a sensible analysis corresponded to an *a priori* assumption that replication of persons within cell belonged in the lowest error term, quite contrary to the trustworthy maxim that "people will be different!")

Actually, the 8 people did behave quite differently, both in slopes against individual factors, and in difference of slopes from day to day. Splitting, at least initially, the data into 8 portions, one for each person, seems to be an essential step in understanding what is going on. This is a simple and important instance of refactoring.

Once we have done this, we can look at sets of 8 numbers, one for each person, for both individual and collective responses, and ask what they seem to show, particularly in terms of the imposed 2 × 2 design. In general, we see little associated with the factors of sex and sight (somewhat confounded, as they were, with age) but strong emphasis on "people will be different".

We turn briefly to the question of seeking limited consistency of behavior across persons in Part E.

Tacit Refactoring

Actually, of course, the original data of Johnson and Tsao is best thought of as having already been refactored, perhaps unwisely, before anyone else ever saw any of it. The original 8 × 56 table, eventually given in Johnson's (1949) book, for 8 persons and 56 condition-date combinations, was a table of means, each of 5 individual trials. The order of trial of the 5 repetitions of 28 conditions for each person was stated to be randomized, though no details were reported. It would be strange indeed, in view of all the other things that appear to have been going on in this data, if there had been no time trends associated with the 140 = 5 × 28 trials for each of the 16 = 2 × 8 date-person combinations. The effects of these trends were buried, in an unknown but reputedly random way, in the table of means, which is all that later analysts have had at their disposal. In a real sense, this is also an instance of refactoring — if not of something still more drastic.

We believe, then, that this example illustrates — in more than one way — the need for, and importance of, refactoring as a standard part of an analyst's tool kit.

Splitting on "Date" in the Example

In the IB1 data, both the weight slope and the date-by-weight slope, if not nominated, would be elected. Indeed, the latter ($DW1$) is nearly as large as the former ($W1$).

The great difference in weight slopes for this subject from one day to the other is easily seen in a simple plot of means for date-weight combinations, as in Figure 12. This suggests splitting on date.

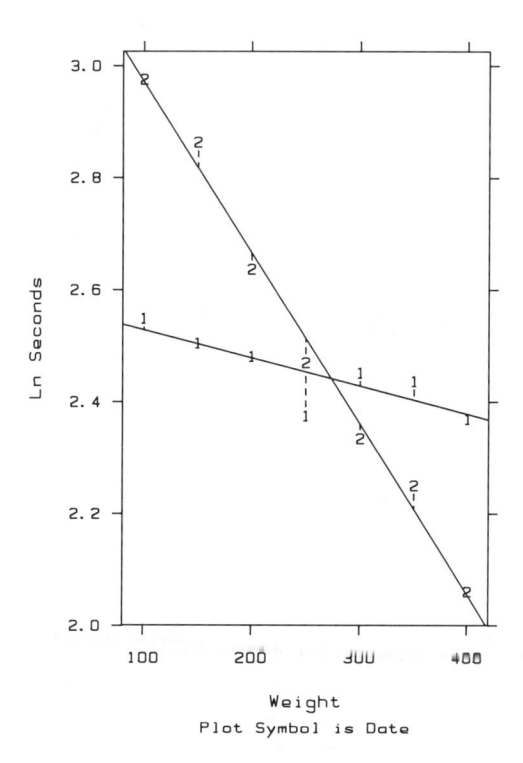

Figure 12. Person IB1 log response time vs weight separated by date (lines are the linear fit).

228   GRAPHICAL EXPLORATORY ANALYSIS OF VARIANCE

The classical analysis of variance, after nomination of all linear-to-the-j contrasts (now only for R, W, and RW) would take the form shown in Table 22 (using parallel columns for the two dates):

TABLE 22. Parallel-column analysis-of-variance table splitting on date.

	df		MS	
Label	(Date 1)	(Date 2)	(Rate 1)	(Rate 2)
Rate slope	1	1	.0322	.1130
Weight slope	1	1	.0704	2.6104
Interaction slope	1	1	.0737	.0022
Trimmed Rate	2	2	.0203	.0362
Trimmed Weight	5	5	.0066	.0059
Trimmed Interaction	17	17	.0114	.0200

It seems natural to present three panels of display ratios, one for rate, one for weight, and one for interaction, as in Figure 13, where we are treating each of the nominated contrasts ($d1R1$, $d1W1$ and $d1RW11$ for day 1, $d2R1$, $d2W1$ and $d2RW11$ for day 2) as separate one-contrast bouquets. The display ratio for the largest of these — $d2W1$, the weight slope for day 2 — is 2.4, which is 4.8 times larger than that of the next largest nominated contrast ($d2R1$).

Super-Election in the Split Example

Collecting the 6 nominated contrasts into a six-contrast nominated bouquet and then computing display ratios produces the first two columns of Table 23. Quite clearly, the weight slope for day 2 stands out from the rest. (The ratio-to-scale for $d2W1$ in the 6-contrast bouquet is 2.4.) Electing this contrast and post-trimming produce the last two columns of Table 23.

If, instead, we use the 3-contrast Helmert SFP bouquet as our scission of rate, we get the horizontalized plots of Figure 14. In this exhibit, we have nominated the linear weight-within-date contrasts ($d1W1$ and $d2W1$) and elected the two rate-50-versus-the-rest Helmert SFP contrasts of rate within date ($d1r1$ and $d2r1$). The election used a threshold value of 2. Notice that no rate-by-weight interaction can be elected with any reasonable threshold. As before, the use of the Helmert contrasts has concentrated the relationship between response and rate largely into a single contrast.

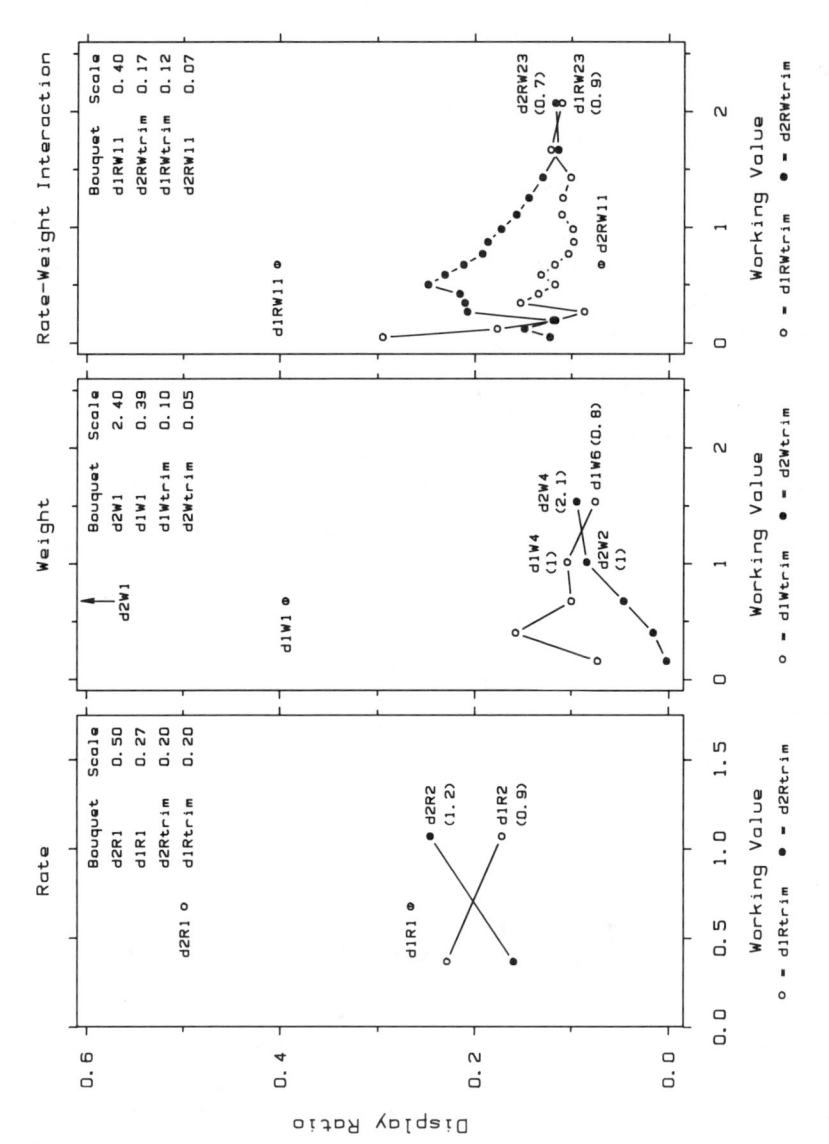

PART D: RETHINKING A SCISSION INTO CONTRASTS 229

Figure 13. Person IB1 — log response time in Ln seconds. Splitting on date; polynomial contrasts for rate and weight within date.

230 GRAPHICAL EXPLORATORY ANALYSIS OF VARIANCE

Combining the two nominated and the two elected contrasts into a 4-contrast nominated-plus-elected bouquet, we get Table 24. The ratio-to-scale of $d2W1$, the linear weight-within-date-2 contrast, within the 4-contrast bouquet is 1.36, so that while this contrast is notable, it is not outstandingly large within the nominated-plus-elected bouquet. In the next section, we will give our final interpretation of the IB1 data, based on what we have now found.

TABLE 23. Display ratios for the nominated bouquet after splitting on date.

Contrast	6-Contrast Bouquet		Electing $d2W1$ and Post-Trimming	
	Display Ratio	Working Value	Display Ratio	Working Value
$d2W1$	.998	(1.620)	2.398	(.674)
$d2R1$	.300	(1.119)	.219	(1.534)
$d1RW11$	.337	(.804)	.268	(1.010)
$d1W1$	.477	(.555)	.393	(.674)
$d1R1$	.533	(.336)	.445	(.402)
$d2RW11$	.356	(.132)	.299	(.157)
	scale = .416		(trim) scale = .299	

TABLE 24. Display ratios for the nominated-plus-elected bouquet after splitting on date with Helmert contrasts for rate.

	4-Contrast Bouquet	
Contrast	Display Ratio	Working Value
$d2W1$	1.133	(1.426)
$d2r1$	.491	(.869)
$d1W1$	.530	(.502)
$d1r1$	1.366	(.194)
	scale = .831	

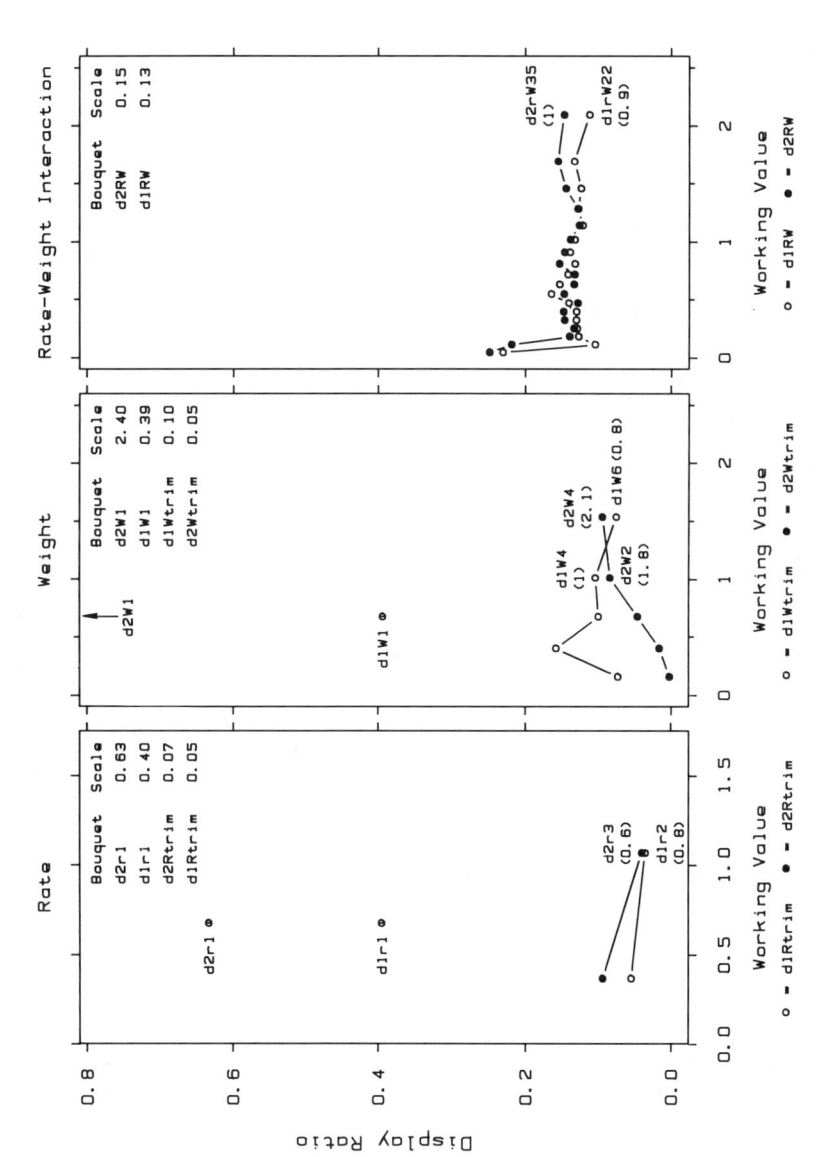

PART D: RETHINKING A SCISSION INTO CONTRASTS 231

Figure 14. Person IB1 — log response time in Ln seconds. Splitting on date. Helmert contrasts for rate — polynomial contrasts for weight.

232 GRAPHICAL EXPLORATORY ANALYSIS OF VARIANCE

Two Further Illustrations

If we give no other example, the choice of the term "refactoring" may come into question. So we offer a few possibilities for 2 × 2 tables: one where an interaction becomes a factor and *vice versa*:

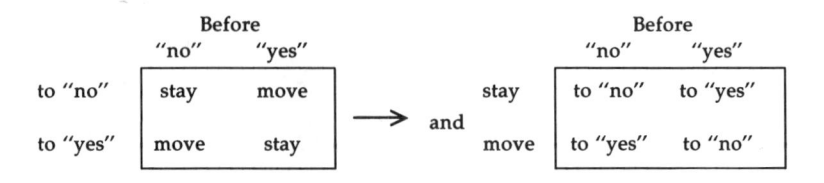

```
                Before                                   Before
             "no"    "yes"                            "no"     "yes"
to "no"    | stay    move  |              stay     | to "no"   to "yes" |
           |               |   ──→  and
to "yes"   | move    stay  |              move     | to "yes"  to "no"  |
```

and one where an interaction is transferred into (a) modifying the A effect, (b) modifying the B effect, and (c) inserting a bonus in one chosen cell (can be any one of the four (cf. Seheult and Tukey, 1982)).

$$\left.\begin{array}{l}\text{A main effect}\\ \text{B main effect}\\ \text{AB interaction}\end{array}\right\} \longrightarrow \left\{\begin{array}{l}\text{A effect}\\ \text{B effect}\\ \text{A–and–B–both–high bonus}\end{array}\right.$$

D6. Recapitulation

Before considering the complete data set (of all 8 persons) and then summarizing the main thrust of this paper, it is likely to be helpful to recapitulate the steps we have taken, as seen in the light of where we now stand.

In Part A we discussed the analysis of the original 2 × 4 × 7 = 56 numbers in terms that could, indeed should, have been planned in advance of seeing those numbers. Our analysis focussed on pictures corresponding to various analyses of variance, where the correspondence was mediated by (a) scission of each "line" into a bouquet of contrasts and (b) a horizontalized version, employing display ratios, of Daniel's half-normal plot. We did this for naive and linear-nominated analyses of variance, both conventional and aggregated. The linear-nominated analyses made clearer what the naive analyses suggested, namely that the essential description was in terms of a few linear-to-the-j slopes, a bending for low rates, and an apparently unstructured mass of residuals.

In Part B we considered election because of behavior in the data set before us, in contrast to nomination based on past experience. We found that much the same interpretations were suggested in our

PART D: RETHINKING A SCISSION INTO CONTRASTS 233

particular example by the results of election as by nomination, with the three largest of what would otherwise be the nominated contrasts, $R1$, $W1$, and $DW11$ being elected as important. We also considered the nominated bouquet consisting of all 7 linear-to-the-j contrasts and found that the rate slope $R1$ could reasonably be super-elected as the most important. By the end of Part B, we had come to the conclusion that, as far as the response of IB1 in grams was concerned, much of the relationship between the response and rate, weight and date could be adequately described by the six largest linear-to-the-j nominated contrasts: $R1$, $W1$, $DW11$, $DRW111$, $RW11$ and $D1$, in that order, where the linear rate slope is by far the most important.

In Part C we considered the possibility of reformulating the response and found that, since the response in grams was approximately proportional to rate, reformulating the response to log response time greatly reduced the apparent importance of the linear rate contrast and allowed other relationships within the data to become more apparent. In particular we discovered the relatively high levels of the display ratios for the trimmed rate bouquet and concluded that a systematic relationship between rate and the response was being spread across the polynomial contrasts.

In Part D we rethought the scission of rate into contrasts. After considering various bouquets which emphasized the ordering of the levels of rate, we concluded that the essential relationship between the response and rate was that person IB1 has a larger response for the smallest rate than the responses for the larger 3 rates, all of which are at the same level. By adopting the Helmert *SFP* scission of rate we found the apparent importance of all interactions involving rate vanished.

Lastly, we have considered the utility of refactoring of the pattern of analysis. We had already split the analysis by person based on the maxim that people are different. When we further split the analysis for person IB1 on date, we discovered that a strong slope in weight for day 2 predominated. Finally, we split over date and used the Helmert contrasts as our scission of rate. This eliminated the rate-by-weight interactions as potentially important.

At the end of our analysis of the response of person IB1 in log seconds, we are left with the following account of the data:

- a strong linear relationship between response and weight within day 2, with the response decreasing in weight. A much weaker, but still notable, linear relationship of the same direction between response and weight within day 1,

- a tendency for the responses at the lowest rate to be significantly higher than the responses at the other three rates, all three of which have responses at much the same level. This relationship is the strongest for day 2 but is still notable at day 1,
- a collection of very much smaller effects, interactions, and noise.

PART E: A LOOK AT THE OTHER 7 PEOPLE

E1. All 16 of the Person-Date Units

We have spent considerable effort on eccentric IB1. What of the other 7 people? With these choices:

response = log response time

no aggregation

nomination = all linear-to-the-j

a nominated bouquet

the horizontalized plots generally show relatively nice behavior. For 5 of the 7 people, the plots of the trimmed bouquets are relatively flat (except, sometimes, for the smallest contrasts) and all at roughly the same level. For these 5 people, the nominated contrasts contain the bulk of the information in the experiment, with little remaining in the trimmed bouquets besides background noise.

Two of the 7 people deserve specific attention: persons IB2 and IIA2. The horizontalized plots for these persons are shown as Figures 15 and 16.

Notice that in both of these figures the plots of the trimmed rate and trimmed date-by-rate bouquet appear at relatively high levels in relation to the levels of the bulk of the other trimmed bouquets. Furthermore, for each person and for each of the trimmed rate and trimmed date-by-rate bouquets, the slope of the line connecting the display ratios of the two contrasts within the bouquet is negative, indicating that the smallest contrast in the bouquet is relatively larger than might be expected. The form of these plots is symptomatic of the spreading of a systematic relationship across the contrasts in a bouquet.

PART E: A LOOK AT THE OTHER 7 PEOPLE 235

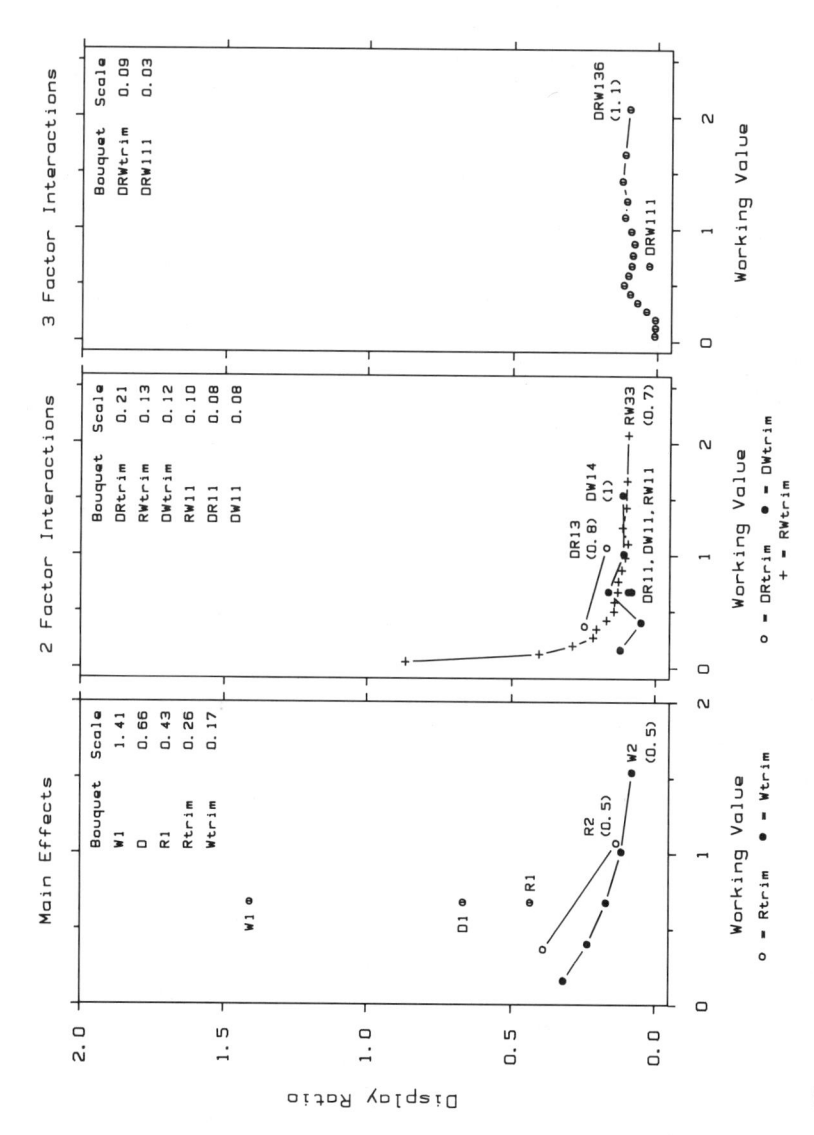

Figure 15. Person IB2 — log response time in Ln seconds. Polynomial contrasts — pretrimmed bouquets.

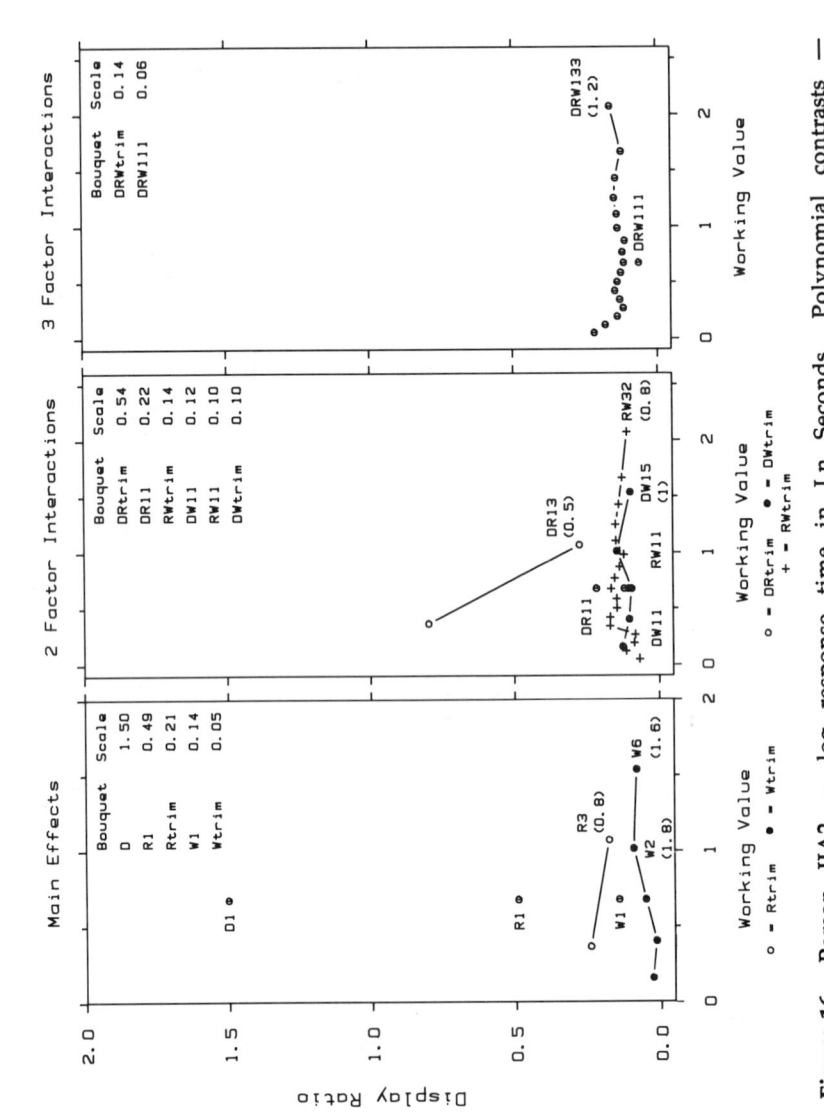

236 GRAPHICAL EXPLORATORY ANALYSIS OF VARIANCE

Figure 16. Person IIA2 — log response time in Ln Seconds. Polynomial contrasts — pretrimmed bouquets.

PART E: A LOOK AT THE OTHER 7 PEOPLE   237

Figure 17 shows the type of spreading for each of the two people. In the plot of log response time versus rate within date for person IB2 shown as the first panel of Figure 17, we can see that the main systematic relationship that is not being well represented by individual polynomial contrasts is the large deviation of his response on date 2 to a rate of 150 gm/30 seconds from the line through the responses for the other three rates (for that date). This is a third-point-off deviation from linearity. In the second panel of Figure 17, there is a second-point-off deviation from linearity in the responses of person IIA2 on date 2. The reasons for these patterns of response for these two people, and the equivalent patterns for person IB1 (Figure 10), are unknown but demonstrate the maxim that people will be different. (We might be suspicious of the randomization.)

Figure 15 also shows a pattern in the display ratios for the trimmed weight bouquet. The monotonically decreasing nature of this plot is also indicative of spreading, of a less obvious kind, as indicated by Figure 18. The spreadings within the rate and weight bouquets are at least partly responsible for the high display ratios

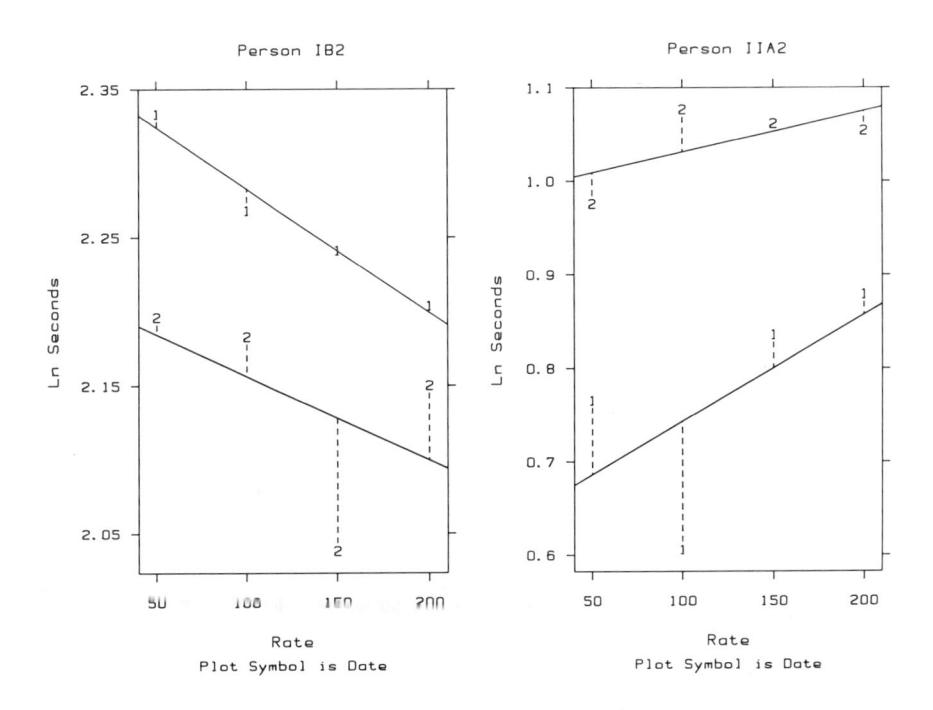

Figure 17. Log response time vs rate by date — persons IB2 and IIA2.

238 GRAPHICAL EXPLORATORY ANALYSIS OF VARIANCE

seen in Figure 15 for the three smallest rate-by-weight contrasts (*RW* 25, *RW* 23 and *RW* 16 in ascending order of size of contrast; descending order in display ratio).

Turning to the nominated bouquets for persons IB2 and IIA2, we note that the ordering of the contrasts is different between these two people and different from that of person IB1. The order of contrasts within the nominated bouquet for person IB2 is, from largest to smallest, *W* 1, *D* 1, *R* 1, *RW* 11, *DW* 11, *DR* 11 and *DRW* 111, where *W* 1 would assuredly be elected, *D* 1 and *R* 1 might also be, and the remaining 4 contrasts, all interactions, are at the background noise level. For person IIA2, the order of contrasts within the nominated bouquet is, from largest to smallest, *D* 1, *R* 1, *DR* 11, *W* 1, *DW* 11, *RW* 11, and *DRW* 111, of which only *D* 1 would be elected.

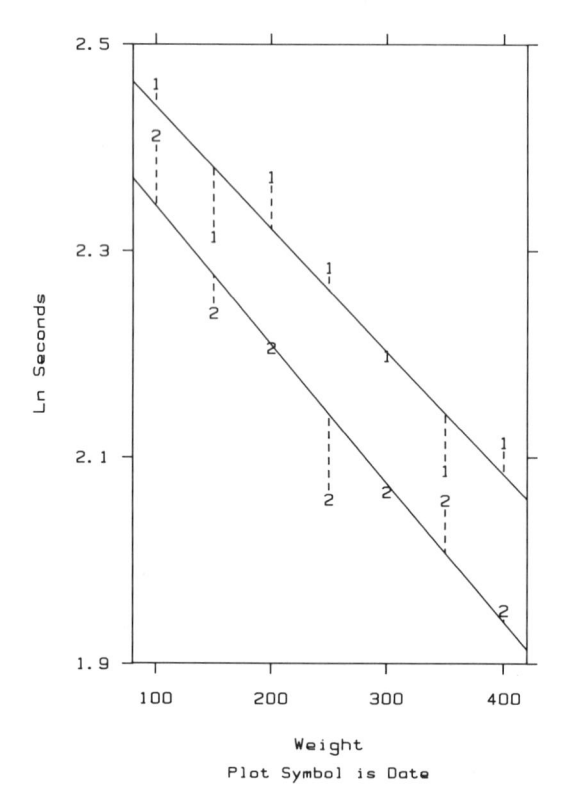

Figure 18. Person IB2: log response time vs weight separated by date.

Let Us Split Again

These analyses have split over person. If we further split over date and adopt a representation analogous to that used in section B5, making the various slope coefficients (and the centercept-multiplied-by-$\sqrt{28}$) equal to plus or minus the square root of the corresponding mean square, we get the results in Table 25. Also included in the table is the median of the 24 display ratios of the three trimmed bouquets within each date.

The major point to notice in Table 25 is that the relationships between response and the linear-to-the-j contrasts, split on date, tend to differ from person to person, and this is true even when we compare the two people of a specified sex and sight combination.

Any thoughts we have about the further analysis of Table 25 will have to wait for another day. If we go to working values of the square root of chi-square as divisors for the 16 observed median display ratios, we find that the picture looks best near 5 to 6 df in the chi-square. Clearly there is more variability here than we would expect for medians of 24 display ratios. We leave this, too, to another time, noting only the large apparent effect of sex × sight.

E2. Reassembly

Let us suppose, for simplicity, that for each of the 8 persons, or, perhaps, for each of the 16 person-date combinations, we have an analysis whose main constituents are:

1) a few fitted constants, say of the linear-to-the-j form for $j = 1, 2$ or 3 (for persons) or $j = 1, 2$ (for person-date combinations);

2) an unresolved mish-mash of residuals.

We understand how to look rather effectively at the sets of 8 or 16 individual responses under (1), or even, perhaps, at the 8 or 16 collective spreads extractable from (2), but how should we look at the 8 or 16 mish-mashes?

Better Matching

If we knew enough about the order of presentation of the treatments, which was once known, and if, also, the effect of order of presentation was somewhat consistent, across persons or across person-date combinations, we could match order of presentation across subjects (or across subject-date combinations) and see what could be extracted. It is probably reasonable to presume that such matching would be more effective than the only matching we can still try, namely that in terms of rate-weight-date or rate-weight combinations.

In either case, we can think of a two-way table of residuals, 8-by-56 or 16-by-28, where we seek to find some matching across persons, or across person-dates, but we do not want to — or dare not — assume that this matching runs right across all 8 persons or all 16 (person-date) combinations. These tables ought, it would seem, to be rescaled (for person or combination) before we tackle them. We need some form of *sub-factorial* analysis, since a plain factorial will not always work.

A first thing to do in such a situation would be to do a resistant row-PLUS-column analysis, say by median polish. If only a few persons, or a few combinations, escape some consistent pattern, such an analysis would tend to find the pattern.

If this fails, it seems natural to begin by dividing the 8 persons or 16 combinations into two or three clusters, and then repeating the first step for the smaller tables that result.

Delineations against Single Splits

Another, quite different approach, would be to select one split and plot the composite of the other splits against it, delineating (Tukey, 1977) the scatter. If the whole Johnson and Tsao data were split into 8 portions, one per subject, with a $2 \times 4 \times 7$ table of working residuals for each, this would mean plotting $7 \times 56 = 392$ residuals for other subjects against the 56 values of the selected subject. Enhanced by delineation, such a plot has a real hope of detecting commonality between the selected subject and a few of the other subjects. Eight such plots would not be too many to look at.

Bear in mind that the purpose of the present section is only to indicate that sub-factorial analyses are possible, and to stress that we need a body of experience in their use and modification.

PART E: A LOOK AT THE OTHER 7 PEOPLE   241

TABLE 25. The results of splitting into 16 pieces (log response time coefficients are the signed square roots of the corresponding MS).

Label	Date	Centercept	R1	W1	RW11	Median Trimmed Display Ratio	Sight	Sex	Age
IA1	1	5.78	0.251	−0.023	−0.041	0.127	sighted	male	21,25*
	2	4.10	0.167	0.189	−0.093	0.060			
IA2	1	11.33	−0.200	0.423	0.116	0.097	sighted	male	25,21*
	2	10.89	0.014	0.114	−0.026	0.076			
IB1	1	12.98	−0.179	−0.265	0.271	0.114	blind	male	21,25*
	2	13.30	−0.336	−1.616	0.047	0.153			
IB2	1	11.97	−0.246	−0.630	0.032	0.105	blind	male	25,21*
	2	11.33	−0.167	−0.711	0.059	0.130			
IIA1	1	9.33	−0.382	−0.413	0.346	0.130	sighted	female	33
	2	8.90	−0.055	−0.285	0.053	0.118			
IIA2	1	4.08	0.338	0.126	−0.020	0.160	sighted	female	33
	2	5.52	0.131	0.011	−0.079	0.121			
IIB1	1	7.29	−0.062	−0.839	−0.022	0.092	blind	female	33
	2	6.33	−0.031	−0.528	−0.066	0.111			
IIB2	1	7.55	−0.049	−0.200	0.064	0.085	blind	female	33
	2	7.13	−0.050	−0.340	0.015	0.052			

* One blind male and one sighted male were 21, the other two males were 25.

PART F: SUMMARY

The overall thrusts of this account are:

1) That simple graphical views of what can easily be calculated from factorial data can guide us in structuring a useful description, one that:

   1a) gives detail, where that is useful,

   1b) avoids detail, where detail would clog our perception,

   1c) alters such parts of the initially concerned expression, formulation, and factoring as need to be changed for increased simplicity of description.

2) That scission of "lines" of an analysis of variance into bouquets of contrasts is a useful tool in doing this, noting that:

   2a) looking at alternative scissions can help, either by making visible something that deserves attention, or by increasing our confidence that we were not missing anything visible,

   2b) the choice of the basic scissions should be responsive to the nature of the corresponding factor: measured, ordered, weakly structured, or unstructured,

   2c) the use of product scissions for interaction lines is the best way we now know in which to begin (splitting or other refactoring may be urged on us by the results of the initial analysis),

   2d) for measured factors, the use of the conventional linear contrast as one of each of our bouquets seems desirable,

   2e) the most promising default may be to combine this contrast with the EPO contrasts (although combination with Helmert contrasts worked best for the rate factor in our example).

3) That modifications and enhancements of Daniel's classical half-normal plot, combined with (2), provide an effective way to do (1), noting that we can make our pictures easier to interpret and understand by:

   3a) "horizontalizing" the plot by plotting "display ratio" against working value,

3b) making separate, sometimes superimposed plots for different lines in the corresponding analysis of variance,

3c) separating lines, for the purpose of (3b), into as meaningful groups as we can find.

4) That enhancing the basic analysis into lines, by nominating *in advance* — or electing *because of the data's behavior* — certain contrasts to become separate "lines" in an enhanced or revised analysis can be very important, noting that:

4a) nomination is "safer" than election, and deserves our careful attention,

4b) the loss from uncalled-for nomination is small, since our procedures will often lead to reabsorption,

4c) the gain from needed nomination can be great, *both* in focussing more attention on the nominated contrast, when such focussing is needed, *and* in avoiding inappropriate dragging upward of the display ratios for other contrasts.

5) That a free hand in rescission, re-expression, reformulation, and refactoring can be of great assistance in such analysis, even though undeserved use of such freedom may produce, with increased frequency, simple descriptions of one data set that later prove not to extend to others, since:

5a) to trust in the establishment of either qualitative (e.g. structures) or quantitative (e.g. slopes) behavior by the analysis of *one* data set collected under *one* set of conditions is very poor science,

5b) the gain in understanding which usually accompanies a simpler description is so frequently helpful in the later use of the results, even when it reflects accidental serendipity.

We believe all of these points apply to the analysis of most factorial data sets with 3 or more factors (for the case of several factors at two levels see Seheult and Tukey 1982), and, as well, to a majority of other instances of analysis of variance of a similar size and complexity.

REFERENCES

Abelson, R. P. and Tukey, J. W. (1963). "Efficient utilization of non-numerical information in quantitative analysis: general theory and the case of simple order," *Annals of Mathematical Statistics*, 34, 1347-1369.

Brownlee, K. A. (1947). *Industrial Experimentation*. New York: Chemical Publishing Company.

Chambers, J. M. (1977). *Computational Methods for Data Analysis*. New York: Wiley.

Daniel, C. (1959). "Use of half-normal plots in interpreting factorial two-level experiments," *Technometrics*, 1, 311-341.

Daniel, C. (1985). "Patterns in residuals from a line through five points." Presented to the Northern New Jersey Chapter of the American Statistical Association, May 6, 1985.

Green, B. F. and Tukey, J. W. (1960). "Complex analyses of variance: general problems," *Psychometrika*, 25, 127-152.

Johnson, P. O. (1949). *Statistical Methods in Research*. New York: Prentice Hall.

Johnson, P. O. and Tsao, F. (1944). "Factorial design in the determination of differential limen values," *Psychometrika*, 9, 107-144.

Kinderman, A. J. and Monahan, J. F. (1976). "Generating random variables from the ratio of two uniform variates." In *Proceedings of the Ninth Interface Symposium on Computer Science and Statistics*. Boston: Prindle, Weber & Schmidt, pp. 197-200.

Pearce, S. C. (1953, revised 1976). *Field experimentation with fruit trees and other perennial plants*. Technical Communication No. 23 of the Commonwealth Bureau of Horticulture and Plantation Crops. Farnham Royal: Commonwealth Agricultural Bureaux.

Seheult, A. and Tukey, J. W. (1982). "Some resistant procedures for analyzing 2^n factorial experiments," *Utilitas Mathematica*, 21B, 57-98.

Tukey, J. W. (1977). *Exploratory Data Analysis*. Reading, MA: Addison-Wesley.

CHAPTER 11

Analysis of a Two-Way Table

John Mandel
National Bureau of Standards

1. INTRODUCTION

In 1974, Derringer (1974) presented a technique for the empirical fit of viscosity measurements of filled and plasticized elastomer compounds. The fit expressed viscosity as a function of naphthenic oil and filler contents. The statistical fitting technique used was based on the Box-Cox transformation (Box and Cox, 1964). One of the three sets of data discussed by Derringer was also used by Draper and Smith (1981), as an example for the illustration of the Box-Cox transformation.

In the present paper, we present an alternative way for the analysis of Derringer's data. Our technique has been published originally in 1961 (Mandel, 1961) and again in several places (Mandel, 1969; Mandel, 1984; Mandel and McCrackin, 1963). This technique has a number of major advantages, to be further discussed below. Above all, it provides considerable insight into the structure of the data. At the end of this paper we discuss briefly the conditions for applicability of the proposed technique. First, we illustrate it by means of one of the three sets of data discussed in Derringer's paper.

2. THE DATA

Table 1 presents the data, consisting of measurements of viscosity of elastomer compounds. The compounds tested represent the combinations of 4 levels of naphthenic oil content with 6 levels of filler content. Thus the data are displayed in a two-way array, the rows representing the 4 levels of naphthenic oil content and the 6 columns, the 6 levels of filler content.

3. THE BOX-COX METHOD

The methods of analysis used by Derringer are based on the following mathematical model:

$$f(\eta) = b_0 + b_1 P + b_2 F \tag{1}$$

where η represents the viscosity measurement, P is the plasticizer level, and F, the filler level. The functive $f(\eta)$ is the one recommended by Box and Cox:

$$f(\eta) = \frac{\eta^\lambda - 1}{\lambda}. \tag{2}$$

The object is to choose the parameter λ in (2), so that (1) represents the data satisfactorily. The method for doing this is based on a double fit of the data for each of a selected set of λ-values. The two fits are the linear one represented by Eq. (1) and a quadratic one, including additional terms in P^2, F^2, and PF. Representing by F' the ratio of the residual mean squares MS_q and MS_L, corresponding to the quadratic and linear fits respectively, a plot is constructed of F' versus λ. The value of λ corresponding to the smallest F' is the one chosen.

Derringer finds a fairly flat minimum region for F' for $-.6 \leq \lambda \leq -.2$, but selects $\lambda = 0$ as a convenient value to fit not only Table 1, but also data corresponding to two other pigments. The value $\lambda = 0$ can easily be shown to correspond to the logarithmic transformation, so that the equation fitted by Derringer is

$$\ln \eta = b_0 + b_1 P + b_2 F. \tag{3}$$

4. THE PROPOSED METHOD

It should first be pointed out that Derringer's method makes no use of the fact that the data are displayed in a two-way array. It would in principle work for any set of data in which η is measured for any set combinations of P and F values (the latter need not follow a simple design such as displayed by Table 1). This is of course an advantage in some respects, but it is also a disadvantage in that it makes no use of the special opportunities provided by such a design for the study of structure.

Our method consists of two stages. In the first stage, the numerical values of P and F are ignored, and only the viscosity measurements themselves are studied, with emphasis on the fact that they are displayed in the form of a two-way table in which each cell contains a measurement. This will allow us to study what will be referred to as the "internal structure" of the table of data. It will also allow us to express the viscosity data as an empirical mathematical function of scalar quantities and of vectors of numerical values. We will refer to these as "structural parameters."

The second stage consists in exploring the relationship between the structural parameters and the variables representing the rows and columns, in this case F and P.

Thus, the first stage results in an equation of the type:

$$\eta_{ij} = f(u_{1i}, u_{2i}, ..., v_{ij}, v_{2j}, ...) \tag{4}$$

where i is a row index, and j is a column index. The symbols u_{ki} and v_{kj} represent vectors associated with the rows and columns respectively; the index k is used only to indicate that more than u_i and one v_i may be required.

The second stage consists in establishing the relationships:

$$u_{ki} = \phi_k(P_i) \tag{5}$$

$$v_{kj} = \psi_k(F_j) . \tag{6}$$

TABLE 1. Mooney viscosity of silica B, at 100° C.

Naphthene Oil phr	Filler, phr					
	0	12	24	36	48	60
0	25	30	35	40	50	60
10	18	21	24	28	33	41
20	13	15	17	20	24	29
30	11	14	15	17	18	25

Introducing (5) and (6) into (4) then yields the desired relation:

$$\eta_{ij} = F(P_i, F_j). \tag{7}$$

The following section deals with the first stage.

5. INTERNAL STRUCTURE

As is common in the ordinary analysis of variance of two-way tables, we begin by calculating the row-averages R_i, the column-averages C_j, and the grand mean M. They are displayed in Table 2. We then calculate the residuals

$$d_{ij} = y_{ij} - M - (R_i - M) - (C_j - M) \tag{8}$$

where we write y_{ij} for the value in the (i,j) cell (rather than η_{ij}). Table 3 displays the residual d_{ij}. A closer look at Table 3 shows at once that the residuals could not possibly represent random

TABLE 2. Row and column averages and grand mean of Table 1.

i	R_i	j	C_j	
1	40.00	1	16.75	
2	27.50	2	20.00	$M = 25.958$
3	19.67	3	22.75	
4	16.67	4	26.25	
		5	31.25	
		6	38.75	

TABLE 3. Residual from Table 1.

i/j	1	2	3	4	5	6
1	−5.79	−4.04	−1.79	−.29	4.71	7.21
2	−.29	−.54	−.29	.21	.21	.71
3	2.54	1.29	.54	.04	−.96	−3.46
4	3.54	3.29	1.54	.04	−3.96	−4.46

experimental error. Indeed, the columns of the original table of data (Table 1) are arranged according to increasing order of C_j (see Table 2), and it is clear that each of the four rows of Table 3 displays a systematic trend, increasing for rows 1 and 2, and decreasing for rows 3 and 4. Now, Eq. (8) is a consequence of the relation:

$$y_{ij} = M + (R_i - M) + (C_j - M) + d_{ij} \qquad (9)$$

which is the sample-equivalent of the population model

$$y_{ij} = \mu + \rho_i + \gamma_j + \epsilon_{ij} \qquad (10)$$

where ρ_i and γ_j are the "row and column effects," respectively.

If, as is usually assumed, the ϵ_{ij} are random experimental errors, then the corresponding residuals should display an approximate random pattern. If this were the case, then the structure of the table would be called "additive." We have seen, however, that the d_{ij} do *not* display this random pattern. Consequently, the additive structure expressed by Eq. (10) does not represent the data adequately.

The behavior of the d_{ij} suggests that it would be reasonable to try to represent each row of d_{ij} by a linear function of the C_j. For example, for the first row, we have:

C_j	16.75	20.00	22.75	26.25	31.25	38.75
d_{ij}	−5.79	−4.04	−1.79	−.29	4.71	7.21

Regressing d_{ij} linearly on C_j, we obtain a straight line whose slope is 0.621. The standard error of this slope is .048, showing that the linear trend in the d_{ij} is highly significant. Performing the same operations also for rows 2, 3, and 4, we obtain the results.

Row	1	2	3	4
Slope (versus C_j)	.621	.052	−.255	−.419

Algebraically, what we have done is expressed by the linear regression equations:

$$d_{ij} = \bar{d}_i + b_i^* (C_j - \bar{C}) + e_{ij}, \quad i = 1, 2, 3, 4,$$

but $\bar{d}_i = 0$, and $\bar{C} = M$; hence, for each i, we have:

$$d_{ij} = b_i^* (C_j - M) + e_{ij} \qquad (11)$$

where b_i^* is the slope, which it should be noted, varies from row to row.

Introducing (11) into (9) gives the more general model:

$$y_{ij} = M + (R_i - M) + (C_j - M) + b_i^* (C_j - M) + e_{ij} \qquad (12)$$

or

$$y_{ij} = M + (R_i - M) + (b_i^* + 1)(C_j - M) + e_{ij}. \qquad (13)$$

Let

$$b_i \equiv b_i^* + 1.$$

Then, we can write:

$$y_{ij} = R_i + b_i (C_j - M) + e_{ij}. \qquad (14)$$

Eq. (14) shows that our analysis results in a set of four linear regressions, one for each row, on the column averages C_j. Whether this is a reasonable model can easily be verified by plots of the entries of each row of Table 1 against the corresponding C_j. If this model holds, we will say that the data of Table 1 have a "row-linear structure."

6. ANALYSIS OF VARIANCE OF A ROW LINEAR STRUCTURE

Using Eq. (14), we first rewrite Eq. (12) as:

$$y_{ij} = M + (R_i - M) + (C_j - M) + (b_i - 1)(C_j - M) + e_{ij}. \qquad (15)$$

This equation clearly indicates that we have *partitioned* the residual d_{ij} into two parts: the *systematic* term $(b_i - 1)(C_j - M)$, and the *random* term e_{ij}.

Squaring each term in Eq. (15) and summing over all i and j, we obtain if p represents the number of rows and q the number of columns:

$$\sum_i \sum_j y_{ij}^2 = pqM^2 + q \sum_i (R_i-M)^2 + p \sum_j (C_j-M)^2 + \sum_i (b_i-1)^2 \sum_j (C_j-M)^2$$

$$+ \sum_i \sum_j e_{ij}^2 . \tag{16}$$

It is indeed readily shown that all cross-product terms vanish.

The two last terms on the right side of Eq. (16) must add up exactly to the usual sum of squares of the residuals d_{ij}, usually denoted as the "sum of squares for row-by-column interaction, R×C." Thus, we obtain the new extended analysis of variance table shown in Table 4.

When applied to our date (Table 1), this yields Table 5.

TABLE 4. Analysis of variance for row linear structure.

Source	DF	SS	MS
Rows	$p-1$	$q \sum_i (R_i-M)^2$	
Columns	$q-1$	$p \sum_j (C_j-M)^2$	
R×C	$(p-1)(q-1)$	$\sum_i \sum_j d_{ij}^2$	$MS = \dfrac{SS}{DF}$
Row Slopes	$p-1$	$\sum_i (b_i-1)^2 \sum_j (C_j-M)^2$	
Remainder	$(p-1)(q-2)$	$\sum_i \sum_j e_{ij}^2$	

TABLE 5. Row linear analysis of variance for Table 1.

Source	DF	SS	MS
Rows	3	1952.7915	650.93
Columns	5	1289.2080	257.84
R×C	15	210.9583	14.060
Row Slopes	3	202.8485	67.616
Remainder	12	8.1098	0.6758

252   ANALYSIS OF A TWO-WAY TABLE

We see by partitioning the interaction term into two terms, we have reduced the "error" mean square from 14.063 to 0.6758. This confirms what we have already noted qualitatively through an examination of the residuals in Table 3. Considering the new mean square 0.6758 as the error-variance, we see that we have fitted the data to a standard deviation of error of $\sqrt{.6758} = 0.82$ units of Mooney viscosity.

7. FURTHER EXPLORATION OF STRUCTURE

We have found that the four slopes of the d_{ij} versus C_j, which we have denoted by b_i^*, were:

$$.621 \quad .053 \quad -.255 \quad -.419.$$

Thus, the slopes of the y_{ij} versus C_j, denoted by b_i, are:

$$1.621 \quad 1.053 \quad .745 \quad .581.$$

We see that they seem to show a trend. This will become ever more apparent when we compare them with the corresponding R_i, as shown in Table 6. Trying a linear regression of b_i on R_i, we obtain

$$b_i = 0.1407 + .0439\, R_i + g_i$$

where $s_{g_i} = .020$, and the standard error of the slope .0439 is .0011. The above equation can also be written as:

$$b_i = 1 + .0439\, (R_i - M) + g_i$$

since the average of the b_i is exactly unity. Denoting the slope .0439 by α_1 we obtain

$$b_i - 1 = \alpha\, (R_i - M) + g_i. \tag{17}$$

Introducing this into (15), we obtain,

$$y_{ij} = M + (R_i - M) + (C_j - M) + \alpha(R_i - M)(C_j - M)$$
$$+ g_i\, (C_j - M) + e_{ij}. \tag{18}$$

FURTHER EXPLORATION OF STRUCTURE 253

TABLE 6. Comparison of b_i with R_i.

Row	R_i	b_i
1	40.00	1.621
2	27.50	1.053
3	19.67	.745
4	16.67	.581

Again we square both members and observe that the cross-products all vanish since $\sum_i g_i = 0$ and $\sum g_i (R_i - m) = 0$ (this follows at once from the regression equation (17) and well-known results in regression theory).

Thus, we obtain:

$$\sum y_{ij}^2 = p.q.M^2 + q \sum_i (R_i - M)^2 + p \sum_j (C_j - M)^2$$

$$+ \alpha^2 \sum_i (R_i - M)^2 \sum_j (C_j - M)^2 + \sum_i g_i^2 \sum_j (c_j - M)^2 + \sum_i \sum_j e_{ij}^2.$$

We see that the term denoted in Table 4 as $\sum_i (b_i - 1)^2 \sum_j (C_j - M)^2$ is itself partitioned into the sum of two terms

$$\alpha^2 \sum_i (R_i - M)^2 \sum_j (C_j - M)^2$$

and

$$\sum_i g_i^2 \sum_j (C_j - M)^2.$$

It can be shown that degrees of freedom can be associated with these terms, as follows.

1 DF for $\alpha^2 \sum_i (R_i - M)^2 \sum_j (C_j - M)^2$

$p-2$ DF for $\sum_i g_i^2 \sum_j (C_j - M)^2$.

254 ANALYSIS OF A TWO-WAY TABLE

Table 5 can now be expanded as follows (Table 7):

TABLE 7. Extended analysis of variance for Table 1.

Source	DF	SS	MS
Rows	3	1952.7915	650.93
Columns	5	1289.2080	257.84
R×C	15	210.9583	14.06
Row Slopes	3	202.8485	67.62
Concurrence	1	202.5830	202.58
Non-concurrence	2	0.2655	0.13
Remainder	12	8.1098	0.68

The mean squares can be tested against their appropriate counterparts by means of F tests. Thus, "concurrence" is tested against "non-concurrence." A formal test is hardly necessary in this case. Moreover, the relation we found between b_i and R_i is far more convincing than the F test, since a significant F could have arisen from a single discrepant point, rather than from a relation valid for all points.

8. THE FINAL MODEL FOR INTERNAL STRUCTURE

The analysis of variance in Table 7 shows that the term labeled Non-Concurrence can be pooled with that labeled Remainder, yielding a pooled mean square of $(.2655 + 8.1098)/(2+12) = .5982 = (.77)^2$. This pooling corresponds to considering the term $g_i(C_j-m)$ in Eq. (18) as experimental error, to be merged with the e_{ij}-term.

Let us write

$$r_i = R_i - M, \quad c_j = C_j - M. \tag{19}$$

Then Eq. (18) becomes:

$$y_{ij} = M + r_i + c_j + \alpha\, r_i c_j + \text{error}. \tag{20}$$

By a simple algebraic transformation, and defining

$$y_0 = M - \frac{1}{\alpha} \qquad (21)$$

equation (20) can be written in the form:

$$y_{ij} = y_0 + \frac{(R_i - y_0)(C_j - y_0)}{M - y_0} + \text{error}. \qquad (22)$$

The interesting fact about Eq. (22) is that for $C_j = y_0$ we have $y = y_0 + \text{error}$, for all i. Thus, when the abscissa in the plot of y_{ij} versus C_j is y_0, *all four* straight lines expressed by Eq. (14) pass, except for error, through the same point, of abscissa C_j and of ordinate y_0. This is why this model is called *concurrent*. We have seen that this concurrent fit is valid to within an error of standard deviation equal to 0.77. Since the data are given to the nearest integer, this fit is as good as can be expected. This is further confirmed by a graph of the four rows of Table 1 against the column averages, as shown in Figure 1. The straight lines are the least squares fit, calculated separately by each row of the data versus the column averages. The concurrence of the lines is strikingly apparent from this graph.

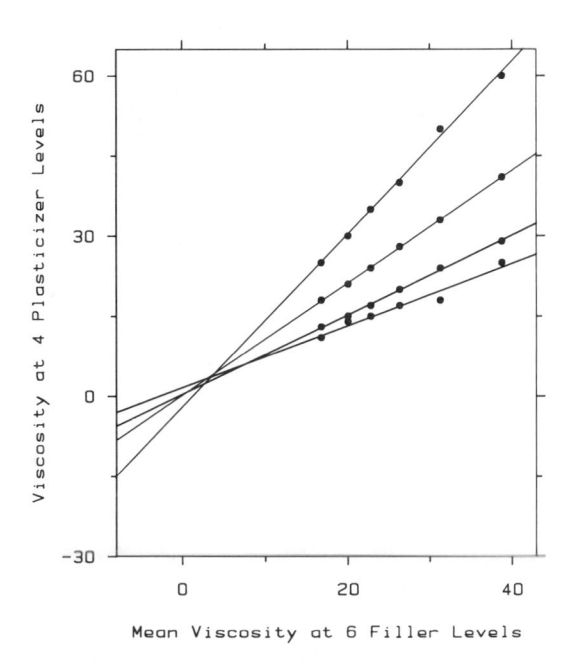

Figure 1. Least squares fits of the four rows of Table 1 versus the column averages.

9. FITTING THE STRUCTURAL PARAMETERS TO THE ROW AND COLUMN VARIABLES

The only remaining task is to express the structural parameters R_i and C_j, occurring in Eq. (22) as functions of naphthenic oil and filler contents. Table 8 provides the data for these fits.

It is apparent that neither the relation between R_i and P nor that between C_j and F is linear. However, both sets are quite well represented by quadratic relations. Least squares fits yield the relations:

$$\hat{R}_i = 40 - 1.4907 + .02375P^2 \tag{23}$$

and

$$\hat{C}_j = 17.2728 + .1216F + .003817F^2 . \tag{24}$$

Introducing the values calculated from these relations into Eq. (22), with $M = 25.958$ and $y_0 = 25.958 - 1/.0439 = 3.179$, we can calculate the "predicted" value $\hat{y}$ for each cell in the table. This yields Table 9.

TABLE 8. Structural parameters versus row and column variables.

P = Naphthene Oil	R_i	F = Filler	C_j
0	40.00	0	16.75
10	27.50	12	20.00
20	19.67	24	22.75
30	16.67	36	26.25
		48	31.25
		60	38.75

TABLE 9. Predicted values based on concurrent model and eqs. (23) and (24).

	0	12	24	36	48	60
0	25.96	29.21	34.23	41.03	49.61	59.97
10	18.21	20.35	23.66	28.15	33.81	40.64
20	13.39	14.85	17.10	20.15	23.99	28.64
30	11.52	12.70	14.54	17.03	20.17	23.96

10. COMPARISON WITH DERRINGER'S FIT

As noted above, Derringer used Eq. (1) where, on the basis of a fit of the statistic F' versus λ, he selected:

$$f(y) = \frac{y^{\lambda-1}}{\lambda} \text{ with } \lambda = 0,$$

which is equivalent to

$$f(y) = \ln(y).$$

Thus, $\ln(y)$ is considered as an *additive* function of P and F.

Applying our method of analysis to $\ln(y)$, it is however readily shown that the additive model is not appropriate. Indeed, the extended analysis of variance, when applied to $\ln(y)$, is shown in Table 10 (the SS column is omitted). It is seen that a concurrent model is more appropriate, *even for* $\ln(y)$, than an additive one.

If one fits an additive model nevertheless, and obtains the least squares solution for the model

$$\ln \eta = a + bP + cF + \text{error} \tag{25}$$

one obtains the estimates

$$\hat{a} = 3.202697$$

$$\hat{b} = -.029263$$

$$\hat{c} = .013237$$

and the estimated values shown in Table 11. These predicted values are considerably poorer as a fit than those obtained by our method of analysis.

It may finally be observed that Eq. (25) can be written in the form:

$$y = K\, P^\alpha\, F^\beta + \text{error}. \tag{26}$$

This equation is of the type:

$$y = f(i)\, g(j) \tag{27}$$

where $f(i)$ is a function of the row variable only and $g(j)$ a function of the column variable only.

TABLE 10. Extended analysis of variance for $\ln(y)$.

Source	DF	MS
Rows	3	.88015
Columns	5	.35654
R×C	15	.0015661
Row Slopes	3	.0022715
Concurrence	1	.0057845
Non-concurrence	2	.0005151
Remainder	12	.0013898

TABLE 11. Predicted values based on additive model for $\ln(y)$.

	0	12	24	36	48	60
0	24.60	28.83	33.80	39.62	46.44	54.43
10	18.36	21.52	25.22	29.57	34.66	40.62
20	13.70	16.06	18.82	22.06	25.86	30.32
30	10.22	11.98	14.05	16.47	19.30	22.62

Eq. (27) represents a *multiplicative* model in terms of y, or, in other words, a concurrent model with the point of concurrence at the abscissa $C_j = 0$, i.e., $y_0 = 0$ (see Eq. (24)).

It may be verified that a fit of Eq. (26), either by least squares, or by using Eq. (22) with $y_0 = 0$ and subsequently fitting the R_i and C_j by Eqs. (23) and (24), will not give as good a fit as the one based on the concurrent model with $y_0 = 3.179$, but better than the one based on the additive model for the logarithm of y. Taking the logarithm of course changes the error structure that is assumed in the analysis, unless one resorts to a weighted analysis. In the latter case, it is still necessary to postulate an error structure for the calculation of the proper weights.

11. CONCLUDING REMARKS

The starting point in our analysis was the observation of *row linearity* for the four rows of Table 1. Further analysis showed that for the data under discussion, we were actually dealing with a special case of row linearity, which we denoted as *concurrence*. Concurrence is present when the data are both row linear *and column linear*; it is equivalent to the case known as "one degree of freedom for non-additivity," first discussed by Tukey in 1949 (Tukey, 1949).

For data that show neither row linearity nor column linearity, and for which additivity cannot be achieved through convenient transformations of scale (e.g., the Box-Cox transformation), other techniques, based on principal component analysis, are indicated (Gollob, 1968; Mandel, 1971; Krishnaiah and Yochmowitz, 1980).

A general discussion of the analysis of two-way tables can be found in Krishnaiah and Yochmowitz (1980).

REFERENCES

Box, G. E. P. and Cox, D. R. (1964). "An analysis of transformations," *Journal of the Royal Statistical Society, Series B*, **26**, 211-243.

Derringer, G. C. (1974). "An empirical model for viscosity of filled and plasticized elastomer compounds," *Journal of Applied Polymer Science*, **18**, 1083-1101.

Draper, N. R. and Smith, H. (1981). *Applied Regression Analysis*, 2nd Edition. New York: Wiley.

Gollob, H. F. (1968). "A statistical model which combines features of factor analytic and analysis of variance techniques," *Psychometrika*, **33**, 73-116.

Krishnaiah, P. R. and Yochmowitz, M. G. (1980). "Inference on the structure of interaction in two-way classification model." In P. R. Krishnaiah (Ed.), *Handbook of Statistics 1*. New York: North-Holland, pp. 973-994.

Mandel, J. (1961). "Non-additivity in two-way analysis of variance," *Journal of the American Statistical Association*, **56**, 878-888.

Mandel, J. (1969). "A method for fitting empirical surfaces to physical or chemical data," *Technometrics*, **11**, 411-429.

Mandel, J. (1971). "A new analysis of variance model for non-additive data," *Technometrics*, **13**, 1-18.

Mandel, J. (1984). *The Statistical Analysis of Experimental Data*. New York: Dover.

Mandel, J. and McCrackin, F. L. (1963). "Analysis of families of curves," *Journal of Research of the National Bureau of Standards*, **67A**, 259-267.

Tukey, J. W. (1949). "One degree of freedom for non-additivity," *Biometrics*, **5**, 232.

CHAPTER 12

Reusing Published Examples: A Case of Caveat Emptor

Barry H. Margolin
National Institute of Environmental Health Sciences

Bruce J. Collings
Montana State University

1. INTRODUCTION

Statisticians commonly reuse each other's published datasets, particularly in papers describing new methodologies. If this is to lead to meaningful reanalyses from which new insights are possible, as opposed to mere numerical illustrations of the evaluation of formulae, reusers need to appreciate fully the true context of the data they are intending to adopt. One of the prime purposes of this volume is to provide examples of data with sufficient accompanying description to permit their intelligent reuse by others. When scrutinizing the existing literature, however, one finds that some datasets, including a few that are well known and have been analyzed by numerous authors, may not be as simple and straightforward as many thought. For example, one may find a feature of the data that raises questions about the way in which the data were obtained. Alternatively, the statistician who originally introduced the example may have taken certain liberties with the data for pedagogical reasons. In some cases this is indicated explicitly, but subsequent users of the example have lost sight of this fact; in other cases, this may become evident only after checking original source documents. Four examples are considered in this paper that reflect some of the issues one faces in adopting previously published data.

2. LOOKING FOR ODDNESS

If the paper or book that initially introduced a set of data into the statistics literature is the only available source document, a simple step to begin the scrutiny of data before their reuse is to look for signs of oddness. A good way to start this examination is, where possible, to look literally at the odd-even pattern of the data.

Table 1 contains a 2^{8-4} resolution IV fractional factorial design and a shrinkage response y for an injection molding experiment that was discussed by Box, Hunter and Hunter (1978, p. 402). If one focuses on the integer to the right of the decimal in y, say z, one notes an oddity: z is even for the first eight responses at the screw speed coded +, and is odd for the remaining eight responses at the screw speed coded −. If the assumed distribution of each observation is neutral to the oddness or evenness of z, and the observations are independent, then the probability of the odd-even pattern of z being identical to the levels of one of the eight experimental factors is 2^{-12}. A cautionary signal is raised by this pattern, but the concern is allayed when the four runs augmenting the initial design are considered (Box et al., 1978, p. 414). These are presented in Table 2. Apparently the observed pattern is not carried into the next four runs, either for factor 8 or any of its low order aliases.

An example in which looking for patterns of oddness does lead to larger issues is the metallurgical experiment and smoothness response in Table 3; this study was originally discussed by Anderson and McLean (1974, p. 233).

The odd-even behavior of the response, when viewed within the 16 paired replicate responses, is summarized in the following 2×2 table:

	Replicate II	
Replicate I	Odd	Even
Odd	6	1
Even	1	8

The two-tailed Fisher exact test for independence in this 2×2 table yields a p value of 0.011. While this is not as extreme a p-value as in the injection molding example, further study of the replicate pairs indicates that there is more complexity here than one might have thought. The values of the difference $\Delta = $ (Rep I − Rep II) for

TABLE 1. A 2^{8-4} resolution IV fractional factorial design for an injection molding experiment.

Run	Mold Temp. 1	Moisture Content 2	Holding Pressure 3	Cavity Thickness 4	Booster Pressure 5	Cycle Time 6	Gate Size 7	Screw Speed 8	Shrinkage y
1	−	−	−	+	+	+	−	+	14.0
2	+	−	−	−	−	+	+	+	16.8
3	−	+	−	−	+	−	−	+	15.0
4	+	+	−	+	−	−	+	+	15.4
5	−	−	+	+	−	−	+	+	27.6
6	+	−	+	−	+	−	−	+	24.0
7	−	+	+	−	−	+	+	−	27.4
8	+	+	+	+	+	+	−	−	22.6
9	−	−	−	+	+	−	−	−	22.3
10	+	−	−	−	−	−	+	−	17.1
11	−	+	−	−	+	+	−	−	21.5
12	+	+	−	+	−	+	+	−	17.5
13	−	−	+	+	−	+	+	−	15.9
14	+	−	+	−	+	+	−	−	21.9
15	−	+	+	−	−	−	+	−	16.7
16	+	+	+	+	+	−	−	−	20.3

TABLE 2. Four additional runs with data, injection molding experiment.

Run	1	2	3	4	5	6	7	8	Shrinkage
17	−	+	+	+	−	−	−	+	29.4
18	−	+	−	−	−	+	+	+	19.7
19	+	+	−	−	+	−	−	+	13.6
20	+	+	+	+	+	+	+	+	24.7

TABLE 3. A 2^4 metallurgical experiment, replicated twice*.

Treatment combination**				Replication		Difference
t	c	r	f	I	II	I−II
L	L	1	L	18	16	2
L	L	1	H	10	12	−2
L	L	2	L	10	12	−2
L	L	2	H	8	19	−11
L	H	1	L	9	7	2
L	H	1	H	9	7	2
L	H	2	L	8	10	−2
L	H	2	H	14	10	4
H	L	1	L	12	16	−4
H	L	1	H	21	14	7
H	L	2	L	15	15	0
H	L	2	H	21	21	0
H	H	1	L	17	15	2
H	H	1	H	24	18	6
H	H	2	L	4	4	0
H	H	2	H	13	13	0

* The response is a score for smoothness of the surface finish, the larger the score the rougher the finish.

** t=solution temperature; c=solution concentration; r=roll size; f=roll tension; L=low; H=high.

each of the 16 replicate pairs are also included in Table 3. It follows from the preceding 2 × 2 table that only two of these differences are odd. What is surprising, however, is the unusual relationship of the magnitude of Δ to the levels of factors t and r:

t	r	Four values of Δ
L	1	2, −2, 2, 2
L	2	−2, −11, −2, 4
H	1	−4, 7, 2, 6
H	2	0, 0, 0, 0

This pattern is clearly indicative of a need to explore further the origins of the data before one adopts this example for one's own purposes; minimally, the usual ANOVA error assumptions are not tenable.

3. IN DATASETS EQUALITY IS NOT ALWAYS DESIRABLE

Searching for odd-even patterns is easy, but limited in its effectiveness. Sometimes the warning flag for an example under consideration for adoption is raised only after one is well into one's own reanalysis of the data. To illustrate, consider Table 4, which contains data presented by Stuart (1953, 1955) on the unaided distance vision of 7477 women. Nearly every author addressing the issue of square contingency tables with similar rows and columns has employed this example. It was used in the 1983 Rietz Memorial Lecture by Goodman (1985), who cited five other books and papers post-1976 that employed the distance vision data. Bishop, Holland and Fienberg (1975, p. 284) considered this example in detail as well, and cited six earlier sets of authors who had analyzed the data prior to 1975.

What is interesting is that nearly all these authors have ignored the corresponding data for men that Stuart (1953) published simultaneously. These data are reproduced in Table 5. In commencing a study of whether there were sex differences in these two sets of data, it became apparent that the data for the two sexes exhibit equality in one unusual respect. The proportions of males and of females whose right eye vision is in the highest two grades are 1835/3242 and 4232/7477, respectively. The difference between these two proportions is 0.6×10^{-5}.

This brings to mind an adage one of us (B.H.M.) heard a long time ago:

> If you stare into a bowl of alphabet soup as it is brought to you in a restaurant, and you see "Happy New Year" spelled out, there is more to the story than meets the eye.[1]

The various authors who have considered the data in Table 4 adopted a multinomial sampling model for their analyses. This would seem the natural model when viewing these data in isolation. In the context of Table 5, however, the model assumptions deserve reexamination. It would be most interesting to be able to trace these data back to the Association of Optical Practitioners, which made them available originally to the statistics community, and to determine an explanation, if one exists, for the identity noted.

TABLE 4. Unaided distance vision (7477 women).

Right Eye / Left Eye	Highest Grade	Second Grade	Third Grade	Lowest Grade	Total
Highest grade	1520	266	124	66	1976
Second grade	234	1512	432	78	2256
Third grade	117	362	1772	205	2456
Lowest grade	36	82	179	492	789
Total	1907	2222	2507	841	7477

TABLE 5. Unaided distance vision (3242 men).

Right eye / Left eye	Highest grade	Second grade	Third grade	Lowest grade	Total
Highest grade	821	112	85	35	1053
Second grade	116	494	145	27	782
Third grade	72	151	583	87	893
Lowest grade	43	34	106	331	514
Total	1052	791	919	480	3242

---

1. The source of this quotation is lost to the authors, but it is believed to be L. J. Savage.

4. SIMPLIFICATION IN THE SERVICE OF PEDAGOGY SHOULD BE NOTED

The last issue to be discussed here regarding the reuse of published datasets is the desirability, where possible, of reviewing initial source documents for the data. Sometimes one knows that the data, upon their introduction to the statistics literature, have been modified to serve a pedagogical end. When clearly noted in print, there is no harm caused by this. In all cases, however, a review of the initial source document is recommended, for it can affect one's statistical reanalysis in a substantive way. A prime illustration of this phenomenon is the statistical treatment by Daniel and Wood (1971, Chapter 9) of data on the setting of Portland cement. Early statistical authors who chose to use this example focused on a small subset of the data, primarily to illustrate a linear regression computation. When Daniel and Wood (1971) resuscitated the full dataset and completed their reanalysis, it was apparent that a linear model was inadequate to describe the joint effect of chemical composition and period of aging on the rate and the amount of heat evolved during hardening. Consideration of the full dataset led in this case to new understanding of the chemistry involved.

Table 6 contains another well-known and oft-analyzed dataset (e.g., Snedecor and Cochran, 1967, p. 495; Bishop et al., 1975, p. 89), this one cited by Bartlett (1935) as a numerical illustration in his fundamental paper on the analysis of interactions in contingency tables with three or more dimensions. The experiment appears to be a 2^2 factorial design with a binary response that is replicated 240 times under each condition. As Bartlett (1935) indicates, however, for simplicity he ignored other treatment classifications in the original, more complex experiment reported by Hoblyn and Palmer (1934).

TABLE 6. Plum rootstock data (Bartlett, 1935).

Time of planting	At Once		In Spring	
Length of cutting	Long	Short	Long	Short
Alive	156	107	84	31
Dead	84	133	156	209
Total	240	240	240	240

Hoblyn and Palmer (1934) set out to conduct a "thorough investigation ... into ... method[s] of facilitating the vegetative propagation of fruit tree stocks" from root cuttings. Their study of the effects of a variety of factors on viability and growth of a root cutting was motivated by the dearth of scientific data available on this topic. Specifically, they considered:

(i) time of making the cutting;

(ii) time of planting the cutting, and

(iii) the size of the cutting.

The primary purpose of this experiment, which was conducted at the East Malling Research Station in Kent, England, was to explore these three factors for two kinds of plum trees. In keeping with Fisher's recommendation to study experimental factors simultaneously in a factorial design, Hoblyn and Palmer constructed an experiment that involved:

Factor a: two varieties of plum tree — Common Mussel, Egg Pershore;

Factor b: six times of making the root cutting — October, November, December, January, February, March;

Factor c: two times of planting the cutting — at once, in April;

Factor d: two lengths of the cutting — long (12 cm.), short (6 cm.);

Factor e: three diameters of the cutting — 3-6 mm., 6-9 mm., 9-12 mm.

While the original design included cuttings at monthly intervals from October 1931 through March 1932, weather conditions necessitated the omission of November's cuttings, and the series of cuttings was extended to include April.

The intended design was a $6 \times 3 \times 2^3$ factorial with 20 replications per factor combination and a binary viability response. A quantitative response assessing growth also was included, but will be ignored here. Results for the Egg Pershore were "to all intents and purposes a complete failure." Few of these root cuttings were viable for any of the factor combinations. Additionally, a planting error invalidated all results for the March cutting time. Finally, all cuttings that were to be planted in April, with one exception, were bedded in sand under cover; all cuttings made in April, however, were planted on the day they were made, so that for this one time of cutting, there was no distinction between the two times of planting. The net effect of these considerations is that the experiment as performed may be viewed as two separate sub-experiments, each with 20 binary replicates per factor setting:

(i) a $4 \times 3 \times 2^2$ factorial design on factors b(4), c(2), d(2) and e(3); and

(ii) a 3×2 factorial design in April on factors d(2) and e(3).

The numbers of surviving plants per 20 tested at the various factor combinations for these two sub-experiments are given in Tables 7 and 8, respectively. Table 6 is derived from Table 7 by collapsing over the 4 and 3 level factors.

Hoblyn and Palmer (1934) drew as one of their main conclusions that "There was no significant difference in the total number alive from the plantings made from cuttings taken in different months ..." They substantiated this inference by a Pearson χ^2 computation involving the total counts of survivors in Table 7 for the cutting times. Summing across other factors before testing for an effect may, at times, be misleading. To check whether that is the case here, one can formally test that the time-of-cutting factor has a negligible effect on survival. This test, whether by a Pearson χ^2 or a likelihood ratio

TABLE 7. Number of surviving plants, each from 20 cuttings (Common Mussel Plum).

Planting Time	Length	Diameter mm	Cuttings Made in Oct	Dec	Jan	Feb	Total for All Cutting Times
At once	Long	3-6	6	5	13	7	31
		6-9	14	16	15	13	58
		9-12	18	17	18	14	67
	Short	3-6	4	4	7	8	23
		6-9	10	10	8	14	42
		9-12	11	10	8	13	42
In Spring	Long	3-6	2	1	1	4	8
		6-9	6	7	4	9	26
		9-12	14	15	10	11	50
	Short	3-6	0	0	0	0	0
		6-9	2	2	3	3	10
		9-12	3	10	2	6	21
Total for each cutting time			90	97	89	102	

test (LRT), amounts to an aggregation across the rows of Table 7 of a test for homogeneity across cutting times within each row. Table 9 presents these results, together with the corresponding test results for the other three factors. The conclusion of Hoblyn and Palmer (1934) that the time of cutting had a negligible effect is substantiated.

Authors subsequent to Bartlett (1935) who adopted the data as presented in Table 6 have inadvertently aggregated the response over

TABLE 8. Number of surviving plants from 20 cuttings in April.

	At Once* of Length		In Spring* of Length	
	Long	Short	Long	Short
Diameter				
3-6 mm	6	4	9	7
6-9 mm	13	2	13	6
9-12 mm	14	7	15	7
Total for Each Length	33	13	37	20
Total For Time of Planting	46		57	

* As reported; actually planted on same date in April.

TABLE 9. Testing each factor in turn for its effect on survival.

Factor	df	Pearson χ^2	(p-value)	LRT	(p-value)
Time of cutting	33*	43.3	(0.109)	43.0	(0.115)
Time of planting	24	137.6	(0.000)	153.5	(0.000)
Length	24	82.3	(0.000)	89.0	(0.000)
Diameter	32	144.1	(0.000)	157.8	(0.000)

* After eliminating the row of four zeros.

SIMPLIFICATION IN THE SERVICE OF PEDAGOGY SHOULD BE NOTED 271

a factor — diameter of cutting — that clearly exhibits a significant effect. One conclusion drawn by these authors (see, e.g., Bishop et al., 1974, p. 90) is that time of planting and length of cutting are lacking in interaction, i.e., they exert their influence on survival independently in the logit scale. In light of the importance of the diameter-of-cutting factor and the original purpose of the experiment, one should reexamine this issue and determine whether the size-of-the-cutting and time-of-planting factors operate independently on survival in the logit scale. Testing this hypothesis yields a Pearson χ^2 statistic value of 11.3 ($p=0.046$) and an LRT statistic value of 15.5 ($p=0.009$), both statistics having 5 degrees of freedom.

Table 10 contains the observations, the fitted values under the assumption of independence of size of the cutting and time of the planting in the logit scale, and the corresponding standardized residuals (Haberman, 1974, p. 139). The lack of independence is largely concentrated in the row relevant to survival of short, small diameter cuttings that have been bedded in sand for later planting in the Spring; the independence model fails to explain the complete failure of any of the 80 short, small diameter root cuttings to survive.

As a concluding point, one should note that various authors have also analyzed the data of Table 6 for additivity directly in the

TABLE 10. Assessment of the fit of the model that assumes independence of size of cutting and time of planting in the logit scale.

Planting Time	Length	Diameter (mm)	Total For All Cutting Times (Alive/Dead)	Fitted Values (Alive/Dead)	Standardized Residuals (Alive/Dead)
At Once	Long	3-6	31 / 49	30.6 / 49.4	0.1 / −0.1
		6-9	58 / 22	57.6 / 22.4	0.1 / −0.1
		9-12	67 / 13	70.4 / 9.6	−0.4 / 1.1
	Short	3-6	23 / 57	18.6 / 61.4	1.0 / −0.6
		6-9	42 / 38	39.5 / 40.5	0.4 / −0.4
		9-12	42 / 38	46.3 / 33.7	−0.6 / 0.7
In Spring	Long	3-6	8 / 72	8.4 / 71.6	−0.2 / 0.1
		6-9	26 / 54	26.4 / 53.6	−0.1 / 0.1
		9-12	50 / 30	46.6 / 33.4	0.5 / 0.6
	Short	3-6	0 / 80	4.4 / 75.6	−2.1 / 0.5
		6-9	10 / 70	12.5 / 67.5	−0.7 / 0.3
		9-12	21 / 59	16.7 / 63.3	1.1 / −0.5

proportion-surviving or probability (*p*) scale (Snedecor and Cochran, 1967, p. 495; Bhapkar and Koch, 1968) rather than in the logit scale in which Bartlett (1935) worked. The statistic used by Bhapkar and Koch is

$$X_A^2 = (q_{111} - q_{121} - q_{112} + q_{122})^2 \bigg/ \sum_{j=1}^{2} \sum_{k=1}^{2} (q_{1jk} q_{2jk} / n_{jk}),$$

where $q_{1jk} = 1 - q_{2jk}$ for all j, k; q_{1jk} is the proportion of surviving plants for time of planting j and length of cutting k; $j = 1$ (at once), 2 (in spring), $k = 1$ (long), 2 (short); and n_{jk} is the number of cuttings made for factor combination (j, k). The X_A^2 statistic is asymptotically distributed as a chi-square random variable with one degree of freedom if additivity of the proportion surviving holds in the *p* scale. X_A^2 is the square of the statistic employed by Snedecor and Cochran for these data. The value of X_A^2 for the data in Table 6 is 0.082; it was reported as 0.085 by Bhapkar and Koch because of rounding in the computation.

If one parallels this additivity analysis in the *p* scale, but treats data for each diameter size separately, one obtains the rather remarkable result that the values of X_A^2 are exactly zero for the small and medium diameter data; the value of X_A^2 for the large diameter data is 0.246. Have we seen "Happy New Year" again? Probably not in view of Table 7, but the extreme conformity with additivity in the *p* scale for the small and medium diameter data is impressive.

REFERENCES

Anderson, V. L. and McLean, R. A. (1974). *Design of Experiments: A Realistic Approach.* New York: Dekker.

Bartlett, M. S. (1935). "Contingency table interactions," *Journal of the Royal Statistical Society, Suppl.* 2, 248-252.

Bhapker, V. P. and Koch, G. G. (1968). "Hypotheses of "No Interaction" in multidimensional contingency tables," *Technometrics*, 10, 107-123.

Bishop, Y. M. M., Fienberg, S. E. and Holland, P. W. (1975). *Discrete Multivariate Analysis: Theory and Practice.* Cambridge, MA: MIT Press.

Box, G. E. P., Hunter, W. G. and Hunter, J. S. (1978). *Statistics for Experimenters: An Introduction to Design, Data Analysis, and Model Building.* New York: Wiley.

Daniel, C. and Wood, F. S. (1971). *Fitting Equations to Data.* New York: Wiley.

REFERENCES

Goodman, L. A. (1985). "The analysis of cross-classified data having ordered and/or unordered categories: Association models, correlation models, and asymmetry models for continency tables with or without missing entries," *Annals of Statistics*, **13**, 10-69.

Haberman, S. J. (1974). *The Analysis of Frequency Data*. Chicago: University of Chicago Press.

Hoblyn, T. N. and Palmer, R. C. (1934). "A complex experiment in the propagation of plum rootstocks from root cuttings," *Journal of Pomology and Horticultural Science*, **12**, 36-56.

Snedecor, G. W. and Cochran, W. G. (1967). *Statistical Methods*, 6th edition. Ames, IA: Iowa State University Press.

Stuart, A. (1953). "The estimation and comparison of strengths of association in contingency tables," *Biometrika*, **40**, 105-110.

Stuart, A. (1955). "A test for homogeneity of the marginal distributions in a two-way classification," *Biometrika*, **42**, 412-416.

CHAPTER 13

Analysis of Bernoulli Data From A 2^5 Design Done in Blocks of Size Four

Lincoln E. Moses
Stanford University

1. INTRODUCTION AND SUMMARY

A pediatrician investigator desired to learn about physicians' attitudes toward holding in confidence sensitive information that came from their adolescent patients; in particular she wished to study factors that would affect physicians' propensity to withhold such information from the family of the adolescent patient. In this study (Lovett and Wald, 1985) she was interested in how the physician gave weight to the patient's age (A), "maturity for her age" (M), and previous length of acquaintance with the family (L). The approach used was a mailed questionnaire containing four standard vignettes, in each of which A, M, and L could plausibly be varied (at two levels) quite freely in any combination. Every respondent was asked to state yes or no to granting confidentiality to each of the same four "fables," though age, maturity, and length of acquaintance were differently associated to those fables.

All four fables involved female patients. Briefly, they presented these situations:

1. An IUD incidentally found in an X-ray that was taken because of back pain.
2. Drug use revealed to the physician.

3. Gonococcal infection identified in the patient.
4. Contraceptive advice requested by the patient.

These fables were simply vehicles on which to carry variations in A, M, and L, each at two levels.

Clearly 32 different questionnaires were possible: the eight combinations of A, M, and L could be applied to each of the basic fables. Eight package types (the "blocks") were constructed, each with all four fables and with the associated A, M, L combinations selected so as to make the design a "2^5 in blocks of 4." The 31 orthogonal contrasts include seven which are computed from the eight block sums; the remaining 24 are intra-block comparisons, in which two responses enter positively and two negatively from every block (and thus from every respondent). It was anticipated that inter-block contrasts would be estimated with lower precision, since they would use inter-person comparisons. Letting D and E be pseudo factors representing the four fables, the design chosen relegated to inter-block comparison the following seven contrasts: DA, EM, DEL, DEAM, EAL, DLM, and ALM. Observe that main effects and two-factor interactions among A, M, and L were estimated as intra-block comparisons. Analysis of the data led to very clear results with regard to the effects and interactions of A, M, and L. But the concern here is with certain features of the data analysis.

First, although the study was large — nearly 4,000 questionnaires entered the analysis — there was only weak indication of any excess of inter-subject variation beyond intra-subject variation. This fits well with the conception that stratification frequently has little effect with Bernoulli observations. If the distinction between inter- and intra-subject variation can be ignored, then more flexible designs are available for such a study. For example, it becomes as straightforward to use three or five fables as to use four.

Second, the 32 distinct kinds of vignette (four basic fables, each with eight combinations of AM and L) yielded proportions of "yes" responses ranging from .360 to .983, with fourteen exceeding .80, and of these six exceeded .90. It was notable that despite the high incidence of proportions outside the middle range, the analyses on the scale of p and on the anglit scale were highly consonant. The sample sizes for the 32 proportions ranged from 102 to 143, with a harmonic mean of 117.9.

The article closes with brief remarks concerning other less technical, but perhaps more important issues, such as response rate and interpretation of studies based on answers to hypothetical questions.

2. DATA ANALYSIS APPLIED TO THE PERCENTS RESPONDING 'YES' TO THE 32 VIGNETTES

The data that are the subject of this discussion appear in column 2 of Table 1, where they are ordered for the application of Yates' algorithm (Box, Hunter and Hunter, 1978). The effects, d_i, obtained by applying that algorithm appear in column (3) with their labels in column (4). Parentheses identify the seven effects that are based on inter-block comparisons. Stars appear against the five effects that are statistically significant, per the following discussion.

The absolute values of the 31 effects appear in Figure 1, where the ith smallest one (in absolute value) $|d|_{(i)}$ is plotted against the two-sided normal percentage point that corresponds to $\frac{3i-1}{3n+1}$ with $n = 31$ (Daniel, 1959; Mosteller and Tukey, 1977). In the figure the seven inter-block effects are shown as crosses, while the 24 intra-block effects are shown as dots. Several features deserve attention. First, there are just five significant effects: A (age), and M (maturity) are the ones involving factors of interest; length of acquaintance with the family showed no effect. The other three significant effects D, E, and DE exhibit different propensities to say "yes" to the four basic fables. No interactions are significant. Second, the seven inter-block effects are about as well mixed with intra-block effects as they could be, apparently attesting to the absence of greater variability in inter-block contrasts. This indication of symmetry between the two sorts of comparison has consequences explored later. The abscissa corresponding to ordinate 1.0 is very near .012 and one might (incautiously) regard it as an estimate of the standard deviation of these contrasts. But, as is clear from the picture, five of the contrasts embody real effects, not simply error. If $n = 31$ as used in the figure be replaced by $n = 26$, the number of null degrees of freedom, then the estimate of the standard deviation, obtained in the same way, is very near .0082, and this figure can be used for assessing the sampling error of the effects A and M. (To set $\Phi^{-1}\left[\frac{3i-1}{3n+1} \times \frac{1}{2} + .5\right] = 1.0$ with $n = 26$, find $i = 18.3$. Among the 26 contrasts left after omitting the five non-null ones, the values of $|d|_{(18)}$ and $|d|_{(19)}$ are .0079 and .0089 — DEM and AL respectively. Interpolation produces .0082.) The foregoing interpretations can be assessed more numerically by collecting the individual squared effects in an analysis of variance format as in panel 1 of Table 2. The figures in that panel exhibit the two mean square errors for intra- and inter-block comparisons. The F ratio is less than 2.0, and not significantly large. If the single degree of freedom, ALM, were pooled into the inter-block error, that would be even smaller. So here we see numerical support for the judgement

278 ANALYSIS OF BERNOULLI DATA FROM A 2^5 DESIGN

TABLE 1. Data and results on scale p.

	DE	ALM	(1) n	(2) p	(3) Effect	(4) Mean
	00	000	119	.445	.7466	
		001	117	.624	.0608*	M.
		010	111	.360	−.0026	L.
DRUG		011	138	.493	−.0109	LM.
		100	115	.513	.0827*	A.
		101	102	.696	−.0122	AM.
		110	118	.534	.0089	AL.
		111	126	.675	−.0050	(ALM)
	01	000	107	.759	.0731*	E.
		001	112	.812	−.0176	(EM)
		010	122	.770	.0128	EL
CONTRACEPTIVE		011	122	.812	−.0034	ELM
		100	126	.857	.00025	EA
		101	124	.968	.0009	EAM
		110	105	.943	−.0018	(EAL)
		111	118	.966	.0014	EALM
	10	000	106	.604	.0449*	D.
		001	117	.795	.0067	DM
		010	124	.589	.0050	DL
IUD		011	121	.818	.0008	(DLM)
		100	120	.850	.0154	(DA)
		101	120	.983	−.0154	DAM
		110	123	.866	−.0091	DAL
		111	114	.930	−.0004	DALM
	11	000	121	.578	−.0861*	DE.
		001	126	.786	.0079	DEM
		010	119	.622	−.0067	(DEL)
G.C.		111	102	.755	−.0028	DELM
		100	113	.814	−.0051	DEA
		101	143	.902	.0008	(DEAM)
		110	122	.869	.0072	DEAL
		111	122	.902	.0065	DEALM

DATA ANALYSIS APPLIED TO THE PERCENTS RESPONDING 'YES' 279

reached visually before — that inter-block variation is not notably different from intra-block. Assuming that both kinds of contrasts may be regarded symmetrically, one could then regard the design as a simple 4 × 8 factorial design, where the four fables are crossed with the 8 combinations of A, L, and M, and proceed to construct a two-way analysis of variance. Panel 2 displays the results. The scales are different in the two panels, though easily reconciled. In panel 2 the basic observation is a proportion, p. In panel 1 the basic observation is one thirty-second of the difference between two sums of 16 distinct p's; it follows that if σ^2 is the variance estimated in panel 2, then $\dfrac{\sigma^2}{32}$ is the variance estimated in panel 1. The two tables were computed independently, and an algebraic relation that holds among the three mean squares is stated in note 2 of panel 2, which satisfies (within rounding error) the algebraic relation.

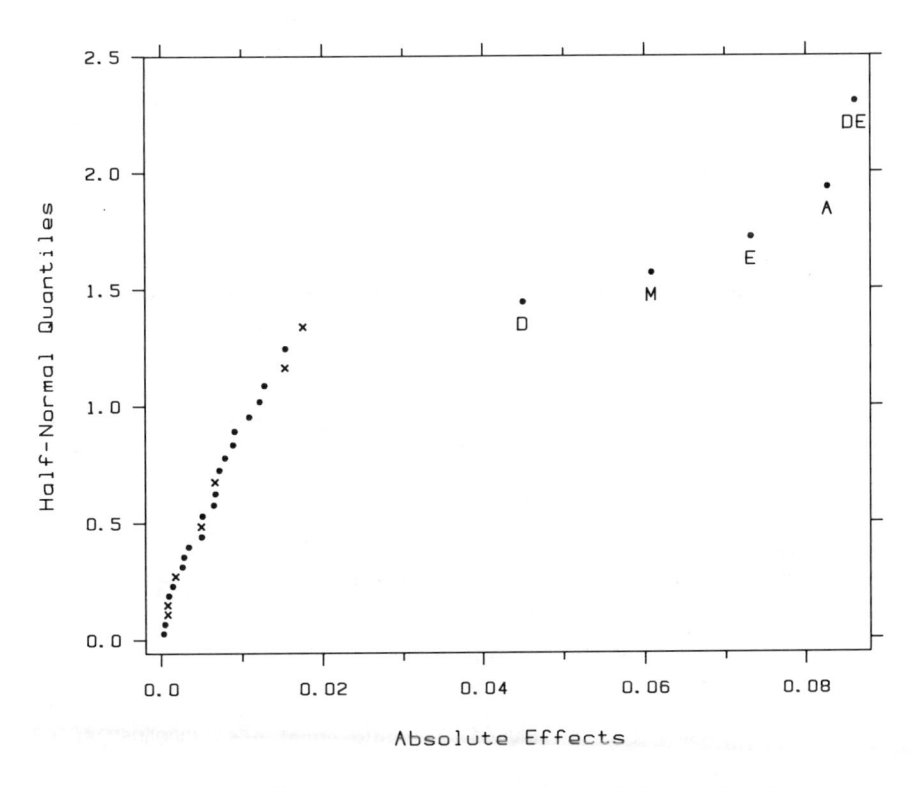

Figure 1. Half-normal plot: absolute effects $|d|_{(\lambda)}$ plotted against $\Phi^{-1}(\dfrac{W_i}{2} + .5)$ where $W_i = \dfrac{3\lambda - 1}{3(31) + 1}$.

TABLE 2. Analyses of variance (scale of *p*).

1. Based on contrasts in Table 1.

Intra-block	SS	df	m.s.
Fables	.01477283	3	
A	.00683929	1	
M	.00369664	1	
L,AL,AM,LM	.00035362	4	
Error	.00075860	15	.0000505735

Inter-block			
ALM	.000025	1	
Error	.00059633	6	.000099388

$F_{6,15} = 1.965 \quad p > .10$

2. Based on two-way analysis of variance of 32 values of *p*, arranged as 4 columns (Fables) × 8 rows (A × L × M combinations).

Source	SS	df	m.s.
Fables	.472569	3	.157523
All A × L × M	.349042	7	.049863
Interaction	.043259	21	.002060

Notes:
1. Sums of squares in this panel must be divided by 32 to be comparable to those in panel 1.
2. $.002060 \div 32 = .000064375$ should equal $\frac{15}{21}$ (.0000505735) + $\frac{6}{21}$ (.000099388) = .000064531; the arithmetic checks.

3. A SECOND DATA ANALYSIS, ON THE ANGLIT SCALE

The methods of analysis that have been used would be well-justified if the individual data (proportions in our case) were independent, normal, and had common variance. Of course the sample proportions are "approximately normal," but their variances are unequal on two counts; first, the binomial probabilities they estimate are manifestly not all equal, and second, the sample sizes vary, from a low of 102 to a high of 143. A further question may attach to whether additivity — an underlying assumption — is unreasonably strained where so many sample proportions exceed .90.

To assess the strength of such considerations, the data were reanalyzed on the anglit scale. That is, each sample proportion p was replaced by its anglit,

$$y = 2 \sin^{-1} \sqrt{p}$$

and the same sorts of analysis were again done. Since $\text{Var}(y) = 1/n$, the inequality in variance due to variation in underlying probabilities is gone, but the variability associated with inequality among the 32 values of n remains. But that degree of heterogeneity of variance is of little concern. Further, the anglit scale "stretches out" the regions where p is near one, or zero, easing the difficulties relating to additivity. So if the results of analysis on the anglit scale differ sharply from our previous results, we should feel reservations about those previous results.

The data, using anglits, appear in Table 3, which is arranged in the format of Table 1; again Yates' algorithm was applied, and the plot of the 31 individual degrees of freedom appears as Figure 2, which resembles Figure 1 strikingly. Again we see the ×'s denoting inter-block effects intermixed; the same five effects appear as the only significant ones, and their relative sizes are very similar in the two analyses. A and DE exchange first and second place; other differences are hard to find. The abscissa corresponding to 1.0 is about .03, but again it is misleading, for we have not 31 but 26 null effects, and calculation on this basis produces (again by interpolating between $|d|_{(18)}$ and $|d|_{(19)}$) .0223 as the estimate of the standard deviation applicable to the effects on the anglit scale.

Table 4 shows in panel 1 the inter-block and intra-block estimates of error, based on the contrasts in Table 3. And panel 2 shows the analysis of variance that results from treating the data as if they had arisen from a simple 4 × 8 factorial design.

282 ANALYSIS OF BERNOULLI DATA FROM A 2^5 DESIGN

TABLE 3. Data and results on anglit scale.

	DE	ALM	(1) n	(2) y	(3) Effect	(4) Mean
DRUG	00	000	119	1.46		
		001	117	1.82	.150*	M
		010	111	1.29	−.005	L
		011	138	1.56	.032	LM
		100	115	1.60	.216*	A
		101	102	1.97	.008	AM
		110	118	1.64	.018	AL
		111	126	1.93	−.021	(ALM)
CONTRACEPTIVE	01	000	107	2.12	.166*	E
		001	112	2.24	−.036	(EM)
		010	122	2.14	.034	EL
		011	122	2.24	.008	ELM
		100	126	2.37	.012	EA
		101	124	2.78	.002	EAM
		110	105	2.66	.007	(EAL)
		111	118	2.77	.004	EALM
IUD	10	000	106	1.78	.098*	D
		001	117	2.20	.023	DM
		010	124	1.75	.003	DL
		011	121	2.26	.001	(DLM)
		100	120	2.35	.038	(DA)
		101	120	2.88	.028	DAM
		110	123	2.39	−.026	DAL
		111	114	2.61	−.004	DALM
G.C.	11	000	121	1.73	−.212*	DE
		001	126	2.18	−.001	DEM
		010	119	1.82	−.011	(DEL)
		111	102	2.11	.002	DELM
		100	113	2.25	.039	DEA
		101	143	2.50	.015	(DEAM)
		110	122	2.40	.018	DEAL
		111	122	2.50	.022	DEALM

Again we see little (indeed less) indication of an excess of inter-block variance as compared with intra-block. When working on the anglit scale, we can readily test for the presence of variability beyond pure binomial variation, as follows. Any contrast has the form $(1/32)(\sum_{i=1}^{32} C_i y_i)$ where C_i is ± 1. y_i has variance $1/n_i$. It follows that every contrast has variance $(1/32)^2 \Sigma(1/n_i) = (1/32)(\bar{n}_h)^{-1}$ where $\bar{n}_h = [1/32 \, \Sigma(1/n_i)]^{-1}$ is the harmonic mean of the sample sizes. So the *a priori* variance for every contrast is $(32\bar{n}_h)^{-1}$. Both the intra- and inter-block error sums of squares when divided by this prior variance have χ^2-distribution, with 15 and 6 degrees-of-freedom, respectively, assuming independent binomial data. Neither χ^2 is significantly large, though their sum, having 21 degrees-of-freedom, lies between the .025 and .05 percentage points of χ^2_{21}. We take this as indicating reliably a modest departure from pure binomial variation.

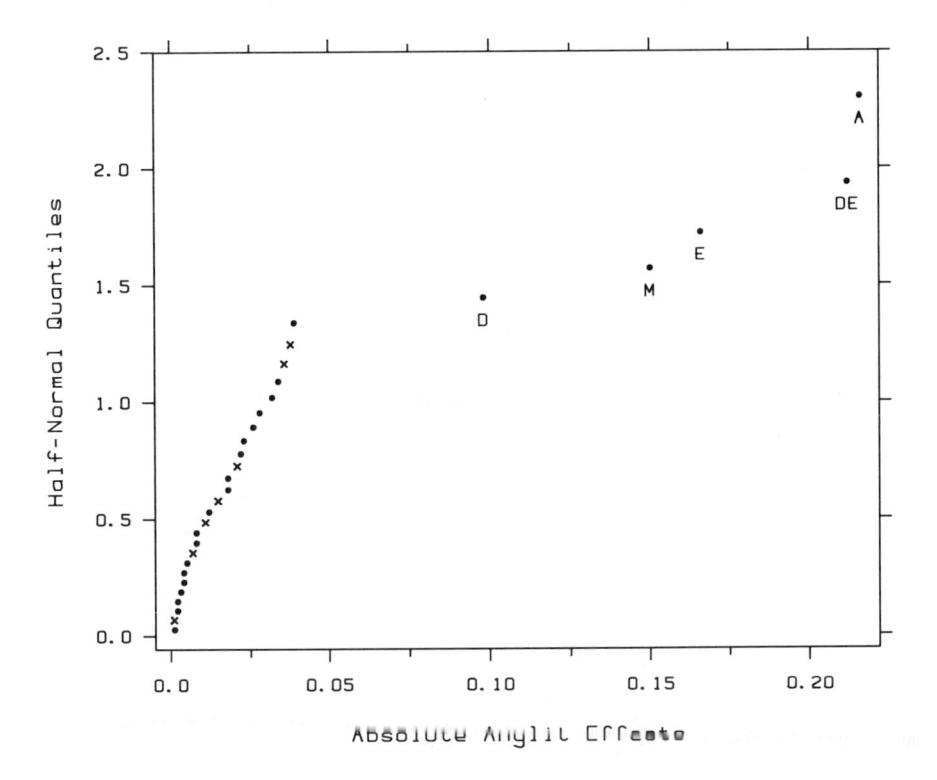

Figure 2. Half-normal plot on anglit scale (inter-person contrasts shown as ×). Vertical scale is $\Phi^{-1}\left[.5 + \dfrac{1}{2}\dfrac{3\lambda - 1}{3N + 1}\right]$ for $N = 31$.

284 ANALYSIS OF BERNOULLI DATA FROM A 2^5 DESIGN

TABLE 4. Analyses of variance (anglit scale).

1. Based on contrasts in Table 3.

Intra-block	SS	df	m.s.
Fables	.082104	3	
A	.046656	1	
M	.022500	1	
L,AL,AM,LM	.001375	4	
Error	.005725	15	.000381667

Inter-block			
ALM	.000441	1	
Error	.003136	6	.000522667

$$F_{6,15} = 1.365 \quad \chi^2_{21} = \frac{.005725 + .003136}{(32\,\bar{n}_h)^{-1}} = (32)(117.9)(.008861)$$

$$= 33.43 \quad .25 < p < .05$$

2. Based on two-way analysis of variance of 32 values of y, arranged as 4 columns (Fables) × 8 rows (A × L × M combinations).

Source	SS	df	m.s.
Fables	2.6251	3	.8750
All A × L × M	2.2662	7	.3237
Interaction	0.2829	21	.01347

Notes:
1. Sums of squares in this panel must be divided by 32 to be comparable to those in panel 1.
2. $.01347 \div 32 = .00042094$ should equal $\frac{1}{21}(.005725 + .003136) = .0042195$.

The main conclusion from this second analysis is that we are less worried now about analysis directly on the scale of p, since conclusions hold up very closely when we look at the problem on the y-scale, which is less liable to objections about homogeneous variance and additivity.

4. WHY IS INTRA-BLOCK ESTIMATION SO LITTLE SUPERIOR TO INTER-BLOCK WITH BERNOULLI VARIABLES?

In our data each subject contributes four Bernoulli responses, and there are 8 *kinds* of such 4-component response vectors. (We write $y_j = (y_1, y_2, y_3, y_4)_j$ with $j = 1,...,8$.) Taken together as a string, they form a 32-vector embodying all combinations of high and low levels of the five factors D, E, A, L, M.

There are seven (of the 31) effects which are estimated as contrasts among the 8 sums, $S_j = y_{1j} + y_{2j} + y_{3j} + y_{4j}$ ($j = 1,...,8$).

The other 24 effects are calculated as linear combinations (with combining coefficients ± 1) of intra-block differences, D_j, which take two of y_{1j}, y_{2j}, y_{3j}, and y_{4j} with coefficient $+1$ and two with coefficient -1.

Now suppose that there are m respondents to each package type; that is, we have m observations on $y_1, y_2,..., y_8$. We seek expressions for the variance of (1) an inter-block contrast and (2) an intra-block contrast. We now may write the kth ($k = 1,...,7$) estimated inter-block effect

$$\frac{1}{32} [C_1^k \bar{S}_1 + C_2^k \bar{S}_2 + ... + C_8^k \bar{S}_8] \qquad (1)$$

where the coefficients $C_1^k = \pm 1$ are characteristic of kth inter-block contrast and where $\bar{S}_j$, is the average of the m block sums of type j. In a similar way the kth intra-block effect ($k = 1,...,24$) is estimated as

$$\frac{1}{32} [a_1^k \bar{D}_1 + a_2^k \bar{D}_2 + ... + a_8^k \bar{D}_8] \qquad (2)$$

in which all a_j^k are ± 1 (though they need not be four of each).

Now, since $\bar{S}_j$ and $\bar{S}_j'$ are from different respondents, we take them as independent, and likewise with $\bar{D}_j$ and $\bar{D}_j'$. Now we introduce the following model, in which for convenience, and with some loss of

286 ANALYSIS OF BERNOULLI DATA FROM A 2^5 DESIGN

generality, we take all true effects as null. Let α index subjects, j index the eight blocks, and i the four components within a block.

$$y_{ij\alpha} = 1 \quad \text{with probability} \quad \Pi_\alpha = \Pi + \delta_\alpha$$
$$\phantom{y_{ij\alpha}} = 0 \quad \text{with probability} \quad \overline{\Pi}_\alpha = 1 - \Pi_\alpha$$

$y_{ij\alpha}$ and $y'_{ij\alpha}$ are conditionally independent, given α. By noting in (1) and (2) that each is a linear combination of eight independent quantities, we see that comparison of the variances of the two reduces to comparing $\text{Var}(\overline{D}_j)$ and $\text{Var}(\overline{S}_j)$, or instead, $\sigma_1^2 = \text{Var}(D_{j\alpha})$ and $\sigma_2^2 = \text{Var}(S_{j\alpha})$

$$\sigma_1^2 = \text{Var}(y_{1\alpha} + y_{2\alpha} - y_{3\alpha} - y_{4\alpha}) \tag{3}$$
$$= 4\sigma_{y_{1\alpha}}^2 - 4\,\text{cov}(y_{1\alpha}, y_{2\alpha}),$$

$$\sigma_2^2 = \text{Var}(y_{1\alpha} + y_{2\alpha} + y_{3\alpha} + y_{4\alpha}) \tag{4}$$
$$= 4\sigma_{y_{1\alpha}}^2 + 12\,\text{cov}(y_{1\alpha}, y_{2\alpha}).$$

We now evaluate $\sigma_{y_{1\alpha}}^2$ and $\text{cov}(y_{1\alpha}, y_{2\alpha})$.

$$\text{Var}(y_{1\alpha}) = \underset{\alpha}{E}\,\text{Var}(y_{1\alpha}) + \underset{\alpha}{\text{Var}}(E(y_{1\alpha}))$$

$$= \underset{\alpha}{E}(\Pi + \delta_\alpha)(\overline{\Pi} - \delta_\alpha) + \underset{\alpha}{\text{Var}}(\Pi + \delta_\alpha)$$

$$= \underset{\alpha}{E}\left[\Pi\overline{\Pi} + \delta_\alpha(\overline{\Pi} - \Pi) - \delta_\alpha^2\right] + \text{Var}(\delta_\alpha)$$

$$= \Pi\overline{\Pi} - \sigma_\delta^2 + \sigma_\delta^2$$

$$= \Pi\overline{\Pi}$$

$$\text{Cov}(y_{1\alpha}, y_{2\alpha}) = \underset{\alpha}{E}\,\text{Cov}(y_{1\alpha}, y_{2\alpha}) + \text{Cov}(E(y_{1\alpha}), E(y_{2\alpha}))$$

$$= 0 + \text{Cov}[(\Pi + \delta_\alpha), (\Pi + \delta_\alpha)]$$

$$= \sigma_\delta^2.$$

Then

$$\sigma_1^2 = 4\Pi\overline{\Pi} - 4\sigma_\delta^2,$$

and

$$\sigma_1^2 = 4\Pi\overline{\Pi} + 12\sigma_\delta^2.$$

Now suppose $\sigma_\delta = .15$ — a rather extreme value if additivity within (0,1) is to hold — and suppose $\Pi = .74$. Then

$$\delta_1^2 = 4(.1924) - .09 = .6796$$

$$\delta_2^2 = 4(.1924) + .27 = 1.0396$$

it appears that *with Bernoulli random variables* one may not expect a large difference between inter- and intra-block variance. The situation is quite otherwise with continuous data, where large values of $\rho = \dfrac{cov}{\sigma^2}$ may produce large differences in σ_1^2 and σ_2^2. Thus, $\rho = .5$ would produce in (3) and (4) the values $\sigma_1^2 = 2\sigma^2$ and $\sigma_2^2 = 10\sigma^2$, and $\rho = .8$ leads to $\sigma_1^2 = .8\sigma^2$ and $\sigma_2^2 = 13.6\sigma^2$.

5. DISCUSSION

In these data, analysis on the scale of p appears reasonable. Further, these data suggest very little excess of inter-block variation over intra-block. If that distinction can indeed be ignored, then design and analysis can both be much simplified; in particular, analysis can be carried on as a simple fables-crossed-with- (A × L × M) design, using the 21 degree-of-freedom interaction mean square for tests and confidence intervals. Moreover, once that paradigm is accepted, it is an easy matter to deal with three or five or twelve fables, rather than strictly with some power of 2. It is only necessary to assure that all eight ALM combinations occur equally often for each fable. Such flexibility could be important if only three plausible fables are developable or if it is desired to assess the variables ALM across very many hypothetical situations.

The data analysis on the scale of p has other implications for design. Formally, the data consisted of somewhat more than 900 4-variate responses across 8 types of underlying multivariate observation (all the respondents to one of the 8 packages belonged to the same type). The analysis in terms of half-normal plots took full account of the actual design. From the half-normal plot we estimated the standard error of any contrast as .0082. But ignoring the complex structure, we might have argued in this way: any effect Δ will be estimated as $\hat{\Delta} = \frac{1}{2}(p_+ - p_-)$ where p_+ and p_- are the proportions of yes responses on the questions that are "high" for the effect and low for it, respectively. There are (except for a slight incidence of missing data) all together 4N questionnaires to be received, with about 2N for p_+ and 2N for p_i so, the s.e. of Δ will be about

$$\frac{1}{2}\sqrt{\left[\frac{p_+q_+}{2N} + \frac{p_-q_-}{2N}\right]}.$$

Now in the actual study 4N was 3795; using that value and the conservative value .25 for both p_+q_+ and p_-q_- produces the value .0081 for this "se" developed on a conservative pure binomial model. From the data analysis by half-normal plot we found a s.e. of .0082, and the s.e. based on the 21 degree-of-freedom interaction mean square is (see note 2, Table 2) equal to $\sqrt{.000064375} = .0080$. The very close agreement of the crude estimate with the two data-based ones is perhaps fortuitous, but nonetheless it encourages planning of sample size using such thinking. Indeed, our experience here says that careful data analysis has not brought us to a point very different from where we would have come by "pure binomial" kind of calculations.

We close with some substantive comments about this kind of study which uses hypothetical vignettes to learn about attitudes. First, the psychological literature gives reasons for much doubt that responses can be taken as predicting actual behavior (Festinger, 1964). Second, if the fables are long enough to be realistic they may be an imposing burden to the respondent, with adverse effects on response rate (and associated biases?). Hence, smaller package size, like two or three may become desirable. Third, the ability largely to ignore the patterning in the data (for example by using the 21 degree-of-freedom m.s.e.) simplifies analysis of yet another kind of comparison that interested the investigator: comparing effects for different subsets of respondents — e.g., males and females, old and young, without doing distinct 2^k analyses on the two sets of respondents.

REFERENCES

Box, G. E. P., Hunter, W. G., and Hunter, J. S. (1978). *Statistics for Experimenters.* New York: Wiley, 342-344.

Daniel, C. (1959). "Use of half-normal plots in interpreting factorial two-level experiments," *Technometrics,* **1,** 311-341.

Festinger, L. (1964). "Behavioral support for opinion change," *Public Opinion Quarterly,* **A78,** 404-17.

Lovett, J. and Wald, M. S. (1985). "Physician attitudes toward confidential care for adolescents," *Journal of Pediatrics,* **106,** 517-521.

Mosteller, F. and Tukey, J. W. (1977). *Data Analysis and Regression.* Reading, MA: Addison-Wesley, p. 111.

CHAPTER 14

A 2-Stage Procedure for Guaranteeing Accuracy with Calibration Standards

Brian R. Schlain
New York, New York

ABSTRACT

Stein's 2-stage procedure was applied to guarantee accuracies of radioimmunoassay Ferritin calibration standards within stated tolerances. The initial samples provided error variance estimates, by which required number of additional replicates were determined for testing calibrator accuracies. When error variances are unknown, 2-stage procedures are the only way to guarantee accuracy. The procedure is especially applicable to immunoassay vendors who experience at a given analyte level nonconstant assay precisions across kit lots. The 2-stage procedure assumes stability of a stored frozen master lot. Formulas, which are extensions of Stein's and Hodges' ideas, are provided for estimating optimal first stage sample sizes, when there is some knowledge of error variance.

A. INTRODUCTION

Immunoassay kit vendors are concerned with manufacturing calibrator lots of consistent accuracy. A popular approach is to choose a "Master Lot" for evaluating new production calibrator lots. Often new calibrators are assayed as unknowns with "master lot" calibrators. It is not uncommon for a new calibrator lot to pass if their assay value averages from a single calibration are within 5%

of their assigned values. Though usually not confronted, this approach is complicated with the variability and bias of fitted calibration curves.

In immunoassay, this calibrator accuracy problem is sometimes further complicated by nonconstant assay precisions at given analytic levels across lots or even across time within lots. With radioimmunoassay (RIA), precision at a given analyte level depends upon changing factors such as tracer specific activity, antibody affinities, and antibody concentrations.

For immunoassay calibrator accuracy problems, we recommend 2-sample tests (Stein, 1945; Healy, 1956; Bishop, 1979; Bishop and Dudewicz, 1978 and 1981). First stage samples are obtained for estimating assay precisions, from which required second stage sample sizes can be determined for comparing a new and master calibration standard within a stated accuracy. If assay precisions are unknown, 2-stage procedures are the only way to guarantee calibrator accuracies (Dantzig, 1940). Both new and master lot standards should be assayed as unknowns in equal replicates within calibration cycles, with master lot standards serving as calibrators.

Two-stage procedures of this type were originated by Stein (1945) in a hypothesis testing context and extended by Healy (1956) to controlling widths of confidence intervals in simultaneous multiple comparisons. Later 2-stage procedures were developed for unequal variance cases by Dudewicz and Bishop (Bishop, 1979; Bishop and Dudewicz, 1978 and 1981), Tamhane (1977), and Hochberg (1975). This paper applies Stein's 2-stage procedure (Stein, 1945) to guaranteeing accuracy of calibration standards relative to a master lot.

B. A 2-SAMPLE PROCEDURE FOR GUARANTEEING ACCURACY OF A NEW CALIBRATOR LOT

Suppose we desire a new standard to be within a stated accuracy, Δ, of its corresponding master standard. We assume the following, which should be checked:

(1) Stability over time of a stored, frozen calibrator master lot;

(2) unchanging assay precisions over 2 consecutive sampling stages;

(3) for each standard level, equal assay precisions across new and master lots.

In sampling stage 1, new and master calibration standards are assayed as unknowns on a current production kit in n_0 replicates, using master standards as calibrators. In section C5 we apply formulas for determining n_0, based on some prior knowledge of error variance. In section C3 we show how precision estimates in stage 1 can be used to determine the number of required replicates for stage 2. Assay run orders should be randomized or determined by trend robust sequences (Daniel and Wilcoxon, 1966). Several calibration cycles may be required to complete sampling stages 1 and 2. To eliminate bias from calibration curve fitting, new and master lot replicate numbers should be equal within calibration cycles.

C. FERRITIN RADIOIMMUNOASSAY CALIBRATOR EXAMPLE

The 2-stage procedure was applied to an actual industrial radioimmunoassay (RIA) calibrator problem. The statistical analysis is provided in sections C3 and C4. The clinical importance of ferritin RIA measurement is given in section C1, and a brief description of biological principles underlying the ferritin test is given in section C2.

C1. Ferritin Test

Ferritin, an iron containing protein, is found in small but clinically significant amounts in human serum. Serum ferritin is secreted in constant proportion to the total iron stores of the body except in certain pathological conditions (Lipschitz et al., 1974). Serum ferritin determination has been suggested as a reliable means of monitoring iron levels and the amount of iron therapy required by patients on hemodialysis (Beallo et al., 1976; Jacobs and Worwood, 1975; Mirahmadietal., 1977). Detection and quantitation of serum ferritin has been made practical through radioimmunoassay procedures (Luxton et al., 1977) (Miles et al., 1974). The advantages of serum ferritin measurement through RIA, in comparison with other means of assessing iron status (e.g., hemoglobin, serum iron, transferring saturation and red cell profoporphyrin) are that it can resolve differences within the physiological range and provide data on certain iron deficiency states that previously were only known after body iron stores were totally depleted (Hochbert, 1975; Jacobs and Worwood, 1975; Tamhane, 1977).

C2. Principles of Ferritin RIA Method

RIA ferritin measurement is based on the competitive binding principles of RIA as developed by Yalow and Berson (1971). Nonradioactive ferritin from patient samples and ferritin standards compete with a constant amount of radio-iodinated ferritin tracer for binding sites on the ferritin antibody, which is held at a limiting concentration. The amount of radio-iodinated ferritin tracer which will bind to the antibody is inversely proportional to the amount of nonradioactive ferritin present in the assay tube.

Radioimmunoassay of a ferritin sample yields a radioactive count measurement which can be interpolated through a calibration curve into nanograms/milliliter units. Ferritin calibration curves can be estimated from measured radioactive counts of standards with known ferritin concentrations.

A radioimmunoassay (RIA) calibrator example was supplied by a vendor with the following standards and accuracy tolerances:

Ferritin Standard (ng/ml)	Accuracy Tolerance (ng/ml)
2	0.6
5	1.5
10	2.0

For each of the above ferritin levels, new and master lot standards were initially assayed randomly in 9-10 replicates Tables (1 and 2) within single calibration cycles. Calibration curves were manually estimated with spline rulers.

To check the statistical assumptions of the 2-stage procedure Shapiro-Wilk tests for normality and F-tests for homogeneous variances were applied to the ferritin data Tables (1 and 2). There were no statistically detectable non-normalities or non-constant variances within ferritin standard levels.

C3. Ferritin 2-Standard

The pooled sample standard deviation for standard 2, S_{p2}, was 0.61 with 16 df (Table 1). We set $\alpha = .05$ and wanted a power of 0.9 against the alternatives that the new 2-standard might be 2 ± 0.6 ng/ml.

Then, applying Stein's procedure (Stein, 1945), we let

$$z_2 = \left\{ \frac{0.6}{t_{.025}(16) + t_{.10}(16)} \right\}^2 / 2 = .015,$$

where $t_{.025}(16)$ and $t_{.10}(16)$ are the 97.5th and 90th percentiles of the Student t-distribution with 16 df.

The total sample sizes required for comparing new and master standards were:

$$N = \max\left\{ \left[\frac{S_{p_2}^2}{z_2} \right] + 1, n_{02} \right\} = 25,$$

where $n_{02} = 9$, the first stage sample size, and $\left[S_{p_2}^2 \right]$ signifies the largest integer in $\left[\frac{S_{p_2}^2}{z_2} \right]$. The required stage 2 sample sizes for new and master standards 2 were then

$$n_2 = N_2 - n_{02} = 16.$$

Stage 2 data for the Ferritin 2-standard are presented in Table 1.

The 2-stage procedure assumption of constant variance across the two stages was checked with the standard F-test, which was not significant at the 0.01-level. The 0.01-level was used since calibration affects the assay value sample variance distribution by perturbing slopes of the calibration line.

Obtaining from Table 1 overall means, $\overline{X}_{n_2} = 2.89$ and $\overline{X}_{m_2} = 2.47$ across both sampling stages, we calculated

$$t = \frac{\overline{X}_{n_2} - \overline{X}_{m_2}}{S_{p_2}\sqrt{\frac{1}{25} + \frac{1}{26}}} = 2.34 > t_{.025}(16) = 2.12.$$

We concluded that new and master standards 2 have different accuracies.

It is not paradoxical to have obtained a statistically significant result when the estimated difference between new and master standards 2 is 0.4 ng/ml, and the accuracy tolerance is 0.6 ng/ml. If the true difference were 0.367 ng/ml, we would have approximately a 50% chance of obtaining statistical significance. For a stated z and n_0, provided $\sigma^2 > z\, n_0$; there is approximately a 50% probability of detection if:

TABLE 1. Ferritin standard 2 data (ng/ml).

Ferritin Standard 2 Stage 1 Data		Ferritin Standard 2 Stage 2 Data	
Master Standard 2 (ng/ml)	New Standard (ng/ml)	Master Standard 2 (ng/ml)	New Standard 2 (ng/ml)
2.21	2.27	3.40	4.21
3.60	2.87	2.97	3.93
2.84	2.97	2.85	2.37
3.27	3.49	2.93	2.82
2.21	2.21	3.88	3.63
2.57	3.34	3.06	3.49
1.81	3.64	1.23	2.18
2.03	2.23	—*	2.40
2.15	2.01	1.51	3.39
		2.13	3.89
		1.72	1.17
		1.69	3.33
		1.42	3.91
		2.11	2.52
		2.56	2.51
		2.23	2.70
		3.47	1.58

Wilk-Shapiro test for normality	n_{02} mean SD	$W = 0.92^{**}$ 9 2.52 0.60	$W = 0.90^{**}$ 9 2.78 0.62	n_2 mean SD	$W = 0.96^{**}$ 16 2.45 0.81	$W = 0.96^{**}$ 17 2.94 0.87
F-test for homogeneous variances within stages		$F = 1.07^{**}$ 0.26 ng/ml 0.61 16		new-master pooled $SD(S_{p2})$ df		$F = 1.15^{**}$ 0.49 0.84 31
F-test for homogeneous variances across stages			$F = 1.90$ Not statistically significant at .01-level.			

* 1 bad value.
** Not statistically significant at .05 level.

TABLE 2. Ferritin standards 5-10 data (ng/ml).

	Ferritin Standard 5		Ferritin Standard 10	
	Master Standard 5 (ng/ml)	New Standard 5 (ng/ml)	Master Standard 10 (ng/ml)	New Standard 10 (ng/ml)
	6.25	5.46	9.70	9.06
	4.35	5.91	9.39	8.55
	5.42	5.68	8.63	9.07
	4.62	6.03	10.38	10.50
	5.32	4.42	10.79	9.29
	5.34	5.92	9.88	9.00
	3.41	4.86	8.99	9.74
	4.42	4.81	9.05	9.31
	6.66	3.77	8.69	8.00
	6.44	4.14	8.74	8.72
Wilk-Shapiro test	$W = 0.95$*	$W = 0.92$*	$W = 0.91$*	$W = 0.95$*
n_{05}	10	10		
mean	5.22	5.10		
SD	1.04	0.81		
df	9	9		
n_{010}			10	10
mean			9.42	9.12
SD			0.75	0.68
df			9	9
F-test		$F = 1.65$*		$F = 1.22$*
new-master		−0.12		−0.30
pooled SD (S_{p5})		0.93		
pooled SD (S_{p10})				0.71
df		18		18

* Not statistically significant at .05 level.

$$\Delta = 2zt_{\frac{\alpha}{2}}(2n_0 - 2).$$

More generally, if $\sigma^2 > z\, n_0$, the power curve of the 2-stage procedure can be approximately determined by solving the following equation for Δ and varying β for fixed α, z and n_0:

$$\Delta = \sqrt{2\left[t_{\frac{\alpha}{2}}(2n_0 - 2) + t_\beta(2n_0 - 2)\right]^2 z}$$

For the ferritin 2-standard,

$$\Delta = \sqrt{2(2.12 + t_\beta(16))^2 0.015},$$

and we obtain the power calculations given in Table 3.

The 2-stage procedure could have been made less sensitive to unimportant accuracy errors by decreasing α. With the ferritin 2-standard, suppose we wanted to reduce the 2-stage procedure's sensitivity to small accuracy errors (< 0.6 ng/ml), maintain $\beta(=0.10)$ and $\Delta(=0.6$ ng/ml), and were willing to increase the total required sample size. Knowing that we must decrease α considerably, we first try $\alpha = .001$. The 99.95th percentile for the Student-t distribution was approximated by Koehler's method (Koehler, 1983). An α-level of 0.001 would have resulted in a considerably improved power curve but would have increased the total required sample size from 25 to 68 (Table 3).

C4. Ferritin 5 and 10 Standards

For new and master Ferritin standards, 5 and 10 ng/ml, first stage sample sizes were fixed at 10. We set $\alpha = .05$ and powers of 0.9 for detecting alternatives outside accuracy tolerances.

Applying

$$z_i = \left\{\frac{\Delta_i}{t_{.025}(18) + t_{.10}(18)}\right\}^2 / 2,$$

where Δ_i was the accuracy tolerance for standard i ($i = 5, 10,$):

$$z_5 = .095$$

$$z_{10} = 0.17.$$

TABLE 3. Ferritin 2-standard power calculations.

$\alpha = .05 \quad N = 25$

β	.01	.025	.05	.10	.20	.30	.40	.50	.60	.70	.80	.90	.95	.975	.99
Δ	0	0	.065	.14	.22	.27	.32	.37	.41	.46	.52	.60	.67	.73	.81

$\alpha = .001 \quad N = 68$

β	.01	.025	.05	.10	.20	.30	.40	.50	.60	.70	.80	.90	.95	.975	.99
Δ	.16	.21	.25	.30	.35	.39	.42	.45	.48	.51	.55	.60	.65	.69	.74

β: probability of rejecting new 2-standard

Δ: accuracy error

Using pooled variance estimators S_{pi}^2 from Table 2 we calculated total required sample sizes:

$$N_i = \max\left\{\left[\frac{S_{pi}^2}{z_i}\right] + 1, 10\right\} = 10.$$

Stage 2 sampling was thus not required.

Obtaining new and master sample means, $\bar{X}_{mi}$ and $\bar{X}_{ni}$, for each standard i (Table 2), we calculated t-statistics using,

$$t_i = \frac{(\bar{X}_{ni} - \bar{X}_{mi})}{S_p \sqrt{\frac{1}{10} + \frac{1}{10}}}$$

$$t_5 = -0.29$$

$$t_{10} = -0.94.$$

Since none of the above t-statistic magnitudes exceeded $t_{.025}(18) = 2.101$, we concluded that there were no detectable accuracy differences between new and master standards 5-10 ng/ml.

C5. Choosing n_0 Given Some Knowledge of σ

If before sampling stage 1, we had assay value error estimates (Tables 1,2), we could have estimated n_0's to minimize expected total sample sizes (Table 4) by extending Hodges' results (Hodges, 1942) to the 2-population case for minimizing $E(N)$, and taking as n_0, the initial sample size, the nearest integer to:

$$3 + 14.2 \left(\frac{\sigma}{\ell}\right)^2 \quad \text{if} \quad \overset{\circ}{\alpha} = .1$$

$$4 + 21 \left(\frac{\sigma}{\ell}\right)^2 \quad \text{if} \quad \overset{\circ}{\alpha} = .05$$

$$5 + 40 \left(\frac{\sigma}{\ell}\right)^2 \quad \text{if} \quad \overset{\circ}{\alpha} = .01$$

where

$$\epsilon/\sigma = \frac{2(t_{\frac{\alpha}{2}}(2n_0 - 2))\Delta}{\sigma(t_{\frac{\alpha}{2}}(2n_0 - 2) + t_\beta(2n_0 - 2))}.$$

Estimated n_0's from the above equations are quite sensitive to small changes in σ. For standard 2, a 38% increase in σ yielded a 71% increase in n_0 (Table 4). For standards 5 and 10 solutions of the above equation ($n_0 = 5$) were invalid, since they failed the condition

$$\sigma^2 > z\,n_0.$$

Setting $n_0 = 2$ for standards 5 and 10 does meet the above condition (Table 4).

Interval estimates of the expected total sample sizes, $E(N)$, which depend upon n_0, σ and z, were calculated by applying Stein's results (Stein, 1945) on the total expected number of observations to the 2-population case (Table 4):

$$n_0 P_r\left\{\chi^2_{2n_0-2} < y\right\} + \frac{\sigma^2}{z} P_r\left\{\chi^2_{2n_0} > y\right\} < E(N) < n_0 P_r\left\{\chi^2_{2n_0-2} < y\right\} \quad (1)$$

$$+ \frac{\sigma^2}{z} P_r\left\{\chi^2_{2n_0} > y\right\} + P_r\left\{\chi^2_{2n_0-2} > y\right\}$$

where $y = 2n_0(n_0 - 1)z/\sigma^2$.

Alternatively we could have used first stage sample sizes equalling largest integers in

$$\max_{n_0} \frac{\sigma^2}{z},$$

where $\sigma^2 > z\,n_0$, which for fixed α, β and Δ would have minimized chances of requiring stage 2 samplings (Table 5). Further increasing the first stage sample size is not recommended, since valid power calculations depend upon

$$\sigma^2 > z\,n_0.$$

Also provided in Table 5 are probabilities of needing second sampling stages, calculated using the distribution of y in equation (1), which is chi-square with $2n_0 - 2$ df.

TABLE 4. Estimated first stage sample sizes for minimizing total expected sample sizes.

Ferritin Standard Level (ng/ml)	$\hat{\sigma}$	$\hat{n}_0$	Interval around $E(N)$ Lower Limit	Upper Limit
2	0.61	17	27.7	28.7
2	0.84	29	50.6	51.6
5	0.31	2	3.2	3.3
10	0.39	2	3.5	4.0

TABLE 5. Estimated first stage sample sizes for reducing need for a second sampling stage.

Ferritin Standard Level (ng/ml)	$\hat{\sigma}$	n_0	$P(N > n_0)$	Interval around $E(N)$ Lower Limit	Upper Limit
2	.61	26	.53	28.5	29.1
2	.84	49	.51	52.1	52.7
5	.31	2	.54	3.2	3.3
10	.39	2	.50	3.5	4.0

ACKNOWLEDGMENT

I thank Cuthbert Daniel, Robert Wheeler and Colin Mallows for their insightful suggestions and sensitive readings of early drafts.

REFERENCES

Beallo, R., Dallman, P. R., Schoenfeld, P. Y., and Humphreys, M. H. (1976). "Serum ferritin and iron deficiency in patients on chronic hemodialysis," *Transactions American Society for Artificial Internal Organs*, 22, 73-79.

Bishop, T. A. (1979). "Some results on simultaneous inference for analysis of variance with unequal variances," *Technometrics*, 21, 337-340.

Bishop, T. A. and Dudewicz, E. J. (1978). "Exact analysis of variance with unequal variances: test procedures and tables," *Technometrics*, 20, 419-430.

Bishop, T. A. and Dudewicz, E. J. (1981). "Heteroscedastic ANOVA," *Sankyā*, Series B, 43, 40-57.

Daniel, C. and Wilcoxon, F. (1966). "Factorial 2^{p-q} plans robust against linear and quadratic trends," *Technometrics*, 8, 259-278.

Dantizig, G. B. (1940). "On the non-existence of tests of 'Student's' hypothesis having power functions independent of σ," *Annals of Mathematical Statistics*, **11**, 186-192.

Healy, W. C. (1956). "Two-sample procedures in simultaneous estimation," *Annals of Mathematical Statistics*, **27**, 687-702.

Hochberg, Y. (1975). "Simultaneous inference under Behrens-Fisher conditions. A two sample approach," *Communications in Statistics*, **4**, 1109-1119.

Hodges, J. L. (1942). "Studies in optimum statistical procedures." Ph.D. thesis, University of California at Berkeley.

Jacobs, A. and Worwood, M. (1975). "Ferritin in serum. Clinical and biological implications," *New England Journal of Medicine*, **292**, 951-956.

Koehler, K. J. (1983). "A simple approximation for the percentiles of the t distribution," *Technometrics*, **25**, 103-105.

Lipschitz, D. A., Cook, J. D., and Finch, C. A. (1974). "A clinical evaluation of serum ferritin as an index of iron stores," *New England Journal of Medicine*, **290**, 1213-1216.

Luxton, A. W., Walker, W. H., Gauldie, J., Ali, A. M., and Pelletier, C. (1977). "A radioimmunoassay for serum ferritin," *Clinical Chemistry*, **23**, 683-689.

Miles, L. E., Lipschitz, D. A., Bieber, C. P., and Cook, J. D. (1974). "Measurement of serum ferritin by a 2-site immunoradiometric assay," *Annals of Biochemistry*, **61**, 209-224.

Mirahmadi, K. S., Paul, W. L., Winer, R. L., Dabir-Vaziri, N., Byer, B., Gorman, J. T., and Rosen, S. M. (1977). "Serum ferritin level. Determinant of iron requirement in hemodialysis," *Journal of the American Medical Association*, **238**, 601-603.

Stein, C. (1945). "A two-sample test for a linear hypothesis whose power is independent of the variance," *Annals of Mathematical Statistics*, **16**, 243-258.

Tamhane, A. C. (1977). "Multiple comparisons in model I one-way ANOVA with unequal variances," *Communications in Statistics-Theory and Methods*, **A6**, 15-32.

Yalow, R. S. and Berson, S. A. (1971). "Introduction and general considerations (on principles of competitive protein-binding assays)." In W. D. Odell and W. H. Daughaday (Eds.), *Principles of Competitive Protein-Binding Assays*. Philadelphia: Lippincott.

CHAPTER 15

Linear Models for Some-Cells-Empty Data: The Cell Means Formulation, A Consultant's Best Friend

Shayle R. Searle[1]
Cornell University

ABSTRACT

Linear model analyses are well known for balanced data, for balanced data having a few missing observations, and for data exhibiting planned unbalancedness, such as those from Latin Squares and balanced incomplete blocks. For data of a more generally unbalanced nature, those that have all cells filled can be usefully analyzed using the weighted-squares-of-means analysis. For some-cells-empty data, analysis based on main-effects-only models are useful whenever interactions are to be ignored. But analyzing some-cells-empty data on the basis of models with interactions is best undertaken using cell means models. Whereas the essential concepts and arithmetic are then easy, the data gatherer and the consulting statistician must work together to decide on, to estimate, and to test hypotheses about, linear combinations of cell means that are of interest. Extensions of cell means models to excluding some (or even all) interactions, and to mixed models, are also available.

---

1 This article was prepared while the author was at the University of Augsburg, Federal Republic of Germany, on a Senior U.S. Scientist Award from the Alexander von Humboldt-Stiftung.

1. INTRODUCTION

Consider the analysis of variance of data classified by two different factors that shall be called rows and columns. Suppose there are a rows and b columns. Data in row i and column j (for i taking values $i = 1,2,...,a$ and for $j = 1,2,...,b$ shall be described as being in cell i,j. Let y_{ijk} be the kth observation in cell i,j, where there are n_{ij} observations in that cell, so that $k = 1,2,...,n_{ij}$.

Data wherein n_{ij} has the same value for every cell, i.e., $n_{ij} = n > 0$ for every cell i,j, are called *balanced data*. Means of the data for cell i,j, row i, column j and for all the data are then

$$\bar{y}_{ij\cdot} = \sum_{k=1}^{n} y_{ijk}/n = y_{ij\cdot}/n, \qquad \bar{y}_{i\cdot\cdot} = \sum_{j=1}^{b}\sum_{k=1}^{n} y_{ijk}/bn = y_{i\cdot\cdot}/bn$$

$$\bar{y}_{\cdot j\cdot} = \sum_{i=1}^{a}\sum_{k=1}^{n} y_{ijk}/an = y_{\cdot j\cdot}/an, \qquad \bar{y}_{\cdots} = \sum_{i=1}^{a}\sum_{j=1}^{b}\sum_{k=1}^{n} y_{ijk}/abn = y_{\cdots}/abn.$$

(1)

In contrast, data where the n_{ij} are not all the same value are called *unbalanced* and the observed means are then

$$\bar{y}_{ij\cdot} = \sum_{k=1}^{n_{ij}} y_{ijk}/n_{ij}$$

$$\bar{y}_{i\cdot\cdot} = \sum_{j=1}^{b}\sum_{k=1}^{n_{ij}} y_{ijk}/n_{i\cdot} = y_{i\cdot\cdot}/n_{i\cdot} \qquad \text{for} \quad n_{i\cdot} = \sum_{j=1}^{b} n_{ij}$$

$$\bar{y}_{\cdot j\cdot} = \sum_{i=1}^{a}\sum_{k=1}^{n_{ij}} y_{ijk}/n_{\cdot j} = y_{\cdot j\cdot}/n_{\cdot j} \qquad \text{for} \quad n_{\cdot j} = \sum_{i=1}^{a} n_{ij} \qquad (2)$$

and

$$\bar{y}_{\cdots} = \sum_{i=1}^{a}\sum_{j=1}^{b}\sum_{k=1}^{n_{ij}} y_{ijk}/n_{\cdot\cdot} = y_{\cdots}/n_{\cdot\cdot} \qquad \text{for} \quad n_{\cdot\cdot} = \sum_{i=1}^{a}\sum_{j=1}^{b} n_{ij}.$$

Clearly, when $n_{ij} = n$ for all i and j, the means in (2) reduce to those in (1).

Several subclasses of unbalanced data deserve distinction. First is when $n_{ij} = n$ for basically all i and j except that in a very few cells (one, two or three, say) the number of observations is one or two less than n. This is usually the case of a very few intended observations being lost or missing from the data due to experimental misadventure; maybe one or two laboratory animals died, or a petri dish got broken, or an experimental plot got eaten when cattle broke a fence. Under these circumstances, there are well-known techniques for estimating such missing observations (e.g., Steel and Torrie, 1980, pp. 209, 227 and 388); we refer to such cases of unbalanced data as data with missing observations.

Second is what can be called planned unbalancedness. This is when there are no observations on certain, carefully planned combinations of levels of the factors involved in an experiment. Latin Squares are examples of this: a Latin Square of order n is a $(1/n)$th replicate of a three-factor factorial experiment with each factor having n levels, an n^3 experiment. Balanced incomplete blocks are also examples of planned unbalancedness.

The third and final class of unbalanced data is where the numbers of observations in the sub-most cells (cells defined by one level of each factor) are not all equal, and may in fact be quite unequal. This can include some cells having no data but, in contrast to planned unbalancedness, with those cells occurring in an unplanned manner. Survey data are an example of this, where data are simply collected because they exist, and so the numbers of observations in the cells are just those that arise in the collection process. Records of most human activities are of this nature; e.g., yearly income for people classified by age, sex, education, education of each parent, and so on. This is the kind of data that shall be called unbalanced data; and within this class of data we make two further divisions. One is for data in which all the sub-most cells contain data; none are empty. We call this all-cells-filled data. Complementary to this is some-cells-empty data, wherein several sub-most cells have no data.

2. BALANCED DATA

Analysis of Variance

The analysis of variance was developed by R. A. Fisher as an analysis of differences among observed means. Its very basis, for the row-by-column example with means given in (1) is the simple algebraic identity

$$\Sigma\Sigma\Sigma(y_{ijk} - \bar{y}_{...})^2$$
$$\equiv \Sigma\Sigma\Sigma(\bar{y}_{i..} - \bar{y}_{...})^2 + \Sigma\Sigma\Sigma(\bar{y}_{.j.} - \bar{y}_{...})^2$$
$$+ \Sigma\Sigma\Sigma(\bar{y}_{ij.} - \bar{y}_{i..} - \bar{y}_{.j.} + \bar{y}_{...})^2 \qquad (3)$$
$$+ \Sigma\Sigma\Sigma(y_{ijk} - \bar{y}_{ij.})^2$$

where, in each case, the triple summation is $\sum_{i=1}^{a} \sum_{j=1}^{b} \sum_{k=1}^{n}$. Under the customary assumptions of homoscedasticity and normality, each sum of squares on the right-hand side of (3) is distributed proportional to a χ^2-variable, independently of the others; and from this come the familiar F-statistics. These and (3) are then summarized in tabular form as an analysis of variance table.

Fisher has an interesting comment on this table. In a letter (on display at the 50th Anniversary Conference of the Statistics Department at Iowa State University, June, 1983) dated "6/Jan/'34" Fisher writes to Snedecor that "the analysis of variance is (not a mathematical theorem but) a simple method of arranging arithmetical facts so as to isolate and display the essential features of a body of data with the utmost simplicity." That the analysis of variance table is indeed, as Fisher says, no more than "a simple method of arranging arithmetical facts" is worth emphasizing in these days of computer-generated tables which too many computer package users are inclined to erroneously treat as sacrosanct.

Models

Fisher's starting point was (3). He seldom, if ever, began with a model, as we so often do today. This current trend is to describe analysis of variance in terms of a model involving parameters in an additive (linear) manner, parameters which, as an aside to analysis of variance, we often seek to estimate. Thus for the row-by-column example we model y_{ijk} using the equation

$$E(y_{ijk}) = \mu + \alpha_i + \beta_j + \gamma_{ij} \tag{4}$$

where μ is a general mean, α_i is an effect due to the ith row, β_j is an effect due to the jth column, γ_{ij} is an effect due to the interaction of the ith row and jth column, and E represents expectation over repeated sampling. Then, on defining $y_{ijk} - E(y_{ijk})$ as a random residual error term, e_{ijk}, the model equation is

$$y_{ijk} = \mu + \alpha_i + \beta_j + \gamma_{ij} + e_{ijk}. \tag{5}$$

The variance-covariance structure usually assumed for the e_{ijk} terms is that each of them has the same variance, σ^2 say, and that covariances between every two of them are zero. Under these conditions, the analysis of variance table based on the sums of squares in (3), for balanced data, can be described in terms of the model (4) and various sub-models thereof. For example, $\Sigma\Sigma\Sigma(\bar{y}_{i..} - \bar{y}_{...})^2$ is the difference between the sums of squares due to fitting $E(y_{ijk}) = \mu + \alpha_i + \beta_j$ and $E(y_{ijk}) = \mu + \beta_j$.

Estimation

One advantage of having (4) is that the parameters in that equation make it easy for us to be specific about what we might like to estimate; for example, concerning row effects, we might be interested in estimating such functions as α_1, $\alpha_1 - \alpha_2$ and $1/3\,(\alpha_1 + \alpha_2 + \alpha_3) - \alpha_4$. However, a counteracting difficulty is that (4) involves more parameters than there are observed means to estimate them from. There are $1 + a + b + ab$ parameters but only ab cell means, $\bar{y}_{ij.}$ for $i=1,...,a$ and $j=1,...,b$. Hence there are too many parameters for us to be able to estimate them all as linear functions of the means, the $\bar{y}_{ij.}$. This is the feature of models such as (4) that is well known as overparameterization.

A consequence of overparameterization is that not all the parameters of a model can be estimated. To circumvent this situation we usually invoke one of two procedures: either we use estimable functions, which has us confine attention to only certain functions of the parameters that can be estimated satisfactorily from the data; or we use reparameterization, wherein we define relationships among parameters of an overparameterized model which implicitly rewrites the model in terms of as many new parameters as can be estimated from the data. Each of these procedures (confinement to estimable functions, or reparameterization) is easily applied and easily interpreted with balanced data.

Estimable Functions

Confinement to estimable functions in the example, for instance, limits us to the functions $\alpha_i - \alpha_h + \bar{\gamma}_{i.} - \bar{\gamma}_{h.}$, $\beta_j - \beta_k + \bar{\gamma}_{.j} - \bar{\gamma}_{.k}$, and $\gamma_{ij} - \gamma_{ik} - \gamma_{hj} + \gamma_{hk}$ where

$$\bar{\gamma}_{i.} = \sum_{j=1}^{b} \gamma_{ij}/b \text{ and } \bar{\gamma}_{.j} = \sum_{i=1}^{a} \gamma_{ij}/a\,.$$

These kinds of functions (and linear combinations of them) are all that can be estimated. This means, unfortunately, that it is not possible, for example, to estimate $\alpha_i - \alpha_h$ free of interactions. It can only be estimated in the presence of averaged interactions $\bar{\gamma}_{i\cdot} - \bar{\gamma}_{h\cdot}$, the estimator being

$$\text{BLUE}(\alpha_i - \alpha_h + \bar{\gamma}_{i\cdot} - \bar{\gamma}_{h\cdot}) = \bar{y}_{i\cdot\cdot} - \bar{y}_{h\cdot\cdot}, \qquad (6)$$

where BLUE($\cdot$) means best linear unbiased estimator.

Reparameterization

One procedure that removes $\bar{\gamma}_{i\cdot} - \bar{\gamma}_{h\cdot}$ from what would otherwise be the estimation of $\alpha_i - \alpha_h$ from (6) is reparameterization using what are coming to be called the Σ restrictions. Although they are often applied directly to elements of $E(y_{ijk}) = \mu + \alpha_i + \beta_j + \gamma_{ij}$ in (4), we introduce them here through first defining a new set of parameters $\dot{\mu}$, $\dot{\alpha}_i$, $\dot{\beta}_j$ and $\dot{\gamma}_{ij}$, which then provide clear distinction between the model with Σ-restrictions and the model without. Sometimes these definitions are displayed when the Σ-restrictions are used, but more often they are not.

The new parameters to be used are as follows:

$$\dot{\mu} = \mu + \bar{\alpha}_{\cdot} + \bar{\beta}_{\cdot} + \bar{\gamma}_{\cdot\cdot} \qquad \dot{\alpha}_i = \alpha_i - \bar{\alpha}_{\cdot} + \bar{\gamma}_{i\cdot} - \bar{\gamma}_{\cdot\cdot} \qquad (7)$$

$$\dot{\gamma}_{ij} = \gamma_{ij} - \bar{\gamma}_{i\cdot} - \bar{\gamma}_{\cdot j} + \bar{\gamma}_{\cdot\cdot} \qquad \dot{\beta}_j = \beta_j - \bar{\beta}_{\cdot} + \bar{\gamma}_{\cdot j} - \bar{\gamma}_{\cdot\cdot}.$$

Then the model (4) can be rewritten as

$$E(y_{ijk}) = \dot{\mu} + \dot{\alpha}_i + \dot{\beta}_j + \dot{\gamma}_{ij} \qquad (8)$$

where, by the nature of the definitions in (7), it is easily seen that

$$\sum_{i=1}^{a} \dot{\alpha}_i = 0, \quad \sum_{j=1}^{b} \dot{\beta}_j = 0, \quad \sum_{j=1}^{b} \dot{\gamma}_{ij} = 0 \ \forall \ i, \quad \text{and} \quad \sum_{i=1}^{a} \dot{\gamma}_{ij} = 0 \ \forall \ j. \qquad (9)$$

These are the Σ-restrictions. They imply, of course, that

$$\bar{\dot{\gamma}}_{i\cdot} = 0 \ \forall \ i \quad \text{and} \quad \bar{\dot{\gamma}}_{\cdot j} = 0 \ \forall \ j. \qquad (10)$$

This leads at once to (6) becoming

$$\text{BLUE}(\dot{\alpha}_i - \dot{\alpha}_h) = \bar{y}_{i\cdot\cdot} - \bar{y}_{h\cdot\cdot}, \qquad (11)$$

after substituting from (7) and (10). Thus by using the Σ-restricted model we have, in the new parameters, achieved removal of interaction terms from the estimation of differences between row effects. More than that, in fact, each one of the new parameters has a BLUE. This is so because one effect of the Σ-restrictions (9) is that those equations involve $1 + 1 + a + b - 1 = a + b + 1$ linearly independent linear conditions on the $1 + a + b + ab$ parameters and so there are only $1 + a + b + ab - (a + b + 1) = ab$ linearly independent parameters — and this is the number of cells means available in the data.

It must also be realized that reparameterizing from $1 + a + b + ab$ parameters of (4) to ab parameters can be done in many more ways than just that which is shown in (7). There is a great deal of arbitrariness in how it is done; for example, another possibility is to define a different set of parameters as $\ddot{\alpha}_i = \alpha_i - \alpha_a$, $\ddot{\beta}_j = \beta_j - \beta_b$ and $\ddot{\gamma}_{ij} = \gamma_{ij} - \gamma_{ib} - \gamma_{aj} + \gamma_{ab}$. These have the restrictions $\ddot{\alpha}_a = 0$, $\ddot{\beta}_b = 0$, $\gamma_{ib} = 0 \;\forall\; i$ and $\gamma_{aj} = 0 \;\forall\; j$, as discussed, for example, by Speed et al. (1976, 1978).

Unfortunately, as we illustrate in Section 3, with unbalanced data that have empty cells, when wanting to consider interactions the niceties of the reparameterization (7) just demonstrated for balanced data do not apply. For example, in $\dot{\alpha}_i = \alpha_i - \bar{\alpha}. - \bar{\gamma}_{i\cdot} + \bar{\gamma}_{\cdot\cdot}$, $\bar{\gamma}_{i\cdot}$ could only have a definition that is different for different values of i — depending on which γ_{ij}s are missing from the data (those corresponding to empty cells). And this would not result in straightforward estimation such as (11).

Analysis of Variance F-tests

For balanced data the use of neither estimable functions nor the Σ-restrictions affects the analysis of variance except for description of the hypotheses that are tested by the F-statistics (based on the usual normality assumptions). For example, the F-statistic that has $\Sigma\Sigma\Sigma(\bar{y}_{i\cdot\cdot} - \bar{y}_{\cdot\cdot\cdot})^2$ as its numerator sum of squares for the model (4) tests the hypothesis

$$H : \text{all } (\alpha_i + \bar{\gamma}_{i\cdot}) \text{ equal for } i = 1,\ldots,a \;. \quad (12)$$

In terms of estimable functions this is equivalent to $H : \alpha_1 - \alpha_i + \bar{\gamma}_{1\cdot} - \bar{\gamma}_{i\cdot} = 0$ for $i = 2,3,\ldots,a$; and in terms of a reparameterized model using the Σ-restrictions (9) the equivalent hypothesis is $H: \dot{\alpha}_1 - \dot{\alpha}_i = 0$ for $i = 2,3,...,a$; and because in this model $\sum_{i=1}^{a} \dot{\alpha}_i = 0$ this is also equivalent to $H: \dot{\alpha}_i = 0$ for $i = 1,...,a$. The distinguishing notation makes it clear that although the hypothesis is $H: \dot{\alpha}_i = 0$ it is not $H: \alpha_i = 0$.

3. UNBALANCED DATA

We here restrict the meaning of unbalanced data to that discussed in the paragraph of Section 1. It does not include data that have just a few missing observations or that exhibit planned unbalancedness. Then, with this meaning, the difficulties caused by overparameterized models are by no means as easily solved for unbalanced data as they are for balanced data, for which using estimable functions or reparameterization with Σ-restrictions provides reasonable alternatives. It is here that the distinction between all-cells-filled data and some-cells-empty data is useful.

All-Cells-Filled Data

Within the framework of analysis of variance, the most useful sums of squares for all-cells-filled data are those coming from Yates' weighted-squares-of-means analysis. For our rows-by-columns example, the sum of squares due to rows in this analysis is

$$SSA_w = \sum_{i=1}^{a} w_i \left[\tilde{y}_{i..} - \sum_{i=1}^{a} w_i \tilde{y}_{i..} \bigg/ \sum_{i=1}^{a} w_i \right]^2 \tag{13}$$

for

$$\tilde{y}_{i..} = \sum_{j=1}^{b} \bar{y}_{ij.}/b \text{ and } w_i = \sigma^2/v(\tilde{y}_{i..}) = b^2 \bigg/ \sum_{j=1}^{b} \frac{1}{n_{ij}}. \tag{14}$$

With $SSE = \sum_{i=1}^{a} \sum_{j=1}^{b} \sum_{k=1}^{n_{ij}} (y_{ijk} - \bar{y}_{ij.})^2$, the hypothesis tested by the F-statistic $(n.. - ab)SSA_w/(a-1)SSE$ is then (12). This is a useful hypothesis.

Insofar as estimation is concerned, since every cell contains data

$$\text{BLUE } (\mu + \alpha_i + \beta_i + \gamma_{ij}) = \bar{y}_{ij.} \tag{15}$$

is true for every cell. Hence any linear combination of the terms $(\mu + \alpha_i + \beta_j + \gamma_{ij})$ can be estimated and, in particular, because every cell contains data,

$$\text{BLUE}(\alpha_i - \alpha_k + \bar{\gamma}_{i\cdot} - \bar{\gamma}_{h\cdot}) = \tilde{y}_{i\cdot\cdot} - \tilde{y}_{h\cdot\cdot} \tag{16}$$

for $\tilde{y}_{i\cdot\cdot}$ defined in (14). Note that (16) differs from (6) in its use of $\tilde{y}_{i\cdot\cdot}$ rather than $\bar{y}_{i\cdot\cdot}$; but, of course, (16) reduces to (6) when the data are balanced, for then $\tilde{y}_{i\cdot\cdot}$ and $\bar{y}_{i\cdot\cdot}$ are the same.

Some-Cells-Empty Data

We distinguish two cases: models without interactions, and those with interactions.

Models Without Interactions

Models having nested fixed effects are not considered; and models with no interactions are then main-effects-only models. Using such models on data that have empty cells demands ascertaining for whatever the main-effects-only model may be, that the data are connected. Unfortunately, the concept of connectedness is not particularly easy, and ascertaining whether data are connected or not is even less so. The essential idea is that connectedness is a property the presence of which ensures that (for main-effects-only models) contrasts among all levels of each factor are estimable. For example, consider Grid 1 where a check mark ($\sqrt{}$) indicates the presence of data.

Grid 1

√	√	√		
√	√	√		
			√	√
			√	√

Expressions $\mu + \alpha_i + \beta_j$ are estimable for each of the filled cells but, for example, because all columns that have filled cells in rows 1 and 2 also have empty cells in rows 3 and 4, it is not possible to estimate any differences between rows 1 and 2 and rows 3 and 4; e.g., $\alpha_2 - \alpha_3$ has no BLUE. These data are not connected. Further elementary ideas about connectedness can be found in Searle (1971), and for more mathematical considerations the reader is referred to Stewart and Wynn (1981). It suffices to say that most data sets are connected, especially when the model consists of just a few (main effect) factors.

Given that some-cells-empty data are connected, their analysis using a main-effects-only model then provides (on the assumption of no interactions) useful results. Those results all come from using estimation by least squares and only in simple cases (e.g., the 1-way classification) can they be stated as simple functions of observed means. Otherwise they involve calculations that are best stated in terms of matrices and vectors, for which the reader is referred to such texts as Searle (1971), Rao (1973) and Guttman (1982). Nevertheless, description of the available results is easily given. (1) First, all contrasts among levels of each factor can be estimated, and tested. (2) Second, population cell means, even of empty cells, can be estimated (but, for filled cells, those estimators are not observed cell means). (3) Equality of all levels of each factor can be tested, using an F-statistic. (4) For a model with f main-effect factors there are $f!$ what-might-be-called analysis of variance tables. Provided the investigator (whose data are being analyzed) is determined that all of the factors included in the analysis do indeed belong in the model, then none of these $f!$ analysis of variance tables is of any particular interest. The only F-statistics in those tables (just one from each table) that test useful hypotheses are those alluded to in (3).

However, it is rare, as Meredith (1985) writes, for all factors included (at least initially) in an analysis to be "desired in the model from which decisions (inferences) are to be made. Many of the factors will act as proxies for other factors and render the suggested F test of little or no worth. Consequently these factors should be removed before further analysis (viz., inferences) is undertaken. This is directly analogous to the full rank multiple regression case where we desire to assess the need of several predictors simultaneously using the additional sums of squares due to these predictors. Factors which act as proxies for other factors ... can be expected to arise whenever a broad survey is undertaken with post-classification of the responses into levels of many factors ... A consultant should have the investigator provide an intelligent (in terms of the subject matter) ordering of the factors and proceed to investigate the corresponding analysis of variance table. Once a reasonable subset of factors has been selected, then one can advance to use the suggested F-test. Granted, there are problems of conditionality with the Type I error levels, but one can minimize these problems by performing the preliminary F-test at a liberal probability level."

Models With Interactions

Consider analyzing data of the nature indicated in Grid 2.

Grid 2

	Col 1	Col 2	Col 3
Row 1	✓	✓	✓
Row 2	✓		✓
Row 3		✓	✓

Based on the model (4), the function $\mu + \alpha_i + \beta_j + \gamma_{ij}$ has a BLUE

$$\text{BLUE}(\mu + \alpha_i + \beta_j + \gamma_{ij}) = \bar{y}_{ij\cdot} \text{ for } n_{ij} > 0.$$

Now row 1 has data in every column, so that there is a BLUE

$$\text{BLUE}\left[\mu + \alpha_1 + \tfrac{1}{3}[\beta_1 + \beta_2 + \beta_3] + \tfrac{1}{3}[\gamma_{11} + \gamma_{12} + \gamma_{13}]\right]$$
$$= \tfrac{1}{3}\left[\bar{y}_{11\cdot} + \bar{y}_{12\cdot} + \bar{y}_{13\cdot}\right].$$

Thus for row 1 there is a BLUE of a function that, along with $\mu + \alpha_1$, includes the mean of all the βs and γs for every column in row 1. But this latter characteristic cannot occur for row 2; because it has an empty cell in column 2, β_2 and γ_{22} cannot occur in a BLUE.

$$\text{BLUE}\left[\mu + \alpha_2 + \tfrac{1}{2}[\beta_1 + \beta_3] + \tfrac{1}{2}[\gamma_{21} + \gamma_{23}]\right] = \tfrac{1}{2}\left[\bar{y}_{21\cdot} + \bar{y}_{23\cdot}\right].$$

Hence the only way to get rid of βs in a BLUE for comparing row 1 with row 2 is to consider a BLUE that involves $\mu + \alpha_1$ and just the βs of columns 1 and 3, the columns that contain data in row 2:

$$\text{BLUE}\left[\mu + \alpha_1 + \tfrac{1}{2}[\beta_1 + \beta_3] + \tfrac{1}{2}[\gamma_{11} + \gamma_{13}]\right] = \tfrac{1}{2}\left[\bar{y}_{11\cdot} + \bar{y}_{13\cdot}\right].$$

Hence

$$\text{BLUE}\left[\alpha_1 - \alpha_2 + \tfrac{1}{2}[\gamma_{11} + \gamma_{13}] - \tfrac{1}{2}[\gamma_{21} + \gamma_{23}]\right] \qquad (17)$$

$$= \tfrac{1}{2}\left[\bar{y}_{11\cdot} + \bar{y}_{13\cdot}\right] - \tfrac{1}{2}\left[\bar{y}_{21\cdot} + \bar{y}_{23\cdot}\right].$$

Thus $\alpha_1 - \alpha_2$ can be estimated in the presence of a difference between average interactions that are in columns 1 and 3 — because these are the only columns wherein there are data in both rows 1 and 2. For similar reasons $\alpha_1 - \alpha_3$ can be estimated only over a different set of columns, columns 2 and 3. This arises solely from the pattern of empty cells. It means, in this example, that no comparison between rows can be made over all columns. Thus no contrast among row effects can be made that involves interaction effects averaged over all columns, i.e., there is no BLUE of $\alpha_i - \alpha_h + \bar{\gamma}_{i\cdot} - \bar{\gamma}_{h\cdot}$ as there is with balanced data and with unbalanced all-cells-filled data.

This inability to make all comparisons between rows across the same set of columns resulting from there being empty cells, also makes it difficult to test hypotheses about row effects (and column effects) — indeed about main effects in general when there are interactions in the model and empty cells in the data. In fact, there is then no test that row effects are all equal, i.e., there is no test of $H : \alpha_i$ *all equal* as in (12) for balanced data, nor even of $H : \alpha_i + \bar{\gamma}_{i\cdot}$ *all equal*, as tested using SSA_w of (13) for all-cells-filled data. The big question, therefore, is what does one do with some-cells-empty data when wanting to be concerned about interactions? The answer is "use the cell means model."

4. CELL MEANS MODELS

Rather than use the overparameterized model (4) when dealing with some-cells-empty data, it is conceptually much easier to just think of the data in each filled cell as being a random sample from a population peculiar to that cell. Thus for cell i,j in which $n_{ij} > 0$ the data $y_{ij1}, \ldots, y_{ijn_{ij}}$ are taken as a random sample of size n_{ij} from a population having mean μ_{ij}. Then the cell means model is

$$E(y_{ijk}) = \mu_{ij} \text{ for } n_{ij} \neq 0. \qquad (18)$$

Promotion of this kind of model since the late 1960s began with Speed (1969), and has continued in papers by Speed and co-workers (e.g., Speed et al. 1976, 1978).

Although on comparing (18) with (4) it is obvious that μ_{ij} and $\mu + \alpha_i + \beta_j + \gamma_{ij}$ are equivalent, it is far easier with some-cells-empty data to concentrate attention on the parameters μ_{ij} of (18) than it is to deal with the μ, α_i, β_j and γ_{ij} terms of (4). It is not only easier through simply making estimation very easy (as it does) but it is also in keeping with a more natural way of looking at data and of providing us with a more straightforward way of seeking interpretation of data than does (4) in the presence of empty cells.

The first thing to notice about (18) is that there are exactly the same number of parameters to be estimated as there are observed cell means to estimate them from. Only for each fitted cell do we have a μ_{ij} in the model for the data, and corresponding thereto is an observed cell mean $\bar{y}_{ij\cdot}$. Insofar as the data gatherer (whom we shall call an experimenter) is concerned, this concept of population cell means, especially compared to the overparameterized model, is right in keeping with one's manner of thinking about some-cells-empty data. For example, with data of Grid 2, no experimenter seeing the pattern of empty cells there would envisage trying to compare rows 1 and 2 over all three columns; nor rows 1 and 3 either. And clearly the only comparison possible between rows 2 and 3 can come from data in column 3. Any good experimenter understands this, simply by scrutinizing the occurrence of empty cells, or more particularly the pattern of occurrence of the filled cells. Statistical consultants who are asked to deal with such data should therefore go along with this understanding; the alternative is to force the experimenter into the forest of overparameterized models with all their mathematical entwinements of estimability, useless F-statistics, reparameterizations and restrictions. Cell means models have none of these. Furthermore, they are directly in line with an experimenter's way of thinking about some-cells-empty data. In addition, the statistician is able, by means of the cell means model, to give the experimenter help and advice that is easy to carry out and which is readily understood, something which cannot be said for the overparameterized model.

Estimation

We have seen that the definition of μ_{ij} is straightforward: it is the population mean for cell i,j. And for every cell i,j that contains data, estimation of its μ_{ij} is easy:

$$\text{BLUE}(\mu_{ij}) = \bar{y}_{ij\cdot} \text{ for } n_{ij} > 0 ; \tag{19}$$

i.e., a population cell mean, when that cell contains data, is estimated by the observed cell mean for that cell. Nothing could be easier.

318 LINEAR MODELS FOR SOME-CELLS-EMPTY DATA

Moreover, for every filled cell the μ_{ij} is estimated in this manner; and every linear combination of those μ_{ij}s is estimated by the same linear combination of the corresponding $\bar{y}_{ij\cdot}$s. For example, for Grid 1,

$$\text{BLUE}(\mu_{11} + 3\mu_{12} - 5\mu_{13}) = \bar{y}_{11\cdot} + 3\bar{y}_{12\cdot} - 5\bar{y}_{13\cdot}.$$

In general, for any values λ_{ij},

$$\text{BLUE}\left(\sum_{i,j}\lambda_{ij}\mu_{ij}\right) = \sum_{i,j}\lambda_{ij}\bar{y}_{ij\cdot} \quad \text{for } n_{ij} > 0. \tag{20}$$

Hypothesis Testing

The model for y_{ijk} based on (19) is

$$y_{ijk} = \mu_{ij} + e_{ijk} \tag{21}$$

with e_{ijk} defined as $y_{ijk} - E(y_{ijk})$ just as is done following (4). On attributing the same variance-covariance properties to the e_{ijk} as there, namely that every e_{ijk} has variance σ^2 and all covariances are zero, the sampling variance of $\bar{y}_{ij\cdot}$ is $v(\bar{y}_{ij\cdot}) = \sigma^2/n_{ij}$ for $n_{ij} > 0$. Furthermore, the $\bar{y}_{ij\cdot}$s are distributed independently of each other so that for (20);

$$v\left(\sum_{i,j}\lambda_{ij}\bar{y}_{ij\cdot}\right) = \sigma^2 \sum_{i,j}\lambda_{ij}^2/n_{ij} \quad \text{for } n_{ij} > 0. \tag{22}$$

The variance σ^2 is estimated, as usual, by the pooled within-cell mean square

$$\hat{\sigma}^2 = \frac{\sum_{i=1}^{a}\sum_{j=1}^{b}\sum_{k=1}^{n_{ij}}(y_{ijk} - \bar{y}_{ij\cdot})^2}{n_{\cdot\cdot} - s} \tag{23}$$

where s is the number of filled cells.

Testing linear hypotheses is done on the basis of customary normality assumptions. Thus the t-statistic (on $n_{\cdot\cdot} - s$ degrees of freedom) for testing the simple linear hypothesis

$$H: \sum_{ij} \lambda_{ij}\mu_{ij} = m \text{ is } t = \frac{\sum_{ij} \lambda_{ij}\bar{y}_{ij\cdot} - m}{\left[\hat{\sigma}^2 \sum_{ij} \lambda_{ij}^2 / n_{ij}\right]^{1/2}}. \quad (24)$$

Testing a composite linear hypothesis is best described in terms of a few simple matrices and vectors, defined as follows:

$\boldsymbol{\mu}$ = vector of μ_{ij}s for $n_{ij} > 0$, in lexicon order.

$\bar{\mathbf{y}}$ = vector of $\bar{y}_{ij\cdot}$s for $n_{ij} > 0$, in lexicon order.

$\mathbf{D}$ = diagonal matrix of terms $1/n_{ij}$ for $n_{ij} > 0$, in lexicon order.

$H: \mathbf{K}'\boldsymbol{\mu} = \mathbf{m}$ is the hypothesis to be tested, where $\mathbf{K}'$ has full row rank $r = < s$.

Then the F-statistic on r and $n.. - s$ degrees of freedom for testing

$$H: \mathbf{K}'\boldsymbol{\mu} = \mathbf{m} \text{ is } F = (\mathbf{K}'(\bar{\mathbf{y}} - \mathbf{m}))'(\mathbf{K}' \mathbf{D} \mathbf{K})^{-1}(\mathbf{K}'(\bar{\mathbf{y}} - \mathbf{m}))/r\hat{\sigma}^2. \quad (25)$$

Essentially this is all there is to estimation and hypothesis testing in the cell means model. (Complexities such as restricted models and mixed models are mentioned in Section 5.) Estimation of means and linear combinations of them is given in (19) and (20), and of σ^2 in (23), and hypothesis testing is set out in (25), with (24) being a special case. Thus, the mechanics of cell means models are patently simple. The problem is how, from this simplicity, does one use a cell means model to answer questions of interest to the experimenter?

Analysis of Variance

First observe that there is no really useful analysis of variance table. The only table available from the model (21) would have but two sums of squares: $\sum_{i=1}^{a} \sum_{j=1}^{b} \sum_{k=1}^{n_{ij}} (\bar{y}_{ij\cdot} - \bar{y}_{\cdots})^2$ and $\sum_{i=1}^{a} \sum_{j=1}^{b} \sum_{k=1}^{n_{ij}} (y_{ijk} - \bar{y}_{ij\cdot})^2$, and its only purpose would be as a summary of the arithmetic for testing the hypothesis H : all μ_{ij} (for $n_{ij} > 0$) equal; and this is so whether the n_{ij} are equal (balanced data) or not. Clearly this is not a hypothesis of very much interest; in fact, in most cases it is of absolutely no interest at all. There is therefore little point in calculating an analysis of variance table for a cell means model.

Hypotheses of Interest

Instead, on the basis of an experimenter's (presumably expert) knowledge of the data at hand, the consulting statistician and the experimenter, working together, formulate what they think are interesting linear combinations of the cell means of the cells that contain data. These combinations can then be estimated using (20), the sampling variance of each estimate can be estimated from (22) and (23), and tests of hypotheses can be made about them by using (25). At the heart of this process is the experimenter's knowledge of the data; in the presence of empty cells the person whose data are being analyzed must contribute knowledge to deciding what combinations of means (of filled cells) are of interest. No longer can the automatic hypotheses like "equality of rows" be tested; considered thought must be given, under the spotlight of having empty cells, as to what combination of the filled cells are interesting. Knowledge of the data and the pattern of filled cells both have to be utilized. What one would like to consider, if all cells were fitted, has to be tempered by what can be considered in the light of certain cells being empty. Since the pattern of empty cells usually differs from one data set to another, the linear combinations of cell means considered in one data set will not necessarily be the same as those in another. Yet in each case they must be combinations that are of interest, and they must also be combinations of filled cells. Different data sets from similar studies might therefore (probably will) have different analyses — depending on which cells in the data grid are empty in each case.

For some examples, consider Grid 2. Although row effects, such as α_i in the overparameterized model (4), are not specifically part of a cell means model, row means can be defined in terms of cell means (as linear combinations of them) and hence they can be studied. Thus for Grid 2

$$\bar{\mu}_{1.} = (\mu_{11} + \mu_{12} + \mu_{13})/3$$

represents a row mean, with estimator

$$\text{BLUE }(\bar{\mu}_{1.}) = (\bar{y}_{11.} + \bar{y}_{12.} + \bar{y}_{13.})/3 .$$

But for comparing rows 1 and 2, $\bar{\mu}_{1.}$ is not suitable because row 2 has no data in column 2. This comparison is confined to columns 1 and 3, which contain data in rows 1 and 2. We therefore consider $\frac{1}{2}(\mu_{11} + \mu_{13}) - \frac{1}{2}(\mu_{21} + \mu_{23})$ with

$$\text{BLUE}\left[\frac{1}{2}(\mu_{11}+\mu_{13})-\frac{1}{2}(\mu_{21}+\mu_{23})\right] = \frac{1}{2}(\bar{y}_{11\cdot}+\bar{y}_{13\cdot})-\frac{1}{2}(\bar{y}_{21\cdot}+\bar{y}_{23\cdot}).$$

This is, of course, the same estimator as (17), but deriving it and understanding it is much easier in terms of cell means μ_{ij} than in terms of the too many parameters of the overparameterized model. This gain in understanding may not be as evident in this small example as it would be in a case of several rows and columns and numerous empty cells.

With Grid 2, every pair of rows has to be compared across a different set of columns. Nevertheless, it is precisely by scrutinizing a pattern of empty cells with a view to comparing means of those cells, that we find it possible to make comparisons that may be of interest. Further illustration of this in Grid 2 is that the interactions $\mu_{11} - \mu_{13} - \mu_{21} + \mu_{23}$ and $\mu_{12} - \mu_{13} - \mu_{32} + \mu_{33}$ can be estimated; and a test of the hypothesis that they are zero can be derived from (25).

Subset Analyses

Analyses of the nature just described (which we call subset analyses) are certainly not as informative overall as either the analysis of variance of balanced data, or the weighted squares of means analysis of unbalanced but all-cells-filled data. But for unbalanced and some-cells-empty data they are much more useful than the analyses of variance of unbalanced data that come from fitting an overparameterized model (4) and its submodels — see, for example, Searle (1971, Chapter 7). Furthermore, these subset analyses for some-cells-empty data are vastly easier to understand, to interpret, and to explain to decision makers than are the analyses using an overparameterized model with interactions. Not only are the latter difficult to interpret, but in most cases of some-cells-empty data they are of no real interest.

Models With Interactions

The analysis of models without interactions (i.e., main-effects-only models) is easy, as has already been described in Section 3. No matter how many factors one has, the use of a main-effects-only model provides, for each factor, a test of equality of the effects of its different levels on the response variable. But such a model implies no interactions and this begs the question "when are we ever in a situation where we *know* there are no interactions?" The answer is probably "never." However, in even the simplest case of only two factors, the use of a with-interaction overparameterized model for some-cells-empty data yields very little (if anything) that is either generally useful or readily interpretable. But the desire and/or need to investigate the occurrence of interactions is often very strong, and whereas the overparameterized model is of little help in this connection when dealing with some-cells-empty data, the use of a cell means model can be very helpful indeed. This is achieved by looking at the data from the cell means model perspective and scrutinizing the data grid to see which subsets of filled cells suggest themselves as possibilities for subset analyses that might yield information about interactions. The information so obtained may not be as far-reaching as when all cells are filled, but it will be better than nothing (which is only what a main-effects-only model can yield, insofar as interactions are concerned) and it will nearly always be better than an overparameterized analysis, because that analysis can, in the face of empty cells, be very difficult to interpret.

The crux of the procedure when wishing to consider interactions with some-cells-empty data is therefore to view the data from the perspective of a cell means model and to seek subsets of data that can yield information about interactions. Then, as consultant to a client who insists (as do some clients) on considering interactions when data have empty cells, the statistician, instead of having to complicate (at least from a client's presumably non-mathematical viewpoint) the analysis of such data by introducing ideas of estimability and/or restricted models, can offer clarification in the form of helping the client decide which subsets of data might provide analyses of interest.

Examples

Suppose data occurred as indicated in Grid 3.

Grid 3

	1	2	3	4
I	√	√		√
II	√	√		√
III		√	√	√

An overparameterized analysis would yield a sum of squares for interaction having three degrees of freedom. But in trying to ascertain which interactions appear to be significant, and to understand their occurrence in the data with more depth than that sum of squares provides, scrutinizing the pattern of filled cells in the data reveals subsets of the data that are easier to interpret; e.g., for Grid 3, the following subsets:

Grid 3a

	1	2	4
I	✓	✓	✓
II	✓	✓	✓

Grid 3b

	2	4
I	✓	✓
II	✓	✓
III	✓	✓

True, analyses of Grids 3a and 3b are not independent of one another; but the analyses are simple and interpretation of each is straightforward.

The preceding example is so simple that it may fail to emphasize just how difficult the search for informative subsets of data can be. But consider Grid 4, of six rows and eight columns, with 19 of the 48 cells containing data.

Grid 4

	1	2	3	4	5	6	7	8
I	✓			✓		✓	✓	
II				✓	✓			✓
III				✓				✓
IV	✓	✓		✓		✓	✓	✓
V								✓
VI			✓	✓				✓

As an example, it illustrates how we can lead ourselves, through "feeling our way," towards analyses that may provide more useful interpretation than does analyzing the full data set "warts and all," in this case the warts being the large number of empty cells: 60% are empty. In this regard the very grid itself is useful, because it provides opportunity to scrutinize just which cells have data and whether or not any of them form subsets of the data that may be open to straightforward analysis. Such scrutiny reveals that columns 2, 3 and 5, and row V each have but a single filled cell. Setting these data aside leaves Grid 4a:

Grid 4a

	1	4	6	7	8
I	√	√	√	√	
II		√			√
III		√			√
IV	√	√	√	√	√
VI		√			√

This, we can easily see, falls into two subsets of data: rows I and IV in columns 1, 4, 6 and 7, and rows II, III, IV and VI in columns 4 and 8. These subsets have but one cell in common and account for all six of the degrees of freedom for interaction available in the analysis of the full data set. But now, in directing attention to these two subsets, we are able to understand, very straightforwardly, what interaction effects are being considered.

Difficulties

Two difficulties with subset analyses are readily envisioned. One is that a data set may not always yield subsets that are useful in the way that those of the preceding examples appear to be. For example, consider Grid 5:

Grid 5

	1	2	3	4
I	√			√
II		√		√
III	√	√	√	

In analyzing the complete data set using an overparameterized model, there will be a 1-degree-of-freedom sum of squares for interaction that will be testing the hypothesis stated, as follows, in three equivalent ways:

$$H : \mu_{11} - \mu_{14} - \mu_{21} + \mu_{24} + (\mu_{21} - \mu_{22} - \mu_{31} + \mu_{32}) = 0$$

$$H : \mu_{11} - \mu_{14} - \mu_{31} + \mu_{34} - (\mu_{22} - \mu_{24} - \mu_{32} + \mu_{34}) = 0$$

$$H : \mu_{11} + \mu_{24} + \mu_{32} - (\mu_{14} + \mu_{22} + \mu_{31}) = 0 \ .$$

The first of these three statements involves the sum of two interactions, whereas the second involves the difference between two such interactions. Whatever the utility of these may be (if any), scrutiny of Grid 5 reveals that no subsets of the data manifest themselves as being candidates for informative analyses. When this kind of situation occurs, the statistician can do little more than persuade the experimenter that this is so, and fall back on the main-effects-only model. Of course with data sets larger than that of Grid 5, coming to the conclusion of no useful subsets may not be as easy as it is with Grid 5, and much resourcefulness might be needed before such a conclusion can be firmly established.

A second and obvious difficulty inherent in subset analyses is that a data set might well be divisible into two or more different subset analyses. For example, Grid 6 can easily be divided into two subsets in two different ways: one way consists of rows I and II, and row III; and the other is columns 1 and 4, and columns 2 and 3.

This situation emphasizes what is so important about analyzing unbalanced data, especially some-cells-empty data: there is seldom just a single, correct way of doing a statistical analysis. Therefore the first responsibility of a consulting statistician to those who have

Grid 6

	1	2	3	4
I	√	√	√	√
II	√	√	√	√
III	√			√

garnered such data is to impress upon them that analyzing those data has no single, easy, umbrella of interpretation. Within that umbra, the statistician can certainly provide advice as to what analyses might be helpful, and two different statisticians might well have two different lines of advice for analyzing the same data set. As with lawyers, the advice of statisticians is not necessarily uniform, let alone uniformly right or uniformly wrong.

The Data Gatherer

Naturally, the person whose data are to be analyzed (the data gatherer) must contribute to deciding on possible divisibility of the total data set into subset analyses. In the preceding examples the pattern of empty cells has been the sole criterion for suggesting subsets. That is always a useful criterion because it can guide us to analyses that are interpretable. But it must not be the sole criterion; data gatherers must be urged, from their prior knowledge of similar data and of the context from which the present data have come, to decide what specific levels of the factors (or pooled combinations thereof) are of prime interest, especially in the context of interactions. Indeed, as an alternative to the statistician's advice being in terms of estimability and estimable functions (as it must for overparameterized models), it seems that that advice should be in terms of helping data gatherers; nay, even cajoling them, perhaps, into deciding what specific subsets of filled cells might be of real interest. One would hope that when faced with empty cells, the combined efforts of statistician and data gatherer would usually reveal some data subsets that provide both easy analysis and straightforward interpretation through the use of the cell means model. Examples of doing this in animal science and in agronomy research are to be found, respectively, in Urquhart and Weeks (1978) and Meredith and Cady (1984).

5. EXTENSIONS

More Than Two Factors

The examples we have used are solely in terms of the 2-way classification, rows and columns. But the cell means model extends very easily and directly to more than two factors: the population mean of a cell defined by one level of each factor is, when that cell contains data, estimated by the mean of those data in the cell. This, for the 2-way classification, is precisely the result (19). Its formal extension to more than two factors simply involves having three or more subscripts in place of i,j in y_{ijk} and μ_{ij}. And its conceptual extension to means of sub-most cells of the data classification is, as already stated, very easy.

Difficulties of overparameterized models for the 2-way classification are simply aggravated when we come to deal with 3-, 4- and more- factor models with empty cells in the data. Although the desire for including interactions may be strong, one must never forget that a main-effects-only model provides straightforward tests about levels of each main effect — as has already been mentioned. Moreover, an alarming feature of interactions is that in a multi-factor situation they can be totally overwhelming, simply by virtue of the sheer number of possible interactions. The example in Searle (1971, Section 8.1) illustrates this. It is taken from the Bureau of Labor Statistics Survey of Consumer Expenditures in which family investment patterns are classified by a total of 56 levels of nine different factors: the numbers of levels of the factors are 12, 11, 4, 3, 4, 6, 6, 6 and 4. This 9-way classification has 5,474,304 possible cells, with 1,354 possible 2-factor interactions and 18,538 possible 3-factor interactions. Yet there were only 8,577 observations in the study! Clearly, then, any desire to "study interactions" in large data sets has to be tempered by the paucity of data relative to the number of possible interactions. Patterns of filled cells and the researcher's knowledge of the data have to be used with great perspicacity to hopefully elucidate subset analyses that provide information about interactions.

Models Without Interactions

Cell means models by their very nature implicitly include interactions in the population means of the sub-most cells. In the 2-way classification, the equivalence of μ_{ij} of the cell means model (18) to $\mu + \alpha_i + \beta_j + \gamma_{ij}$ of the overparameterized model (4) has already been noted; and in models for more than two factors the cell means model includes implicitly all interactions of all orders. Contrasted to this are the main-effects-only models that have no interactions. Sometimes a middle ground may be suitable with some but not all interactions wanted in a model. This can be done with a cell means model by defining in terms of the population cell means those interactions which are not wanted, and then excluding them from the model by having, as part of the model, restrictions that put those interactions equal to zero. For example, in the case of just two rows and two columns the no-interaction form of the cell means model is

$$E(y_{ijk}) = \mu_{ij} \text{ for } i,j = 1,2 \text{ and } \mu_{11} - \mu_{12} - \mu_{21} + \mu_{11} = 0. \quad (26)$$

The standard procedure of restricted least squares can then be used to estimate the μ_{ij}s, subject to the no-interaction restriction $\mu_{11} - \mu_{12} - \mu_{21} + \mu_{22} = 0$. And, of course, this use of a restricted model such as (26) generalizes very directly to more complicated cases.

In a case like (26), where all interactions are to be excluded, the model is of course equivalent to a main-effects-only model. This is also true when, in cases of more than two factors, all interactions of all orders are to be excluded; but when in those many-factor cases only some interactions are to be excluded, then the estimability of linear combinations of cell means is affected both by the pattern of empty cells and by which interactions are excluded. Searle and Speed (1982) have a theorem that gives detail of this situation.

Mixed Models

The preceding discussion has been based on assuming that observations all have the same variance, σ^2, and that covariances between all pairs of observations are zero. This is conventional for fixed effects models. In contrast, a mixed model consists of both fixed effects and random effects. So far as estimation of fixed effects is concerned, the consequence of also having random effects in the model is that they contribute structure to the pattern of variances and covariances among the observations. Using this structure, estimation of the fixed effects can nevertheless be dealt with by generalized least squares (equivalent to BLU estimation). Thus can cell means models be extended to mixed models: population cell means are defined for the sub-most cells defined by the levels of the fixed effects factors. Those cell means are then estimated by generalized least squares. Searle (1984a,b) shows details, including two useful results: (i) in using mixed models with balanced data, the BLUE of any contrast is the same as the ordinary least squares estimator; (ii) analytic expressions have been derived for the BLUE of treatment means in randomized complete blocks having unequal numbers of observations on the treatments in the blocks. These expressions simplify for balanced incomplete blocks to be equivalent to the results of Scheffé (1959).

REFERENCES

Guttman, I. (1982). *Linear Models: An Introduction*. New York: Wiley.

Meredith, M. P. (1985). Personal Communication.

Meredith, M. P. and Cady, F. B. (1984). "Methodology analysis of treatment means from factorial experiments with unequal replication." Technical Report BU-859-M, Biometrics Unit, Cornell University.

Rao, C. R. (1973). *Linear Statistical Inference and its Applications*, 2nd Edition. New York: Wiley.

Scheffé, H. (1959). *The Analysis of Variance*. New York: Wiley

Searle, S. R. (1971). *Linear Models*. New York: Wiley.

Searle, S. R. (1984a). "Cell means formulation of mixed models in the analysis of variance." Technical Report BU-862-M, Biometrics Unit, Cornell University.

Searle, S. R. (1984b). "Best linear unbiased estimation in mixed models of the analysis of variance." Technical Report BU-864-M, Biometrics Unit, Cornell University.

Searle, S. R. and Speed, F. M. (1982). "Estimability in the cell means general linear model." Technical Report BU-730-M. Biometrics Unit, Cornell University.

Speed, F. M. (1969). "A new approach to the analysis of linear models." Ph. D. Thesis, Texas A. and M. University, College Station, Texas.

Speed, F. M. and Hocking, R. R. (1976). "The use of the R( )-notation with unbalanced data," *The American Statistician*, **30**, 30-34.

Speed, F. M., Hocking, R. R., and Hackney, O. P. (1978). "Methods of analysis of linear models with unbalanced data," *Journal of American Statistical Association*, **73**, 105-112.

Steel, R. G. D. and Torrie, J. H. (1980). *Principles and Procedures of Statistics: A Biometrical Approach*, 2nd Edition. New York: McGraw-Hill.

Stewart, I. and Wynn, H. P. (1981). "The estimability structure of linear models and submodels," *Journal of the Royal Statistical Society, Series B*, **43**, 197-207.

Urquhart, N. S. and Weeks, D. L. (1978). "Linear models in messy data: some problems and alternatives," *Biometrics*, **34**, 696-705.

CHAPTER 16

Six-Sequence Carry-Over Design for The Determination of the Effect of a Drug in Reducing Food Intake

John C. Thornton
The Mount Sinai School of Medicine

Harry Smith
Durham, North Carolina

Harry R. Kissileff
Columbia University

Administration of the synthetic octapeptide of cholecystokinin (CCK-8) for reduction of food intake in man has produced variable results (1). In 1981, Kissileff et al. (Kissileff et al., 1981) reported that slow intravenous infusions of relatively low doses of CCK-8 significantly reduced food intake in 12 non-obese men, when compared to a placebo. This paper analyzes the data from that experiment and compares the experimental design used in that paper to an alternative design of Berenblut that could have been used.

1. THE EXPERIMENT

Complete details of the experiment can be found in Kissileff et al. (1981). A summary of the procedures sufficient for understanding the statistical discussion of the alternative designs is presented below.

Twelve men were selected for relative uniformity in liking the same test food, by means of a procedure in which they rated the test food on a 9-point scale (Peryam and Pilgrim, 1957). Each man was then given two test meals of this food (Kissileff, Klingsberg and Van Italie, 1980) in conjunction with an intravenous saline infusion to adapt him to the procedure, since previous results (Kissileff, Thorton and Becker, 1982) indicated that two days are necessary for stabilization of the amount of food consumed in this laboratory setting. Following adaptation, four additional test meals were given at the same time of day on nonconsecutive days. The dependent variable in the present analysis was the amount of food consumed on each of these four days. The amount consumed was determined by the difference in the weight of the food container before and after the meal. During two of these test meals CCK-8 was infused, beginning just as the man started eating the meal, and terminating when he stopped eating for 5 minutes. During the other two meals saline was infused over the same period of time. The key point for the following analysis is that there were two blocks of six subjects each, and each subject in each block received one of the six possible sequences of two CCK-8 and two saline infusions accompanying the meal.

2. THE STATISTICAL ANALYSIS OF THE EXPERIMENT

One replicate of this six-sequence design is shown symbolically as follows: S = CCK-8,   P = Placebo.

Period	Sequence					
1	S	S	S	P	P	P
2	P	P	S	S	S	P
3	P	S	P	S	P	S
4	S	P	P	P	S	S

The sequences were randomly allocated to subjects so that two subjects received each sequence. The experiment was a double-blinded one; i.e., neither the experimenter nor the subject knew which sequence was being used at any time.

The mathematical model used for analyzing this experiment was:

$$Y_{ijk} = \mu + \eta_i + \xi_{j(i)} + \pi_k + \phi_\ell + \lambda_\ell + \epsilon_{ijk},$$

where

μ	=	population mean
η_i	=	effect of sequence i; $i = 1,2,...,6$.
$\xi_{j(i)}$	=	effect of subject j within the ith sequence; $j = 1,2$. Effect assumed to be normal with mean 0 and variance σ_s^2.
π_k	=	effect of period k; $k = 1,2,3,4$.
ϕ_ℓ	=	direct effect of treatments ℓ; $\ell = 1,2$.
λ_ℓ	=	one-period carry-over effect of treatment ℓ.
ϵ_{ijk}	=	random variable assumed to be normal with mean 0 and variance σ_e^2.

The following additional assumptions are made:

$$\sum_{i=1}^{6}\eta_i = 0, \quad \sum_{k=1}^{4}\pi_k = 0, \quad \sum_{\ell=1}^{2}\phi_\ell = 0, \quad \sum_{\ell=1}^{2}\lambda_\ell = 0, \quad \text{and}$$

$\xi_{j(i)}$ and ϵ_{ijk} are independent random variables. The data obtained from this experiment are shown in Table 1.

Rearranging the data to show replicates of the same sequence, the response vector $Y(48 \times 1)$, design matrix $X(48 \times 17)$, $X'X(17 \times 17)$ and $X'Y(48 \times 1)$ are shown in Tables 2 and 3.

Inspection of the $X'X$ matrix shows that direct and carry-over effects cannot be estimated independently. Further, since the total effect of CCK-8 is desired, a generalized linear model analysis was used. The SAS PROC GLM procedure provides the analyst with the expected mean squares and the necessary quadratic forms needed to do hypothesis testing. The SAS PROC REG procedure provides the necessary covariance matrix of the parameter estimates needed for calculating variance estimates of linear functions of the parameter estimates.

The analysis of variance for this six-sequence design that one gets from the PROC GLM procedure used to obtain the expected mean squares in Table 4 is shown in Table 5. This is calculated assuming a completely fixed effects model. Thus, this design and its corresponding model assumptions require different calculations for various tests of hypotheses than are given in the SAS output. The overall analysis of variance at the top of Table 5 is correct. This shows that the 16 parameter model (excluding the mean) is statistically significant [$F(16,31) = 5.84$, $P<.0001$)]. Further, the model explains 75% of the variation in the intake data. The coefficient of variation indicates that 31% of the variation relative to the observed mean remains unexplained. These latter two results are consistent with our experience in well-controlled biological experiments.

The F-test for sequences is an approximate F-test based on the Type III expected mean squares in Table 4, due to the difference between the 3.927 and 4.000 coefficients of the variance of subj(seq). The test is as follows: F(5,6) = [m.s.seq./m.s.subj(seq)] = 2.97, which shows no significant difference among sequences. [Note that if the PROC GLM procedure is used for any mixed model, one should use the random effects option which generates the expected mean squares to determine the correct ratios for calculating the proper F's for testing hypotheses.] Period effects are not significant. Our interest now focuses on direct and carry-over effects. Regardless of the results of the significance tests, we want to make inferences about the magnitude of the total effects of both CCK-8 and Placebo.

Using the results in Tables 5 and 6, the estimates of the direct, carry-over, and total difference between the effects of CCK-8 and Placebo with their standard errors are as follows:

Mean Difference	[CCK-8 - PLACEBO] (±std. error)
Effects	Mean Difference
Direct	−136.38 (±54.56)
Carry-over	−57.20 (±65.80)
Total	−183.58 (±97.32)

The covariance of the coefficients for direct and carry-over effects is shown in Table 6. Here,

$$\text{Var(Total)} = 4[\text{Var(D)} + \text{Var(CO)} + 2\text{Cov(D,CO)}]$$
$$= 4[744.103 + 1082.232 + 2(270.583)]$$
$$= 9470.004$$
$$\text{Std. Error} = 97.31.$$

Using the 17 parameter model (including the mean), SAS PROC REG was used to do a residual analysis. These residuals and a selected number of the many analytical options available are shown in Table 7. Since our concern is with patterns, outliers, influential data points, etc., we've removed decimals without rounding and restricted the number of digits recorded. For example, the standard errors of predicted values are either 105, 109, or 115 when rounded. We do not think any further detail is warranted.

There are four possible outliers in this table. The four points are concentrated on two subjects, one using the SPPS sequence and the other using the SPSP sequence. There doesn't seem to be much information in the sequence aspect of these residuals. However, these two subjects were the largest eaters among the twelve subjects, and they vary a great deal in the amount eaten. The DFITS elements in the residual analysis are the largest for these two, and as one would expect the DBETA elements for direct and carry-over coefficients are also the largest. That is, when each of these four data points are eliminated one at a time, all four of them affect both the predictive result and both the direct and carry-over coefficients. One other data point should be noticed; namely observation #28. It also has a large effect on the two beta coefficients of interest.

TABLE 1. Luncheon food intake (gms.).

Subj.	Seq.	Y	Subj.	Seq.	Y	Subj.	Seq.	Y
1	S	715	5	P	659	10	S	360
	P	1130		S	664		S	416
	P	1319		S	663		P	519
	S	1483		P	491		P	584
2	S	887	9	P	517	8	S	263
	P	882		S	444		S	139
	P	954		S	362		P	401
	S	582		P	362		P	431
11	P	378	7	P	538	4	P	521
	P	449		P	449		S	466
	S	474		S	397		P	417
	S	500		S	192		S	255
6	P	610	12	C	550	3	S	531
	S	471		P	1427		P	525
	P	589		S	536		S	472
	S	690		P	1009		P	289

TABLE 2.

Y (48×1)	$\hat{\mu}$	$\hat{\eta}_1$	$\hat{\eta}_2$	$\hat{\eta}_3$	$\hat{\eta}_4$	$\hat{\eta}_5$	$\hat{\xi}_{11}$	$\hat{\xi}_{12}$	$\hat{\xi}_{13}$	$\hat{\xi}_{14}$	$\hat{\xi}_{15}$	$\hat{\xi}_{16}$	$\hat{\pi}_1$	$\hat{\pi}_2$	$\hat{\pi}_3$	$\hat{\phi}_1$	$\hat{\lambda}_1$
715	1	1	0	0	0	0	1	0	0	0	0	0	1	0	0	1	0
1130	1	1	0	0	0	0	1	0	0	0	0	0	0	1	0	−1	1
1319	1	1	0	0	0	0	1	0	0	0	0	0	0	0	1	−1	−1
1483	1	1	0	0	0	0	1	0	0	0	0	0	−1	−1	−1	−1	−1
887	1	1	0	0	0	0	−1	0	0	0	0	0	1	0	0	1	0
882	1	1	0	0	0	0	−1	0	0	0	0	0	0	1	0	1	1
954	1	1	0	0	0	0	−1	0	0	0	0	0	0	0	1	−1	1
582	1	1	0	0	0	0	−1	0	0	0	0	0	−1	−1	−1	−1	1
659	1	0	1	0	0	0	0	1	0	0	0	0	1	0	0	1	0
664	1	0	1	0	0	0	0	1	0	0	0	0	0	1	0	1	−1
663	1	0	1	0	0	0	0	1	0	0	0	0	0	0	1	1	−1
491	1	0	1	0	0	0	0	1	0	0	0	0	−1	−1	−1	1	0
517	1	0	1	0	0	0	0	−1	0	0	0	0	1	0	0	−1	−1
444	1	0	1	0	0	0	0	−1	0	0	0	0	0	1	0	−1	1
362	1	0	1	0	0	0	0	−1	0	0	0	0	0	0	1	−1	1
362	1	0	1	0	0	0	0	−1	0	0	0	0	−1	−1	−1	−1	1
360	1	0	0	1	0	0	0	0	1	0	0	0	1	0	0	1	0
416	1	0	0	1	0	0	0	0	1	0	0	0	0	1	0	1	−1
519	1	0	0	1	0	0	0	0	1	0	0	0	0	−1	1	−1	1
584	1	0	0	1	0	0	0	0	1	0	0	0	1	1	−1	−1	0
263	1	0	0	1	0	0	0	0	−1	0	0	0	1	0	0	1	0

X (48 × 17)

THE STATISTICAL ANALYSIS OF THE EXPERIMENT 337

TABLE 3.

X'X (17×17)							X'Y (17×1)
48	0		0		0	0	27970
	16 8 8 8 8					−4	2605
	8 16 8 8 8	8 8 8 8 8				0	−1185
	8 8 16 8 8	8 8 16 8 8				0	−2234
	8 8 8 8 8	8 8 8 16 8				−4	−1970
	8 8 8 8 8	8 8 8 8 16				−4	−1328
0			8 0				1342
			8 8 0				792
			8 8 8 0				645
			8 8 8 8 0			0	225
			8 8 8 8 8 0				−701
			8 8 8 8 8 8				1713
0	0		0	24 12 12			−331
				12 24 12	12 12 12	0	594
				12 12 24	24 12 24		235
0	0		0		0	48	−2930
0	−4 −4		0		0	−12	−807
0	0 0 −4 −4		0		0	36	

The studentized residuals were next plotted on normal probability paper [Figure 1]. This plot shows an ogive shape indicating the need for transforming the response variable (Daniel and Wood, 1980). This shape plus the increased variance with large eaters suggests using the logarithm of food intake as the needed transformation. The complete model was reanalyzed using ln(intake) as the response.

The analysis of variance for ln(food intake) is shown in Table 8. The results show that there is a significant effect of CCK-8 in reducing food intake when compared to a placebo. Before drawing final conclusions, this complete model was fitted using a regression model program and the residuals analysis is shown in Table 9. A plot of the studentized residuals is shown in Figure 2. The transformation has accomplished its purpose; i.e., making the variance more homogeneous and reducing the influence of the possible outliers indicated in the original analysis.

It is our position in doing residual analysis in a biological experiment with human subjects that extreme values usually occur. Investigations on reasons why these outliers occur rarely yield helpful information. The reasons given are complex and difficult.

TABLE 4. Expected mean squares for six-sequence carry-over design.

DEPENDENT VARIABLE: INTAKE

SOURCE	TYPE I EXPECTED MEAN SQUARE (SEQUENTIAL)
SEQ	VAR(ERROR) + 4 VAR(SUBJ(SEQ)) + Q(SEQ, CO)
SUBJ(SEQ)	VAR(ERROR) + 4 VAR(SUBJ(SEQ))
PERIOD	VAR(ERROR) + Q(PERIOD, CO)
DIR	VAR(ERROR) + Q(DIR, CO)
CO	VAR(ERROR) + Q(CO)

SOURCE	TYPE III EXPECTED MEAN SQUARE (PARTIAL)
SEQ	VAR(ERROR) + 3.92727 VAR(SUBJ(SEQ)) + Q(SEQ)
SUBJ(SEQ)	VAR(ERROR) + 4 VAR(SUBJ(SEQ))
PERIOD	VAR(ERROR) + Q(PERIOD)
DIR	VAR(ERROR) + Q(DIR)
CO	VAR(ERROR) + Q(CO)

TABLE 5. Analysis of variance for the six-sequence design with 48 observations.

DEPENDENT VARIABLE: INTAKE

SOURCE	DF	SUM OF SQUARES	MEAN SQUARE	F VALUE	PROB>F
MODEL	16	3032365.22	189522.83	5.84	0.0001
ERROR	31	1006568.70	32469.96		
TOTAL(CORR)	47	4038933.92			

R-SQUARE	C.V.	ROOT MSE	INTAKE MEAN
0.75	30.92	180.19	582.71

SOURCE	DF	TYPE III SS (PARTIAL)	F VALUE	PROB>F
SEQ	5	1953643.709	12.03	0.0001
SUBJ(SEQ)	6	790081.000	4.06	0.0041
PERIOD	2*	14915.056	0.23	0.7961
DIR	1	202913.603	6.25	0.0179
CO	1	24538.800	0.76	0.3913

PARAMETER		ESTIMATE	T-TEST	PROB>|T|	STD ERR
INTERCEPT		529.517	4.85	0.0001	109.113
SEQ	SPPS	33.800	0.26	0.7942	128.474
	PSSP	18.300	0.14	0.8877	128.474
	SSPP	711.500	5.58	0.0001	127.417
	PPSS	183.300	1.43	0.1636	128.474
	PSPS	139.750	1.10	0.2812	127.417
SUBJ(SEQ)	SSPP	−161.250	−1.27	0.2151	127.417
	SPSP	428.250	3.36	0.0021	127.417
	SPPS	−335.500	−2.63	0.0131	127.417
	PSSP	−198.000	−1.55	0.1303	127.417
	PSPS	−175.250	−1.38	0.1789	127.417
	PPSS	−56.250	−0.44	0.6619	127.417
PERIOD	1	−56.183	−0.70	0.4909	80.585
	2	49.500	0.67	0.5060	73.564
	3	19.583	0.27	0.7918	73.564
DIR	S	−136.383	−2.50	0.0179	54.557
CO	S	−57.200	−0.87	0.3913	65.798

Note: The results for period, as given here by the raw SAS output, are incorrect. See the text.

Thus, we prefer to take the classical quality control position and unless a point is at least 3 sigma units beyond the predicted value, we rarely bother to do much more than note the large residuals, live with the problem, and design a better experiment the next time. The results from the analysis of the ln(intake) data yield the following estimates of the direct, carry-over, and total effects of the difference between ln(CCK-8) and ln(Placebo):

Mean Difference	[ln(CCK-8) - ln(PLACEBO)] (±std. error)
Direct	−.2756 (±.0869)
Carry-over	−.1817 (±.0869)
Total	−.4573 (±.1550)

Placing a 95% confidence limit on the true difference of the total effect of the drug when compared to a placebo where the response is ln(intake), one obtains:

$$-.4573 \pm (2.04)(.1550)$$
$$-.4573 \pm .3162$$
$$[-.7735 < \delta < -.1411].$$

TABLE 6. Covariance of estimates (direct and carry-over only).

SIX-SEQUENCE MODEL WITH ALL 48 OBSERVATIONS		
COVB	DIRECT	CARRY-OVER
DIRECT	744.103	270.583
CARRY-OVER	270.583	1082.332

TABLE 7. Residual analysis for complete six-sequence model.

	INTAKE OBS	INTAKE PRED	SE PRED	RES	SE RES	STU RES	−2−1−0 1 2	COOK D	R STU	DF FITS	DFBETAS D	DFBETAS C
1	715	1048	105	−333	146	−2.28	****	0.15	−2.45	−1.77	−0.50	−0.27
2	1130	1233	109	−103	143	−0.72	*	0.01	−0.71	−0.54	0.07	−0.16
3	1319	1261	109	58	143	0.40		0.00	0.40	0.30	−0.09	−0.09
4	1483	1105	105	378	146	2.58	*****	0.20	2.87	2.07	0.39	−0.32
5	887	712	105	174	146	1.19	**	0.04	1.19	0.86	0.24	0.13
6	882	897	109	−15	143	−0.11		0.00	−0.10	−0.08	0.01	−0.02
7	954	925	109	28	143	0.20		0.00	0.19	0.15	−0.04	−0.04
8	582	769	105	−187	146	−1.28	**	0.05	−1.29	−0.93	−0.17	0.14
9	659	656	105	2	146	0.01		0.00	0.01	0.01	−0.00	−0.00
10	664	625	105	38	146	0.26		0.00	0.26	0.19	0.02	−0.06
11	663	538	109	124	143	0.86	*	0.02	0.86	0.65	0.20	0.19
12	491	655	105	−164	146	−1.12	**	0.03	−1.13	−0.81	0.15	−0.12
13	517	458	105	58	146	0.39		0.00	0.39	0.28	−0.08	−0.04
14	444	427	109	16	143	0.11		0.00	0.11	0.08	0.01	−0.02
15	362	340	109	21	143	0.14		0.00	0.14	0.11	0.03	0.03
16	362	457	105	−95	146	−0.65	*	0.01	−0.64	−0.46	0.08	−0.07
17	360	370	104	−10	147	−0.07		0.00	−0.07	−0.05	−0.01	−0.00
18	416	419	109	−3	143	−0.02		0.00	−0.02	−0.01	−0.00	−0.00
19	519	525	105	−6	146	−0.04		0.00	−0.04	−0.03	0.00	−0.00
20	584	563	115	20	138	0.14		0.00	0.14	0.12	−0.04	−0.05
21	263	209	104	53	147	0.36		0.00	0.35	0.25	0.06	0.00
22	139	257	109	−118	143	−0.83	*	0.02	−0.82	−0.62	−0.19	−0.18

THE STATISTICAL ANALYSIS OF THE EXPERIMENT 343

23	401	364	105	36	146	0.25		0.00	0.24	0.17	-0.03	0.02
24	431	402	115	28	138	0.20		0.00	0.20	0.17	-0.05	-0.07
25	373	473	104	-95	147	-0.64		0.01	-0.64	-0.45	0.10	0.00
26	449	579	109	-130	143	-0.90		0.02	-0.90	-0.68	0.21	0.20
27	474	412	105	61	146	0.41		0.00	0.41	0.29	0.05	-0.04
28	500	335	115	164	138	1.18	**	0.05	1.19	0.99	0.34	0.42
29	538	417	104	120	147	0.82	*	0.02	0.81	0.57	-0.13	-0.00
30	449	522	109	-73	143	-0.51		0.00	-0.50	-0.38	0.12	0.11
31	397	356	105	40	146	0.27		0.00	0.27	0.19	0.03	-0.03
32	192	279	115	-87	138	-0.63	*	0.01	-0.62	-0.52	-0.17	-0.22
33	525	437	104	83	147	0.56	*	0.00	0.55	0.39	-0.09	-0.00
34	466	407	105	58	146	0.40		0.00	0.39	0.28	0.05	-0.04
35	417	456	109	-39	143	-0.27		0.00	-0.27	-0.20	0.02	-0.06
36	255	357	105	-102	146	-0.70	*	0.01	-0.69	-0.50	-0.09	0.07
37	610	613	104	-3	147	-0.02		0.00	-0.02	-0.01	0.00	0.00
38	471	582	105	-111	146	-0.76	**	0.01	-0.75	-0.54	-0.10	0.08
39	589	631	109	-42	143	-0.29		0.00	-0.29	-0.22	0.03	-0.06
40	690	532	105	157	146	1.07	***	0.03	1.07	0.77	0.14	-0.12
41	558	783	104	-225	147	-1.53	****	0.06	-1.56	-1.10	-0.26	0.00
42	1427	968	105	458	146	3.13	******	0.30	3.73	2.69	-0.50	0.42
43	536	859	109	-323	143	-2.25		0.17	-2.42	-1.84	-0.25	0.55
44	1009	918	105	90	146	0.61	*	0.01	0.61	0.43	-0.08	0.06
45	531	355	104	175	147	1.19	**	0.04	1.20	0.85	0.20	-0.00
46	525	540	105	-15	146	-0.10		0.00	-0.10	-0.07	0.01	-0.01
47	472	431	109	40	143	0.28		0.00	0.28	0.21	0.02	-0.06
48	289	490	105	-201	146	-1.37	**	0.05	-1.40	-1.00	0.19	-0.15

Thus, one can say that the true percent reduction in food intake when taking CCK-8 is between 13% and 54%. Based on the average food intake of 582.71 g in this study, this represents a range of decrease in food intake due to CCK-8 of 76 to 315 g.

3. FURTHER ANALYSIS CONSIDERATIONS (THE BERENBLUT ALTERNATIVE)

The Berenblut (Berenblut, 1964) carry-over design for two treatments with direct and carry-over effects estimated independently is:

	Sequence
Period	
1	S S P P
2	S P P S
3	P P S S
4	P S S P

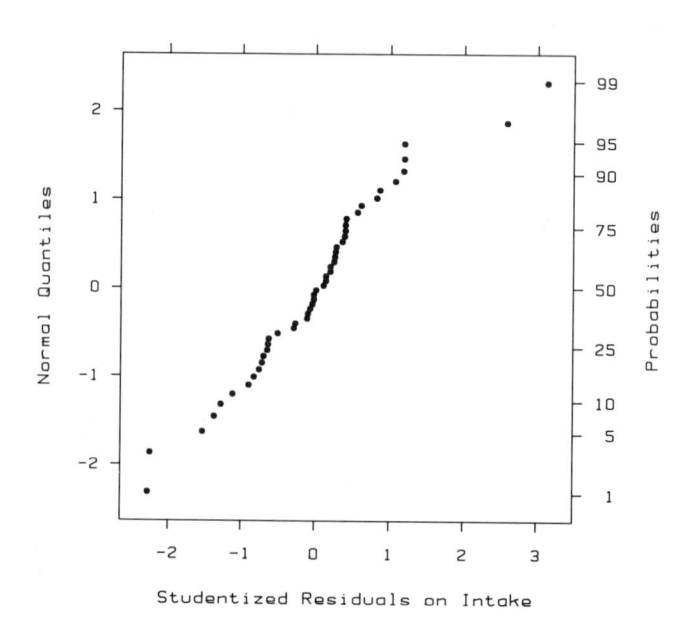

Figure 1. Studentized residuals on intake (Six-Sequence Model).

TABLE 8. Analysis of variance for ln(intake) six-sequence model with 48 observations.

DEPENDENT VARIABLE: LN(Y)

SOURCE	DF	SUM OF SQUARES	MEAN SQUARE	F VALUE	PROB>F
MODEL	16	7.7706	0.4857	5.90	0.0001
ERROR	31	2.5541	0.0824		
TOTAL(CORR)	47	10.3246			

ROOT MSE	ADJ R-SQ	C.V.	LN(INTAKE) MEAN
0.2870	0.62	30.9	6.2596

VARIABLE		DF	PARAM EST	STAND ERR	T-TEST	PROB>|T|
INTERCEPT		1	6.2596	0.0414	151.090	0.0001
SEQ	SSPP	1	0.5784	0.0936	6.182	0.0001
	PSSP	1	−0.0107	0.0936	−0.115	0.9093
	SSPP	1	−0.3488	0.0936	−3.728	0.0008
	PPSS	1	−0.2756	0.0936	−2.946	0.0061
	PSPS	1	−0.1001	0.0936	−1.070	0.2928
SUB(SEQ)	SSPP	1	0.1614	0.1015	1.591	0.1218
	PSSP	1	0.1944	0.1015	1.915	0.0647
	SSPP	1	0.2465	0.1015	2.429	0.0211
	PPSS	1	0.0977	0.1015	0.963	0.3432
	PSPS	1	−0.1886	0.1015	−1.859	0.0726
	SPSP	1	0.3034	0.1015	2.989	0.0054
PERIOD	1	1	−0.0056	0.0718	−0.078	0.9381
	2	1	0.0246	0.0718	0.343	0.7337
	3	1	0.0468	0.0718	0.652	0.5190
DIR	S	1	−0.1378	0.0435	−3.172	0.0034
CO	S	1	−0.0909	0.0525	−1.734	0.0929

346 SIX-SEQUENCE CARRY-OVER DESIGN

TABLE 9. Residual analysis for ln(intake) six-sequence model.

	LN(INTAKE) OBS	PRED	SE PRED	RES	SE RES	STU RES	−2−1−0 1 2	COOK D	DF FITS	DFBETAS D	C
1	6.57	6.85	0.16	−0.28	0.23	−1.21	**	0.04	−0.88	−0.25	−0.13
2	7.03	7.07	0.17	−0.04	0.22	−0.18		0.00	−0.13	0.01	−0.04
3	7.18	7.27	0.17	−0.09	0.22	−0.39		0.00	−0.29	0.09	0.08
4	7.30	6.88	0.16	0.41	0.23	1.78	***	0.09	1.33	0.25	−0.20
5	6.78	6.53	0.16	0.25	0.23	1.09	**	0.03	0.79	0.22	0.12
6	6.78	6.74	0.17	0.03	0.22	0.14		0.00	0.11	−0.01	0.03
7	6.86	6.95	0.17	−0.09	0.22	−0.40		0.00	−0.30	0.09	0.09
8	6.36	6.56	0.16	−0.19	0.23	−0.84	*	0.02	−0.60	−0.11	0.09
9	6.49	6.57	0.16	−0.08	0.23	−0.36		0.00	−0.25	0.07	0.04
10	6.49	6.42	0.17	0.07	0.22	0.33		0.00	0.25	0.03	−0.07
11	6.49	6.26	0.17	0.23	0.22	1.03	**	0.03	0.78	0.24	0.23
12	6.19	6.42	0.16	−0.22	0.23	−0.97	*	0.02	−0.70	0.13	−0.11
13	6.24	6.18	0.16	0.06	0.23	0.26		0.00	0.18	−0.05	−0.02
14	6.09	6.03	0.17	0.06	0.22	0.27		0.00	0.20	0.02	−0.06
15	5.89	5.87	0.17	0.01	0.22	0.08		0.00	0.06	0.01	0.01
16	5.89	6.03	0.16	−0.14	0.23	−0.61	* *	0.01	−0.44	0.08	−0.06
17	5.88	6.01	0.16	−0.12	0.23	−0.54		0.00	−0.38	−0.09	−0.00
18	6.03	5.95	0.17	0.07	0.22	0.33		0.00	0.25	0.08	0.07
19	6.25	6.25	0.16	0.00	0.23	0.00		0.00	0.00	0.00	0.00
20	6.37	6.32	0.18	0.04	0.22	0.22		0.00	0.18	−0.06	−0.07
21	5.57	5.52	0.16	0.05	0.23	0.21		0.00	0.15	0.03	0.00
22	4.93	5.46	0.17	−0.52	0.22	−2.30	****	0.18	−1.89	−0.60	−0.57

FURTHER CONSIDERATIONS (THE BERENBLUT ALTERNATIVE) 347

23	5.99	5.75	0.16	0.23	0.23	1.01		* *	0.03	0.72	−0.13	0.11
24	6.06	5.82	0.18	0.23	0.22	1.08		* *	0.04	0.90	−0.31	−0.38
25	5.93	6.21	0.16	−0.27	0.23	−1.19	* *		0.04	−0.84	0.20	0.00
26	6.10	6.33	0.17	−0.22	0.22	−0.99	*		0.03	−0.75	0.24	0.22
27	6.16	6.08	0.16	0.07	0.23	0.34			0.00	0.24	0.04	−0.03
28	6.21	5.78	0.18	0.42	0.22	1.93		* * *	0.15	1.68	0.58	0.72
29	6.28	6.01	0.16	0.26	0.23	1.14		* *	0.03	0.81	−0.19	−0.00
30	6.10	6.14	0.17	−0.03	0.22	−0.14			0.00	−0.10	0.03	0.03
31	5.98	5.88	0.16	0.09	0.23	0.42			0.00	0.29	0.05	−0.04
32	5.25	5.59	0.18	−0.33	0.22	−1.51	* *		0.09	−1.28	−0.44	−0.55
33	6.25	6.10	0.16	0.15	0.23	0.65			0.01	0.45	−0.10	−0.00
34	6.14	5.94	0.16	0.19	0.23	0.84		*	0.02	0.60	0.11	−0.09
35	6.03	6.06	0.17	−0.03	0.22	−0.13		*	0.00	−0.10	0.01	−0.03
36	5.54	5.85	0.16	−0.31	0.23	−1.36	* *		0.05	−0.99	−0.18	0.15
37	6.41	6.48	0.16	−0.06	0.23	−0.28			0.00	−0.19	0.04	0.00
38	6.15	6.32	0.16	−0.17	0.23	−0.73	*		0.01	−0.52	−0.09	0.08
39	6.37	6.44	0.17	−0.06	0.22	−0.27			0.00	−0.20	0.02	−0.06
40	6.53	6.23	0.16	0.30	0.23	1.29		* *	0.05	0.94	0.17	−0.14
41	6.32	6.57	0.16	−0.25	0.23	−1.07	* *		0.03	−0.76	−0.18	0.00
42	7.26	6.79	0.16	0.47	0.23	2.02		* * * *	0.12	1.54	−0.29	0.24
43	6.28	6.72	0.17	−0.43	0.22	−1.90	* *		0.12	−1.51	−0.20	0.45
44	6.91	6.70	0.16	0.21	0.23	0.92		*	0.02	0.66	−0.12	0.10
45	6.27	5.97	0.16	0.30	0.23	1.30		* *	0.05	0.93	0.22	−0.00
46	6.26	6.18	0.16	0.07	0.23	0.33			0.00	0.23	−0.04	0.03
47	6.15	6.11	0.17	0.04	0.22	0.19			0.00	0.14	0.01	−0.04
48	5.66	6.09	0.16	−0.42	0.23	−1.83	* * *		0.10	−1.37	0.25	−0.21

This design utilizes only four of the six sequences of the design used in this experiment. Thus, by using only the eight subjects for the four sequences corresponding to the Berenblut design, a similar analysis can be done on ln(food intake). The expected mean squares for this design are shown in Table 10 and indicate that the direct and carry-over effects are estimated independently of each other. The analysis of variance for this subset of data is shown in Table 11. The results of this analysis show similar effects with smaller standard errors. These are as follows:

Effects	Mean Difference [ln(CCK-8) - ln(PLACEBO)] (±std. err.)
	Mean Difference
Direct	−0.2345 (±.0941)
Carry-over	−0.2386 (±.1134)
Total	−0.4731 (±.1474)

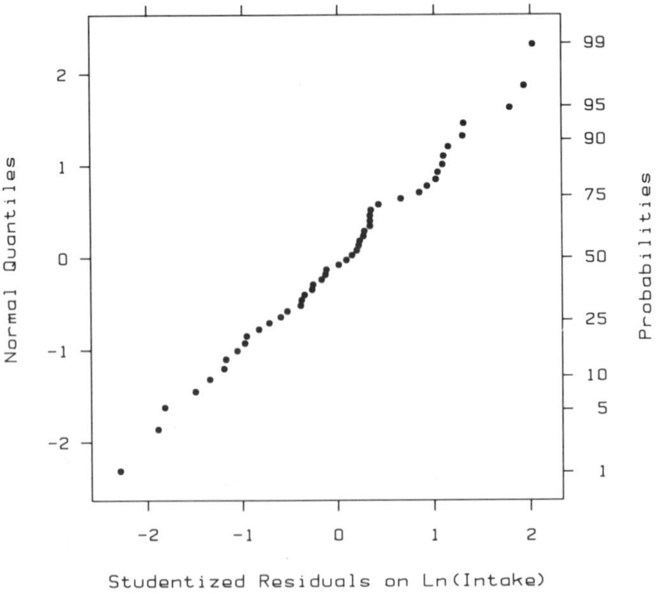

Figure 2. Studentized residuals on ln(intake) (Six-Sequence Model).

Placing a 95% confidence limit on the true difference of the total effect of the drug when compared to a placebo in the log transformed space, one obtains:

$$-0.4731 \pm (2.093)(0.1471)$$
$$= -0.4731 \pm 0.3085$$
$$[-.7816 < \delta < -0.1646].$$

Thus, one can say the true percent reduction in food intake when taking CCK-8 is between 15% and 54%, which represents a decrease in food intake in this study of between 88 and 315 g.

TABLE 10. Expected mean squares for the subset of 8 patients (Berenblut design).

NUMBER OF OBSERVATIONS IN DATA SET = 32

DEPENDENT VARIABLE: INTAKE

SOURCE	TYPE I EXPECTED MEAN SQUARE (SEQUENTIAL)
SEQ	VAR(ERROR) + 4 VAR(SUBJ(SEQ)) + Q(SEQ, CO)
SUBJ(SEQ)	VAR(ERROR) + 4 VAR(SUBJ(SEQ))
PERIOD	VAR(ERROR) + Q(PERIOD, CO)
DIR	VAR(ERROR) + Q(DIR)
CO	VAR(ERROR) + Q(CO)

SOURCE	TYPE III EXPECTED MEAN SQUARE (PARTIAL)
SEQ	VAR(ERROR) + 3.88889 VAR(SUBJ(SEQ)) + Q(SEQ)
SUBJ(SEQ)	VAR(ERROR) + 4 VAR(SUBJ(SEQ))
PERIOD	VAR(ERROR) + Q(PERIOD)
DIR	VAR(ERROR) + Q(DIR)
CO	VAR(ERROR) + Q(CO)

TABLE 11. Analysis of variance for the subset of 8 patients (Berenblut design).

DEPENDENT VARIABLE: LN(INTAKE)

SOURCE	DF	SUM OF SQUARES	MEAN SQUARE	F VALUE	PROB>F
MODEL	12	6.4607	0.5384	7.61	0.0001
ERROR	19	1.3447	0.0708		
TOTAL(CORR)	31	7.8053			

R-SQUARE	C.V.	ROOT MSE	LN(INTAKE) MEAN
0.828	4.26	0.2660	6.2455

SOURCE	DF	TYPE I SS (SEQUENTIAL)	F VALUE	PROB>F
SEQ	3	4.5086	21.24	0.0001
SUBJ(SEQ)	4	1.0732	3.79	0.0198
PERIOD	3	0.1260	0.59	0.6270
DIR	1	0.4398	6.21	0.0221
CO	1	0.3132	4.42	0.0490

SOURCE	DF	TYPE III SS (PARTIAL)	F VALUE	PROB>F
SEQ	3	4.1107	19.36	0.0001
SUBJ(SEQ)	4	1.0732	3.79	0.0198
PERIOD	2	0.1203	0.85	0.4430
DIR	1	0.4398	6.21	0.0221
CO	1	0.3132	4.42	0.0490

PARAMETER		ESTIMATE	T-TEST	PROB>|T|	STD ERR
INTERCEPT		6.2738	37.26	0.0001	0.1684
SEQ	SSPP	0.0899	0.47	0.6420	0.1902
	SPPS	0.9177	4.88	0.0001	0.1881
	PSSP	0.3758	1.98	0.0629	0.1902
SUBJ(SEQ)	SSPP	−0.4930	−2.62	0.0168	0.1881
	SPPS	−0.3229	−1.72	0.1023	0.1881
	PSSP	−0.3888	−2.07	0.0527	0.1881
	PPSS	−0.1954	−1.04	0.3121	0.1881
PERIOD	1	−0.1049	−0.73	0.4771	0.1446
	2	−0.0099	−0.07	0.9416	0.1330
	3	0.1450	1.09	0.2892	0.1330
DIR	S	−0.2345	−2.49	0.0221	0.0941
CO	S	−0.2386	−2.10	0.0490	0.1134

4. DISCUSSION

The above analysis has concentrated on the problem of estimation rather than testing of hypotheses. While the analysis of variance shows no significant carry-over effects (P>.05), in both analyses the direction of the carry-over is the same and confirm what was expected. Because it is difficult to conduct experiments of this kind and because the number of subjects is small, the estimation of effects is the most important element of the analysis.

Design Comments

In retrospect, if one were to design a study similar to the nutrition experiment above, the design which we would recommend is the Berenblut design replicated three times rather than the six-sequence design replicated twice. In addition to being simpler to administer, the Berenblut design estimates direct and carry-over effects independently and has smaller variances of the effects as shown below:

Effects	Variances	
	Six Sequences	Berenblut
Direct	$\sigma^2/43.64$	$\sigma^2/48$
Carry-over	$\sigma^2/30$	$\sigma^2/33$
Total	$\sigma^2/13.71$	$\sigma^2/19.56$

REFERENCES

Berenblut, I. I. (1964). "Change-over designs with complete balance for first residual effects," *Biometrics*, **20**, 707-712.

Daniel, C. and Wood, F. S. (1980). *Fitting Equations to Data*, 2nd edition. New York: Wiley.

Kissileff, H. R., Klingsberg, G., and Van Italie, T. B. (1980). "Universal eating monitor for continuous recording of solid or liquid consumption in man," *American Journal of Physiology*, **238**, R 14-22.

Kissileff, H. R., Pi-Sunyer, F. X., Thornton, J., and Smith, G. P. (1981). "C-Terminal octapeptide of cholectystokinin decreases food intake in man," *American Journal of Clinical Nutrition*, **34**, 154-160.

Kissileff, H. R., Thornton, J., and Becker, E. (1982) "A quadratic equation adequately describes the cumulative food intake curve in man," *Appetite: Journal for Intake Research*, 3, 255-272.

Peryam, D. R. and Pilgrim, F. J. (1957). "Hedonic scale measuring food preferences," *Food Technology, Supplement 11*, 9-14.

CHAPTER 17

Statistics in a Court of Law

Hans Zeisel
University of Chicago

One Randy Gometz appealed his conviction after jury trial in an Illinois federal court primarily on the ground that the process by which his jury had been selected violated the 1968 Federal Jury Service and Selection Act.

The facts were these. The jury clerk had sent some fourteen thousand questionnaires to prospective jurors who in accordance with the Act had been randomly selected from the voter list. Only 30 percent of these persons returned the questionnaire, and it was from them that the Gometz jury was selected. Gometz complained that restriction of the juror pool to the 30 percent who had responded to the questionnaire violated the provision for random selection of the Act; a 30 percent first wave of returns could not be relied upon to produce a random sample of the original voter list. The jury clerk's failure to increase the return rate by a second mailing, so Gometz's appeal claimed, violated the Act. The Illinois Court of Appeals, sitting en banc, voting 7 to 2, denied the appeal. Judge Richard A. Posner wrote the majority opinion.[1]

Judge Posner, who before he came on the bench had been a colleague of mine and knew of my interest in juries and statistics, generously invited me to comment on his opinion. The following letter, here somewhat enlarged and rearranged, was my response.

---

[1] U.S. v. Gometz, 730 F.2d 475.

354 STATISTICS IN A COURT OF LAW

Dear Richard:

Prior to the 1968 Federal Jury Service and Selection Act, most jurisdictions used the so called key-man system; the jury clerk would ask key members of the community to recommend citizens who would make good jurors. It was the primary goal of the 1968 Act to replace that system by one that would select jurors without prejudice from the entire eligible citizenry. Juries henceforth would bring to the courts the community's sense of justice, not one distorted by a biased selection process. The Act tries to accomplish this aim by four key provisions:

* by declaring the voter list as the normal basic list from which jurors are to be selected. In communities in which the voter list is not a reasonable representation of the eligible population, it is to be supplemented by other lists.

* by insisting that from the basic list or lists the prospective jurors be selected "at random".

* by establishing ground rules for the subsequent excuses of certain of these randomly selected jurors because of physical incapacity or economic hardship.

* by entitling the defendant in criminal cases to a dismissal of the indictment or other stay of the proceedings, if there was substantial failure to comply with the provisions of the Act.

The Argument

Your arguments can be summarized as follows; I will try to answer in turn:

(1) "At random," as used in the Act, is not to be interpreted in the statistician's technical understanding of the term.

(2) The jury clerk's acceptance of the first wave of respondents constitutes no substantial violation of the Act because there is no evidence that it biased the selection process.

(3) Even if these jurors were different from what a true cross-section would have been, this difference would benefit the judicial process.

(4) The Act specifically leaves to the discretion of the clerk (he "may") the decision whether or not to follow-up non-respondents. Hence the clerk's decision is not reviewable.

(5) Even if the clerk's decision were reviewable, in this case there is no ground for it, since the 30 percent return,

yielding more than 4000 names, was satisfactory under the circumstances. It is the absolute size of a sample that determines its reliability, not its relative size.

What Is The Meaning of "At Random"?

To the statistician, random selection means a mode of selection that gives each unit or person on the basic list (the "sampling frame") an equal likelihood of falling into the sample. This is achieved, as we all know from lottery or military service drafts, by entrusting the selection to chance.

You argue that this is not the meaning in which the Federal Jury Service and Selection Act uses the term. You quote paragraph 2 of footnote 9 in the Senate Report[2] which indeed seems to support you:

> "It is also true that, to the extent that the bill does provide for random selection, it does not insist upon randomness is the sense in which that term might be understood by statisticians."

However, the paragraph that follows explains the "sense" in which randomness may be understood.

> "Thus, for example, the plan may specify selection of every 76th name from the voter list, or every name at the bottom of a page in the list, or all the names on the list, even though in certain cases statisticians might not agree that truly random selection would be the result."

What footnote 9 refers to is the difference between what statisticians call a pure random sample and what they call a systematic sample. Both, in spite of their different names, are designed to produce random selection.

In the pure design each person on the list is given a number, and then some lottery device makes the selection. Because no such direct lottery device is easily applicable to large numbers, especially before automation is introduced, the Act suggests the use of the systematic sample. Except for the unrealistic possibility that the n'th number interval is related to a relevant juror characteristic, the systematic sample produces random selection and has the enormous advantage of easy application.

---

2 Senate Report No. 891, 90th Congress, 1st Session, p. 10 (1967).

Thus, the seeming support from footnote 9 fades. By explicating the range of allowable deviation, the technical meaning of random selection and the concern for it are in fact reaffirmed.

You make a second argument in support of a loose interpretation of "random selection." You point to the Act's acceptance of the voter list as a basic sampling frame, although it is obvious that the citizens who vote are not a random sample of all citizens who could vote. You quote a passage from the Congressional debate, as evidence that the Congress even saw merit in what you call the "non-random" character of the voter list.

> "Voter lists contain an important built-in screening element in that they eliminate those individuals who are either unqualified to vote or insufficiently interested in the world about them to do so."[3]

But this remark was not made in support of the imperfection of the voter list. It was made to show that the imperfection is not an unmitigated evil. Congress was well aware of the potential dangers of that imperfection. That is why it insisted that in districts where the voter list is grossly imperfect, it must be supplemented by other lists, such as lists of driver licensees and of public utility customers.

To conclude from the conditional acceptance of the voter list as basis for juror selection, that the selection *from* that list need not be random, is unjustified. You might as well have come to that conclusion by pointing out that the non-random voir dire challenges in the final phase of the jury selection reenforces your argument.

The Act quite clearly limits the random requirement to one phase of the selection process: the random selection of prospective jurors from the basic list.

But in this phase, the Act both in its language and its policy declaration insists on the principle. Here, for instance, is the Act's preamble.

Declaration of policy:
> "It is the policy of the United States that all litigants in Federal Courts entitled to trial by jury shall have the right to grand and petit juries selected at random [!] from a fair cross section of the community . . . wherein the court convenes." (§1861)

---

3 See preceding note 2, at p. 22.

And later on §1863 reads:

Plan for random jury selection

> "Each United States district court shall devise and put into operation a written plan for random selection[!] of grand and petit jurors. . . . .
> [Among other things, such plans shall —] specify detailed procedures to be followed by the jury commission or clerk in selecting names. . . . These procedures shall be designed to ensure the random selection[!] of a fair cross-section of the persons residing on the community.

If the language of the Act is not sufficiently convincing, its documented intent leaves no doubt as to how the term "random selection" is to be interpreted.

The Act marks the replacement of the old system of asking elite citizens to serve as jurors by a system which aims, as far as this is practically feasible, at selecting jurors randomly from the total population of eligible jurors. Harry Kalven and I had a modest but insightful role in shaping the Federal Jury Selection and Service Act when we testified before the Senate Subcommittee that held hearings on the bill.[4] Several findings from the Jury Project of the University of Chicago Law School[5] had a bearing on the issue. The first was that the intellectual task of fact finding posed no problem in the vast majority of criminal cases; the cumulative, shared intelligence of the jurors proved to be sufficient. The second relevant finding was that the jury's major contribution to the judicial process — the one that causes the occasional difference between the jury's verdict and what the trial judge without a jury would have done — is the injection of the jurors' sense of justice. When the facts allow some leeway, the jury will try to shape its verdict in the direction of what it sees as substantive justice in the particular case, even if it deviates from the letter of the law.

Furthermore, it turned out that "the jury's sense of justice" is not a homogeneous, predefined position. Rather, it evolves in the individual juries in the following complex and interesting manner.

---

4 *Testimony on Federal Jury Selection Methods*, Subcommittee on Improvements of Judicial Machinery, Committee on the Judiciary, U.S. Senate, 90th Congress, 1st Session, 1967 (with Harry Kalven, Jr.).

5 Kalven H., Jr. and Zeisel, H. (1968). *The American Jury*. Chicago: University of Chicago Press.

358 STATISTICS IN A COURT OF LAW

In roughly one-third of all cases, the jury's first ballot is unanimous, indicating that the facts were so clear that no difference of opinion arose. In two-thirds of the cases, the jury's first ballot is split; some jurors say "guilty", others say "not guilty". How is that to be explained since every juror heard and saw the same witnesses, the same lawyers, and received the same instruction from the judge? By definition, the difference can arise only from the jurors themselves, who differ with respect to the experiences and values they bring to the trial.

Since the law has no way of deciding which values and experiences are the right ones, it aims at making the jury as representative of the community as possible within the framework of legal and practical constraints. The requirement of random selection in the Jury Service and Selection Act therefore represents the very root of its intent.

Does Non-response Create Bias?

The appellant argues that the prospective jurors who respond to the first wave of questionnaires are likely to be different in important respects from the jurors who would have responded to a follow-up mailing. On this point the appellant is on firm ground.

For experts who seek a representative sample from a predefined list, non-response is a well-known and important hazard; as a rule, self-selection will produce bias. Ascertaining public opinion on any issue, through voluntarily returned questionnaires or other mail initiative, will tend to reflect the opinion of strong partisans, possibly even those from only one side. Follow-up waves in any mail survey operation, have long since become standard procedure.[6]

There is no published study that analyzes specifically the first wave respondents to a jury questionnaire, with those who failed to respond. However, the general experience with non-respondents heavily favors the presumption that they are different both with respect to demographics and to some less visible but equally important attitudinal characteristics. Two of my own research experiences bear on the issue.

Some years ago, I examined the jury selection process in Cook County (Chicago) Illinois, which at the time indulged in the very

---

[6] I myself have contributed to the early literature of the problem. ["Bias in Mail Questionnaires Cannot Be Controlled by One Mailing," (with R. N. Ford), *Public Opinion Quarterly*, **13**, (1949), p. 495.] Today the point is firmly established. See Frederick Mosteller (1968). "Nonsampling errors." In D. L. Sills (Ed.), *International Encyclopedia of the Social Sciences*, Volume 5. New York: Free Press, pp. 113-132.

practice complained of in the present case. Citizens who did not want to serve as jurors simply disregarded their summons; there never was a follow-up. This procedure yielded juries demographically different from the electorate of which they were a part.

My second research experience, reflected not on the demographic but on the attitudinal bias appellant claims, was created by accepting voluntary first wave respondents. At one time, jury service by women in New York state was optional. They were allowed to serve but were not required to. As a result, the women who did serve were volunteers, very much like the jurors in the present case who returned the first wave of questionnaires. These women volunteers had an interesting bias. The New York juror questionnaire at the time asked, among other things, whether the respondent had any difficulties with the death penalty. Generally at the time, and still today, the proportion of women who favor the death penalty is lower than the corresponding proportion among men. Among the New York jurors at the time, the situation was reversed. The proportion of women favoring the death penalty was substantially higher than that of the men, indicating that the self-selection had brought the tough, more prosecution prone women to the fore.

For all these reasons, the presumption is heavy that restricting juror service to those who respond to the first wave biases the venire.

A New Version of "Good" and "Not so Good" Jurors

You yourself instinctively acknowledge that first wave respondents are likely to differ from the rest. You prefer the former and would grudgingly admit the latter. Yet there is no ground for either reaction.

You frankly admit that if you had the choice between a system with 30 percent response to one wave of questionnaires, and a system with 80 percent response to several waves, you would prefer the former, because the citizens who reply without delay to the first invitation will serve more voluntarily than the citizens who replied only to repeated invitation. These latter, you write, would be persons "forced to serve against [their] will" and such persons "as anyone with experience as trial judge knows, [are] apt to be angry juror[s] and . . . an angry juror is a bad juror. Yet there is no evidence anywhere that a citizen who is reminded by a follow-up letter of his civic duty to serve as a juror would be a "forced," "angry" and therefore undesirable juror. The root position which you impute to the authors of the Act, I suspect is only your own.

Your negative view of the non-respondents is triggered by a claim of the appellant. You write:

> Gometz also argues that a certain type of personality is bound to be underrepresented on the qualified jury wheel when some people do not return their juror qualification forms — namely the "antiauthoritarian" personality, who thumbs his nose at the law and is therefore likely to ignore the requirement (see 28 U.S.C. § 1864(a)) of completing and returning the form. But nothing in the Jury Selection and Service Act suggests that Congress thought that a cross-section of the community, to be fairly representative, must include the antisocial elements in the community. Although for obvious practical reasons people who have "antiauthoritarian" personalities are not forbidden to serve on juries (as convicted felons whose civil rights have not been restored are, see 28 U.S.C. § 1865(b) (5), neither the letter nor the spirit of the Act requires that they be represented on the qualified jury wheel, let alone in the same proportion that they bear to the population).

It is well established through many studies that the population of prospective jurors can be arrayed along a spectrum ranging from extreme sympathy for the goals of the prosecution at one end, to similar extreme sympathy for the goals of the defense at the other end. This ranking is done by the response to poll questions that ask, for instance, whether what prosecutor and defense lawyer says would carry equal weight, or whether one would be trusted more than the other. Different people will give different answers, and there are no grounds why the system should prefer either. It is the very purpose of the Act not to make this distinction. It is, however, the purpose of the last phase of the jury selection process, the voir dire, to remove jurors at the extreme of either side.

Filling a Gap

It is obvious that the legislators had not thought of the problem created by substantial non-response. It therefore behoves the courts to fill this gap. You say that establishing a minimum percentage of response "would be arbitrary. Legislatures are permitted to be arbitrary; courts are not."

The argument is not convincing. If the court must decide whether the acceptance of a 30 percent return "substantially violates" the Act, the court must establish a numerical level which exonerates the system. That this is a feasible way is confirmed by the juror selection plans filed with the Administrative Office of the U.S. Courts by the various district courts under its supervision. Most of them establish such minimum response levels. The dissenting minority opinion in your court cites chapter and verse:

> "the touchstone of a defendant's rights are a 'substantial failure' to comply with the provisions of the Jury Selection and Service Act. Congress has relegated enforcement of the Act to the judicial branch through the procedures provided in 28 U.S.C. § 1867 . . . The applicable House Committee Report specifically 'leave[s] the definition of substantial' to the process of judicial decision. . . Common sense suggests that we need not require 100% of return of jury questionnaires but, when the return rate drops as low as 30% so as to conspicuously impair the principle of randomness it seems to me that we may find at least on prong of a 'substantial failure to comply.' . . . 'Substantial compliance' suggests some reasonable standard, less than 100% but appreciably greater than zero." (p. 15)

By refusing to impose a modest burden on the clerk, which the vast majority of districts has adopted as a matter of routine, you have thwarted the very core of the Act's intent — to select jurors at random from the basic list.

Another Reason For Strengthening Random Selection

There is another good reason why the courts should support the random selection process instead of impeding it. It is the best and indeed the only way to insure fair representation. We have learned to appreciate this fact by watching the uncanny power of the election polls. A sample of 1500 prospective voters allows us to predict what 60 millions of them will do. Except that this example makes us look through the other end of the telescope: we appreciate that the population will behave as the sample does. In our case, we know the population list, and want to be sure that the sample represents it fairly.

Both the law and common sense suggest that one cannot expect every individual 12-member jury, not to speak of one of 6 members, to be a true representation of the population list. But on the average, random selection will result in optimal representation.

The courts should appreciate this and insist on random selection because it is then relatively easy to establish whether its rules were observed or violated. The cumbersome proofs of discrimination in the individual case or type of case is necessary only in the absence of formal selection. In complaints of discrimination, the observed discrepancy is being used to prove the absence of impartial random selection at the outset. Proof of random selection at the outset will be a powerful defense against observed discrepancies at the end of the process.

A Misunderstanding

You defend the jury clerk's action or inaction on still another ground. You point out that the response to the first wave yielded a sufficient number of jurors for the court's needs. You then try to bolster your argument by claiming that the substantial absolute size of the response brings also some guarantee of its quality with respect to representing the list:

> "This is a large sample of the eligible population, bearing in mind that it is the absolute size of a sample rather than its ratio to the population from which it is drawn that determines the sample's reliability."

By reliability, you explain, you mean the fidelity with which the sample represents the list. You cite the best authority[7] but you overlooked the context. The statement is correct only with respect to an unbiased sample. Size can never cure a biased sample. You briefly discuss the bias problem but in the end you repeat your position unchanged, failing to see that the size-theorem does not apply to biased samples.

Conclusion

For sound reasons, most jury selection plans filed with the Administrative Office of the United States Courts commit the clerk to follow-up mailings, often to a minimum response percentage. These are routine performances in no way particularly onerous. The jury clerk of the U.S. District Court for the Northern District of Illinois, for instance, obtains responses from over ninety percent of the original mailing.

---

7 Freedman, D., Pisani, R., and Purves, R. (1980). *Statistics.* New York: Norton, pp. 332-333.

By refusing to impose this modest burden on the clerk, which the vast majority of districts has adopted as a matter of routine, I believe, you have thwarted the very core of the Federal Jury Service and Selection Act, to broaden and democratize our jury venires by insuring their random selection from the basic list.

Sincerely,

Hans

Index

Page numbers for illustrations are in italics.

Abelson, R. P., 178
Accuracy, guaranteeing, of new
　calibrator lot, 2-sample procedure,
　　292-293
　assumptions, 292
　sampling stages 1 and 2, 293
Additivity, 271, 272, 281
Aggregation, 172
　"above," notion of, 193-195
　after nomination, 194, 197-198, *198*
　analysis, opening, 193
　definition, 195
　effect of, 193-196
　in example, 196-199
　Interpretation One, 194, 195
　Interpretation Two, 195, 199
　overall picture, 198-199
　procedure, 195-196
　results, 198-199, *198*
　rules for, 195-196
Agricultural cash crops, 35
　calf production, 35-38
　cows, health of, 35-38
　vaccination for virus, 35-38
Algorithm(s)
　forward selection, hierarchical
　　clustering, 17, 19-32

　in regression, 17
　variable selection, 15-18
Alphabet soup adage, 266
Analyses, linear model
　main-effects-only models, 305
　weighted-squares-of-means, 305
Analysis
　refactoring, 172
　resistant row-plus-column, 240
　subset, 321
Analysis considerations, farther (the
　　Berenblut alternative), 344-350
　ANOVA for subset of 8 patients, 350
　expected mean squares, 349
Analysis of variance (ANOVA), 62, 71, 75,
　　76, 77, 87, 88, 171-172, 232, 243, 277,
　　279, 280, 281, 284, 308
　after aggregation, 197
　aggregated, 176, 177, 196, 197
　anglit scale, 284
　classical, 172
　columns, 306
　decomposition, 172
　described in terms of a model, 308
　error-variance, 252
　extended, 254, 257
　factorial, ingredients for, 172

365

Analysis of variance (*Continued*)
  Fisher's letter, 308
  for food intake, 339, 345
  F-tests, 311-312
  nonstandard, 104-106
  no really useful table, 319
  parallel column table, 228
  post-nomination, 193, 194
  of row linear structure, 250-252
  rows, 306
  for six-sequence design, 333, 340
  standard, 176-177
  table (Fisher's letter), 308
  two-way, 74, 75
Anderson, V. L., 262
Anglits, 281
  scale, 281-285, *283*
Approximations, percent point values, 202
  estimated error, 202
Arithmetic, 172
  graphic display and, 171
Arrhenius relationship, 137
Assumptions, strong, 120
Asymmetry, 98
  quasi-symmetry, 98, 100
Automobile example, variable selection, 18, 19-32, *23-26, 28-29, 31-32*
  Opel-Chevette anomaly, 23-24

Balance, experiment design, 47
Balanced data, 306, 307-312
  ANOVA, 307-308
  ANOVA F-tests, 311-312
  estimable functions, 309-310
  estimation, 309
  models, 308-309
  reparameterization, 310-311
Bartlett, M. S., 267, 270, 272
Bates, D. M., 135
  multiresponse data analysis, 135, 136, 137
Bemesderfer, John L.
  Explaining Experimental Design Fundamentals to Engineers: A Modern Approach (coauthor), 41-69
Benchmarks, analytical determination, 17
Berenblut alternative, 331
Berenblut, I. I., 331
Berger, L., 107
Bernoulli
  observations, 276
  random variables, 287
  responses, 285
  stratifications, 276
  variables, 285-287
Bernoulli data, analysis, from a 2^5 design done in blocks of size four, 275-288
  data analysis, percents responding "yes," 277-280
  data analysis, second, on anglit scale, 281-285
  discussion, 287-288
  introduction and summary, 275
  intra-block and inter-block estimation, Bernoulli variables, 285-287
Berra, Yogi, 45
Berson, S. A., 294
Bezzel, E., 113
Bhapkar, V. P., 272
Biological data sets, design, modelling, and analysis, 93-126
  abstract, 94
  crowding data, 107-109
  desperado designs, 120-123
  factorials, scale-split, 123-126
  grooming rates of monkeys, 104-106
  introduction, 95
  marriage data, 95-100
  mice, home ranges, 115-120
  migrating birds, resting periods, 109-115
  personal preface and dedication, 93-94
  sucking rates, young fallow deer, 101-104
Birds, migrating, distribution example, 109-115
  analysis, recapture data, 113-115
  quantitative assessment, migration, 109-110
  true and observed distribution of resting periods, 111-112
Bishop, T. A., 292
Bishop, Y. M. M., 98, 265
Blackwell, David, 93
Blankenhorn, H., 107, 108
Block designs
  randomized complete and incomplete, 48, 49
Blocking designs, 68
Blocking designs and full factorial plans, 47, 48-51
  evaluating process variables, 50
  major points, 48
Blocks, balanced incomplete, 305
BLUE (best linear unbiased estimator),

INDEX 367

310, 311, 312, 313, 315, 316, 317, 318, 319, 320, 321, 328, 329
Borrowing strength, 100
Bouquet(s)
of contrasts, 214-217, 232, 242. *See also* Contrasts
general inflation in, 212
high levels, 234
nominated, 172, 188, 234
nominated-plus-elected, 230
post-trimmed, 213
pretrimmed, 211
pretrimmed: nomination, 184, 185, *186*
seven-contrast, 188, 212, 213
single-contrast, 185
six-contrast, 188
size reduced, 193
spreading, systematic relationship, 234
trimmed, 184, 188-189, 191
trimmed rate, 212
Bouquets, data-guided trimming, 199-207
election (post-trimming) in example, 204-206
final outcomes, first 56 numbers, 206-207
null behavior of ratio-to-scale, 200-202
post-trimmed bouquets; election, 203-204
scales and ratios-to-scale, 199-200
Box-Behnken design, 167, *168*
Box-Behnken response surface plans, 68
Box-Cox transformation, 245, 246, 259
Box, George E. P., 45, 52, 59, 135, 262
Analysis of Unreplicated Factorials, Allowing for Possibly Faulty Observations, (coauthor), 1-11
random balance, 123
Brownlee, K. A., 225
Industrial Experimentation, 225
splitting, advantages of, 225

Cady, F. B., 326
Calf production, experiments to improve, 35-38
industrial conclusion, 38
Calibrator lots
consistent accuracy, 291-292
master lots, 291, 292
2-sample tests, 292
Campbell, N. A., 16
discriminant analysis, 15
Caveat emptor, 261
CCK-8, administration of, 331-332

percent reduction of food intake, 344, 349
Cell means
linear combinations, 305, 320
models, extensions, 305
Cell means models, 316-326, 327-328
ANOVA, 319-320
data gatherer, 326
difficulties, 324-326
estimation, 317-318
hypotheses of interest, 320-321
hypothesis testing, 318-319
models with interaction, 321-324
subset analyses, 321
Cells, pattern of filled, 320
Chambers, J. M., 19
variable selection, 19
Cleveland, W. S., 19
variable selection, 19
Client, 322. *See also* Data gatherer; Experimenter
Cluster(s), 240
analysis, 16, 33
five, 27
hierarchical trees, 25, *28*
nine-variable, 25-26
outliers, *29*, 30
separation plots, 17, *18*, 23-25
structure, 16, 32
Clustering
complete linkage method, 19
hierarchical, 19
Clustering, variable selection in, 13-33
abstract, 13
algorithms, variable selection, 15-18
conclusion, 33
example, three variable selection contexts, 19-32
introduction, 13-14
Cochran, W. G., 272
Cole-Cole plots, 129, 130
Collaborative experiments, 89-91. *See also* Interlaboratory studies
Collings, Bruce J.
Reusing Published Examples: A Case of Caveat Emptor (coauthor), 261-273
Column
averages, 255
linearity, 259
variables, 256, 257
Comparison(s)
of contrasts, 180
internal, 178, 180

Comparison(s) (*Continued*)
  linear, 183
  of material types, 49
  valid, provided by experiment, 46
Complex plane dielectric plot, *131*, 136, 138
Complex plane plots, 129, 130
  parameter choices, 133, *133*, 134
  for polycarbonate, 130, *131*
  for syndiotactic PMMA, 130, *132*
Computer programs, experiment design, 68
Concurrence, 254, 255, 259
Conditionality, 315
Confidence interval, 47
Connectedness, 314
Contingency tables, square, 265
Contrast(s), 176, 177,178, 203, 214-217.
  See also Bouquets
  display ratios, 179, 180, 182
  double-ended, 216, 217, 218
  election, 204, 213, 223
  EPO's, 216, 221, 242
  FPO's, 216, 217, 221
  Helmert, 214, 217, 218, 228, 242
  largest, 190
  linear, 183, 184, 208, 214, 220, 221, 242
  linear-by-linear, 184
  linear-by-linear-by-linear, 184
  LPO's, 214-215, 216, 217, 221
  nominated, 184, 185-187, 212, 213
  one-factor, 178
  ordering, 238
  orthogonal, 214, 220
  polynomial, 180, *181*, 182, 185, *186*, 233
  quadratic, 220
  ratios-to-scale, 212, 213
  scission of rate, 233
  SEPO's, 217
  sizes of, 221, 222
  super-elected, 204
  systematic relationship, 213-214
  three-factor, 183, 192
  working values, 187
Contributions, spreading across contrasts, 213-214
Cook County (Chicago), Illinois, jury selection process, 358-359
Cox, D. R., 123
C_p plot, 29, *31*
  subset regressions, 29, *29*, 30, *31*
Crowding data: 4x3 with diagonal and Winsorized variances, 107-109

  analysis, 108-109
  background and data, 107-108
  testing interactions, 109

Daniel, Cuthbert, 8, 10, 44, 45, 55, 93-94, 95, 172, 214, 215
  data on setting of Portland cement, 267
  FPO's, 215
  Free-Wilson model, 39
  half-normal plot modifications and enhancements, 242-243
  half-normal plots, 68, 171, 178, 232
  LPO's, 214-215
  normal plot analysis, 1, 4, 38
  observations, possible faulty, 3-4
  variable selection for multiple regression analysis, 14
Data
  anticipation of revision, 172
  balanced, 305
  description of behavior, 171
  gaps in, 110
  hazards, analysis of unplanned, 69
  intelligent reuse, 261
  internal structure, 247, 248-250, 254-255
  marriage: several layers, 95-100
  planned unbalance, 305
  sets, 261
  some-cells-empty, 317
  subsets, 322, 323, 324, 326
Data analysis, 53, 93, 95
  applied to percents responding "yes" to the 32 vignettes, 277-280, *279*
  five significant effects, 277
  improvisation, 95
  multivariate observations, 13-14
  no faulty observations, 7, 8
  possibility of faulty observations, 8-10
  posterior probabilities, 8-10, *8-10*
  second, on anglit scale, 281-285
  variables, 13, 14
Data gatherer, 305, 317, 326. *See also*
  Client; Experimenter
Data, qualitative
  weighting, 35-39
Data sets, 261, 265-266
  equality not always desirable, 265-266
Decomposition
  orthogonal, 220, 222
  polynomial, 220
Deer, sucking rates of young: statistical and social interactions, 101-104

analysis, 101-104
  data background, 101
  least squares, 101, 103
  median polishing, 103
Delineating, 240
  against single splits, 240
Deming, W. Edwards, 42, 48
Dendrogram, 25, *28*
Derringer, G. C., 245, 246, 257
  analysis, alternative to, 245, 246-248
  mathematical model, 246
  technique, empirical fit of viscosity measurements of filled and plasticized elastomer compounds, 245
Design(s), 42, 93, 95. *See also* Experiment(s); Experimental design fundamentals, explaining to engineers
  blocking, 46
  complete factorial, 121
  first order, 126
  second order, 126
  supersaturated, 120-123
Desperado designs: the utmost in supersaturated designs, 120-123
  aspects, supersaturated designs, 121-123
  construction, 120
  introduction, 120-121
  research questions, 122
Dielectric constants, analytical representation of, 129-157
  abstract, 129
  analysis, polycarbonate and s-PMMA, 137-138
  appendixes, 155-157
  data sets, 155
  discussion, 148
  gradient of the Havriliak-Negami function, 156-157
  introduction, 130-135
  multiresponse estimation, 135-137
  s-PMMA, 138-148
Dielectric measuring equipment
  inaccuracies, 138
  nonlinearities, 145
Difference limen (D.L.), 174, 175, *175*, 208, 209
  relationship to rate, 175, 176, 182
Dimensionality, reduction of, 13-14, 33
Discriminant analysis, 13, 14, 26, 30, 33
  Q_{p-p} plot, 30, 32

Discrimination problems
  multi-group, 15, 16
  two-group, 15
Discussions, value of, 45
  with experimenter, 52
Display ratios, 179-180, 199, 211, 212, 213, *219*, 221, 222, 228, *229*, 230
  after trimming, 191
  decline in value, 193
  estimating residual variability, 199
  example, 180-183
  Helmert SFP bouquet, 223
  increases in value, 185, 187
  nominated contrasts, 187, 188, 196-197
  polynomial contrasts, 180, *181*
  scale, 213, 214
  typical size, changing, 189-190
  values, 182
Distance vision data, 265-266
  Association of Optical Practitioners, 266
  for men, 265-266
  for women, 265-266
Distribution, 89-90, *90*
  Gaussian cumulative, 179
  half-Gaussian, 178, 179, 184, 200
  of mice, 115-120
  modelling connection between observed and actual, 109-115
  resting periods, bird migrations, 110
  triangular, 111
Dragging upward, 183, 189, 190-191, 200
  denominators, 191
  in initial plot, 192
  undragging, 192, *192*
Draper, N. R., 1, 55, 59, 135, 245
  multiple regression analysis, 15
Dudewicz, E. J., 292

Effect sparsity, hypothesis of, 4
  model, 4-6
Efficiencies (efficiency), 122, 123, 125, 126
  loss of, 123
Election, 233
  behavior of data, 232, 243
Election, post-trimmed bouquets, 203
  in the example, 204-206, 205
Engineers, course on experimental design fundamentals, 41-69
Error(s), 180
  estimates, 177
  isolated, 177
Estimable functions, 311, 312

370 INDEX

Estimation, 309, 310
  BLUE, 310
  multiresponse, 129, 135-137
Estimator, 321. *See also* BLUE (best linear unbiased estimator)
Evolutionary operation (EVOP), 46, 57-60, 61, 69
  characteristics, 59-60
  example, 59
  response surface experiments and, 57-60
  simplex and factorial, 60
  test plan results, *61*
  tinkering, 60
Exceedance probabilities, 90, *90*, 91
Exotic values, 171, 180
  after aggregation, 199
Expectations, 77, 90, 99, 100, 112
Experiment(s). *See also* Design(s)
  best design, statistically, 73
  broad-based, 47
  calling in an expert, 42
  CCK-8 used to reduce food intake in man, 331-332
  comparative, 46
  design, 42. *See also* Design listings
  factorial, 61
  foundations for, 46-47
  initial pilot runs, 65
  interlaboratory or collaborative, 71, 73, 86-88, 91
  materials for future runs, 65
  nested, 61
  predicting results, 65
  redesign, 58
  scope, 64
  variables, 64
Experimental design, 42, 47
  Latin Squares, 163-169
Experimental design fundamentals, explaining to engineers, 41-69
  abstract, 41
  basic philosophy, 44-45
  concluding remarks, 68-69
  examples, 45, 46, 47
  graphical techniques, 45
  introduction and setting, 42-44
  major purposes, 42
  moderator, 43, 69
  on-site interests and applications, 69
  overview, 63-67
  principle of KISS, 44

quality problems, 43
time factors, 68
topics, 46
what we selected and why, 46-68
Experimental plans, 41, 42, 64, 65, 66-67
  concepts, 47, 52
  fractional factorial, 51-53
  practical considerations, 52
Experimentation
  physical evaluation, 63
  response surface, 46
  sequential, 47
Experimenter, 317, 319, 320, 325. *See also* Client; Data gatherer
Extensions, 327-329
  mixed models, 328-329
  models without interactions, 327-328
  more than two factors, 327
Extrapolations, bird migration, 110

Fables, in pediatrician's study, 275-276, 280, 287, 288
Factorial
  designs, 121
  splitting, 123
  3^3, 163, *164*, 165, 167, 168
Factorial data, 243
  graphical views, 242
Factorial plans
  fractional, 46, 51-53
  full, 46, 47, 48-51
Factorials, analysis
  conclusion, 10
  introduction, 1-4
  more formal solution, 4-10
  sub-factorial, 240
Factorials, analysis of unreplicated, 1-11
  effect sparsity hypothesis, model 4-6
  example, 1-4
  observations, possibility of faulty, 6-11
Factorials, scale-split: measuring curvature in response surface exploration, 123-126
  reconsideration of published example, 123
  scale-splitting 2^3, 124-126
  some additional remarks, 126
Factors, 314-315
  more than two, 327
  ordered and unordered, 178
  proxies for other factors, 314
  testing, 120

Farmers, 35, 38
  health of cows, 35
Federal Jury Service and Selection Act
    (1968), 353, 354, 355, 363
  four key provisions, 354
  interpretation of "random selection,"
    357
  voter list provisions, 356
Federov, V. D., 123
Ferritin. *See also* Serum ferritin
  calibration curves, 294
  radio-iodinated, 294
  RIA method, 294
  tests, 293, 294
Ferritin 5 and 10 standards, 294, 298,
    299-301
  pooled variance estimators, 298, 301
  t-statistics, 301
Ferritin radioimmunoassay calibrator
    example, 293-303
  choosing n_0, 301-303
  ferritin standards, 294-301
  ferritin test, 293
  RIA method, 294
Ferritin 2-standard, 294-297, 299, 300
  errors, 299
  stage 2 data, 296-297
  Student-t distribution, 295, 299
Fienberg, S. E., 265
Fisher exact test for independence, two-
    tailed, 262
Fisher, R. A.
  analysis of variance (ANOVA), 307
  letter to Snedecor (1934), 308
Fitting
  iterative proportional, 98
  statistical technique, 245
  structural parameters to row and
    column variables, 256
Fowlkes, Edward B.
  algorithms, 17
  clustering, 16
  *Variable Selection in Clustering and Other
    Contexts* (coauthor), 13-33
Fractional factorial(s), 121, 123
  applications, 51
  concepts and practical considerations,
    52
  mixed, 52
  plans, 51-53
  two-level plans, 51
Free, Spencer M.
  Weighting Qualitative Data, 35-39

Free-Wilson model, 39
F-statistics, 308, 311, 312, 319
F-tests, 314, 315
  mean squares and, 254

Gaussian random noise with
    homogeneous variability, 198
Gauss-Newton minimization techniques,
    156
General Electric Company
  Corporate Engineering and
    Manufacturing, 42
  Quality Leadership Curriculum, 42
Gnanadesikan, Ramanathan
  clustering, 16
  *Variable Selection in Clustering and Other
    Concepts* (coauthor),13-33
Gometz, Randy, 353, 360
Goodman, L. A., 97, 98, 265
  1983 Rietz Memorial Lecture, 265
Gordon Conference on Statistics, 39
Granularity, 180, 183, 212
Graphical analysis, 4, 10, 53, 65, 137, 138,
    148
  of data, 41
  estimating variability, 62
  EVOP application, 60
Graphical exploratory analysis of
    variance
  better matching, 239-240
  the other seven people, 234-241
  people will be different, 226, 233, 237,
    239
  summary, 242-243
Graphical methods, 43, 45, 46, 47, 53
Graphical views, calculations from
    factorial data, 242
Graphic display, 172, 173
  arithmetic and, 171
Green, B. F., 175, 209
  aggregation, 195
Guttman, I., 314

Hahn, Gerald J.
  *Explaining Experimental Design
    Fundamentals to Engineers: A Modern
    Approach* (coauthor), 41-69
Half-normal plot(s), 171, 172, 178, 283,
    288
  absolute effects, 279
  on anglit scale, 283
  display ratios, 232
  modifications and enhancements, 232

372   INDEX

Hamaker, Hugo C.
  Repeatability and Reproducibility: Some Problems in Applied Statistics, 71-91
Hampel, Frank R.
  Design, Modelling, and Analysis of Some Biological Data Sets, 93-126
Hand, D. J.
  discriminant analysis, 15
Hartigan, J. A.
  clustering, 16
Havriliak-Negami expression, 133, *133*, 134, 135
Havriliak, Stephen Jr., 133
  Analytical Representation of Dielectric Constants: A Complex Multiresponse Problem (coauthor), 129-157
Healy, W. C., 292
Helmert
  SFP bouquet, 228, *231*
  SFP scission of rate, 233
Helmert contrasts
  double-ended, 217, 218, 223
  nomination and, 223
  SFP, 214, 222, 223, 228
  SLP, 214
Hoblyn, T. N., 267, 269, 270
  plum root stock data, 267-272
Hochberg, Y., 292
Hodges, J. L., 291, 301
Holland, P. W., 265
Horizontalized plots, 172, 178-179, 200, 205, 211, 224, 232, 242
  display ratios, 179
Hovik, Mary B.
  Indirect Measurement of Work (coauthor), 159-162
Huber, P. J., 109
Hunter, J. Stuart, 45, 52, 262
  Are Some Latin Squares Better Than Others?, 163-169
  "Partially Replicated Latin Squares," 165
  pioneering videotaped course, Westinghouse, 43-44
Hunter, W. G., 45, 52, 262
Hypotheses
  automatic, 320
  tests, 320

Immunoassay
  kit vendors, 291
  master lot, 291, 292
  precision factors, 292

Independence, 96-100
  deviations from, 96, 98
  quasi-independence, 98, 99, 100
Insight, long-term, 172
Interblock
  comparisons, 277, 279, 280
  estimates of error, 281, 284
  variance, 283, 287
Interlaboratory studies
  purpose, 89-91
  standards, 86-88
International standards
  ISO 4259, 75, 86-88, 91
  ISO 5725, 86-88, 91
Intra-block
  comparison, 277, 279, 280
  estimates of error, 281, 284
  variation, 283, 287
Intra-block estimation
  why so little superior to inter-block, with Bernoulli variables, 285-287
Iron, monitoring levels, 293

Jackknife
  multihalving, 201
Japan, 42
Johnson, Eugene G.
  Graphical Exploratory Analysis of Variance Illustrated On a Splitting of the Johnson and Tsao Data (coauthor), 171-243
Johnson, Palmer O., 175, 240
  data refactored, 226
  methodological experiment, 171
Jury selection, 353-363
  key man system, 354
  non-respondents, 358-359
  numerical level of response, 361
  at random, 354, 355-358

Kalven, Harry, 357
Kettenring, Jon R.
  clustering, 16
  Variable Selection in Clustering and Other Contexts, 13-33
Kinderman, A. J.
  random normal generator, 201
Kissileff, Harry R.
  Six-Sequence Carry-Over Design for the Determination of the Effect of a Drug in Reducing Food Intake (coauthor), 331-351
KISS principle, 44-45

Kleiner, B., 19
  variable selection, 19
Koch, G. G., 272
Koehler, K. J., 299
Krishnaiah, P. R., 259
Kummer, H., 104, 106
Kutner, M. H., 55

Laboratory variations, 71, 72
  repeatability, 72
  reproducibility, 72
  standard deviations for, 72
Latin Squares, 48, 49, 163-169, *164*
  augmented design, 167, 168, *168*
  investigating unknown response, 163, 164, 166-169
  main effect clear design, 167
  plan for comparison of materials, 49
  some better than others? 163-169
  3^3 factorial design, 163, *164*, 165
  Type A, 163, 164, 165, 167, 168
  Type B, 163, 164, 165, 167, 168
Likelihood ratio test (LRT), 269-270, 271
Linear
  contrast, 242
  hypothesis, testing, 318-319
  model analyses, 305
Linear models for some-cells-empty data: the cell means formulation, a consultant's best friend, 305-329
  abstract, 305
  balanced data, 307-312
  cell means models, 316-326
  extensions, 327-329
  introduction, 306-307
  unbalanced data, 312-316
Lines of an analysis, 242, 243
Log-response rate effect
  alternative descriptions, 217-228
  results for various bouquets, 220-223
Log (response time), 209, *210*, 211-213, *219*
  comparison of analyses, 212
  first analysis, 211-213
  general levels, 212-213
  plot, average values by rate for each date, 220, *221*, *222*

McCabe, G. P.
  ordering, multi-group discrimination problem, 16
McKay, R. J., 16
  discriminant analysis, 15

McLaughlin, D. H., 109
McLean, R. A., 262
Main effects, 120
Main-effects-only models, 313, 321, 325.
  See also Models without interactions
Mallows, Colin L.
  C_p plot, 15
Mandel, John, 91
  Analysis of a Two-Way Table, 245-259
Mansfield, M. L., 134
Margolin, Barry H.
  Reusing Published Examples: A Case of Caveat Emptor (coauthor), 261-273
Marriage data, 95-100
  data and design structure, 95-96
  first coarse analysis, 96
  religion of spouse, 95-100
  sizes of diagonal elements, 99-100
  structure of off-diagonal elements, 96-99
Mean effects, 122
Mean squares
  expected, 333, 339
  F-tests and, 254
  pooled, 254
Measurement of work, indirect, 159-162
  comments, 162
  data, 159-160
  methods, 160-162
  productivity, 161, 162
Meier, Erwin, 101, 103
Meredith, M. P., 326
  quote from personal communication, 314
Meyer, R. Daniel
  Analysis of Unreplicated Factorials, Allowing for Possibly Faulty Observations, (coauthor), 1-11
Mice, home ranges of: traps of systematic errors, 115-120
  African mouse, 119-120
  altitudinal distribution of rodents, 115-118
  estimation of home range, 119-120
  various statistical methods used, 116-118
Mixed models, 328-329
  fixed and random effects, 328
Model(s), 54-56, 57
  alternative, 55
  evaluating, 55
  fitting to data, 55
  possible inadequacies, 4

374 INDEX

Model(s) (*Continued*)
  selecting, 54-55
  statistical, 69
  variability, 56
  without interactions, 313-315
Modelling, 93, 95
Models with interactions, 315-316
  empty cells, 316
Monahan, J. F.
  random normal generator, 201
Monkeys, grooming rates: a
    nonstandard analysis of variance
    with incomplete triangular data,
    104-106
  design and model, 104-105
  main effects model, 105, 106
  results, 105-106
Monro, Sutton
  Indirect Measurement of Work
    (coauthor), 159-162
Mooney viscosity, 247, 252
Moses, Lincoln E.
  *Analysis of Bernoulli Data From a 2^5
    Design Done in Blocks of Size Four*,
    275-288
Müller, Jürg Paul, 115, 118, 119, 120
Multiple linear regression, 160, 161
  disadvantages, work measurement,
    160-161
Multiple regression, 33
  models, 54-56
  quantifying relationships, 53-57
  Session 4, 68
  turbine wheel example, 53-54
Multiple regression analysis, 13, 14
  variable selection, 14, 15
Multiplicity, 223
  elected contrasts and, 204
Multiresponse data, analysis, 135
  estimation, 135-137
  Gauss-Newton procedure, 135
Multiresponse estimation 129, 135-137
  program, 137

Negami, S., 129, 133, 134
  graphical analyses, 137
Neter, J., 55
New York State jury, women volunteers,
    359
Noise, 1, 3, 16, 234
  background, 214
  measuring, 212
  random Gaussian, 198

Nominating
  in advance, 243
Nomination, 190, 191, 232, 233, 234
  linear contrasts, 223
Nonadditivities, 104
Non-concurrence, 254
Nonlinearities, 145
  within a decade, 145
Normal plot, 1, 3, *3*
  faulty observations, pattern, 1
  primary objective, 1

Observations
  grouping, clustering, 13
  testing factors and, 120
Observations, faulty, 1, 6-7
  no possibility of, 7, *8*
  possibility of, 3, 8-10
Oddness, looking for, 262-265
  alphabet soup adage, 266
  injection molding experiment, 262,
    263, 264
  metallurgical experiment and
    smoothness response, 262
  odd-even pattern of data, 262
Olsson, Donald M.
  *Explaining Experimental Design
    Fundamentals to Engineers: A Modern
    Approach* (coauthor), 41-69
On-line experiments, 69
On-line process improvement, using
    EVOP, 59-60
  characteristics, 59-60
  limitations, 59
Operational protocol, 57
  documentation, 65
Order statistics, 178, 179
Ornithologists, 110
Orthogonal contrasts, 187, 194
Orthogonal decomposition, 220, 222
Orthogonal polynomials, 178, 187, 194,
    211
  contrasts, 207
Outliers, 50, 56, 71, 85, 138, 145
  Dixon's test, 85
  Grubb's test, 85
Overparameterization, 309
  difficulties, multiple factors, 327
Overparameterized model, 317

Palmer, R. C., 267, 269, 270
  plum root stock data, 267-272
Pareto Chart, 62

INDEX 375

Parsimony, 55
Pearson X^2, 269, 271
Percent points
  approximations, 202
  $d = 2$ is special, 202
  half-samples, 202
Periodicity, 138, 145
Person IB1, 171-234, 242-243
  analysis of response in log seconds, 233-234
  analyzing performance in grams, 174-199
  analyzing performance in other terms, 208-213
  classical ANOVA, 228
  date-by-weight slope, 227, *227*
  deviation in response, 237
  D.L. in grams, *175, 181, 186, 189, 192, 198, 205, 210, 219, 221, 224, 227, 229, 231*
  log response time, first analysis, 211-213
  partial summary of responses, 206-207
  polynomial contrasts, pretrimmed bouquets, 185, *186*, 205
  recapitulation 230, 232-234
  reformulating the response, 208-209
  responses, 174, 175, *175*
  splitting on date, 227, 233
  weight slope, 227
Person IB2, 234, *235-236*, 237, *237*, *238*
  deviation in response, 237
  nominated bouquets, 238
Person IIA2, 234, *235-236*, 237, *237*
  deviation in response, 237
  nominated bouquets, 238
Pfanzagl, J., 95
Pfister, H., 120
Pillai, K. C. S.
  trace statistic, 17
Planning
  experiments, 43
  statistical, 44
Plans, nested (hierarchal), 46, 60
  estimating sources, 60-62
  partially, 61
Plots, partial residual, 55-56
Plum root stock experiment, Kent, England, 267-272
  additivity, 271, 272
  independence, 271
  survival factors, 271
  test results, 269-270

Poisson point process, 111, 112, 113, 115
Polycarbonate
  analysis, 137-138, *139-144*
  residuals, 138, *139-143*
  scaled determinants, 137
  summary statistics, 136
Polymer chain rotation, 134
Polymers, 129
  analysis of dielectric coefficients, 148
  structure-property relationships, 130
Polynomial contrasts, 180, *181*, 182
  post-trimmed bouquets, 205
Polynomial decomposition, of rate main effect, 220
Pooling, 254
Posner, Judge Richard A., 353
  letter to, 354-363
Posterior probabilities, 8-10, *8-10*
Post-trimmed bouquets; election, 203-204
  elected contrasts, 204
  election process, 203
  threshold values, 203
Post-trimming, 188, 191
  a bouquet, 187
  by election, 172
Precision
  lack of, 91
  sample size and, 47
Precision measures, 71, 72
  repeatability, 71
  reproducibility, 71
Pretrimming, 187
  by nomination, 172
Probabilities (probability), 89
  exceedance, 90, *90*, 91
Process, tinkering, 60
Process data, 59
  interfering with, 59
Protocol, 65
Psychological literature, responses to studies, 288
Published examples, reusing, 261-273
  data sets, equality not always desirable, 265-266
  introduction, 261
  oddness, looking for, 262-265
  simplification in the service of pedagogy, 267-272

Qualitative data, weighting, 35-39
Quality improvement, 41, 42, 43
  off-line quality control, 43
  statistics, 42

376 INDEX

Quality improvement (*Continued*)
  training in modern methods, 42
  variability and, 60

Radioimmunoassay (RIA), 293, 294
  competitive binding, 294
  ferritin measurement, 294
Random balance designs, 123
Randomization, 47, 48, 50, 52, 64-65
  comparison of material types, 49
  variables, 65
Random number generator, 201
Random selection, 355-358
  and optimal representation, 361
  size of a sample, 362
Random variates, half-Gaussian, 201
Random variation, concept of, 46
Rao, C. R., 314
Rate effect, 220, 221, 222
  main, 220, 225
  scission of, 223, 224
  scission into contrasts, 233
Ratios-to-scale, 199, 200, 212, 213
Ratio-to-scale null behavior, 200-202
  approximations, 202
  $d = 2$ is special, 202
  simulation details, 200-201
  simulation error, 201-202
Ray, A. A., 137
Recapitulation, Person IB1
  data, 232-234
Re-expression, 243
  of factors, 225
  of response, 225
Refactoring, 225-232, 242, 243
  illustrations, 232
  instances of, 226, 227
  pattern of analysis, 225, 233
  splitting, 225-226
  splitting on date in the example, 227-228
  splitting into persons, 226
  super-election in split example, 228-231
  tacit refactoring, 226-227
  two further illustrations, 232
Reference value, 193
Reformulation, 243
  of response, 225, 233
Regression, 26, 33, 71
  curve, 71, 85
  equation, 82, 83
  least squares, 81

linear, 82, 84
  problem, 80-85, *80, 81, 84*
  weighted, 83
Regression analysis, 32
  of historical data, 56
  of interlaboratory problem, 78
Rejecting data, 108
Relationships, quantifying using multiple regression, 46
Reparameterization, 309, 310-311
  Σ restrictions, 310, 311, 312
Repeatability, 65, 71, 72, 89, 91
  conditions, 73
Repeatability and reproducibility, 71-91
  example, 74-78
  interlaboratory or collaborative experiments, 73
  introduction, 72-73
  outliers, 85
  purpose of interlaboratory studies, 89-91
  regression problem, 80-85
  second example, 78-79
  summary, 71-72
  two international standards, 86-88
Repeat runs, 50, 52, 65
Replication, 47
Reproducibility, 71, 72, 89, 91
  definition, 75
  variance, 76, 78
Rescission, 223, 243
  contrasts and, 225
  example after, 223-225
Residual analysis, 341
  six-sequence model, 334, 342-343, 346
  studentized residuals, 339, *344, 348*
Residuals, 138, *139-143*, 145
  frequency dependence, 138
  two-way table, 240
  typical size, changing, 189-190
Response
  log response time, 234
  reformulating, 172
Response, reformulating IB1's, 208-209
  reexpressing, 209-210, 233
Response surface experimentation
  and EVOP, 57-60
  example, machine tool optimization, 57-59
  plan, 57-58
  plot data, 58
  use of model, 57-58
  variables, 57

Response surface models, first- and
    second-order, 69
Response time, 209
    rate and, 209
Response variable, 208
    approximately homogeneous, 208
    D.L., 209
Richardson, W. J., 159
    *Cost Improvement, Work Sampling, and
    Short Interval Scheduling*, 159
Robustness, 123
Row linearity, 249, 250, 257, 259
    ANOVA, 250-252

Scale-splitting the 2^3, 124-126
    curvature in, 126
    second-order designs, 126
Scales and ratios-to-scale, 199-200
Scanning response surface, 52
Scatter plots, variable selection contexts, 24, 26
Scheffé, Henry, 93, 329
Schlain, Brian R.
    *A 2-Stage Procedure for Guaranteeing
    Accuracy with Calibration Standards*,
    291-303
Scission, 232
    into bouquets of contrasts, 172
    of lines of ANOVA, 242
    of rate, 223, 228, 231
    rethinking, 172
Scission, rethinking into contrasts, 213-234
    alternative descriptions, log response
    rate effect, 217-220
    example after recission, 223-225
    recapitulation, 232-234
    refactoring, 225-232
    spreading of contributions across
    contrasts, 213-214
    useful bouquets of contrasts, 214-217
Searle, Shayle R.
    *Linear Models for Some-Cells-Empty Data:
    The Cell Means Formulation, A
    Consultant's Best Friend*, 305-329
Seber, G. A. F.
    discriminant analysis, 15
Seheult, A., 243
Selection, variable
    clustering and other contexts, 13-33
    forward process, 19, 23, 24, 25
Serendipity, accidental, 243
Serum ferritin. *See also* Ferritin
    determination, 293
    measurement through RIA, 293, 294
Seven people, the other, 234-241
    all 16 person-date units, 234-238, 235-236
    better matching, 239-240
    reassembly, 239-241
    single splits, delineations against, 240-242
    splitting, 239
Shortdth, 121
Simplification in the service of
    pedagogy, 267-272
    source documents, review, 267
Simulation, 17, 200-202
    error, 201-202
    percent points, 201-202
Single-degree-of-freedom
    components, 176-177, 178
    contrasts, 176, 177
    error estimates, 177
Six-sequence carry-over design for the
    determination of the effect of a drug
    in reducing food intake, 331-351
    design comments, 351
    discussion, 351
    experiment, 331-332
    further analysis considerations
    (Berenblut alternative), 344-350
    statistical analysis of the experiment, 332-344
Smith, Harry, 55, 245
    multiple regression analysis, 15
    *Six-Sequence Carry-Over Design for the
    Determination of the Effect of a Drug in
    Reducing Food Intake* (coauthor), 331-351
Snedecor, George W., 272, 308
Snee, R., 62
Snell, E. J., 123
Social interactions, analysis of, 103-104, 106
Some-cells-empty data, 322
Source documents, desirability of review, 267
    example, setting of Portland cement, 267
    plum root stock data, 267-272
Speed, F. M., 311
    cell means models, 316
Spjøtvoll, E.
    alternatives, multiple regression
    plotting, 15

Spjøtvoll, E. (*Continued*)
  multiple regression plotting, 15-16
Splitters, 197
Splitting, 242
  advantages of, 225
  disappearance of, 226
  into persons, 226
  over date, 259
  proper reason for, 225
  results, into 16 pieces, 241
s-PMMA
  analysis, 138, 145, *146-147*, 148
  decade factor, 145, 148
  dial nonuniformity, 148
  function by frequency, *149-150*
  graphical analysis, 148
  natural log radian frequency, 138, *146-147*
  residuals, 148, *149, 150, 151*
  summary statistics, 145
  values, 148, *152-153*
Spreading, 234, 237, *237, 238*
Stammboch, E., 106
Standard Methods for Testing Tar and Its Products, 91
Standards
  for products and materials, 72
  tests, precision of, 72
Standards, international
  ISO 5725 and ISO 4259, 86-88, 91
Statistical analysis, CCK-8 experiment, 332-344
  assumptions, 333, 335
  estimation of effects, 351
  F tests, 334
  mathematical design, 332-333
  percent reduction, food intake, 344-349
  SAS PROC GLM procedure, 333, 334
  SAS PROC REG procedure, 333, 334
  six-sequence design, 332
Statistical consultants, 317
Statistical data analysis, 93, 95
  variables, 13, 14
Statistician, 305, 320, 326
  reuse of others' published papers, 261
  working with client, 322, 325
Statistics
  applied: repeatability and reproducibility, 71-91
  discriminant analysis and, 17
  gap between applied and theoretical, 91
  new quality philosophy, 42

Statistics in a court of law, 353-363
  argument, 354-355
  conclusion, 362-363
  does non-response create bias? 358-359
  filling a gap, 360-361
  "good" and "not so good" jurors, 359-360
  meaning of "at random," 355-358
  misunderstanding, 362
  reason for strengthening random selection, 361-362
Stein, C., 291, 292, 295, 302
Stewart, I., 314
Stochastic model, 110, 115
Stuart, A., 265
  data, distance vision of women, 265
Subsets, 322, 323, 326
  two difficulties, 324-326
Super-election, 232
  in split example, 228-231, *229*
Symmetry, 217, 277, 279
  SEPO contrasts, 217, 221
Systematic relationship
  rate and response, 233
  spreading, 234, 237, *237*

Taguchi, Genichi, 42
  concepts, 46
  concepts of parameter design, 62
  fractional factorial experiments, 63
  multivariable experimental design, 62-63
  parameter design, 68
Tambane, A. C., 292
Techniques
  good, from many ideas, 172
  twelve ingredients, 172
Test
  examples, 10 laboratories, material tests, 74-78, 78-79
  good plan, 62
  homogeneity of samples, 72
  measurement or observation, 72
  method, standard of, 73
  standards, precision, 71
  validation of method, 91
Thornton, John C.
  Six-Sequence Carry-Over Design For The Determination of the Effect of a Drug in Reducing Food Intake (coauthor), 331-351
Threshold values, 203
Transformation, ISO standards, 86-88

INDEX 379

Trees, hierarchical
  for clusterings, 28
  forward selection, 17
  P hierarchical, 17
Trimming
  data, 108
  second order (super-election), 172
Tsao, F., 175, 226, 240
  data refactored, 226
  methodological experiment, 171
Tukey, John W., 93, 109
  borrow strength, 100
  Graphical Exploratory Analysis of Variance Illustrated on a Splitting of the Johnson and Tsao Data (coauthor), 171-243
  median polishing, 103
  one degree of freedom for nonadditivity, 259
Tukey, Paul A., 19
  variable selection, 19
Two-stage procedure for guaranteeing accuracy with calibration standards, 291-303
  abstract, 291
  Ferritin radioimmunoassay calibrator example, 293-303
  introduction, 291-292
  2-sample procedure for guaranteeing accuracy of new calibrator lot, 292-293
Two-way table, analysis of, 245-259
  additive function, 249, 257, 258, 259
  ANOVA, 248, 250-252
  Box-Cox method, 246
  comparison with Derringer's fit, 257-258
  concluding remarks, 257
  concurrence, 254
  data, 245-246
  degrees of freedom, 253
  final model for internal structure, 254-255
  fitting structural parameters to row and column variables, 256
  further exploration of structure, 252-254
  internal structure, 248-250
  introduction, 245
  linear regression, 249, 250, 252, 253
  non-concurrence, 254
  proposed method, 246-248
  residuals, 248, 249, 250, 253

two-stage method, 247

Unbalanced data, 306, 312-316
  all-cells-filled data, 307, 312-313
  balanced incomplete blocks, 307
  experimental misadventure, 306
  importance of analysis, 325-326
  Latin Squares, 307
  missing observations, 306, 307
  models with interactions, 315-316
  models without interactions, 313-315
  planned, 307
  some-cells-empty data, 313
  survey data, 307
Undragging, 192, *192*
Uniformity
  of performance, 62-63
  in product performance, 60
United States Bureau of Labor Statistics
  Survey of Consumer Expenditures, 327
United States Congress
  House Committee Report, 361
  Senate Report 891, 355
United States Courts, Administrative Office, 361, 362
  minimum response levels, 361
United States District Court, Northern District of Illinois, 362
University of California at Berkeley, 93
University of Chicago
  Law School Jury Project, 357
  two relevant findings, 357-358
Urquhart, N. S., 326

Variability
  homogeneous, 209
  jackknife, 201
  laboratories, 71
  reducing, 60
  residual, 199, 200
  of test errors, 72
  test for the presence of, 283
Variability, sources
  estimating, 46, 60-62
  example, integrated circuit crystals, 61-62
  nested data arrangement, 60-61
Variables, 64
  define, 64
  dependent, 209
  estimating, 46, 60-62
  example, integrated circuit crystals, 61-62

380 INDEX

Variables (*Continued*)
  extraneous, 48
  inner and outer array, 63
  interaction between, 50
  linear combinations, 14
  negligible weights, 14
  predictor, 53-54, 56
  prime, 48
  process, 50
  randomization, 64-65
  reduction, 14
  three or more levels, 52
  weights, 14
Variable selection
  algorithms for, 15-18
  data on 9 variables, 56 autos, 19-32
  discriminant analysis, 15-16
  example, three contexts, 19-32
  graphical approaches, 33
  multiple regression analysis, 15
Variance, graphical exploratory analysis illustrated on a splitting of the Johnson and Tsao data, 171-243
  analyzing IB1's performance in grams, 174-199
  analyzing IB1's performance in other terms, 208-213
  contents, 173
  data-guided trimming of bouquets, 199-207
  introduction, 171-173
  the other 7 people, 234-241
  rethinking a scission into contrasts, 213-234
  summary, 242-243

Vienna marriage data, example, 95-100
Viscosity, 245
  elastomer compounds, measurements, 245-246, 247
  measurements, 247
  Mooney, 247, 252
  two-way table, 247
Volterra-type integral equation, 112

Wasserman, W., 55
Watts, Donald G.
  Analytical Representation of Dielectric Constants: A Complex Multiresponse Problem (coauthor), 129-157
Weeks, D. L., 326
Wermuth, N., 95
Wilson, J. W., 39
Winsorizing, 109
  definition, 109
Wood, F. S., 55
  data, setting of Portland cement, 267
Wynn, H. P., 314

Yalow, R. S., 294
Yates, Frank, 312
  algorithm, 277, 281
Yen, John K. C., 39
Yochmowitz, M. G., 259
Youden, W. J., 44
  "Partially Replicated Latin Squares," 165

Zeisel, Hans
  Statistics in a Court of Law, 353-363

Applied Probability and Statistics (Continued)

JOHNSON and KOTZ • Distributions in Statistics
  Discrete Distributions
  Continuous Univariate Distributions—1
  Continuous Univariate Distributions—2
  Continuous Multivariate Distributions
JUDGE, HILL, GRIFFITHS, LÜTKEPOHL and LEE • Introduction to the Theory and Practice of Econometrics
JUDGE, GRIFFITHS, HILL, LÜTKEPOHL and LEE • The Theory and Practice of Econometrics, *Second Edition*
KALBFLEISCH and PRENTICE • The Statistical Analysis of Failure Time Data
KISH • Statistical Design for Research
KISH • Survey Sampling
KUH, NEESE, and HOLLINGER • Structural Sensitivity in Econometric Models
KEENEY and RAIFFA • Decisions with Multiple Objectives
LAWLESS • Statistical Models and Methods for Lifetime Data
LEAMER • Specification Searches: Ad Hoc Inference with Nonexperimental Data
LEBART, MORINEAU, and WARWICK • Multivariate Descriptive Statistical Analysis: Correspondence Analysis and Related Techniques for Large Matrices
LINHART and ZUCCHINI • Model Selection
LITTLE and RUBIN • Statistical Analysis with Missing Data
McNEIL • Interactive Data Analysis
MAINDONALD • Statistical Computation
MALLOWS • Design, Data, and Analysis by Some Friends of Cuthbert Daniel
MANN, SCHAFER and SINGPURWALLA • Methods for Statistical Analysis of Reliability and Life Data
MARTZ and WALLER • Bayesian Reliability Analysis
MIKÉ and STANLEY • Statistics in Medical Research: Methods and Issues with Applications in Cancer Research
MILLER • Beyond ANOVA, Basics of Applied Statistics
MILLER • Survival Analysis
MILLER, EFRON, BROWN, and MOSES • Biostatistics Casebook
MONTGOMERY and PECK • Introduction to Linear Regression Analysis
NELSON • Applied Life Data Analysis
OSBORNE • Finite Algorithms in Optimization and Data Analysis
OTNES and ENOCHSON • Applied Time Series Analysis: Volume I, Basic Techniques
OTNES and ENOCHSON • Digital Time Series Analysis
PANKRATZ • Forecasting with Univariate Box-Jenkins Models: Concepts and Cases
PIELOU • Interpretation of Ecological Data: A Primer on Classification and Ordination
PLATEK, RAO, SARNDAL and SINGH • Small Area Statistics: An International Symposium
POLLOCK • The Algebra of Econometrics
PRENTER • Splines and Variational Methods
RAO and MITRA • Generalized Inverse of Matrices and Its Applications
RÉNYI • A Diary on Information Theory
RIPLEY • Spatial Statistics
RIPLEY • Stochastic Simulation
ROSS • Introduction to Probability and Statistics for Engineers and Scientists
RUBIN • Multiple Imputation for Nonresponse in Surveys
RUBINSTEIN • Monte Carlo Optimization, Simulation, and Sensitivity of Queueing Networks
SCHUSS • Theory and Applications of Stochastic Differential Equations

(continued from front)